Globalizing America

NEW HORIZONS IN INTERNATIONAL BUSINESS

General Editor: Peter J. Buckley
Centre for International Business,
University of Leeds (CIBUL), UK

The New Horizons in International Business series has established itself as the world's leading forum for the presentation of new ideas in international business research. It offers pre-eminent contributions in the areas of multinational enterprise – including foreign direct investment, business strategy and corporate alliances, global competitive strategies, and entrepreneurship. In short, this series constitutes essential reading for academics, business strategists and policy makers alike.

Titles in the series include:

Direct Investment in Economies in Transition
Klaus Meyer

Taiwanese Firms in Southeast Asia
Networking Across Borders
Edited by Tain-Jy Chen

Global Competitive Strategies in the New World Economy
Multilateralism, Regionalization and the Transnational Firm
Edited by Hafiz Mirza

Foreign Direct Investment and Corporate Networking
A Framework for Spatial Analysis of Investment Conditions
Robert L.A. Morsink

Structural Change and Cooperation in the Global Economy
Edited by Gavin Boyd and John H. Dunning

Managing the Multinationals
An International Study of Control Mechanisms
Anne-Wil Käthe Harzing

The Origins of the International Competitiveness of Firms
The Impact of Location and Ownership in the Professional Service Industries
Lilach Nachum

Deepening Integration in the Pacific Economies
Corporate Alliances, Contestable Markets and Free Trade
Edited by Alan M. Rugman and Gavin Boyd

The Global Integration of Europe and East Asia
Studies of International Trade and Investment
Edited by Sang-Gon Lee and Pierre-Bruno Ruffini

Foreign Direct Investment and Economic Growth in China
Edited by Yanrui Wu

Multinationals, Technology and National Competitiveness
Marina Papanastassiou and Robert Pearce

Globalizing America
The USA in World Integration
Edited by Thomas L. Brewer and Gavin Boyd

Globalizing America

The USA in World Integration

Edited by

Thomas L. Brewer

Editor, Journal of International Business Studies *and Professor, Department of International Economics and Management, Copenhagen Business School, Denmark*

Gavin Boyd

Honorary Professor in the Political Science Department, Rutgers University, Newark, USA and Research Associate, Centre for International Business Studies (HEC), University of Montreal, Canada

NEW HORIZONS IN INTERNATIONAL BUSINESS

Edward Elgar
Cheltenham, UK • Northampton, MA, USA

Globalizing America :
 the USA in world

© Thomas L. Brewer and Gavin Boyd, 2000

Published by
Edward Elgar Publishing Limited
Glensanda House
Montpellier Parade
Cheltenham
Glos GL50 1UA
UK

Edward Elgar Publishing, Inc.
136 West Street
Suite 202
Northampton
Massachusetts 01060
USA

A catalogue record for this book
is available from the British Library

Library of Congress Cataloguing in Publication Data

Globalizing America : the USA in world integration / edited by Thomas L. Brewer,
    Gavin Boyd.
    (New horizons in international business)
    Includes index.
        1. United States—Foreign economic relations.   2. International economic
    relations.   I. Series.   II. Brewer, Thomas L., 1941–   III. Boyd, Gavin.

HF 1455.G58 2000
337.73 21—dc21   99–044832

ISBN 1 85898 981 7

Typeset by Manton Typesetters, Louth, Lincolnshire, UK.
Printed and bound by MPG Books Ltd, Bodmin Cornwall.

Contents

Figures

Tables

Contributors

Sven Arndt is at the Lowe Institute of Political Economy, Claremont McKenna College, Claremont, California.

Gavin Boyd is an Honorary Professor in the Political Science Department, Rutgers University, Newark, New Jersey.

Thomas L. Brewer is Professor, Department of International Economics and Management, Copenhagen Business School, Denmark.

Joseph P. Daniels is Professor, Economics Department, Marquette University, Milwaukee, Wisconsin.

John B. Davis is Dean, Faculty of Commerce, Marquette University, Milwaukee, Wisconsin.

John Kirton is Professor of Political Science, University of Toronto, Canada.

Mona Makhija is Professor in the Graduate School of Business, University of Pittsburgh, Pennsylvania and in the Fisher College of Business, The Ohio State University.

Maria Papadakis is Professor in the Integrated Science and Technology Program, James Madison University, Harrisonburg, Virginia.

Frederic L. Pryor is Professor of Economics, Swarthmore College, Swarthmore, Pennsylvania.

Willem Thorbecke is in the Economics Department, George Mason University, Fairfax, Virginia.

Sandra Williamson is Professor, Graduate School of Public and International Affairs, University of Pittsburgh, Pennsylvania.

Ronald J. Wonnacott is Professor of Economics, University of Western Ontario, London, Ontario, Canada.

Stephen Young is Professor, International Business Unit, Department of Marketing, University of Strathclyde, Scotland.

Introduction

Thomas L. Brewer and Gavin Boyd

The term 'globalization' has taken on diverse meanings in the empirical social science literature as well as a variety of connotations in more evaluative semi-popular books and articles. In this volume, each author has been granted the liberty of adopting his or her own preferred notion – either explicitly or implicitly. However, for the most part, the concepts that are evident in the individual chapters fall into one or more of the following elements of the concept.

A relatively comprehensive concept of globalization is that it is a process involving three spheres – economic, political and cultural. Within the economic sphere, there are both quantitative and qualitative aspects to each of two dimensions at the macro level. One dimension concerns the countries that are involved in international economic relationships – in which the quantitative aspect is the number of countries and the qualitative aspect is the diversity of the countries. This dimension is the geographic dimension. The second includes the economic relationships among countries – in which the quantitative aspect is the number of interactions among countries and the qualitative aspect is the variety of the interactions. At the macro level, there are thus four sets of indicators, with both quantitative and qualitative aspects for each of the two dimensions: number and diversity of countries for the geographic dimension; volume and variety of interactions for the relationship dimension.

As parallels to these macro-level dimensions, there are micro-level dimensions concerning corporations' strategies and operations. Indeed, many of the macro-level aspects of economic globalization are aggregations of corporate-level international interactions – in terms of the quantity and diversity of their interactions as well as the number and diversity of the countries involved. Thus, a corporation that is headquartered in one country with foreign affiliates and other business interests in most countries and in all regions of the world and that has an enormous volume of transactions of many types among them every day can be reasonably called a 'global' corporation.

At the same time, there is often an additional element of globalization at the corporate level – a strategic element – that is used as the basis of identifying a corporation as 'global'. That is, a global corporate strategy takes into account the interdependencies and similarities of its markets and other interests in all countries in an integrative way. Such a strategy is often contrasted with a 'multi-domestic' strategy, according to which each national market and national production system is treated more or less independently. To the extent, then, that a corporation's marketing, production, government-relations, financial and other functions are globally integrated, the firm has a 'global' strategy; to the extent that these functions are focused on individual countries separately, the firm has a 'multi-domestic' strategy.

Use of these corporate, strategy-based, conceptualizations of globalization, however, needs to take into account two complicating factors. First, just as with the macro-level conceptualization, the micro-level concept has several dimensions – for instance the marketing, production, government-relations and finance functions. Within any one corporation, some management functions are more globalized than others. Second, there is a tendency for corporations to declare themselves as having global strategies when, in fact, they do not have such strategies by an explicit definition of the term; the tendency is both cause and consequence of the term's having acquired a certain degree of faddishness.

The chapters in this volume address a variety of questions about the nature, extent and consequences of the globalization of the US economy. Multiple levels of analysis are represented in the chapters – within some individual chapters as well as among the chapters in the totality. There are obviously differences in emphasis in the notions of globalization that are represented here. At the same time, there are also some recurrent core elements that are common to many of the chapters.

The authors are themselves a diverse group in terms of their professional backgrounds and interests – a diversity that is appropriate to such a multidimensional topic. Some are trade economists, some are international politics specialists, some are international business scholars, some are US political economy specialists. Rather than summarize their contributions, we will let them speak for themselves.

The preparation of this volume benefited greatly from a workshop sponsored by the Center for Global Change and Convergence at Rutgers University, Newark, New Jersey, in January 1999. We are especially grateful for the hospitality provided by Professor Richard Langhorn, Director of the Center, and Professor Yale Ferguson, Chairman of the Political Science Department. Their contributions to our discussions, and those by Professor John H. Dunning, Director of the Center for International Business at Rutgers University, Newark, were greatly appreciated.

1. Internationalization and globalization of the American economy

Frederic L. Pryor

Although the meaning of 'globalization' varies among those using the term, most would agree that it is a process occurring when communications between peoples of different nations increase, when economic decision-makers develop a wider orientation taking into account a larger group of nations and the constraints of geography on economic, political, social, and cultural arrangements gradually become less important.[1] Such a 'taking account' of other nations may occur, not just because of greater opportunities to do so, but also because of greater vulnerability of the nation to the actions of others. Such globalization can be manifested either by an increasing scope of cross-border linkages or a greater intensity of such interaction.

In this chapter I spend the major part of the analysis on the measurement of economic dimensions of globalization. Although in the final section I focus on some particular impacts of globalization on the US economy, I leave to others the more difficult task of determining globalization's *overall* economic impact.[2]

In going about the task of measurement, it is analytically convenient to distinguish between two particular aspects of the process which, for short, will be called the 'old' and the 'new' globalization. The former (often called 'internationalization') deals with international trade of goods and services as well as the international flows of labour and capital; the latter deals more directly with the changing orientation of economic decision-making by governments, productive units and individuals, as manifested by increased international communications and the flow of money. The old globalization, of course, has waxed and waned over the millennium; the new globalization, I show below, started to become particularly important in the 1970s. The two types of globalization are, of course, related but they have rather different time profiles. We can, of course, define still other dimensions of globalization that focus on more micro-economic aspects of the process, for instance the number and diversity of nations involved and the various types of interactions. In later chapters other contributors discuss these issues.

My approach differs from that of others, who have defined globalization in terms of an end result rather than a process. For instance, certain commentators see globalization as total economic integration and the movement toward one reigning price for a particular good in different nations of the world. This not only raises difficulties of measurement, especially when some markets are integrated but others are not, but places too high a standard against which to measure current trends since, even within the United States, such integration has not been achieved (Pryor, 1995). Others see globalization as convergence of economic, political, social, or cultural systems. Such homogenization of institutions may certainly occur, and we can argue that this type of change certainly aids the globalization process. Nevertheless, it is certainly does not seem essential to globalization, except in a very broad sense.

This chapter has five parts: (1) a brief survey of long-term trends in the old globalization of the US economy; (2) a similar discussion of the new globalization; (3) a brief look at some institutional manifestations of these trends; (4) an analysis of certain critical policy problems raised by these trends in recent years; and (5) an assessment of the significance of these trends for the economy in the 21st century, a tentative journey into the murky realm of economic futurology.

THE OLD GLOBALIZATION (INTERNATIONALIZATION)

To gain some perspective on the old globalization, it is useful to consider how John Maynard Keynes (1971, pp. 6–7) described the international economy shortly before the beginning of World War I:

> The inhabitant of London could order by telephone, sipping his morning tea in bed, the various products of the whole earth, in such quantity as he might see fit, and could reasonably expect their early delivery upon his doorstep; he could at the same moment and by the same means adventure his wealth in the natural resources and new enterprises of any quarter of the world, and share, without exertion or even trouble, in their prospective fruits and advantages; or he could decide to couple the security of his fortunes with the good faith of the townspeople of any substantial municipality in any continent that fancy or information might recommend. He could secure forthwith, if he wished it, cheap and comfortable means of transit to any country or climate without passport or other formality, could despatch his servant to the neighbouring office of a bank for such supply of the precious metals as might seem convenient, and could then proceed abroad to foreign quarters, without knowledge of their religion, language, or customs.

Our first task is to determine in what ways the old globalization has changed since that glittering period. I focus primarily on the flow of foreign trade and the international flow of labour, showing as many others have before me that internationalization was at roughly the same level in 1970 as in 1900, but that since then a dramatic increase has occurred.

Flow of Foreign Trade

Figure 1.1(a) shows that the openness of the US economy, as measured by the share of exports or imports in the gross domestic product (GDP), has varied considerably over the years since 1900. The trade ratios of both imports and exports to GDP were very roughly the same in the early 1970s as in 1900, but since then this measure of openness has risen considerably. By the mid-1990s exports began to exceed the peaks occasioned by World War I. Campa and Goldberg (1997) show that this recent increasing external orientation of manufacturing is parallelled in most industries and their input–output analysis also shows that the percentage of imported inputs (raw materials and intermediate products) of most industries has increased as well since the mid-1970s. In this volume Makhija and Williamson show other aspects of the process on a four-digit level.

Most trade is in manufactured and primary goods, and it is well known that these sectors have greatly declined as a share of total GDP over the period. Thus any increase in the trade/GDP ratio is accompanied by a much faster external orientation in those sectors where the traded goods and services are actually produced. Figure 1.1(b) presents some very rough estimations of the ratio of the trade of goods to total goods production and the ratio of services to total production of tradable services over the century. For goods, the ratio of trade to domestic production only began to exceed the 1900 levels by the mid 1970s. For tradable services, the trade/production ratios are much lower but, by way of contrast, have increased slowly over the century – and much faster for exports than for imports.

These ratios of trade to GDP or to merchandise production are considerably lower in the United States than in most industrialized nations, a result that can be traced to the much larger internal market in the US than in these other nations. Like those in the US, however, the ratios of merchandise exports to merchandise value-added have risen in most of these nations (Japan and the UK are exceptions), even if the ratios of such trade to GDP have not, as shown by Feenstra (1998).

Several additional and major differences between the beginning and the end of the 20th century must be noted:

Changing composition of trade
The major change in the composition of US trade since 1929 has been from a raw material exporter to a raw material importer. In 1929 net exports of raw

Figure 1.1(a)   US exports and imports as a percentage of GDP, 1900–96

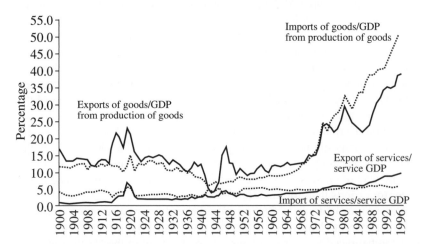

Note: Exportable goods are agriculture, mining and manufactured goods; exportable services are transportation, wholesale trade and finance. Other notes are in the Statistical Appendix.

Figure 1.1(b)   US exports and imports of goods and services as a ratio of exportable goods and services, 1900–96

materials amounted to about 6.5 per cent of domestic production. By the end of World War I, however, the United States had become a net importer of raw materials and, by 1996, such imports constituted 38.5 per cent of domestic production of these products.[3] As a share of total imports, however, raw materials have fallen because such inputs constitute a decreasing share of total manufacturing production.

Increasing vertical specialization (disintegration of the production chain)

Since the mid-1970s there has been a disintegration of the vertical chain of production and a rise in the importance of outsourcing of intermediate products abroad (global sourcing). This can occur in the situation of sequential production where a country imports a good from another country and uses it in the production of a good which is exported. Hummels et al. (1998) show for industries defined on a two-digit level that the share in total trade of such vertically specialized goods has risen dramatically in US trade with certain nations such as Mexico; as a share of total trade, however, these goods have only increased from roughly 3.8 per cent to 7.4 per cent between 1972 and 1990. Between 1975 and 1995, Campa and Goldberg estimate that the share of imports in total intermediate inputs in manufacturing rose from 4.1 per cent to 8.2 per cent. A similar calculation by Feenstra and Hanson (1996) for total US manufacturing industries finds imported inputs increasing from 5.7 per cent of total intermediate inputs in 1972 to 8.6 per cent in 1979 to 13.9 per cent in 1990. Such studies also show that this rising degree of vertical specialization has occurred in most major trading nations except Japan and is, moreover, much more important in smaller trading nations such as the Netherlands than in the US

Changing location of trade transactions

Comparable data on the agents of foreign trade and the manner in which this trade has been institutionalized are not available over the century. One receives the impression, however, that in the early part of the 20th century, foreign trade was carried out primarily by businesspeople in the coastal cities. At the end of the century a considerable part of US trade was carried out by multinational corporations located all over the country.[4] For instance, in the mid-1990s US-owned multinational enterprises carried out about two-thirds of all exports and about 40 per cent of all imports. Indeed, exports of US-owned multinationals to their affiliates abroad comprised about one-quarter of US exports and, if we add the exports of branches of foreign multinationals operating in the USA to their parent and affiliated enterprises abroad, this rises to about one-third of total US exports. Similarly, imports from affiliates of US multinational enterprises abroad to their parent company constituted about 16 per cent of total imports and, if we add the imports of foreign multinationals to their affiliates in the USA, this increases to about 40 per cent. Although the shares of intra-company trade of both exports and imports have not markedly changed between the mid-1970s and the mid-

1990s and we have no data for earlier dates, it seems likely that this is a post-World War II phenomenon.

Shifting direction of trade

At the beginning of the century most US foreign trade was with Europe.[5] By the middle of the century about 25 per cent of US trade turnover was with its immediate neighbours (Canada and Mexico), about 30 per cent with other industrialized nations and about 45 per cent with non-industrialized nations. By the late 1990s, trade with neighbouring countries had increased to about 30 per cent, trade with industrialized nations remained roughly the same (although Japan's share soared at the expense of Europe), about 15 per cent was with the newly industrialized nations and about one-quarter with non-industrialized nations. In sum, the growth of various regional trade blocs throughout the world (as shown in various essays in Frankel (1998) or by Coleman and Underhill (1998)), has resulted in a rise in the share of US trade with its North American Free Trade Area (NAFTA) partners, a rise in its share of trade with developing nations not strongly affiliated with trade blocs and a dramatic fall in the share of trade with West European nations. These trends have been in evidence throughout the entire post-World War II period, and not just since the 1970s. Whether full globalization of trade in the future will be throttled by increasing regionalization or whether such regional blocs are only an intermediate point toward a full globalization is an open question with strong opinions and little hard evidence on both sides of the debate.

Growth of intra-industry trade

Intra-industry trade reflects the share of imports that are in the same category of goods that are exported, in contrast to inter-industry trade where a country exports one type of good and imports another. If there is no intra-industry trade (so that all trade is inter-industry) the trade pattern in a particular industry will be either exports or imports, but not both, a result predicted by the Heckscher–Ohlin approach. Complete intra-industry trade occurs when exports of a particular good equal imports of the same good. The degree of intra-industry trade is commonly measured by the Grubel–Lloyd statistic (1971), whose numerator is the sum of the absolute values of exports minus imports of goods of the same industry for all industries and whose denominator is the average value of exports and imports. This fraction is subtracted from 1 so that 0 indicates no intra-industry trade and 1 indicates that all trade is intra-industry.

Defining industries at the three-digit level, the Organization for Economic Cooperation and Development (OECD) (1996) calculated that the Grubel–Lloyd index for the United States had increased from 44.4 per cent in 1970 to 46.5 per cent in 1980 and to 71.8 per cent in 1990. Part of this growth represents an increasing vertical specialization (company X imports half-finished clothing and exports fully finished clothing, both of which are classified as trade in clothing). Nevertheless, a major part appears to represent an increase in the variety of goods available to consumers (either individuals or companies) that are produced by a single industrial sector. Although many years ago this phenomenon was predicted theoretically by Staffen B. Linder (1961), it still raises many theoretical puzzles (Pryor, 1992).

These trade trends, combined with other information, give us some important clues about why the trade/GDP ratio has risen since the 1970s. Using a gravity model and bilateral trade data of OECD nations from 1958 to 1988, Bauer and Bergstrand (1998) estimate that roughly one-third of the growth of the trade/GDP ratio has occurred as a result of the combined effect of falling tariffs and transport costs, of which the former were roughly twice as important as the latter. Assuming that all of the vertical specialization represents new trade, this phenomenon probably accounted for roughly 5 to 8 per cent of the rise in the trade/GDP ratio. If we guess that one-third of the exports of multinational enterprises across borders represents trade that otherwise would not have occurred without the growth of affiliates abroad, then this would account for 5 per cent of the growth of the exports/trade ratio and 13 per cent of the growth of the imports/trade ratio. Although a considerable part of the growth of the trade/GDP ratio still remains unexplained, it seems likely that the growth of intra-industry trade, which has greatly increased the variety of goods to consumers, has been the most important causal factor.

In sum, if we focus just on trade it should be clear that the old globalization (internationalization) has become more important since the 1970s but that, a number of important features of this trade have changed. These shifts have, of course, occurred in most other major trading nations and reflect a changing global environment of trade.

Flow of Labour

Figure 1.2(a) focuses on the gross flows of immigrants into the United States from 1900 to 1992; comparable data for the period for the subsequent outflow of any of these immigrants or of emigration of US citizens are not available. These data show quite clearly that the legal immigrant flow into the United States is considerably less at the end of the century than at the beginning. The spike in the late 1980s represents a legalization of the status of many who were in the country illegally. The composition of immigrants has also changed over the century; for instance, a much higher percentage of legal immigrants are educated and have professional backgrounds and an increasing percentage are also from Asia or Latin America.

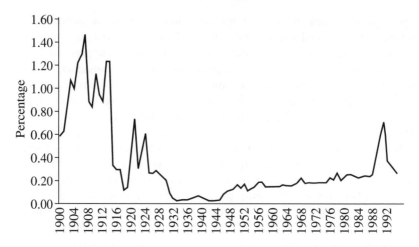

Figure 1.2(a)   Annual flow of legal immigrants as a percentage of total US population, 1900–92

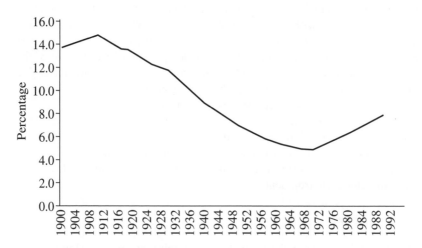

Note: Data sources and other notes are given in the Statistical Appendix.

Figure 1.2(b)   Percentage of foreign-born in the USA, 1900–92

Figure 1.2(b) shows the percentage of foreign-born in the USA. These data are from the decennial census and include many, but not all, of non-documented immigrants. Again, the data show that the percentage of foreign-born in the country in 1900 was considerably higher than at the end of the 20th century, but that an upturn occurred around 1970.

Several factors encourage greater immigration flows in the future. Of course, population pressures occurring in various developing nations and widening income gaps between these nations and the United States are important, particularly because it is difficult to prevent illegal immigration. But another factor that appears to be assuming increasing importance since 1970 deserves mention. Journalists (for example, Kaplan, 1998, p. 95) report being repeatedly told by businesspeople that 'it is far more cost-efficient to import [labour] from the rest of the world's talent [pool] than to train citizens at home, especially as weak or nonexistent national education standards and insufficient tax revenues make a mockery of many local American schools'. In future decades educated labour may become even more internationally mobile than now.

In brief, the data at the beginning and the end of the century show no long-run increase in internationalization of the economy, at least when internationalization is defined in terms of population flows across national boundaries. Nevertheless, 1970 appears to mark an inflection point.

Flow of Capital

In contrast to the flow of labour, US international capital flows (combined short and long term) are greater at the end of the century than at the beginning, a phenomenon we would expect because of the greater fungibility of capital.[6] The two solid lines in Figure 1.3(a) show the net outflow of US capital abroad. Aside from a brief period during and after World War I, the outflow of US capital amounted to less than 1 per cent of the US GDP until the 1970s, when it began to rise dramatically. The two broken lines show the net inflow of foreign capital to the United States. This series is much more volatile since periods of net foreign capital outflows occurred on several different occasions. Again, the absolute quantity seldom amounted to more than 1 per cent until the late 1960s when it began to increase dramatically.

This process is also reflected in types of data on capital stocks which, it must be emphasized, are very problematic because of issues of measurement and valuation. A rough picture of US long-term investment abroad and foreign long-term investment in the USA is shown in Figure 1.3(b). Although the data are not very good, they do provide some rough orders of magnitude.[7]

At the beginning of the century, foreign investment, measured as a ratio of GDP, was high. During World War I, considerable disinvestment took place, and the relative amount of such investment remained low until the 1970s when, with the advent of large US trade deficits, foreign investment took off. US investment abroad has taken some curious zigs and zags, but again it took off in the early 1970s and has continued rising ever since. By the end of the

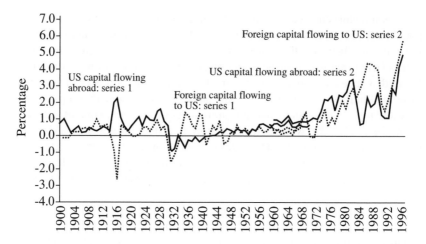

*Figure 1.3(a)   International capital flows as a percentage of US GDP,
1900–96*

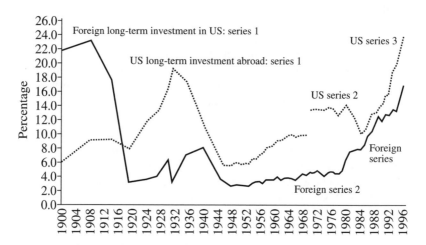

Note: Data sources and other notes are given in the Statistical Appendix.

*Figure 1.3(b)   Long-term foreign investment as a percentage of US GDP,
1900–96*

20th century, the previous highs of the early part of the century had been
exceeded. Even more important, a considerable share of this investment is
direct, and foreign markets appear to be increasingly served by affiliate sales
of multinational enterprises rather than exports from the home enterprise.

The composition of long-term capital flows between direct and portfolio investment has fluctuated considerably over the years. From the beginning of the century to the present, however, direct investment appears to account for a very slowly declining share of both US long-term investment abroad and foreign investment in the USA,[8] a trend that stands in contrast to what is happening in many other countries. The geographical composition of foreign investment has not greatly changed: from 1929 to the late 1990s, somewhat more than half of US foreign investment has gone either to Canada or to Western Europe.[9] The relative business risks and investment opportunities do not seem to have greatly changed over the period.

A Brief Summary

The old globalization (internationalization) of the US economy was not a unidimensional process: indicators of trade and capital flows on the one hand and flows of labour and capital on the other show rather different behaviour over the 20th century. For trade and capital, internationalization remained roughly the same from 1900 to 1970 when it began to increase; for labour flows, internationalization was greater at the beginning than at the end of the century, although an inflection point occurred around 1970. In both cases, however, the 1970s proved to be a decisive decade.

It would require too great a digression to discuss in detail why internationalization of the economy seemed to change in the 1970s. Certainly the two oil shocks, combined with a falling share of US domestic oil production, played a key role. This was also the decade in which foreign multinational enterprises became highly competitive on world markets. Finally, an ideological change also occurred, reflected in both the increasing market-orientation of government policies of industrialized nations and the dismantling of controls over the international flow of capital.

THE NEW GLOBALIZATION

Although increased international communication certainly underlies the internationalization of the economy, I would like to focus more directly on such communication disregarding for a moment its economic content. In particular, I shall deal with flows of information and money, two phenomena which have changed much more dramatically than the internationalizations which have been discussed up to now. These indicators show more clearly that a new orientation is emerging.

Information Flows

Figure 1.4 presents an index of per capita international communications and consists of four separate components. These components, I must add, cover not only commercial and business matters but also social, political and cultural matters. The results of such calculations can be quickly summarized. The first component is international mail flows. For the United States, we have such data from the early part of the century and from these series we can estimate the number of letters sent. Per capita international mail flows were roughly the same at the end of the century.[10] The second component is international tel-

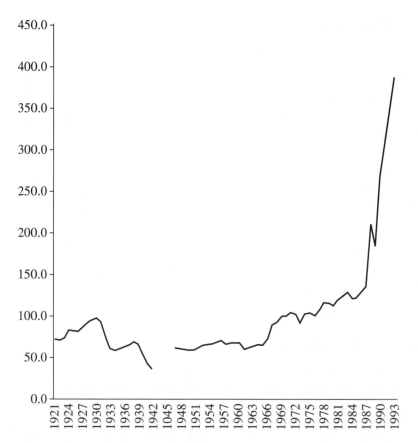

Notes:
Data sources and other notes are given in the Statistical Appendix.
1970 = 100.

Figure 1.4   Index of per capita US international communications, 1921–93

ephone calls, which first became economic in the early 1920s. From 1921 to 1970 per capita international calls rose at an annual rate of about 17 per cent, accelerating thereafter to an average annual rate of 22 per cent. These numbers represent a substitution of telephone calls for mail communication. A third component of the communication index is international travel since travel provides an important means of international communication. In the 73 years between 1921 and 1994, per capita international travel (excluding Mexico and Canada) of US citizens increased at about 4.5 per cent a year. To convert such trips into 'message units', I have assigned each traveller an arbitrary number of 'messages' which remain the same throughout the period. The final component of the index was a very rough estimate of international fax messages and e-mails. Given the paucity of data, this estimate is very crude. Its inclusion illustrates a problem arising in the 1990s, namely that with the development of the World Wide Web, it has become impossible to measure messages any more. For instance, a person might 'visit' six countries in one day when searching for a document over the Internet, and yet none of these 'visits' can be measured. As a result, by the 1990s the communication index shown in the graph becomes anachronistic.

Although the index of international communication requires some very heroic assumptions,[11] the results of such a rough statistical exercise are, nevertheless, illuminating. Over the entire 73-year period from 1921 to 1973, per capita direct international communications increased at 2.3 per cent a year, roughly the same rate as per capita GDP and considerably slower than the annual increase in real per capita foreign trade of 3.5 per cent.[12] Nevertheless, the growth of per capita international communications differed greatly in various sub-periods. Between 1921 and 1970, such communications rose at roughly 0.7 per cent a year, while both per capita GDP (and foreign trade) were experiencing an average annual increase of roughly 2.7 per cent a year. From 1970 to 1994, per capita direct international communications rose at roughly 5.8 per cent a year, while real per capita GDP and foreign trade grew at rates of 1.8 per cent and 4.9 per cent a year respectively. So globalization of the US, defined in terms of per capita direct international communications flows, lagged behind internationalization before 1970 and led internationalization thereafter.

Of course, this index does not include indirect communications through newspapers, news wire services or radio and TV broadcasts via satellite technology. We know that these have also increased but measurement problems seem insurmountable.

Comparing the results of this exercise with previous results, we can see quite graphically the different temporal patterns of globalization and internationalization. In particular globalization increased much more slowly than per capita GDP from the beginning of the century to 1970, while it increased much faster thereafter. Internationalization, as measured by the ratio of trade to GDP remained stagnant until about 1970 when it began to increase, albeit at a much slower rate than my globalization measure.

Unfortunately, this kind of statistical exercise does not tell us the content of new messages flowing between the United States and foreign nations. We do not know, for instance, what share are strictly business and trade communications or whether they deal with management issues such as the coordination of production or financial decisions. On a qualitative basis, however, two aspects of such business communications deserve brief mention. First, flows of business intelligence, in which US financial and consulting firms have played a major role, have greatly increased. Second, business communication has grown rapidly because the changing nature of the multinational enterprise (MNE) has had a major impact on international communications. The older model of MNE, pioneered by the Singer Sewing Machine Company, featured roughly similar plants in many countries, each serving national markets. Except for standardizing products and determining which factory should service which countries, such an arrangement required relatively little international communication and coordination from the home office. By way of contrast, the newer model of MNE, where factories in different nations of a given company specialize in different parts of production or in different functions of management, requires much more coordination. For instance, Hewlett-Packard manages certain parts of its product line from France, and IBM has a research laboratory in Sweden drawing upon the skilled technicians of that nation which supplies R&D to IBM factories in other nations. Indeed, the share of R&D of the world's largest firms undertaken outside the home country increased considerably from the early 1970s to the mid-1980s (some useful data are presented by Cantwell (1995)) and it seems likely that this trend will continue. This international disaggregation of production and management functions requires, of course, much more international communication than the old model of MNE.

Flows of Money

A very direct type of economic communication is the exchange of money. Figure 1.5 shows a critical feature in the increasing globalization of the capital market, namely the increasingly greater gross flows of foreign short-term investment entering US markets. As a percentage of the monetary base, the total daily foreign exchange turnover rose from less than 5 per cent in 1977 to more than 50 per cent by 1995. As a percentage of annual GDP, this daily turnover rose from 0.2 per cent to 3.4 per cent in the same period. The turnover of foreign exchange also dwarfed the sales of domestic securities, as shown by the comparison between the daily foreign exchange turnover and the monthly sales of stocks in all US stock exchanges.

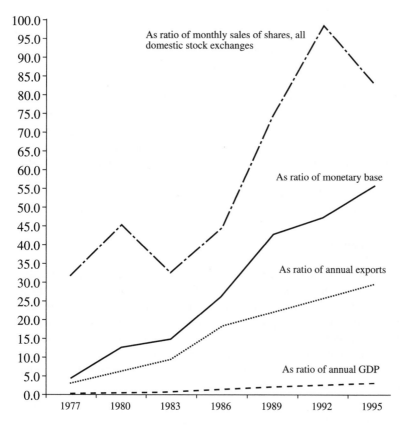

Note: The data on foreign exchange turnover come from a review of the foreign exchange market carried out every three years by the Federal Reserve Bank of New York and they were supplied to me in a personal letter from the bank. The data apply either to March or April of the particular year. The data on the monetary base of the corresponding month come from the web pages of the Board of Governors of the Federal Reserve. Other data come from the Department of Commerce, Bureau of the Census (annual), various years.

Figure 1.5   Average daily foreign exchange turnover in the USA, 1977–95

A major part of this short-term capital flow is, by and large, between the United States and a relatively small number of industrialized nations. This capital flow is not aimed at investment and, I should add, since profit rates do not seem to have converged between these industrialized nations, it seems premature to speak of a fully integrated market.

Some idea of the importance of these short-term capital flows can be seen from US Treasury data on the holdings of Treasury securities. In 1970 the share held by non-US citizens amounted to almost 9 per cent; by the end of

1997 this share had increased to almost 38 per cent. Indeed, from 1995 through 1997, the amount of new bonds purchased by foreigners exceeded those purchased by US citizens.[13] Two nations, the UK and Japan, own almost half of these foreign holdings. Thus, in June 1997 when Prime Minister Hashimoto mused about finding it necessary to sell some of Japan's large holding of these bonds, the Dow-Jones stock index fell 192 points in the next day as investors feared a rapid fall in the price of bonds and soaring interest rates. It should be clear that the USA had not previously witnessed such an impact of a casual foreign action on its economy and we are now forced to pay attention to others. As I argue below, these data on capital flow point to an increasing macroeconomic vulnerability of the US economy to economic events abroad. Other authors in this book, such as John Kirton, analyse a number of microeconomic aspects of this increased vulnerability.

A Brief Summary

Discussion of the new globalization focuses on communications and a shift in the orientation of decision-making of various organizations toward an international, rather than a domestic, environment. More specifically, economic globalization is a process in which a growing portion of a given population becomes oriented in its decision-making to international economic conditions. Measuring such communications through the flow of messages or money, we see vast changes in globalization of the US economy from the beginning to the end of the century.

SOME INSTITUTIONAL DIMENSIONS OF GLOBALIZATION IN THE USA

For private business organizations the new globalism implies a growing integration of markets and a greater necessity to take the actions of enterprises in other nations into account. For other types of organization, such as governments or non-governmental groups, it implies increasing cooperation and consultation. Both of these phenomenon represents a greater structural complexity of the economy.

In looking at the institutional dimensions of globalization, the definition of globalization is quite important. If we define globalization in terms of the elimination of national boundaries so that, for instance, the facilities of a large multinational corporation would be 'evenly spread' throughout the world, or so that governmental policy-making would make no distinctions between domestic and foreign economic circumstances, then we would find that globalization has not proceeded very far. Similar negative results would also occur if we were to view globalization as a type of convergence or homogenization of economic decision-making units, this would indicate, for instance, a growing similarity of enterprise structures, business practices or corporate strategies, or a convergence in various nations of the level of technology or R&D systems. Indeed, with such approaches it is doubtful whether globalization would ever be achieved in the foreseeable future.

Because other chapters in this book deal with many specific institutional aspects of globalization, such as the growth of international banking, I shall deal below only with some critical general issues that will place this later discussion in a broader context. I focus first on issues involving the private sector and then turn to certain parts of the public sector.

Globalization and the Private Sector

The obvious example of the increasing globalization of the private sector is the growing importance in the world economy of the multinational enterprise (MNE), those firms with production facilities, offices and markets in two or more nations. These MNEs, feared by many as the precursor to global monopolies, praised by others as the precursor to the emerging global economy, have received enormous public attention. Nevertheless, in the last few years several books have appeared (for example, Hirst and Thompson, 1996; Doremus et al., 1998) arguing that the relative importance of these firms and, hence, the globalization process have been vastly overrated. They argue on the basis of two points.

Location

Most corporations classified as multinational have a predominant share of their economic base in one country. In 1987 (Hirst and Thompson, 1996, Chapter 4), 70 per cent of sales and 67 per cent of the assets of MNEs with headquarters in the USA were in the USA or Canada; for Canadian, German or Japanese-based MNEs, a similar proportion of sales and assets were in nearby countries. The shares of research facilities in the home country are usually higher. Nevertheless, the interaction between the home and foreign facilities can be intense: both can participate in the design or manufacture of a given product, and facilities in both can draw upon the others' marketing experience. For instance, Levi Strauss and Häagen-Dazs have recently introduced new products into the USA that were first designed for Japanese and Argentinian markets respectively (*Business Week*, 7 September 1988, pp. 56–8). It seems clear that international communications and interaction, rather than share of facilities or sales in one country or another, is the critical change.

One particular aspect of the location of MNEs deserves brief comment, namely the ability of those MNEs which have broken the dominant-nation pattern and have sales all over the world to move their headquarters from one nation to another. For instance, in 1998 the Swedish company Ericsson moved its headquarters to London to avoid high Swedish taxes and to help with recruitment; in the next year ABB in Sweden, Allianz (a giant insurance company) in Germany and three other large German firms also threatened to move their headquarters unless certain changes in tax regulations were made. In brief, globalization has increased the bargaining power of enterprises against a national government and, consequently, globalization is beginning to shift the balance of power between governments and enterprises by making it increasingly easier for MNEs to play one government off against another. This, of course, is the same game some US companies have used against individual US states to obtain tax or other concessions.

Governance

Because most MNEs are closely tied to a single territorial base, the national political and economic structures continue to shape their ownership structure, operations, their internal governance, long-term financing, research and development, direct investment, intra-firm trading strategies and other aspects of their structure and operations. This means that MNEs are not converging toward a single type of global behaviour norms, as Doremus et al. (1998) and La Porta et al. (1998) have forcefully pointed out. But such convergence of structure and operation, while important to keep in mind, does not seem to be a phenomenon of primary importance because many different kinds of firms can compete in the same markets if they can agree on certain basic rules of the game. For instance, many different types of firms have competed against each other in the US domestic market. In some circumstances, competitive forces determine a clear winner, but in other cases the various firms remain quite different and no convergence can be seen. Whatever the structure of ownership and management or strategies of operation, it should be clear that the successful firms will be those with highly sophisticated information systems which allow them not only to know what is happening in markets in every nation and what their competitors are doing but also to have a close eye on all of their own far flung operations.

For many, the key issue in the emergence of the MNE is not the convergence of their structure or policies but their potential for the global monopolization of certain industries. And, or course, every large-scale international purchase or merger revives this worry; for instance, those involving British Petroleum and Amoco or Random House and Bertelsmann AG or, just in the auto industry, the recent cross-border mergers of Chrysler and Mercedes-Benz, Ford and Volvo, and BMW and Rover. Several empirical remarks on the topic of enterprise size are in order.

In the US domestic economy up to now, the share of enterprises with more than 10 000 workers, as well as other measurements of enterprise size, began to decline from the 1970s, as has the share of workers in the hundred or thousand largest enterprises (Pryor, 1999b). Taking account of the publicity given to a number of mega-mergers during the first part of the 1990s, these results may seem puzzling. Along with the merger trend, however, there is also a divestment trend in which the merged enterprises focus more upon their core business and sell off miscellaneous pieces of their enlarged company. Or large corporations such as AT&T will spin-off pieces of their company, such as Lucent Technology, so that management efforts can be focused on a narrower range of problems.

Trends in the rest of the world, however, are quite different. In the 22 leading industrial nations as a whole, the average size of the work force in the hundred largest industrial enterprises has risen steadily from 1958 through 1995, (Pryor, 1999b). Nevertheless, in the same period the share of the labour force working in the top hundred manufacturing and mining firms as a share of total workers in these two sectors for the world capitalist system as a whole remained about 6 per cent in both sectors. Although this represents, of course, a remarkable concentration of production, the data suggest that the growth of manufacturing and mining employment in the developing nations is offsetting the growth of large corporations whose headquarters are in the industrial nations.

If we look at the top hundred firms in 91 sectors world-wide (unfortunately, comparable data for 1958 are not available), we find that in 1995 these firms employed about 2.5 per cent of total workers outside of agriculture, personal services and government and communal services. Three aspects of these calculations are notable: only about half of the world's largest employers are in manufacturing and mining. It seems likely that the largest source of concentration of capital will come outside the traditional smokestack industries. Second, a major source of this concentration of employment has occurred as a result of activities of firms outside of the United States. For instance in 1958, 44 of the top employers in manufacturing and mining were US firms, while only three were Japanese. By 1995, firms in the two countries represented respectively 38 and 16 of the total enterprises on the list. Finally, the average size of the world's largest employers has increased dramatically. Among the largest employers in the mining and manufacturing sectors, employee numbers in the average firm have risen from 83 000 to 134 000. If we look at the largest employers in all sectors, the top hundred firms averaged 196 000 employees.

Since we do not have a complete set of global concentration ratios, but only calculations for individual industries, it is difficult to gain an overall view of changing global competition. Anecdotal evidence such as the examples of multinational intra-industrial mergers mentioned above suggests that such industrial concentration on a world-scale is already occurring. Further, the United Nations Conference on Trade and Development (UNCTAD) estimates that the largest 100 MNEs (excluding those in banking and finance) account for about one-third of global foreign direct investment (Dunning, 1967, p. 23). In addition, two additional forms of globalizing activities of MNEs are becoming increasingly common: cross-border mergers and strategic alliances (Ibid). By way of contrast, some economists such as Lester Thurow (1992) argue that such competition has actually increased as a result of the long-term struggle between the USA, Japan and Europe for economic hegemony. Although I find the arguments for a growing concentration of production more convincing, the literature has an apocalyptic quality and, of course, with selected anecdotes, it is possible to 'prove' that anything is now occurring.

Other changing institutional features in the private sector accompanying globalization also deserve brief consideration. One critical aspect of the integration of the markets for goods and services on a world-wide basis is, of course, the implication that the 'law of one price' will hold, so that no gains from arbitrage can be gained by buying at a low price in one country and selling at a high price in another. With the considerable fall in transportation and communications costs, which have constituted an important real barrier to trade, and the creation of the euro which will make price comparisons in Europe considerably easier, such arbitrage possibilities should decline. Moreover, artificial barriers to trade appear to be falling. For instance, in 1996 the percentage of goods entering the USA duty free was somewhat higher than at the beginning of the century;[14] moreover, the share of tariffs on the price of goods on which the duties were placed fell from 49 per cent in 1900 to 13 per cent in 1950 to 4.7 per cent in 1996. The impact of this phenomenon on the degree of market competition receives attention below.

Despite these trends, however, many artificial non-tariff barriers to trade remain that can be traced to policies (such as pricing to market) pursued by particular firms or governments. At present, for instance, the prices of Levi jeans or Ford Escort cars are twice as high in London as in New York, when only a small part of the difference can be explained by higher consumption taxes, shipping costs or custom duties. Price disparities between Britain and Ireland range as high as 40 per cent. Moreover, certain forces are reinforcing these artificial barriers that are created by company or governmental policies. For instance, the European Court of Justice upheld the right of an Austrian spectacles maker to sell at a lower price outside the EU and to sue anyone who reimported the discounted goods for resale in any EU member country (*Economist*, 22 August 1998, p. 17). In Europe the introduction of the euro on 1 January 1999 is, of course, reducing these price differences between the

11 Euroland countries because all prices in each country will be quoted in a common currency and price comparisons will be easier to make. Nevertheless, for the sake of perspective it is useful to note that price differences of different goods between cities have persisted at the same level for the last four decades (Pryor, 1996, pp. 159–70), even when transportation costs appear to be taken into account.

Broader empirical attempts to study the law of one price, for instance, on an international level (Engel and Rogers, 1998) show that there are still large divergences in prices between various market economies. Market integration has many steps to take and is complicated especially by floating exchange rates, sticky prices and such business practices as 'pricing to market'.

Increasing integration of capital markets should be reflected in a similar movement of real interest rates and a narrowing of their spread. Certainly in the post-World War II period there has been a rough movement of these rates. Moreover, the variation between such interest rates has slightly narrowed. Among industrial nations the standard deviation of these rates in the periods from 1955 through 1972 and from 1989 through 1995 were respectively 2.0 and 1.8 percentage points.[15] Of course, the new European Central Bank in Frankfurt will act to unify European interest rates and banking regulations. For the world as a whole, an important step toward integration of the capital market was the drive by the Basle Committee on Banking Supervision in 1988 to set up uniform banking standards for the world economy so that a certain harmonization of banking regulations can be achieved in the major industrial countries on all continents. Obstfeld (1998) shows that the standard deviation of the difference in interest rates between the USA and the UK has declined markedly between the late 1960s and the mid-1990s; however, they are still somewhat higher than they were at the beginning of the century. Under perfect capital mobility, of course, the differential and its variation should be zero.

The integration of labour markets has several dimensions. It is commonly argued that foreign imports have led to unemployment of unskilled workers in the USA so that, in this indirect manner, factor markets are becoming integrated via a Heckscher–Ohlin mechanism. I provide lengthy empirical evidence elsewhere (Pryor and Schaffer, 1999; Pryor, 1999a) that neither foreign trade nor, for that matter, immigration have much impact on overall unemployment rates in the USA. Moreover, although wages in the EU are catching up to those in the USA, this appears to be due more to faster technological change than to trade or immigration, especially since immigration between the two areas is not high. And certainly wages in most developing countries which are sending large numbers of immigrants to the USA do not appear to be converging at a very rapid rate, suggesting that integration of factor markets in these cases is low. Finally, as Ehrenberg (1994) points out, labour legislation and standards, not to mention social legislation, are still quite different in various industrialized nations.

Globalization and the Government Sector

The most obvious example of globalization in the field of government is the growth of international organizations. In 1900 only a few such organizations existed and these dealt primarily with specialized problems: for instance, the International Telecommunications Union, the International Institute of Agriculture (predecessor to the UN Food and Agriculture Organization) or the International Rail Transport Committee. In the 1920s the creation of the League of Nations brought into existence several other new international organizations such as the International Labour Office (ILO). By the end of the 20th century the United Nations had 18 affiliated international organizations such as the ILO, UNESCO, the International Fund for Agricultural Development and the World Trade Organization not to mention five regional commissions, 68 information offices, more than 120 centres, institutions and other bodies.

The US government is enmeshed in a dense network of treaties, not just multilateral but bilateral as well, and the number of such treaties is increasing every year. For instance, from 1955 to 1997, the US State Department's annual publication *Treaties in Force* has more than doubled in length, and, it should be added, in later years the pages are bigger and the type is smaller. Of particular interest are the creation of intergovernmental agencies that have the potential to evolve into global economic regulators. In just the financial sector, for instance, these include the Basle Committee on Banking Supervision, the Committee on the Global Financial System, the Committee on Payments and Settlement Systems, the International Association of Insurance Supervisors and the International Organization of Securities Commission. In the area of trade, the USA has entered into a number of international treaties directed toward economic integration through the reduction of trade barriers, ranging from agreements with particular countries (for example, Israel), to regional agreements (for example, NAFTA), to a world-wide basis (the World Trade Organization).[16]

But such globalization through the creation of new international entities extends, of course, far beyond various intergovernmental agencies. The *Yearbook of International Organizations* for 1998/99 lists more than 13 000 international non-governmental organizations (INGOs) covering the spectrum of human endeavour. One example of particular importance to expanding world trade is the creation of the development of a network of international commercial arbitration courts – in 127 countries by 1993 – which are slowly developing world legal standards for such disputes (Sassen, 1996). Undoubtedly, many more INGOs exist but have not been registered and, moreover, this listing does not include various business international non-governmental organizations (BINGOs).

In short, both public and private agencies, or organizations which are carrying out delegated governmental functions, must increasingly take into account their obligations to other nations. On a vast spectrum of policies – environmental, banking regulation, product standards, trade rules, labour regulations, antitrust policies, taxation and subsidy measures and so forth – various international organizations and groups have been at work harmonizing or coordinating the governmental policies of various nations.

THE ECONOMIC IMPACT OF GLOBALIZATION AND INTERNATIONALIZATION ON THE US ECONOMY

The discussion below separates some important short-term micro- and macroeconomic effects of increased globalization and internationalization on the US economy. I end with a discussion of the loss of government economic autonomy. The long-term impacts of globalization and internationalization depend on what the shape of the US economy will be in the future, a matter discussed in the following section.

Microeconomic Impacts of Increased Globalization and Internationalization

The most important microeconomic impact of increased globalization and internationalization is increased competition for goods on domestic markets. This is brought about by the increasing share of imports in the US economy and the greater attention that US producers pay to their foreign competitors. Several empirical indicators of this increased competition are readily available.

Four-firm, four-digit concentration ratios measure the share of domestic shipments accounted for by the top four domestic producers and are a standard measure of market competition. It is possible to adjust these ratios to take account of the impact of foreign trade by adding imports to domestic shipments and to weight the results by the value added in each industry to calculate an overall index. The results of such an exercise (Pryor, 1994) can be quickly summarized.

Between 1958 and 1982, the weighted average four-firm, four-digit concentration ratios decreased by only one per cent, which means that the degree of competition by this measure did not greatly change. By way of contrast, the same statistic adjusted for the impact of imports decreased by almost 9 per cent which indicates a considerable increase in market competition. A statistical analysis of which industries experienced the greatest changes can explain a considerable portion of the differences between industries, but further consideration of these issues would take us too far afield.

Another simple indicator is the growth of intra-industry trade, which was discussed above. The dramatic increase in the Grubel–Lloyd index of 27 percentage points attests to the greater competition occurring in many industries which had experienced few imports in the years prior to the 1970s, although most of this increase in intra-industry trade occurred in the 1980s, when both internationalization and globalization had already taken off. Nevertheless, this phenomenon is extremely important because it means that American manufacturers are facing stiffer competition both in their domestic and their foreign sales.

Macroeconomic Impacts of Increased Globalization and Internationalization

Several facets of the decreasing autonomy of the American economy deserve our attention: in particular, the declining effectiveness of fiscal and monetary policy and the greater potential for economic instability induced by outside shocks. The Mundell–Fleming model has served as the basis of much of the conventional wisdom on these matters – for instance, that fiscal policy is more effective under a fixed rate, rather than a floating exchange rate regime, while the reverse is the case for monetary policy.[17] Such stark conclusions have been considerably modified over the years with the loosening of particular assumptions of the model and the introduction of other considerations. Without delving into the intricacies of international macroeconomics, it is nevertheless useful to review briefly several important policy effects of increasing globalization on the effectiveness of macroeconomic policy.

Fiscal policy
The effectiveness of fiscal policy depends critically upon the marginal propensity to import (MPM), because this is one of the determinants of the fiscal policy multiplier. For instance, if the MPM is high, the purchasing power pumped into the economy by expansionary fiscal policy gets rapidly spent abroad, rather than circulating within the domestic economy to create new jobs. In the United States, cities and states do not engage in fiscal policy because at their level of the economy the marginal propensity to import is very high and such aggregate tax and expenditure policies would not be an effective way of regulating the real income in the political area.

Globalization should raise the MPM, not only because our awareness of foreign goods is greater but because of increased foreign competition in US markets. And a rising MPM is exactly what we find since the MPM in the USA has increased in each decade following World War II.[18] More specifically, in the 1950s the MPM was .08; in the 1960s, .09; in the 1970s, .10; in the 1980s, .21; and, from 1990 through 1996, .42.

As a result, the effectiveness of fiscal policy has decreased in each decade, especially after the 1970s. It is unclear whether discretionary fiscal policy was ever an effective policy tool; but whatever the situation in the period from 1950 through 1980, its force appears to have dramatically worsened since them.

Monetary policy

For monetary policy the implications of globalization can be seen most clearly by looking briefly at cities and states in the United States. Such political units do not engage in monetary policy because they have no control over the money supply. If, for instance, a state buys bonds in order to raise their price and lower the interest rate in its area, state residents would sell their bonds to the government at these higher prices and then would export their capital to other states to buy bonds at lower prices. The lower the barriers to capital flows and the lower the costs of information about investment returns in other political units, the more sensitive are monetary flows to changes in interest rates.

For the federal government the policy situation differs in several essential ways. Of course, the government has more control over the money supply since it can print money if necessary. Moreover, capital flows between the USA and other countries are still hindered by some barriers that do not exist between individual states in the USA. For instance, in certain countries financial intermediaries such as insurance companies and mutual funds must maintain a minimum share of investments in the home country.

Nevertheless, the daily flow of foreign capital into the New York money markets shown in Figure 1.5 reflects the falling barriers to such transactions. This means that not only is it more difficult for the government to maintain interest rate differentials between the USA and other nations but it is also more difficult to control the volume of the money supply. Thus, even with a floating exchange system where the government is not constrained to use monetary policy to maintain the exchange rate, monetary policy is complicated by several factors of increased importance.

First, monetary policy effects the exchange rate. Of course, this can aid the policy process in the short run: For instance, expansionary monetary policy lowering the interest rate can encourage an outward flow of capital which, in turn, can lead to a depreciation of the currency that encourages exports and discourages imports. In the long run, however, interest rates between nations converge.

Second, because of these exchange rates associated with policy changes, speculative flows of capital become increasingly important and, depending on circumstances, these can be stabilizing or destabilizing. In a situation without speculation, as noted above, expansionary monetary policy leads to a net outflow of capital and a depreciation of the exchange rate. If speculators believe that such monetary policies will lead to greater long-term investment opportunities in the USA or if they believe that the dollar depreciation is only temporary so that by buying cheap dollars they could make profits when the dollar appreciates, then an expansionary monetary policy might lead to a net inflow of foreign funds and an appreciation of the currency. Given the huge volume of foreign exchange turnover – much greater than trade – both the potential for speculative flows dominating the exchange rate and the difficulties of carrying out monetary policy increase.

As noted above, real interest rates between the USA and other nations have not converged so that monetary policy-makers still have some leeway. But if this process continues, the US monetary authorities may have increasingly less control over money supply, irrespective of the exchange rate regime, and monetary policy as an instrument to influence aggregate demand would become ineffective, just as it now is for individual US states.

One last consideration deserves brief mention. In a recent book Benjamin Cohen (1998) argues that the notion that all currencies are national ('One nation/one money') is becoming obsolete since in many countries several types of money (for instance, dollars and the national currency) are used. One dramatic indicator is foreign holdings of US dollars which, at the end of 1995, represented more than half of total outstanding currency (Jefferson, 1998). In future years globalization may lead to greater use of foreign moneys in America which will further weaken domestic US monetary policy.

Greater potential for economic instability

The rapidly increasing international flows of money, as shown in Figure 1.5, signify not only increasing international liquidity but also point toward increasing fragility of the financial structure. From 1950 through 1990 a number of variables indicating the degree of intermediation have increased as well and, under certain circumstances, this can also lead to instability. For instance, household debt as a percentage of total assets or disposable income has risen; productive enterprises and banks are more leveraged; and key macroeconomic ratios such as the ratio of total financial assets to total physical assets or the ratio of assets of financial institutions to total financial assets have risen (see Pryor, 1996, p. 105). The increasing integration of the world capital market, whereby cross-border transactions of bonds and equity as a percentage of GDP and other indicators has risen dramatically in all industrial nations of course has also led to greater fragility. For instance, according to Crockett (1997), in the USA this ratio rose from 4.1 per cent in 1975 to 151.5 per cent in 1996. The dramatic expansion in various financial derivatives since the mid-1980s can also, under certain circumstances, increase financial fragility. Finally, the decline of a highly regulated banking industry and the rising importance of other financial institutions that are less regulated adds to the potential instability (Mishkin, 1994).

As might be feared, increasing fragility has also been accompanied by increasing financial instability. For instance, in a study of volatility of 59 monthly and quarterly series from 1950 through 1990, Pryor and Sulcove (1995) show that, in general, financial variables such as bond yields, outstanding credit or exchange rates have become increasingly volatile. In addition, a variety of domestic indicators such as business failures, failed banks, delinquent mortgages and personal bankruptcies show a dramatic increase from 1950 through 1990 (Pryor, 1996, p. 112). Wolfson (1986, 1990) also presents data showing that the number of 'financial crises' in the US economy, while infrequent, has steadily increased over the same period. Finally, as shown in Figure 1.5, the average daily turnover in US foreign exchange markets has risen dramatically.

From the mid-1990s the world as a whole has also faced a series of major financial crises. First was the 1994/5 Mexican currency emergency, followed by currency difficulties in various South-East Asian nations in 1997, by the rouble crisis in Russia in 1998 and, in early 1999, by the Brazilian meltdown. In the 1990s, financial interdependency has been accompanied by a serious contagion effect (the Kirton chapter in this volume provides a more detailed analysis of America's increasing vulnerability to external currency shocks).

At the same time, major foreign exchange rates have experienced some wild swings. Looking, for instance, just at Japan and the USA from 1990 to 1999, while domestic price indices in the two countries moved roughly in tandem, the exchange rate has swung from 160 yen to the dollar (17 April 1990) to 82 (18 April 1995) to 146 (14 August 1998) to 112 (4 February 1999).[19] Following European Monetary Union at the beginning of 1999, the euro/dollar exchange rate may take similar swings, particularly if international financial speculators become more sensitive to interest rate differentials between the two areas, if short-term capital controls are not imposed and the European Central Bank adopts the same indifference to exchange rate swings as the Central Bank of Japan.

The theoretical literature on currency and balance of payments crises is rich, and a literature on the role of expectations in international finance is developing. Using quite different approaches various analysts – to pick two recent examples, George Soros (1998) and Maurice Obstfeld (1998) – argue that an unregulated international payments system has some inherent instabilities. Given the increasing international flows of capital, such approaches suggest that these crises will occur with ever increasing frequency unless some type of capital controls is imposed.

What has not received sufficient theoretical or empirical attention, however, is the relation between greater financial instability and greater instability in production, wages and unemployment. Up to now these parallel developments have not occurred, at least in the United States. Indeed, from 1950 through 1990, 27 monthly and quarterly series reflecting real variables such as GDP, industrial production and employment became less volatile, even as financial instability increased. There is, indeed, theoretical evidence (Pryor, 1981) that increasing world trade can diminish volatility in the real economy since supply or demand shocks in a particular region can be absorbed over a wider area. Nevertheless, the stability of real variables in the emerging global economy has yet to be tested.

In sum, increasing globalization of financial markets raises two critical questions for policy-makers: To what extent will financial instability continue and worsen? And to what extent will financial instability lead to instability in the productive sphere? The proper answers are far from clear.

Declining sovereignty as a result of increased globalization and internationalization?

Patrick Buchanan (1998) has written: 'The question ... that is presented to every American is whether the United States will take the opportunity which is offered to shape her own life in her own way and in accord with her own ideals, or whether this opportunity will be thrust aside for an elusive and delusive old-world concept of sordid international shopkeeping.'[20] In less striking language other American populists ask in the same way whether we want dependence on foreign imports, markets, and capital which limit our sphere of action and which bring unemployment, trade deficits, loss of government revenue, income inequality and other economic ills. Such views reflect a more general phenomenon than merely the decreasing effectiveness of monetary and fiscal policy.

The notion that globalization will emasculate all domestic institutions does not warrant serious discussion. Nevertheless, a number of Europeans have raised a less extreme issue, namely that globalization will lead to an increasing attack on their welfare states, which will gradually be dismantled under a wave of global neoliberalism (Rhodes, 1998). Two brief rebuttals are in order. First, there is little evidence that 'lagging international competitiveness' is related to high welfare state spending (Pfaller et al., 1991). Second, changing exchange rates and real wages net of taxes can adjust to compensate for increased wage taxes used to finance higher welfare state spending (Ehrenberg, 1994).

This is also certainly not the place to rehearse the arguments for and against free trade, which seem to play an important role in these decline-of-sovereignty arguments.[21] Nor is it appropriate to worry here about whether multinational enterprises have forgotten how to 'salute the flag' and have become companies without a country, menacing the economic security of their US workers in an unprincipled search for higher profits. Nevertheless, the sovereignty argument against internationalization and globalization requires some deconstruction because in a limited sense it is correct. A cost/benefit approach is in order.

If we were living in isolated cubicles without contact with others, our sovereignty would be complete. Any contact with others brings a loss of such autonomy, but the benefits of such loss of autonomy should also be apparent. Broadening our view, a ban against murder reduces personal autonomy since I lose an important means of getting even with my neighbours, but I also gain an increased personal security for myself and my family.

It is obvious that the rules of the World Trade Organization limit our sovereignty by restricting our ability to impose tariffs or other trade restrictions while, at the same time, they limit the ability of our trading partners to take domestic actions which hurt our exports to that nation. A basic idea underlying the WTO's existence is that once trade retaliation begins it is difficult to stop and, as a result, both nations end up in a worse economic position. The rules of other international organizations regarding labour and product standards or environmental practices limit the US government's ability to act on its own but, at the same time, prevent certain kinds of unfair competition when governments lower such standards in order to capture export markets.

Unrestricted imports limit the ability of inefficient domestic producers to remain in business, and the closing of their plants can cause some painful adjustments. Economic dependency on foreign capital, imports or markets limits both private and governmental actions in certain spheres and thus acts as a limitation of our sovereignty. Nevertheless, sovereignty is not costless and competing values and goals are involved as well. Once a trade-off between sovereignty and other values is recognized, we can then deal with the advisability of undertaking particular policies in specific circumstances that may result in an increase or a decrease of internationalization or globalization of the US economy. The sovereignty issue, as posed by Buchanan and other enemies of globalization, obscures the problem.[22]

THE SIGNIFICANCE OF GLOBALIZATION FOR THE US ECONOMY

In this chapter I sketch a number of macroeconomic aspects of globalization – increased flows of trade, labour, capital, information, and money – and show how these have had quite different temporal patterns over the century. Nevertheless, all of these indicators of internationalization and globalization have experienced a dramatic increase. On a microeconomic level in the private sector such globalization has been accompanied up to now by increasing competition in domestic markets and a greater extension of domestic firm activity into other countries. Further, such globalization has been accompanied by an increasingly dense web of international treaties and various types of international organization – both public and private – that are creating and enforcing rules and regulations for the global economy.

After describing these changes and trying to explain some of the underlying causes, I show how such trends have some serious macroeconomic policy implications. In particular, the effectiveness of both fiscal and monetary policy to stabilize the domestic economy appears to be diminishing, part of a general trend toward declining political sovereignty. I also argue that the structural fragility of the international financial structure has increased, leading in turn to increased volatility of certain financial variables such as interest rates and exchange rates. In some circumstances, such increased financial volatility might have adverse effects on the production side of the economy as well.

The microeconomic policy implications are more difficult to sketch. The increased importance of foreign investment, especially by a relatively small number of multinational enterprises, combined with the growing importance of cross-border mergers and strategic alliances, might lead to a decline in global market competition in the future.

The progress the USA has made toward internationalization and globalization during the 1980s and 1990s is the product of a particular set of circumstances which are not permanent and which may not last. The real significance of the current globalization of the US economy is whether such trends will continue and how, as a result, the economy will evolve in the future.

Trend extrapolation about these matters is dangerous and we must be cautious. For instance, the movement toward free trade, which appeared invincible in the 1870s, experienced a political backlash and was reversed soon thereafter with rising protectionism in Europe, the 'marriage of iron and rye' in Germany and the beginning of immigration restrictions in America and other countries (Williamson, 1995, 1998).

Current trends toward globalization and internationalization are, of course, different from those in the 19th century. In particular, architects of the current system have attempted to make such trends irreversible by building international institutions to ensure that the new rules of the economic game will be enforced and that no national backlash will endanger them. Nevertheless, the permanence – or malleability – of such institutions depends very much on the international environment in which they are functioning.

To determine whether globalization will continue, the key question is whether the emerging global economy will be able to solve some key economic problems. Will the major industrial nations in the world be able to sustain a real growth in income and a decline in unemployment? Will they be able to contain the international transmission of financial crises? Will they be able to solve world-wide environmental problems? Will they be able to prevent a planetary social breakdown arising from growing poverty in the developing nations or, in industrial nations, an increasing disintegration of the social order and key institutions such as marriage? Will they be able to dampen international conflicts and to limit vicious civil wars – Kosovo, Sierra Leone, Congo – from widening to other countries?

Without hope for amelioration of these kinds of economic, environmental, social and political problems, definite constraints are placed on the extent of globalization, which will always be a convenient political target. A backlash against current globalization trends is certainly possible and the trends identified can always be reversed: domestic protectionism can increase, restrictions can be placed on the international flows of labour or capital or on the activities of multinational enterprises; and current international agreements in various functional areas can always be ignored. The future of globalization is far from certain.

STATISTICAL APPENDIX

Figures 1.1(a) and 1.1(b):   For 1929–96, GDP data come from the US Department of Commerce, Bureau of Economic Analysis (1997). For earlier years I spliced on data from series F-1, US Department of Commerce, Census Bureau (1975). For GDP originating from individual industrials, for 1948–96, the data come from Lum and Yaskavage (1997). For 1920–47 I spliced on sectoral data of national income without capital consumption adjustments from the US Department of Commerce, Bureau of Economic Analysis (1998), Table 6-1A. And for data from 1900–29 I spliced on sectoral national income data from the US Department of Commerce, Census Bureau (1949), Series A154–164. For production of goods I use the agriculture, forestry and fishing, mining and manufacturing sectors. For production of exportable services I use the transportation, communications and public utility, wholesaling and finance, insurance and real estate sectors.

For trade in goods and services comparable to the GDP data for 1929–96, the data come from the Department of Commerce, Bureau of Economic Analysis (1997). For 1900 to 1920 I spliced on data on merchandise trade and selected services from the Department of Commerce, Census Bureau (1975), Series U-2 to U-11.

Figure 1.2(a): Data on legal immigrants come from the US Immigration and Naturalization Service (1996).

Figure 1.2(b): Data on foreign-born population come from the Bureau of the Census (1975), Series C-228 and the Bureau of the Census (annual, 1995), p. 52. The stock of foreign-born is available only in the census years, so interpolations based on the assumption of a constant growth rate were made in the inter-census years.

Figure 1.3(a): Data for 1900 to 1970 come from Bureau of the Census (1975), Series U19–U23. Data for 1960 through 1996 come from the *Survey of Current Business*, 78, July 1998, pp. 70–71 and the Council of Economic Advisors (1998), p. 399. These two series are not quite comparable, but since they are in the same order of magnitude, no adjustments have been made.

Figure 1.3(b): The data for 1900 to 1970 come from Bureau of the Census (1975), Series U26–U39. The data from 1982 (estimated back to 1980) to 1996 come from the *Survey of Current Business*, 77, July 1997, p. 39. In order to make these series roughly comparable with the earlier series, it was necessary to estimate 'long-term' investment that was not foreign direct investment and for this purpose I employed the series on investment in corporate stocks. All other types of foreign investment I considered as 'short term.' Moreover, since the comparisons are with GDP, I believed it useful to use the current cost, rather than the historic cost, estimates. Problems arose, however, for the data between 1970 and 1980 which are based on data from the *Survey of Current Business*, 64, August 1984. The series on direct investment use historic cost data which, for US investment abroad, are hopelessly out of date. Therefore, I made a rough estimate by taking the ratio of current cost to historic cost estimates in 1980 and adjusting upward the foreign direct investment data for 1970 to 1980.

Figure 1.4: For mail, the data between 1910 and 1915, between 1915 and 1920 and between 1920 and 1922 are interpolated; the data come from the Bureau of the Census (annual, various issues). The two series for telephone calls come from the Bureau of the Census (1975), Series and the Bureau of the Census (annual various issues). Data on international travel come from Bureau of the Census (1975), Series H-932 and the Bureau of the Census (annual, various issues). The assumptions used to combine the three series plus the estimate for e-mail and fax are specified in Note 9. Given the nature of the data and the estimates used to combine them in one index, Chart 4 can only be viewed as a very rough estimate.

Figure 1.5:   Data on the foreign exchange turnover in the New York money market come from the Bank of International Settlements (1996), Table 2-E. Data on the monetary base come from US Council of Economic Advisors (1998), p. 364. Data on the market value of sale of all securities come from the Bureau of the Census (annual, various issues).

Note on multinational enterprises   The discussion about global concentration of production draws on various databases presented in Pryor (1999b) and Pryor (1996). In particular, for calculating the concentration of production on a world-wide basis, I used lists published in *Fortune*, July 1958, August 1958 and August 1996. For 1958 I combined the separate lists for the United States and the rest of the world in order to determine the largest enterprises by numbers of employed.

For calculating the relevant size of the labour force for the capitalist world, I used data from censuses and labour force surveys that includes the entire economically active population. Manufacturing and mining are usually specified separately. As a comparison base for the 'all firms' calculation, I subtracted from the total all economically active workers in agriculture and in personal and communal services (which includes public administration). After making an adjustment to remove the unemployed and the armed forces, I then took the fraction of workers to the total population in the countries for which I had data and applied this fraction to the population of the countries for which I did not have data. For these calculations of the labour force I included all countries except Cuba and the former communist countries in Europe and Asia so as to achieve comparability for both years. The final estimates are rough, but they give the appropriate orders of magnitudes.

The underlying data come from: ILO (annual, various editions) and (1990); OECD (1965) and (1997); Republic of China (1996); and United Nations, *Demographic Yearbook* (annual, various editions). Again, I include all nations in the world except Cuba and the former communist nations in Europe and Asia.

NOTES

1. This particular definition draws upon the discussion of Waters (1995, p. 5).
2. Although a considerable literature focuses on the impact of particular aspects of globalization such as foreign trade on unemployment or other specific facets of the US economy, the assessment of the overall impact of globalization, either on a single economy or on the world in general, is still in its infancy. Some interesting attempts along these lines are contained in a recent edited collection by Chen (1998).
3. Raw materials include petroleum, coal products and primary metals but exclude agricultural, forestry and fishing products. The generalizations in this paragraph are based on data series presented in Pryor (1996, p. 189), the Department of Commerce, Bureau of the

Census (annual, 1997, p. 809) and data on GDP originating from various sectors from the Bureau of Economic Analysis web site (http://www.bea.doc.gov/bea/dn2/gpoc.htm).

4. The discussion in this paragraph combines data drawn from Mataloni (1998) and Zeile (1997).

5. The data underlying these generalizations come from the US Department of Commerce, Bureau of the Census (1975, pp. 903–6), and various issues of US Department of Commerce, Bureau of the Census (annual). This represents an extension of the series presented in Pryor (1996, p. 329) from 1900 to 1929 and from 1988 to 1996.

6. Net capital flows, of course, are different and no apparent trend for the USA is observable. For 12 industrial nations as a whole, Obstfeld (1988, table 1) shows a decline in the ratio of such flows to GDP over the 20th century.

7. Problems arise both in determining how much investment is where and how to evaluate such investment. From 1970 onward I have tried to measure this long-term investment in current prices. Cantwell and Bellak (1998) have rather different estimates of the current values of the data shown in the table and, for instance, estimate a faster growth of US FDI (Foreign Direct Investment) and a slower growth of FDI in the United States than that shown in Graph 3b.

8. The data come from the US Department of Commerce, Bureau of the Census (1975, series U-28 to U-36) and (annual, 1996, p. 791). The two series, however, are not comparable and the conclusions drawn in the text are highly tentative.

9. The US Department of Commerce, Bureau of the Census (1975, p. 870); and (annual, 1997, p. 795).

10. Between these end points, however, such flows spiked dramatically upward during World War II, fell rapidly back to prewar levels, rose slowly until 1970, and then declined. The data have a bizarre artifact in that until 1950 the volume of international mail was measured by the weight of such flows and the World War II spike reflects the parcels, rather than letters, mailed to US soldiers abroad. I have, for this reason, omitted the war years.

11. These include: (a) one phone call equals one letter; (b) the average weight of overseas letters did not change between 1921 and 1950; (c) one visit overseas equals 10 letters or phone calls; (d) the omission of Canada and Mexico from these various series does not essentially change the results; and (e) that in 1975 there were one million fax or e-mail messages overseas and that these increased by 20 per cent a year thereafter.

12. Data on real exports and imports from 1921 through 1996 come from the US Department of Commerce, Bureau of Economic Analysis (1997). These were extended back to 1921 by splicing data on real exports and imports from the Census Bureau (1975), Series U225 and U237.

13. The information on bond holdings comes from Sobol (1998).

14. Data come from the Census Bureau (1975), Series U207–U212, and the Census Bureau (annual, 1997, p. 808).

15. The interest rates used to make these comparisons for the different countries are: *United States*, three-month T-bills and three-year government bond rate; *Belgium*, T-bills and the average government bond rate; *Canada*, T-bills and the average rate on three- to five-year government bonds; *France*, three-month lending rate and average yield on government bonds; *Germany*, T-bill rate and average government bond yield; *Italy*, average T-bill rate before taxes and average rate on medium-term government bonds; *Japan*, the government bond yield (no short-term rates comparable to the other countries were available); *Netherlands*, T-bills and average government bonds; *Switzerland*, T-bills and government bond yields; and *United Kingdom*, T-bills and short-term government bond rate.

Data on interest rates come from *World Investment Report* (1997). I calculated real interest rates for a given year by subtracting the change in the GDP price deflator from the interest rate. Real interest rates for a given year for the long term were calculated by subtracting the average annual change in the GDP price deflator for that year and the two previous years. The variations in these interest rates are an unweighted standard deviation. Other types of calculations along these lines are carried out by Herring and Litan (1995).

16. Regional agreements are proliferating, although many are not in force. According to Lawrence (1996), in 1994 the IMF listed 68 preferential economic agreements, running from the ASEAN Free Trade Area (AFTA), the Andean Pact (ANCOM) through to the West African Economic and Monetary Union (WAEMU).

17. Among other things the Mundell–Fleming model assumes perfect capital mobility between nations. Under a fixed exchange rate regime, expansionary fiscal policy would stimulate home output but would have a negative effect on the balance of trade because of higher imports (which might require open market operations to decrease the money supply to protect the exchange rate). An increase in the money supply through open market operations would give rise to an equal fall in foreign reserves as domestic capital would flow abroad to higher interest rates, with no final impact on the interest rate. With a floating exchange rate expansionary fiscal policy would give rise to imports of equal size (plus a downward pressure on the exchange rate which might offset this movement), while expansionary monetary policy would stimulate production by lowering the exchange rate, even though interest rates would not be affected. Such an static approach makes a considerable number of assumptions that are open to challenge. It also does not take into account the impact of portfolio balance, speculation or other real-world phenomena.

18. These results report the 'b' coefficient in regressions specified as: $M = a + bY$, where M and Y refer respectively to imports and GDP in fixed prices. The data come from the Department of Commerce, Bureau of Economic Analysis (1997).

19. These exchange rates are taken from the web site of the Board of Governors of the Federal Reserve Bank.

20. The statement is cited by Patrick J. Buchanan (1998, p. 257) and is taken from a 1933 book, *America Self-Contained*, by Samuel Crowthers.

21. The battle rages as fiercely today as in yesteryear. Recently, Burtless et al. (1998) provide arguments supporting open trade while Buchanan (1998) supplies arguments against. I have yet to find a popular book opposed to tariff reduction or free trade that does not cite Abraham Lincoln's famous remark: 'I don't know much about the tariff. But I know this much. When we buy manufactured goods abroad, we get the goods and the foreigner gets the money. When we buy the manufactured goods at home, we get both the goods and the money.'

22. One other issue about state sovereignty deserves brief mention. According to Daniel Bell (1987), 'The nation-state is becoming too small for big problems of life and too big for small problems of life.' There is, in brief, a growing mismatch of scale. Regarding the first misalignment, the increase in the power of weapons of mass destruction, global pollution problems, the shocks on financial systems of one nation if other nations experience economic panic and other difficulties cannot be dealt with by individual governments. From this perspective, globalization allows us as citizens of the world to deal more effectively with our problems.

   Some have offered interesting reasons why the nation state may disappear entirely in the future. For instance, Kaplan (1998) argues that given the increasing economic and geographical stratification of American society, educated Americans may have more in common with their counterparts throughout the world than with their less-educated fellow Americans. Omae (1995) claims that nation states are too heterogeneous and that regional entities, often covering several nations, will play ever-growing strategic roles in the increasingly globalized and interregionalized economy.

   The growing power of Scottish nationalism is, perhaps, the most glaring example of the growing power of such regionalism. Nevertheless, let me state without argument that to me the death of the nation state seems premature and that national governments will continue to have an important role in structuring and regulating economic activity for at least the next century.

REFERENCES

Bank of International Settlements, Monetary and Economics Department (1996), *Central Bank Survey of Foreign Exchange and Derivatives Market Activity*, Basel.

Bauer, Scott and Jeffrey H. Bergstrand (1998), 'The growth of world trade', unpublished paper, Notre Dame University.

Bell, Daniel (1987), 'The world and the United States in 2013', *Daedalus*, **116** (3), 1–33.

Buchanan, Patrick J. (1998), *The Great Betrayal: How American Sovereignty and Social Justice are Being Sacrificed to the Gods of a Global Economy*, Boston: Little, Brown and Company.

Burtless, Gary, Robert Z. Lawrence, Robert E. Litan and Robert J. Shapiro (1998), *Globaphobia: Confronting Fears about Open Trade*, Washington, DC: Brookings Institution, The Progressive Policy Institute and The Twentieth Century Fund.

Campa, José and Linda S. Goldberg (1997), 'The evolving external orientation of manufacturing: a profile of four countries', Federal Reserve Bank of New York, *Economic Policy Review*, **3** (2), 53–81.

Cantwell, John (1995), 'Multinational Corporations and Innovatory Activities: Toward a New, Evolutionary Approach', in José Molero (ed.), *Technological Innovation, Multinational Corporations and New International Competitiveness*, Newark, NJ: Harwood Academic Publisher.

Cantwell, John and Christian Bellak (1998), 'How important is foreign direct investment?', *Oxford Bulletin of Economics and Statistics*, **60** (1), 99–106.

Chen, John-Ren (ed.) (1998), *Economic Effects of Globalization*, Aldershot: Ashgate.

Cohen, Benjamin J. (1998), *The Geography of Money*, Ithaca: Cornell University Press.

Coleman, William D. and Geoffrey R.D. Underhill (eds) (1998), *Regionalism and Global Integration: Europe, Asia and the Americas*, New York: Routledge.

Crockett, Andrew (1997), 'Global Capital Markets and the Stability of Banking and Financial Systems', in Charles Enoch and John H. Green (eds), *Banking Soundness and Monetary Policy: Issues and Experiences in the Global Economy*, Washington, DC: IMF.

Doremus, Paul N., William W. Keller, Louis W. Pauly and Simon Reich (1998), *The Myth of the Global Corporation*, Princeton, NJ: Princeton University Press.

Dunning, John H. (1997), 'The Advent of Alliance Capitalism', in John H. Dunning and Khalil A. Hamdani (eds), *The New Globalism and Developing Countries*, New York: United Nations University Press, pp. 12–51.

Ehrenberg, Ronald G. (1994), *Labour Markets and Integrating National Economies*, Washington, DC: Brookings Institution.

Engel, Charles and John H. Rogers (1998), 'Regional Patterns in the Law of One Price: The Roles of Geography versus Currencies', in Frankel (1998), pp. 153–83.

Enoch, Charles and John H. Green (eds) (1997), *Banking Soundness and Monetary Policy: Issues and Experiences in the Global Economy*, Washington, DC: IMF Institute.

Feenstra, Robert C. (1998), 'Integration of trade and disintegration of production in the global economy', *Journal of Economic Perspectives*, **12** (3), 31–51.

Feenstra, Robert C. and Gordon H. Hanson (1996), 'Foreign Investment, Outsourcing and Relative Wages', in Robert C. Feenstra, Gene M. Grossman and Douglas A. Irwin (eds), *The Political Economy of Trade Policy: Papers in Honour of Jagdish Bhagwati*, Cambridge: MIT Press, pp. 98–127.

Frankel, Jeffrey A. (ed.) (1998), *The Regionalization of the World Economy*, Chicago: University of Chicago Press for the National Bureau of Economic Research.

Grubel, Herbert G. and P.J. Lloyd (1971), 'The empirical measurement of intra-industry trade', *Economic Record*, **47** (120), 494–517.

Herring, Richard J. and Robert E. Litan (1995), *Financial Regulation in the Global Economy*, Washington, DC: Brookings Institution.

Hindrich, Harley H. (1966), *A General Theory of Tax Structure Change during Economic Development*, Cambridge, MA: Harvard University Law School.

Hirst, Paul and Grahame Thompson (1996), *Globalization in Question: The International Economy and the Possibilities of Governance*, Cambridge, MA: Blackwell Publishers.

Hummels, David, Dana Rapoport and Kei-Mu Yi (1998), 'Vertical Specialization and the Changing Nature of World Trade', Federal Reserve Bank of New York, *Economic Policy Review*, **4** (2), 79–99.

International Labour Office (ILO) (annual), *Year Book of Labour Statistics*, Geneva.

International Labour Office (ILO) (1990), *Retrospective Edition on Population Censuses, 1945–1989*, Geneva.

International Monetary Fund (1996), *International Financial Statistics CD Data Diskette*, Washington, DC, June.

Jefferson, Philip N. (1998), 'Seigniorage payments for use of the dollar: 1977–1995', *Economic Letters*, **58**, 225–30.

Kaplan, Robert D. (1998), *An Empire Wilderness: Travels into America's Future*, New York: Random House.

Keynes, John Maynard ([1919] 1971), *The Economic Consequences of the Peace*, Volume 11, *The Collected Writings of John Maynard Keynes*, London: Macmillan.

Krugman, Paul and Anthony J. Venables (1995), 'Globalization and the inequality of nations', *NBER Working Paper*, 5098, Cambridge, MA.

La Porta, Rafael, Florencio Lopez-de-Silanes and Andrei Shleifer (1998), 'Corporate ownership around the world', *NBER Working Paper*, 6625, Cambridge, MA.

Lawrence, Robert Z. (1996), *Regionalism Multilateralism and Deeper Integration*, Washington, DC: Brookings Institution.

Linder, Staffan Burenstam (1961), *An Essay on Trade and Transformation*, New York: Wiley.

Lum, Sherlene K.S. and Robert E. Yuskavage (1997), 'Gross product by industry, 1947–1996', *Survey of Current Business*, **77** (11), 30–36.

Mataloni, Raymond J. (1998), 'US multinational companies: operations in 1996', *Survey of Current Business*, **78** (9), 47–73.

Mishkin, Frederic S. (1994), 'Preventing Financial Crises: An International Perspective', *The Manchester School*, Supplement, *Papers in Money, Macroeconomics and Finance*, 1–40.

Obstfeld, Maurice (1988), 'The global capital market: benefactor or menace', *The Journal of Economic Perspectives*, **12** (4), 9–31.

Omae, Kenichi (1995), *The End of the Nation State: The Rise of Regional Economies*, New York: Free Press.

Organization of Economic Cooperation and Development (OECD) (1965), *Manpower Statistics 1954–1964*, Paris.

Organization of Economic Cooperation and Development (OECD) (1997) *Labour Force Statistics, 1976–1996*, Paris.

Pfaller, Alfred, Ian Gough and Goran Therborn (1991), *Can the Welfare State Compete?*, London: Macmillan.

Pryor, Frederic L. (1981), 'Static and dynamic effects of different types of trade barriers: a synthesis using a general equilibrium model', *Eastern Economic Journal*, **7** (2), 59–74.

Pryor, Frederic L. (1992), 'A puzzle about intra-industry trade: a comment', *Weltwirtschaftliches Archiv*, **128** (4), 742–6.

Pryor, Frederic L. (1994), 'The evolution of competition in the United States', *The Review of Industrial Organization*, **25** (2), 121–33.

Pryor, Frederic L. (1995), 'Behaviour of retail prices: a note on market integration in the US', *Eastern Economic Journal*, **21** (1), 83–97.

Pryor, Frederic L. (1996), *Economic Evolution and Structure: The Impact of Complexity on the US Economic System*, New York: Cambridge University Press.

Pryor, Frederic L. (1999a), 'The impact of foreign trade on the employment of unskilled US workers: some new evidence', *Southern Economic Journal*, **65** (3), 47–93.

Pryor, Frederic L. (1999b), 'Will we all be working for giant enterprises by 2028?', forthcoming.

Pryor, Frederic L. and David Schaffer (1999), *Who's Not Working and Why: Employment, Cognitive Skills, Wages, and the Changing US Labour Market*, New York: Cambridge University Press.

Pryor, Frederic L. and Elliott Sulcove (1995), 'A note on volatility', *Journal of Post-Keynesian Economics*, **17** (4), 525–44.

Republic of China (1996), *Statistical Yearbook of the Republic of China, 1996*, Taipai.

Rhodes, Martin (1998), '"Subversive Liberalism": Market Integration, Globalization and West European Welfare States', in Coleman and Underhill (1998), pp. 99–121.

Rodrik, Dani (1997), *Has Globalization Gone too Far?*, Washington, DC: Institute for International Economics.

Sassen, Saskia (1996), *Losing Control? Sovereignty in an Age of Globalization*, New York: Columbia University Press.

Sobol, Dorothy Meadow (1998), 'Foreign ownership of US treasury securities: what the data show and do not show', Federal Reserve Bank of New York, *Current Issues in Economics and Finance*, **4** (3), 1–6.

Soros, George (1998), *The Crisis of Global Capitalism: Open Society Endangered*, New York: Public Affairs Press.

Thurow, Lester C. (1992), *Head to Head: The Coming Economic Battle Among Japan, Europe, and America*, New York: Morrow.

United Nations (annual), *Demographic Yearbook*, New York.

US Council of Economic Advisors (annual), *Economic Report of the President*, Washington, DC: GPO.

US Department of Commerce, Bureau of the Census (1949), *Historical Statistics of the United States 1879–1945*, Washington, DC: GPO.

US Department of Commerce, Bureau of the Census (1975), *Historical Statistics of the United States*, Washington, DC: GPO.

US Department of Commerce, Bureau of the Census (annual), *Statistical Abstract of the United States*, Washington, DC: GPO.

US Department of Commerce, Bureau of Economic Analysis (1997), *US National Income and Product Accounts*, diskette BE-54 (September 1997).

US Department of Commerce, Bureau of Economic Analysis (1998), *National Income and Product Accounts of the United States, 1929–94*, Washington, DC: GPO.

US Department of Justice, Immigration and Naturalization Service (1996), *Statistical Yearbook*, Washington, DC: GPO.

Waters, Malcolm (1995), *Globalization*, London: Routledge.

Williamson, Jeffrey G. (1995), 'Globalization, convergence, and history', *NBER Working Paper* 5259, Cambridge, MA.

Williamson, Jeffrey G. (1996), 'Globalization and inequality then and now: the late 19th and late 20th centuries compared', *NBER Working Paper* 5491, Cambridge, MA.

Williamson, Jeffrey G. (1998), 'Globalization, labour markets and policy backlash in the past', *The Journal of Economic Perspectives*, **12** (4), 61–73.

Wolfson, Martin E. (1986), *Financial Crises: Understanding the Postwar US Experience*, Armonk, New York: M.E. Sharpe.

Wolfson, Martin E. (1990), 'The causes of financial instability', *Journal of Post-Keynesian Economics*, **12** (3), 333–55.

Wood, Adrian (1994), *North–South Trade, Employment and Inequality*, Oxford: Clarendon Press.

World Investment Report 1997, New York and Geneva, United Nations Conference on Trade and Development.

Zeile, William J. (1997), 'US intrafirm trade in goods,' *Survey of Current Business*, **77** (2), 23–38.

2. Deepening integration and global governance: America as a globalized partner

John Kirton

INTRODUCTION

The argument that intensifying transnational flows of private sector forces are altering and eroding the capacity of states to manage their national economies and the multinational firms operating or based within them has long been a standard claim in international political economy (Angell, 1912; Stanley, 1939; Cooper, 1968; Vernon, 1971; Keohane and Nye, 1977). In its current manifestation, with the rubric of 'globalization' replacing earlier concepts of 'interdependence', the debate over the force of such flows and their implications for the American economy, its multinationals and the management of both, has passed through several stages.

The first asserted that the new communications technologies, initially evident in the realm of globalized finance and subsequently in integrated transnational production, produced a seamless global economy and polity in which multinationals and markets would converge toward a new single set of prices, practices, characteristics and ultimately identities designed to maximize wealth in the single global environment, with little regard for their distinctive national origins, or efforts at national government control (Reich, 1990; Ohmae, 1995). The second stage emphasized how, in the face of the new global orientation and power of multinationals and markets, even the more powerful governments in the world were suffering a substantial diminution of their ability to manage the global, and even their own domestic economy, to the point where they were reluctant even to attempt interventions they now calculated would fail (Peterson, 1995; Strange, 1996; Bergsten and Henning, 1996). The third stage, in reaction to the occasionally excessive claims of government impotence in the face of globalized markets and multinationals, pointed to how limited the processes of globalization still were, as technology produced at best only an internationalized rather than globalized economy (Weiss, 1998). To some analysts in this third stage, the world's leading multinationals and national political systems, far from being common global actors with convergent features, retained the distinctive entrenched features of their original and continuing national base (Doremus, et al., 1998; Soskice, 1998).

Throughout this debate, America as an empirical entity maintained an exceptional status (Krugman, 1999). The forces of globalization, long a reality for smaller states, were felt to have become more broadly dominant when they propelled Japanese firms to move abroad in the 1980s and compelled major European governments to devalue their national currencies in the early 1990s. Even then, the most ardent advocates of the advent-of-globalization argument judged that America, with appropriate unilateral policy adjustments, could equip itself to prevail in the new competitive environment (Peterson, 1995). For others, globalization, based on technological innovation and the liberalization of international barriers and national regulations for finance, trade and investment, was, in effect, Americanization. It constituted an American-inspired and guided project that spread the American ideology of neo-liberalism and the American business system as the triumph model to be adopted on a global scale (Wade, 1998–9; Helleiner, 1994). For still others, the world remained one of relative isolation, with America and its multinationals, along with those of its major rivals, able to maintain their distinctive character and flourish, within and beyond their home regions, in so doing. Amid this debate there were few who offered a vision, seen briefly in the political realm in the mid-1970s, of America as an ordinary country, equally affected by, equally vulnerable to and reacting in similar ways to the forces of globalization along with, and in cooperation with, other consequential countries in the world. (Rosecrance, 1975; Kapstein, 1994). Indeed, as the 1990s progressed, America, with its uniquely large, nationally insulated economy, exceptionally vibrant growth and self-confident isolationist and unilateralist political traditions, seemed to be a country that created or contained globalization by national choice, rather than one seriously constrained by it through international necessity.

At the dawn of the new millennium, however, proliferating forces of globalization are indeed rapidly transforming America into an ordinary country. Transnational flows of capital, goods, services, technology and information have now acquired a speed, intensity, comprehensive and self-reinforcing character, and fully global reach that make them qualitatively different than their precursors of even proximate decades past. Rather, they have become a defining feature of the international system as a whole. They are thus much more able to constrain a relatively less powerful but far more globally connected America, and to impact more on its domestic economy, society and polity than in the earlier eras of interdependence (Rodrik, 1997). They have given the United States an equality of vulnerability, alongside lesser powers, to processes originating outside American borders. But they have also endowed America with an equality of incentive to develop, along with its major market democratic partners, effective international cooperation and institutions whose resources, decisions and constraints display far more balance than in the past.

In short, America is already effectively globalized. Its economy is sufficiently vulnerable to the outside world, in ways that its governments, managers and citizens recognize, that it has developed a reluctant attachment to international collaboration through mutual adjustment and has allowed its national policies and practices to be constrained by international regimes. Globalization has created a vulnerable American economy, but it has not thereby bred an impotent American polity or management. Rather, it has at both levels fostered an America compelled to cooperate, through concert governance and alliance capitalism, to resist, shape and create the processes of globalization that it and most other countries desire (Kirton and Daniels, 1999; Dunning, 1997).

To support this thesis, this chapter first assesses the structural foundations of America's globalization by identifying America's modest capabilities and its ensuing requirements for external resources to maintain its position, relative to the global system, major country competitors and collaborators and private sector actors on key dimensions of the international political economy. It explores, second, a critical test case – the response of the US economy and government to the 1997–8 crisis in the global financial system – to demonstrate the acute vulnerability of an apparently dominant American economy to market contagion from abroad, the need of the US government for major assistance from G7 governments to stem the crisis and the US government's forced adjustment to the preferences of its partners in its crisis response and the construction of a new international financial architecture. It examines, thirdly, the effective international dependence of US firms on foreign capital and business alliances, not only through a static snapshot or examination of trends in American behaviour over time but also by means of an analysis of changes in the American position relative to that of its G7 partners. It reviews, fourth, the broad popular foundations of America's new acceptance of globalization by showing how Americans, at the elite and mass public level, have reluctantly come to accept and support the policies of cooperation-as-equals that a globalized America now demands. It finally considers the equal adjustment of American governments and firms to the preferences of others in the regimes embedded in international institutions, both at the global level in the G7 and at the regional level in NAFTA.

THE STRUCTURAL FOUNDATIONS OF AMERICA'S GLOBALIZATION: RELATIVE CAPABILITY RETREAT

America's emergence in the 1990s as a globalized partner rests on solid structural foundations, notably the reduction to modest levels of America's capabilities relative to the global system, major country competitors and collaborators, and private sector actors, on key dimensions of the international political economy. This reduction has bred a reliance on others for external resources that an earlier, more hegemonic America, could do without. The transition began during the mid-1980s (Kirton, 1986). It has experienced a small and recent Clinton reversal. However, the absence of any genuine post-cold war unipolar moment for America as the world's only superpower has produced, for well over a decade, a less capable and hence more cooperative America

The first sign of America's relative decline is apparent in its overall economic capabilities, measured by GDP in US$ at current exchange rates (a measure which well reflects the advent of floating exchange rates and national capital liberalization after 1971). In 1970 the USA possessed a majority 54.6 per cent of economic capabilities among what was to become the G7 with the formation of the group in 1975 (Kirton, 1999a; Kirton, 1999b). Following a decline to 41.1 per cent in 1980, and the 'Reagan rise' to a renewed majority 51.7 per cent in 1985, the US declined rather steadily to a post-World War II low of 38.2 per cent by 1995. Although it experienced a small rise to 42.1 per cent by 1997, this 'Clinton revival' is but a tiny replica of the ultimately ephemeral 'Reagan restoration' of 1980–85. By this measure of capability Japan had risen to reach 68.4 per cent of America's capabilities by 1994, with Germany commanding 26.1 per cent. Together the two ranking rivals were almost as powerful as America alone.

America's declining and modest share of G7 and global capabilities is even more apparent in the core economic components of finance, trade, foreign direct investment and aid. In the realm of finance, the US$ share of G5 currencies in world foreign exchange reserves dropped from 76.1 per cent in 1973 to 63.3 per cent in 1994, while that of the German mark rose from 7.1 per cent to 15.5 per cent over the same period (Bergsten and Henning, 1996). The 1999 introduction of the euro could well take the still hegemonic US position down below 50 per cent. The US share of world private transactions (outside external bank loans) was by 1992–3 already well below 50 per cent. Its share of international monetary reserves dropped from 13.2 per cent in 1973 to 10 per cent in 1995, whereas that of Japan doubled from 5.5 per cent to 10. 6 per cent during the same period. Similarly, the US share of total IMF quotas fell from 34.2 per cent to 18.3 per cent over the same period. The USA now accounts for 22.9 per cent of the $18.5 billion total of the General

Arrangements to Borrow (GAB), down from 33 per cent of the $6 billion total when the GAB was created in 1962.

In the realm of trade, in 1997 the USA had only 12.6 per cent of global exports, compared to 9.4 per cent for Germany, 7.7 per cent for Japan and 48.8 per cent for the G7 as a whole (Kirton, 1999b). Exports as a share of GDP rose for the United States from 1992 to 1997 at a more rapid pace than those of its largest (if not its smallest) G7 partners, as follows: USA 15.7 per cent, Germany 12.2 per cent, Japan 10 per cent, France 15.8 per cent, Britain 19.3 per cent, Italy 37 per cent, and Canada 47.8 per cent. Given the relative overall size of these economies, and the natural tendency for smaller economies to be more open, this represents a rapid relative US rise toward openness. Indeed, the United States Trade Representative (USTR) has estimated that by the early years of the 21st century, trade will represent one-third of US GDP.

In the realm of foreign direct investment, on a global basis the inward plus outward stock of Foreign Direct Investment (FDI) as a share of global production rose from 9.5 per cent in 1980, to 15.8 per cent in 1990, to 21.4 per cent in 1996 (United Nations, 1997, p. 8). For the USA, it rose, over the same intervals, from 11.2 per cent through 14.5 per cent to 18.6 per cent. In contrast, for Japan it rose from 2.2 per cent to 7.3 per cent, but then declined to 6.3 per cent in 1996. Although the US growth of FDI in the 1990s has not quite kept pace with the global average or with G7 partners such as France, it continues to expand relative to the US economy, and remains close to the average global level.

In the realm of official development assistance, a measure of the surplus capacity a country has to secure influence abroad, the USA had fallen to second and then third place among the ranks of donors during the 1990s (Kirton, 1999b). In 1997, the USA provided only $6.1 billion in Overseas Direct Aid (ODA), compared with $9.4 billion for Japan, $6.2 billion for France and $6.0 billion for Germany. In 1997 the US share represented only 16.8 per cent of the G7 total; in 1993 it had accounted for 20.9 per cent. It is thus hardly surprising that the European Union provided three-quarters of the assistance to the former Soviet Union and Central and Eastern Europe in the 1990s, 70 per cent of the budget for peacekeeping and civil construction in Bosnia and over half the international assistance to the West Bank and Gaza in support of the Middle East peace process from 1994–7, whereas the US offered only 10 per cent of the latter (Wallace and Zielonka, 1998).

Indeed, should the ongoing process of European integration make it useful to consider the European Union a single unit, it is possible to see the emergence of a new trans-Atlantic bi-powerness and potential bipolarity, with Europe serving as an equal to a post-cold war United States. In high-technology fields, Europe rivals the USA in pharmaceuticals and new materials if not in information technology. In the security sphere European NATO members spend two-thirds of the US defence budget, and the EU provides 80 per cent of the peacekeepers on the ground in Bosnia (Wallace and Zielonka, 1998). Yet globalization means connections too close, unlike old bipolarity or that which may emerge across the Pacific with China.

THE GLOBAL FINANCIAL CRISIS OF 1997–98

Given America's relative remaining predominance in the realm of finance, where the dynamics of globalization first flourished, it is instructive to determine whether the USA, even with superior capabilities, has passed a critical threshold that has rendered its economy vulnerable, rather than merely sensitive, to the now much more intense and extensive flows of global finance. An appropriate test case is the 1997–98 Asian-turned-global financial crisis, and the response of the US economy and government to it. An analysis of the crisis from its origins with the devaluation of the Thai baht in July 1997, through the mobilization of a $41.5 billion international support package for Brazil in November 1998, to the conclusions of the G7 finance ministers meeting in Bonn on 20 February 1999 reveal three features of America's new equal vulnerability to financial globalization. These are: the acute exposure of an apparently dominant American economy to market contagion from abroad; the need of the US government for major assistance from G7 partner governments to stem the crisis; and the US government's forced adjustment to the preferences of its partners in its crisis response and in the contemporaneous construction of a new international financial architecture.

The American economy, throughout its private sector agents, both multinationals and markets, proved to be vulnerable to what President Clinton himself described as the most serious financial crisis in 50 years. Its underlying exposure to the general deflation and collapse in commodity prices stemming from Asian currency devaluation is evident in America's substantial share of commodity exports as a percentage of total exports. Here the US figure of 21 per cent compares with only 5 per cent for Japan and 15 per cent for Germany, although 24 per cent for the UK and 35 per cent for Canada (Hale, 1998a). The peak of the crisis in September 1998 – the contagion throughout Asia, the mid-August de facto default and devaluation in Russia and the continuing inability of the US Congress to authorize the US share of an agreed upon IMF quota increase – culminated in the US Federal Reserve orchestrated rescue of the virtually bankrupt LTCM hedge fund. Its action was precipitated by the panic a collapse of LTCM was causing in the US domestic credit market, amid a flight to quality and liquidity that had even large and profitable US firms experiencing difficulties in maintaining access to their usual lines of credit (Soros, 1998–9; Krugman, 1999). As one analyst described the progression: 'In an ironic twist of fate, the global financial contagion which began with the New York hedge funds' attack on the Thai baht in the spring of 1997 had gone full circle back to a near collapse of the New York markets themselves' (Hale, 1998b). At the peak of the crisis, with the prospect of a frozen US credit system amid a full-blown crisis of confidence, the USA was no longer a Kindlebergerian stabilizer of last resort but an equally vulnerable economy (Kindleberger, 1973).

In response to the crisis, the USA no longer alone possessed the resources to provide global stability but needed a collective response to rescue both its own economy and that of the world. At the peak of the crisis, the USA led with an interest rate reduction on 29 September and two subsequent downward moves. But its initial response was accompanied by virtually simultaneous moves in the UK and Canada. By the end of the year, a broad array of countries had joined to produce a total of 34 interest rate reductions. Moreover, it was only in response to the evident domestic crisis that the US Congress finally passed the US IMF quota share increase.

Second, the US need for its G7 partners' support in the face of the crisis was further apparent in the packages assembled to support the major infected countries. Here, the need, especially given congressional reluctance for the USA to provide its IMF quota share increase, was so great as to force the USA to reach beyond the resources of the IMF, where its influence was exceptionally strong, to mobilize additional support from its G7 partners. In early December 1997, the G7 countries agreed to support a beleaguered South Korea with a package of US$35 billion from the IMF, the World Bank, and the Asian Development Bank, reinforced if necessary by a second line of defence. To this second line Japan committed US$10 billion, the United States US$5 billion, each of the European G7 members US$1.25 billion and Canada up to US$1 billion (Kirton and Kokotsis, 1997–8). In the case of Thailand, among non-Asian G7 members only Canada, in April 1998, provided additional national funds, whereas the United States, fearful of congressional criticism, remained uninvolved. By the time of the Brazilian package in November 1998, of the US$41.5 billion total, the IMF provided $18 billion, the IBRD $4.5 billion, the IDB $4.5 billion and bilateral contributions funneled through the BIS, $14.5 billion. The US provided only $5 billion of these bilateral contributions (Kirton, 1999c).

A third sign of America's equal vulnerability was its willingness to adjust to the preferences of its G7 partners to combat the crisis and construct a new international financial architecture to govern the global economy of the new millennium. America's adjustment was first evident at the G7 finance ministers' gathering in Hong Kong in September 1997, where the Asian financial crisis dominated the agenda. Here G7 finance ministers agreed to increase the IMF quota share by 45 per cent; to amend the IMF Articles of Agreement within the year to make the IMF responsible for capital account liberalization; to strengthen IMF involvement in banking and financial sector reform; to improve national governance by reducing corruption; and to expand the allocation of special drawing rights (SDRs) (Sachs, 1998). On the IMF quota share increase, G7 members induced a reluctant United States, which feared congressional opposition, to accept a large 45 per cent addition. On capital account liberalization, which was a UK initiative supported by the USA, strong opposition from Canada, first evident in Canadian views on the treatment of capital flows at the 1995 Halifax G7 Summit, blunted initial enthusiasm for a blanket grant of authority to the IMF for rapid, unrestricted liberalization. The United States, Japan and Canada reinforced their initiative, begun at the G7 summit in Lyons in 1996, to emphasize banking and financial sector reform. A United States' desire to address national governance issues, supported by Canada, succeeded when the IMF agreed to take up the question. On the issue of an additional 'equity allocation' of IMF Special Drawing Rights (SDRs), the IMF, in accord with the G7 position at Halifax, agreed to double the allocation and to devote the proceeds to the new members of the IMF.

During the autumn of 1998, at the height of the global crisis, America was induced to share leadership and the shaping of collective outcomes with its G7 partners to an even greater degree. The traditional portrait of an America able and willing to lead appeared in the form of a speech given by President Clinton in New York on 14 September 1998, in which he emphasized the desirability of interest rate cuts, a new IMF precautionary lending facility and support for Brazil. Yet other countries, including smallest Canada on 29 September, were equally active in asserting intellectual and policy leadership by presenting comprehensive visions or concrete proposals on core items. In the realm of process, a UK desire for a special G7 Summit to reassure markets, after it was clear the regular 3 October G7 finance minister's meeting had failed to do so, met with US, Japanese and Canadian resistance, but led to the compromise of three special G7 statements on 30 October by leaders, by finance ministers and by the G7 executive directors of the IMF to the organization's managing director. This last statement represented not only an unusually public manifestation of the G7's control within the IMF, but the G7's provision to the USA of the support it needed to ensure that congressional conditions for the transfer of the IMF's quota share increase would be fulfilled.

In the realm of substance, by November the USA had prevailed in only a few of the preferences which it pioneered. The G7 accepted the use of a 'preventative' approach in regard to Brazilian support resisted, however, moving to entrench a precautionary facility within the IMF (Eichengreen and Ghironi, 1998, p. 97). Indeed, by the conclusion of the 20 February G7 finance minister's meeting in Bonn, it was clear that no such facility would be created within the IMF. American leadership, supported by the Japanese, the British and more cautiously by the Canadians, proved unable to overcome the strong resistance of Germany, France and Italy, their concerns of moral hazard and the spectre of a further Russian request. The compromise result was a possible contingent credit facility, with money lent for very short terms at high and escalating interest rates, with strong IMF conditionality applied throughout.

Nor was the USA markedly more successful on most of the other major issues: lower interest rates within the G7; fiscal stimulus in affected Asian economies; social targeting of expenditures; financial system supervision; capital controls and governance of the international financial architecture. On interest rate stimulus, the US–Canadian–UK preference for lower interest rates was readily adopted, especially after the election of a social-democratic government in Germany. The preference of Canada, initially resisted by the USA, for the IMF to allow fiscal deficits in affected Asian economies, to use the additional spending for targeted social safety nets and to have the World Bank join to reinforce this objective, prevailed (Krugman, 1999). On arrangements for enhanced international supervision of national financial institutions, Canadian, UK and French proposals competed, with the USA having no hard preference but leaning toward an IMF-centred regime. The result, approved at the February 1999 G7 finance ministers meeting, was the creation of a new financial stability forum, in which the supervisory authorities for banks, securities, insurance and mutual funds and finance ministers and central bankers in about 34 countries would meet twice a year with the IMF, BIS and other international institutions on the margins of the IMF to set policy. On capital controls, the Anglo–American plan that prevailed at Hong Kong was substantially overturned, as Canada succeeded in securing a G7 consensus for a properly sequenced, 'roadmap' to capital liberalization (Wade, 1998–9). On governance of the international financial architecture, at Bonn in February 1999, the G7 set aside a French proposal for a leaders'-level summit of the IMF Interim Committee in favour of an Italian proposal, supported by the Americans, for a greater decisional role for the IMF Interim Committee, with finance deputies meeting two weeks in advance to prepare the meetings.

AMERICAN MULTINATIONALS IN ALLIANCE

A further sign of America's equal globalization is the increasing international dependence of US firms on foreign capital and business alliances. This is evident when examined, not only through a static snapshot or a look at trends in American behaviour alone over time, but also in changes in the America position relative to that of its G7 partners. A static snapshot of the international spread of exposure of US-based firms to the global economy still provides evidence for the traditional portrait of a relatively unique and insulated American business system. A consideration of trends in American FDI and multinationals' behaviour in isolation over recent decades provides evidence of a slow, and often steady, internationalization. However an examination of such trends in relation to those of America's G7 partners reveals a dynamic of genuine globalization – the move of the United States towards an effective equality of involvement in and dependence upon international operations and alliances.

A static snapshot of the American economy at present suggests an American business system still heavily based on the national market and well insulated from, rather than dependent upon, the outside world. The outward stock of US FDI as a percentage of US GDP, at 10 per cent, (and US FDI outflows as a percentage of fixed capital formation) is substantially smaller than that of most of its OECD partners, reflecting the sheer size of the US economy. In the mid-1990s US TNCs produced 74.6 per cent of their gross product, had 75.7 per cent of their employment and conducted 76.4 per cent of their capital expenditures within the United States, while US parent companies' inputs purchased from abroad represented only 6 per cent of the parent's output (United Nations, 1998, p. 153).

Not surprisingly, of the over 2800 technology alliances among firms from the USA, Europe or Japan from 1980 to 1994, the largest number were between firms from the USA alone: 37 per cent (and 57 per cent in 1994 alone) in the case of information technology and almost 40 per cent in biotechnology. But the second largest share – a total of 22 per cent overall – were alliances between US and European firms (Doremus et al., 1998, pp. 113–4). Moreover, in the field of biotechnology, the US–EU share was 28 per cent.

When the US trend over time is examined, however, there is evidence of a steady, if slow, internationalization. From 1982 to 1995, the US TNC parent companies' national share had fallen from 78.1 per cent to 64.6 per cent of gross product, 78.8 per cent to 75.7 per cent of employment. In the field of biotechnology, since 1989, trans-Atlantic alliances have rivalled or surpassed intra-US ones (Doremus et al., 1998, p. 114).

When this slow internationalization of the USA is placed in the context of trends in other G7 countries, however, the American move toward effective globalization becomes more clear. As Table 2.1 shows, the USA in 1980 had close to a globally dominant position, and loomed far above any of its G7 partners, in its outward stock of FDI. Moreover, its share of the world's outward FDI stock, at 42 per cent, vastly exceeded its share of inward stock, at 25.6 per cent. It was then in a *de facto* hegemonic position, as a provider of capital and embedded management and technology to the rest of the world.

By 1997, however, its position had changed dramatically. Its share of the world total of outward FDI stock had fallen to a still leading but non-hegemonic

Table 2.1   *Outward and inward stock of FDI, G7 countries and world, 1980 and 1997 (US$)*

	1980	World %	1997	World %
FDI outward stock				
USA	220 178	42.0	907 497	25.6
Canada	23 783	4.5	137 715	3.9
Germany	43 127	8.2	326 028	9.2
France	23 604	4.5	226 799	6.4
Italy	7 319	1.3	125 074	3.5
Japan	19 610	3.7	284 605	8.0
UK	80 434	15.3	413 229	11.8
World	524 636		3 541 384	
FDI inward Stock				
USA	83 046	17.3	720 793	20.8
UK	63 014	13.3	274 369	7.9
Canada	54 163	11.3	137 113	4.0
Germany	36 630	7.6	137 731	4.0
France	22 617	4.7	174 152	5.0
Italy	8 892	1.8	78 514	2.2
Japan	3 270	0.007	33 164	0.01
World	479 985		3 455 509	

Source: United Nations, United Nations Conference on Trade and Development (1998), *World Investment report 1998: Trends and Determinants*, New York: United Nations, pp. 373–9.

25.6 per cent. The lead the United States had over its second-place rival (the UK in both instances) had fallen from a ratio of 2.7 to 2.1. Moreover the combined Anglo–American total had fallen from 57.3 per cent of the world total to 37.4 per cent. By 1997, both Germany and Japan in particular had emerged as substantial global investors.

Even more striking was the change by 1997 in the ratio of US outward to inward FDI. In 1980 the USA had 42 per cent of the world's outward investment but only 17.1 per cent of its inward investment – a portrait of an America relying on its own capital for investment at home, with a substantial surplus to spread abroad. By 1997, the US world share had fallen to 25.6 per cent of outward FDI but risen to 20.8 per cent of inward FDI. There had been a vast reduction in the US surplus and an increasingly reliance on foreign capital within the USA itself.

This new reliance of the USA on foreign firms can be seen in the sharp surge in 1998 in merger and acquisition activity between US and European firms. From 1995 through 1997 both US firms acquiring in Europe and European firms acquiring in the USA had acquisitions valued at under US$50 billion annually, with a relatively even balance in the flow each way. In 1998, however, US acquisitions in Europe jumped to over US$80 billion, while those of European companies in the USA soared to US$170 billion (*Business Week*, 1999).

In the field of technology alliances, since 1980 Japanese firms, traditionally reluctant to engage in strategic alliances internationally, have produced a share of alliances with US firms about half as large as that for USA–Europe partnerships in information technology and biotechnology. A hub and spoke pattern, with the USA at the centre, has come to prevail. In the third high-technology field of new materials, however, where the number of alliances is lower, the pattern is substantially more international than intranational. Indeed, it is fully trilateral among the three triad regions (Doremus et al., 1998, p. 113).

This globalization of the USA is, however, far from geographically complete. An examination of the sources and recipients of US FDI (by stock) shows that from the early 1980s to 1995 the share of FDI G7 members had, in other G7 members, increased substantially to the point where in 1995 all G7 members had between 62 per cent and 83 per cent of their FDI within the club (Kirton, 1999a). The increased concentration within the USA, amidst an era of apparent enthusiasm for 'emerging markets', was led by Japan, Italy and the United Kingdom. The USA increased its share within each G7 country save for Canada, despite having concluded the bilateral FTA and trilateral NAFTA with its northern neighbour. This globalization of America is thus not *de facto* territorial regionalism; rather, it is G7 globalization, taking place among major powers, on a transoceanic, plurilateral basis, instead of one which flows more equally across the north–south or major power–lesser power divide. By way of contrast, in the field of trade from 1990 to 1994 there was some deconcentration within the G7 both overall and for each member.

THE POPULAR FOUNDATION OF AMERICA'S GLOBALIZED PARTNERSHIP

Although there are overwhelming incentives for the US to recognize its reduced capabilities, its vulnerabilities to global financial crises and the deepening investment and alliance ties of its firms with those in Europe and Japan, there are recurrent concerns that the US policy process is unable to generate positions in its international economic and other policies that give appropriately strong expression to an orientation of cooperative international engagement. Indeed, the singularly strong American economy during the

1990s, and the lack of any serious rivals in a post-European cold war era, has generated a United States policy process within the administration, the Congress and associated interest groups and policy communities that is inwardly focused, and prone to unilateralist outbursts (Wallace and Zielonka, 1998).

A domestically distracted president, a parochial Congress, and a fragmented set of policy communities with relatively few international affiliations of consequence do indeed impede America from reacting with the appropriate speed and strength to the demands of a globalized world. However, the domestic foundations for such a movement clearly exist. The longer-term depth, durability and particular shape of America's acceptance of globalization by governors and managers can be assessed by exploring its cognitive and affective embeddedness among American business and foreign policy elites, and ultimately within the mass public where international awareness and orientations are least likely to exist. Here the evidence suggests that American business elites overwhelmingly prefer an equal partnership in active international leadership as an American foreign policy stance. Other American elites largely share this attitude. And even the mass public has, if reluctantly, come to accept the case for America's equal globalized partnerships.

American business and finance elites are overwhelming advocates of American engagement in a globalized economy (Toth, 1997). They rank trade as America's most important international problem, and declare America's top foreign policy priorities to be, in order, preventing the spread of nuclear weapons, ensuring adequate energy supplies, combating international drug trafficking, protecting the jobs of American workers and reducing the trade deficit. They identify the trade and economic agenda as President Clinton's greatest foreign policy success. They give the USA high marks for protecting the global environment, aiding the interests of US business abroad, dealing with trade and economic disputes with Japan, stopping the flow of illegal immigrants and bringing peace to the Middle East. Business leaders are least likely to support Europe's economic and political integration, suggesting their preference is for a world with a single global economy and polity, rather than one divided into competitive regional blocs.

These business leaders thus show a preference for global engagement. They do so in recognition of an intense interdependence that directly threatens America from beyond the economic realm. This sense of vulnerability includes the embedded memory of the oil shocks that first generated America's steep 1970s' decline. But it embraces the contemporary 'common enemies' or global issues of nuclear proliferation and drug trafficking.

These views are generally shared by the broader foreign policy elite. This elite expresses moderate concern about global international problems and views the major international problems as the proliferation of weapons of mass destruction, the need to ensure adequate energy supplies for the USA and the need to combat international drug trafficking. Their key priorities thus also point to a recognition of a globally exposed America. Their views are not grounded in a defensive or isolationist response, as reducing foreign trade deficits has lost its urgency for the elite. Rather, they feel vulnerable on non-economic issues, and give the Clinton administration poor grades in stopping illegal immigration and international drug trafficking and protecting the global environment. They give their highest approval rating to the Clinton administration's foreign affairs performance in promoting US business abroad and in dealing with trade and economic issues. Consistent with this attitude, overwhelming majorities of the elite, in all categories save union leaders, believe NAFTA is a good thing and favour expanding it to other nations in the hemisphere. Most groups of the elite chose the Pacific Rim nations over Europe as a preferred regional partner, overwhelmingly for economic reasons.

The US mass public, at first glance, would appear to doubt the fact, value or implications of globalization. They have little knowledge of international affairs and doubt the relevance of international events to their own lives. For example, majorities say events in neighbouring NAFTA partners Canada (66 per cent) and Mexico (55 per cent) and more distant Asia and Western Europe (61 per cent each) do not matter to their lives. Yet beneath this surface ignorance and lack of interest is a firm internationalist consensus, grounded in a recognition that America must be globally engaged but should be so in equal partnership with other leading nations.

In the first instance, there is an enduring internationalist consensus among the American mass public. Only a minority think the USA 'should mind its own business internationally' (37 per cent), go its own way in international affairs (32 per cent), or not take allies' views into account when formulating US foreign policy (18 per cent). There has been no increase in these isolationist and unilateralist views during the 1990s.

Second, in considering a desired US leadership role, a preference for balanced multilateralism prevails. Four out of five Americans prefer a shared leadership role for the USA rather than that of single world leader. At the elite level, one-half (50 per cent and down from 58 per cent in 1993) prefer assertive multilateralism – that the USA should be the most assertive power among a group of countries sharing the responsibilities of leadership. Over one-quarter (27 per cent) prefer balanced multilateralism – or equal assertiveness in leadership. Only 15 per cent wish the USA to be the single leader. Here the general public is equally reluctant to embrace a single leadership role but far more supportive of balanced multilateralism (50 per cent) than assertive multilateralism (22 per cent).

The mass public agrees with its elites on America's foreign policy priorities, with the striking exception that the mass public's top foreign policy priority is protecting American jobs. However this is not a sign of a general mercantilist mentality. Among the mass public a plurality think NAFTA is a good thing (47 per cent to 30 per cent), with even union members sharing this view (51 per cent to 34 per cent). While they remain focused on Europe regionally, a full 59 per cent feel the US should cooperate fully with the UN.

It is noteworthy that the US mass public rejects the view that the end of the cold war, and its apparent isolationist implications, is a more powerful force than the advent of globalization (Kull et al., 1997, p. 24). Only 36 per cent agree that the collapse of the Cold War and communism mean embassies should be closed so more money could be spent at home. In contrast, 59 per cent agree with the statement that 'The end of the cold war has unleashed new problems so that the world is still a dangerous place. Also, the US economy has become more interdependent with the world economy. Thus it is important for the US to maintain vigorous diplomatic efforts.'

The American mass public's acceptance of, and affection for, globalization can be further assessed by examining their views on two salient issues at the core of the globalization process – support for trade liberalization and a US contribution to the IMF in the wake of the Asian financial crisis. When given a choice (by the Angus Reid Group) between restricting imports or removing import restrictions to improve 'our' international trade, Americans in 1998 chose the protectionist option by a 56 per cent to 37 per cent margin. Yet support for protectionism increased only marginally over the year, despite the turmoil in the global economy. Moreover, this was only slightly above the global average of 47 per cent to 42 per cent support for protectionism. Finally, when given a choice between open competition or government subsidies, controls and regulations, North Americans chose the liberalization option by a four-to-one margin, compared to the global average of two to one.

Nor are Americans, in the realm of finance, distrustful of the capacity of established multilateral institutions to deal with world economic problems. When asked in late 1998, over 70 per cent of Americans trusted the capacity of the United States to deal with such problems. But a majority 50 per cent also trusted the United Nations. Receiving less support (and net distrust) were the World Bank and International Monetary Fund.

Further evidence of the American mass public's reluctant acceptance of globalization, at least in the face of visible crisis, comes in its attitudes towards the USA providing its share of the IMF quota share increase and New Arrangements to Borrow (NAB) contribution. When initially asked in December 1997 in an NBC/*Wall Street Journal* poll if the USA should participate in a plan with the IMF and other nations to help countries suffering financial collapse such as South Korea and Thailand, 51 per cent said 'no' and only 34 per cent said 'yes'. When asked in mid-April 1998 whether they approved of congress providing such funding to 'help back up the economies of Asian countries', a modest majority of 56 per cent said 'no' and only 38 per cent said 'yes' (Kull, 1998). Yet by April a relatively high 48 per cent of respondents were paying attention to the issue, and among those 52 per cent favoured a US contribution. Moreover, when all respondents were given two arguments for a contribution, and two against it, support climbed to a majority 56 per cent (with 41 per cent opposed). Two-thirds of respondents had overestimated the amount the USA was being asked to give, compared to only 28 per cent who had provided an accurate estimate. Among the latter, 52 per cent favoured the contribution. Americans' informed support for equal partnership in the face of a clear crisis of globalization appeared to be firm.

CONVERGENCE AND COMPLIANCE WITHIN INTERNATIONAL INSTITUTIONS

A final test of the advent of America as an equally globalized partner is the adjustment of its governments and firms to the constraints of international institutions, and its compliance with the collective commitments made within and by such centres of global governance. Traditionally, the United States has shown a marked isolationist reluctance to join broadly based, binding multilateral international institutions and legal regimes, from its refusal to join the League of Nations in 1919 to its failure to accept the International Trade Organization in the late 1940s, to President Reagan's withdrawal from the United Nations' Law of the Sea Convention in the early 1990s and President Bush's rejection of the United Nations Convention on Biodiversity in 1992. This tradition has continued during the Clinton administration, with the US refusal to accept a new concentration on anti-personnel landmines and the establishment of an International Criminal Court. Yet such actions have been offset by recent, major US decisions to accept new and far-reaching international institutional and legal obligations, such as the surveillance policies and dispute settlement judgements of the World Trade Organization created in 1994, and the United Nations Convention on High Seas Overfishing and Straddling Stocks concluded in 1995.

In the field of international political economy, America's record in regard to two institutions serves a critical test case of US willingness to accept the constraints of globalization in the 1990s. The first, in the field of trade, is the relatively recent treaty-based, bureaucratized, regional NAFTA regime, which came into effect amidst much domestic political controversy in the United States on 1 January 1994. The second is the G7, an informal global institution active in the realm of finance but with a fully comprehensive agenda, which America helped create in 1975. In both cases there are clear signs that America, despite its strong insular, isolationist and unilateralist traditions, had, by the 1990s, come to accept international institutional constraints. Global governance had come to apply to America to a degree long experienced by other less powerful countries.

In the case of NAFTA, the constraints can be assessed by examining the impact of the novel and potentially far reaching trade-environment regime which NAFTA pioneered. The NAFTA regime had, during its first few years in operation, created or catalyzed about 50 trilateral, intergovernmental institutions among the USA, Canada and Mexico, and done much to engender a convergence of national environmental regulations on the basis of mutual adjustment (Kirton and Fernandez de Castro, 1997; Rugman and Kirton, 1998). From 1980 to 1998, the NAFTA partners of the United States, Canada and Mexico dealt, on at least a bilateral basis, with 84 cases of environmental regulatory protection – environmental regulatory actions by one government which had implications for its trade with a fellow North American partner or, reciprocally, trade actions with environmental impact (Rugman et al., 1999). Such cases involved both the imposition of national import-restricting regulations (and the disputes which arose from them) and proactive moves to produce new or convergent environmental regulations between the countries so as to prevent trade barriers from arising.

Of these 84 disputes, 81 involved the United States. Of the 84 cases, 50 had come to an effective resolution by mid-1998, permitting judgements about whether the outcome reflected the initial preferences and interests of one country rather than the other. As 12 were resolved prior to the advent of NAFTA, and 37 were resolved in the post-NAFTA period (or in the immediate lead-up to and under the clear anticipation of NAFTA), it is possible to assess how the introduction and operation of the NAFTA regime altered the balance of outcomes.

For the entire period, the USA prevailed in 29 cases, Canada in seven and Mexico in seven, while eight were resolved to the mutual benefit of at least two of the three North American parties. Such a pattern, with the USA prevailing in 58 per cent of the cases, would appear to affirm the realist portrait of a relatively unconstrained America, whose superior power allows it to prevail most of the time.

However this first order finding requires several immediate qualifications. American relative economic capability (85 per cent of regional GNP) is far greater than its success rate. America tends to prevail in cases involving sectors dominated by US-owned firms, such as automotive and manufacturing recycling, but lose in those, such as forestry, where foreign-owned firms loom relatively large. Third, US victories are in part attributable to its role as a beneficent hegemon, with the capability to first recognize regional ecological problems and pioneer a region-wide solution that its partner countries readily accept. Finally, in contrast to the environmentally related trade disputes, where the USA prevails 64 per cent of the time, in trade-related environmental cases there is an equality of outcome, reflecting the relatively larger ecological power of Canada and Mexico, the ecological vulnerability of the USA and the relative strength of NAFTA's environmental organization, the Commission for Environmental Cooperation (CEC), relative to its trade institutions. Where America's relative power is low, its ecological vulnerability high and international institutions strong, America is an equally constrained partner.

The autonomous influence of international institutions over America is further indicated by the pattern of their non-NAFTA rather than NAFTA resolution. In the 13 cases resolved before NAFTA (with the USA involved in all), the USA prevailed 77 per cent of the time, a proportion fairly close to the ratio of relative economic capability within the region. In the 37 cases from the NAFTA era however, the USA (directly involved in all), won only 51 per cent. The portion of cases in which all countries won equally rose from none to 22 per cent.

Further evidence of the constraining influence of the NAFTA institutions comes by examining those post-NAFTA cases dealt with through the NAFTA institutions, rather than outside (where the deterrent or normative force of the regime remains influential). A majority 51 per cent of the resolved cases were dealt with by the NAFTA institutions (although in some cases other instruments of firm and government strategy may have proved decisive in securing particular outcomes). Of these cases the USA prevailed in only 39 per cent, Canada in 26 per cent, Mexico in 16 per cent and all three countries equally in 21 per cent.

A final indication of the new 1990s' international institutional constraints on the United States is the difference in outcomes, in the cases where the NAFTA institutions were the actual nest for resolution, when NAFTA's trade as opposed to its environmental institutions were involved. In the former cases, the USA prevailed in 55 per cent. In the latter cases, where the more powerful CEC was used, the USA prevailed in only 25 per cent.

In the case of the G7, the many collective commitments made by the leaders at their annual summits in the field of economics and energy from 1975 to 1989 met with a widely varying degree of compliance as the members returned to implement their promises during the ensuing year, as follows:

UK	.413
Canada	.409
Germany	.346
Italy	.274
Japan	.262
USA	.246
France	.240

The economically smaller and more globally open economies, Canada and the UK, have relatively high compliance rates. That of the United States is substantially lower, and ranks as the second lowest in the group.

During the subsequent decade, from 1988 to 1995, however, there is evidence of a substantial rise in America's compliance rate (Kokotsis, 1999; Kokotsis and Daniels, 1999). Here the results for the United States and Canada, the G7's largest and smallest members, across four issues areas, are as follows:

Issue area	Total	Canada	USA
Biodiversity	15	+1	–5
Climate change	34	+17	+6
Debt	13	+13	+6
Russia assistance	21	+13	+21
Total	83	+34 (41%)	+28 (34%)

These data show that the overall score of a smaller and much more internationally open Canada remains higher than that of the USA. However Canada's overall score is essentially unchanged over the two periods. In sharp contrast, the US score rises substantially from one-quarter (25 per cent) to over one-third (34 per cent). This suggests that the 1990s have brought an America that has become equally constrained by collective commitments made in international institutions and has joined its less powerful partners in becoming an equal citizen within a globalized world and governance system. Indeed, in some issues areas, notably financial assistance to Russia, the USA may have become more constrained than its smaller partners.

This evidence of substantial and rising US compliance is sustained by more recent findings. An analysis of compliance with commitments at the 1996 Lyons Summit in 19 issue areas indicates the highest compliance came from Germany, Canada, the USA and the UK. A similar analysis of six priority commitments made at the Denver 1997 Summit suggests a similar result (Kirton, 1999b).

CONCLUSION

In some intellectually ambitious analyses, the power and proliferation of new communications technologies are presented as leading to a major, half-millennial-long transformation of the very nature of international politics, in which even the most powerful nation states will have their authority, loyalties and identity eroded to the point of effective emasculation in many domains

(Ruggie, 1993; Deibert, 1997; Ferguson and Mansbach, 1996). In contrast, this chapter argues, more modestly, that America is likely to endure as an authoritative and effective national actor well into the new millennium. However it is an America that will be diminished in capability, more open and exposed to forces and flows from the outside world, and thus forced to cooperate with other leading countries to manage and shape the international order and secure its values at home and abroad.

Whether the powerful international incentives for collective management, combined with the embedded consensus for cooperative and engaged globalism within the American public, will prevail depends on two factors. The first is the existence of appropriate international institutions which enable America easily to engage in cooperative management of a newly globalized order. The second is whether the American policy process will sufficiently recognize and value the role of these new international centres, in ways that overcome the prevailing parochialism in the Washington-centred policy process.

The institutions of the G7 and now G8 network of international institutions provide the required institutionalized centre of global action. As the data on compliance with G7 commitments indicates, it is a forum, unlike those of broad UN- and Bretton Woods-based multilateralism, in which America is willing to be constrained and alter its domestic policies in response to cooperatively agreed international imperatives. As signified by President Clinton's decision to hold Denver as a 'Summit of the Eight' with Russia included as a virtually full member, the G7 has been a forum where America has comfortably and confidently practised cooperative leadership in the 1990s. As the modern international expression of a concert system of governance, its effectiveness is likely to endure and expand, as there are few contemporary equivalents of the forces which overcame the classic nineteenth-century concert currently in evidence (Wallace, 1984; Kirton, 1999a; Langhorne, 1981).

Of more concern is the ability of America to help construct a supportive, internationally cooperative policy community to strengthen and sustain an outwardly engaged orientation within the US administration and congress. Here the G7 provides an appropriate array of members, agenda items and deliberative, directional and decision-making actions to serve as the appropriate international institutional nest for such a community to develop. Yet it is striking how underdeveloped are the existing mechanisms for civil society engagement, especially on a cooperative international level, in the G7/8 process. Only recently has the business community become directly engaged in the work of the G7/8, through ministerial meetings for a global information society and energy (Kirton, 1999b). There is a clear need for enhanced involvement, including in the annual summit process itself (Bayne, 1999). One form this might take is the creation of a G7 Business Council, composed of senior business figures from each country, to meet regularly and on the eve of each summit, to arrive at consensus and to forward recommendations to leaders.

A second useful device would be the creation of a G7 Interparliamentary Group, similar to those that have long existed for other international institutions. This would involve G7 legislators, including those at the subfederal level where appropriate, in the process. Such a group would have an important educational and community building role. It is all the more needed now that a majority of government departments in each member country are directly involved in G7/8 activity. Indeed, the G7/8 has become an international centre of domestic governance.

Finally, it is important to involve civil society actors, including interest groups and individual citizens, more directly in G7-centred processes of consultation and community building. Such an incorporation could begin, following the US experience within NAFTA's environmental institution, the Commission for Environmental Co-operation, within the G7 environment ministers' forum. It could further extend using Internet technologies and other devices, to involve individual citizens. For it is here, in the United States in particular, that the support for the policies which a globalized America and international community need is most robust.

REFERENCES

Angell, Norman (1912), *The Great Illusion*, New York: Garland.
Bayne, Nicholas (1999), 'Continuity and Leadership in an Age of Globalization', in Michael Hodges, John Kirton and Joseph Daniels (eds), *The G8's Role in the New Millenium*, Aldershot: Ashgate, pp. 21–44.
Bergsten, Fred and Randall Henning (1996), *Global Economic Leadership and the Group of Seven*, Washington, DC: Institute for International Economics.
Business Week (1999), 'The Atlantic Century', 8 February 1999, 64–70.
Cooper, Richard (1968), *The Economics of Interdependence*, New York: McGraw-Hill.
Deibert, Ronald (1997), *Parchment, Printing and Hypermedia: Communication in World Order Transformation*, New York: Columbia University Press.
Doremus, Paul, William Keller, Louis Pauly and Simon Reich (1998), *The Myth of the Global Corporation*, Princeton: Princeton University Press.
Dunning, John (1997), *Alliance Capitalism and Global Business*, London and New York: Routledge.
Eichengreen, Barry (1989), 'Hegemonic Stability Theories of the International Monetary System', in Richard Cooper et al. (eds), *Can Nations Agree? Issues in International Economic Co-operation*, Washington, DC: Brookings Institution, pp. 255–98.
Eichengreen, Barry and Fabio Ghironi (1998), 'European Monetary Unification and International Monetary Co-operation', in Barry Eichengreen (ed.), *Transatlantic Economic Relations in the Post-Cold War Era*, New York: Council of Foreign Relations, pp. 69–98.

Ferguson, Yale and Richard Mansbach (1996), *Polities: Authority, Identities and Change*, Columbia, SC: University of South Carolina Press.

Hale, David (1998a), 'Can the G-7 restrain global deflation without a recovery in Japan?', *The Global Economic Observer*, **15**, 17 July.

Hale, David (1998b), 'Will Russia's default produce a global recession?', *The Global Economic Observer*, **16**, 8 October.

Helleiner, Eric (1994), *States and the Reemergence of Global Finance*, Ithaca: Cornell University Press.

Kapstein, Ethan (1994), 'Governing global finance', *The Washington Quarterly*, **17** (2).

Keohane, Robert and Joseph Nye (1977), *Power and Interdependence: World Politics in Transition*, Boston: Little-Brown.

Kindleberger, Charles (1973), *The World in Depression. 1929–1931*, Berkeley: University of California Press.

Kirton, John (1986), 'America's Hegemonic Decline and the Reagan Revival', in David Flaherty and Will McKercher (eds), *Southern Exposure: Canadian Perspectives on the United States*, Toronto: McGraw-Hill Ryerson.

Kirton, John (1999a), 'Economic Co-operation: Summitry, Institutions and Structural Change', in John Dunning and Gavin Boyd (eds), *Structural Change and Cooperation in the Global Economy*, Cheltenham, UK and Lyme, US: Edward Elgar.

Kirton, John (1999b), 'Explaining G8 Effectiveness', in Michael Hodges, John Kirton and Joseph Daniels (eds), *The G8's Role in the New Millennium*, Aldershot: Ashgate, pp. 45–68.

Kirton, John (1999c), 'Canada and the global financial crisis: G7 and APEC diplomacy', *The Canadian Studies Journal*, **4** (forthcoming).

Kirton, John and Joseph Daniels (1999), 'The Role of the G8 in the New Millennium', in Michael Hodges, John Kirton and Joseph Daniels (eds), *The G8's Role in the New Millennium*, Aldershot: Ashgate, pp. 3–18.

Kirton, John and Raphael Fernandez de Castro (1997), *NAFTA's Institutions: The Environmental Potential and Performance of the NAFTA Free Trade Commission and Related Bodies*, Montreal: Commission for Environmental Cooperation.

Kirton, John and Ella Kokotsis (1997–8), 'Revitalizing the G7: prospects for the Birmingham summit of the Eight', *International Journal*, **53**, Winter, 38–56.

Kokotsis, Ella (1999), *Keeping International Promises: National Compliance with G7 Environment and Development Commitments, 1988–1995*, New York: Garland Publishing.

Kokotsis, Ella and Joseph Daniels (1999), 'G8 Summits and Compliance', in Michael Hodges, John Kirton and Joseph Daniels (eds), *The G8's Role in the New Millennium*, Aldershot: Ashgate, pp. 75–92.

Krugman, Paul (1999), 'The return of depression economics', *Foreign Affairs*, January/February, 56–74.

Kull, Steven (1998), *Americans on UN Dues and IMF Funding: A Study of Public Attitudes*, School of Public Affairs, University of Maryland, 24 April 1998.

Kull, Steven, I.M. Destler and Clay Ramsay (1997), *The Foreign Policy Gap: How Policymakers Misread the Public*, Centre for International and Security Studies, University of Maryland, October.

Langhorne, Richard (1981), *The Collapse of the Concert of Europe: International Politics, 1890–1914*, New York: St. Martin's Press.

Ohmae, Kenichi (1995), *The End of the Nation State: The Rise of Regional Economies*, New York: The Free Press.

Peterson, Erik (1995), 'Surrendering to markets', *The Washington Quarterly*, 18.

Reich, Robert (1990), 'Who is us?', *Harvard Business Review*, **68**, January–February.

Rodrik, Dani (1997), *Has Globalization Gone Too Far?*, Washington, DC: Institute for International Economics.

Rosecrance, Richard (1975), *America as an Ordinary Country*, Ithaca: Cornell University Press.

Ruggie, John (1993), 'Territoriality and beyond: problematizing modernity in international relations', *International Organization*, **47**, Winter, 139–74.

Rugman, Alan and John Kirton (1998), 'Multinational enterprise strategy and the NAFTA trade and environment regime', *Journal of World Business*, **33** (4), 438–54.

Rugman, Alan, John Kirton and Julie Soloway (1999), *Environmental Regulations and Corporate Strategy: A NAFTA Perspective*, Oxford: Oxford University Press.

Sachs, Jeffrey (1998), 'International economics: unlocking the mysteries of globalization', *Foreign Policy*, **110**, Spring, 97–111.

Soros, George (1998–9), 'Capitalism's last chance', *Foreign Policy*, **113**, Winter, 55–66.

Soskice, David (1998), 'Openness and Diversity in Transatlantic Economic Relations', in Barry Eichengreen (ed.), *Transatlantic Economic Relations in the Post-Cold War Era*, New York: Council of Foreign Relations, pp. 8–35.

Stanley, Eugene (1939), *World Economy in Transition*, New York: Council on Foreign Relations.

Strange, Susan (1996), *The Retreat of the State: The Diffusion of Power in the World Economy*, Cambridge: Cambridge University Press.

Toth, Robert (1997), *America's Place in the World*, Washington, DC: Pew Research Center for the People and the Press, October.

USTR (1997), *Study on the Operation and Effect of the North American Free Trade Agreement*, Washington, DC: US Trade Representative.

Vernon, Raymond (1971), *Sovereignty at Bay*, New York: Basic Books.

Wade, Robert (1998–9), 'The coming fight over capital controls', *Foreign Policy*, **113**, Winter, 41–53.

Wallace, William (1984), 'Political Issues at the Summits: A New Concert of Powers', in Cesare Merlini (ed.), *Economic Summits and Western Decisionmaking*, London: Croom–Helm), pp. 137–52.

Wallace, William and Jan Zielonka (1998), 'Misunderstanding Europe', *Foreign Affairs*, November/December, 65–79.

Weiss, Linda (1998), *The Myth of the Powerless State*, Ithaca: Cornell University Press.

World Investment Report 1997, New York and Geneva: United Nations Conference on Trade and Development.

3. The USA in the world trading system

Sven Arndt

The USA has been an important player on the post-war world economic stage, but for much of that period what happened in the world economy was not of much consequence to the majority of the country's citizens. Trade was, and in many ways still is, a small part of overall economic activity. To assess the importance of trade one has to go to sector- and industry-specific levels, where shifts in world demand and supply can affect wages, profits, employment and output. The public at large has a general sense that the US economy is becoming more 'globalized' and that this process could have important implications, but most would be hard-pressed to come up with hard evidence from personal experience.

The term 'globalization' is used here in the broadest sense to refer to the totality of ways in which an economy becomes more integrated into the world trading system. In the realm of goods and services, this usually means that exports and imports come to make up a growing share of GNP.[1] In the realm of factors of production, it means that cross-border flows of capital and labour play a rising role in domestic economic activity. In the process, domestic markets become more sensitive to developments in the world economy. In the realm of economic policy, it means that the conduct and efficacy of domestic economic policies are increasingly influenced by developments in other countries and in the world economy generally.

Although changes in all three dimensions are taking place in the current phase of globalization, none is entirely new as a phenomenon.[2] Trade liberalization at home and abroad, as well as the gradual removal of capital controls and of constraints on the movement of persons, is playing a significant role in facilitating the integration of the US economy into the global system. While the dismantling everywhere of protectionist policies has been a key element in this process, technological advances in transportation and communication have contributed by greatly reducing the cost of cross-border transactions.

Although the current phase of globalization has features that have been seen before, their relative importance has changed. More important now than before, is the globalization of production and the consequent rise of trade in parts and components. While outsourcing of components has always been an important part of production, it was long confined mainly to the domestic economy. This meant that the international division of labour could not be pushed much beyond the level of products. This limitation is reflected in traditional trade theory and its strong focus on trade in finished products.

This chapter begins with a review of the domestic sources of US trade policy and the external influences on that policy. It then examines changes in the external orientation of US manufacturing, focusing in particular on the rapidly spreading phenomenon of offshore production of parts and components. Although the latter has been criticized as inimical to the interests of American workers, it is, on the contrary, capable of improving the lot of workers and strengthening the competitive position of US manufacturers. It generates positive overall welfare effects by making resource utilization more efficient. The chapter moves next to consideration of competition policies and their role in affecting trade patterns and the distribution of the gains from trade. Next on the agenda is a discussion of the political economy of globalization and its implications for the future of economic policy. A brief summary section wraps up the discussion.

DOMESTIC SOURCES OF US TRADE POLICY

Traditionally, the dominant influence on US trade policy has come from import-competing industries.[3] Pressures for protection have traditionally come from producers rather than consumers and from producers of import-competing products rather than exports. Agriculture, industries associated with the first industrial revolution, especially coal and steel, and industries producing standardized mass-consumption goods such as automobiles, textiles, apparel and household appliances have been the primary sources of policy activism over the years and for much of the post-war period.

Among main trade policy instruments, tariffs and quotas played major roles in earlier years, and quotas continue to be important in the Multifibre Arrangement covering trade in textiles and apparel. As multilateral trade negotiations gradually reduced tariffs and limited the use of quotas, American policy-makers turned increasingly to other instruments such as voluntary export restraints (VERs) and anti-dumping procedures, and to contingent protection generally. American trade policy gradually moved away from multilateral, non-discriminatory approaches to more selective, more discriminatory and more bilateral or unilateral initiatives.

In the more recent past, however, the focus of trade policy has shifted from protecting the home market to opening foreign markets. Pressures on trade policy have increasingly come from export industries. US makers of communications equipment, computers, construction machinery and various other capital- and human capital-intensive products have looked to trade policy for opening foreign markets. In this effort, goods producers have increasingly been joined by service providers from industries such as banking and finance, entertainment and telecommunications. The objective has been to open foreign markets to US goods and services and to prevent foreign producers from infringing on US patents and copyrights. As a result, the tool kit of trade policy has been expanded to include market-opening initiatives, enforcement of intellectual property rights and Section 301 proceedings.

The stress on opening foreign markets naturally forces trade negotiators to think in product- or sector-specific terms. In the USA, thinking along these lines has developed to the point where policy-makers view such approaches as the most promising for achieving current objectives. Sector-specific approaches simplify the bargaining process by reducing the number and complexity of issues that need to be dealt with simultaneously, but they often leave little to 'bargain' over in the sense of reciprocity. When everything is on the bargaining table, there is no need to search for reciprocity within a sector. When the USA wants a developing country to open its telecommunications market, for example, it has little to offer in that sector which would be of much interest and value to such a country. But a concession offering greater access to the US apparel market would be of interest.

Overall, therefore, the shift in the sources of trade policy has been from parties suffering from comparative disadvantage and bent on preventing imported products from cutting into their share of the home market, that is, bent on keeping the US economy closed, to parties with strong comparative advantage intent on using policy to increase their share of foreign markets. Although all this has brought major changes to US trade and trade policy, international trade is even today relatively unimportant in relation to overall US GNP.

EXTERNAL INFLUENCES ON US TRADE POLICY

In the early decades after World War II, political and strategic considerations often dominated US foreign economic relations. For example, US support for waivers under GATT rules to permit discriminatory trade policies in the European Economic Community (EEC) and European Free Trade Association (EFTA) was motivated by Cold War strategic rather than national economic considerations. For an extended period of post-war history, US trade policy adopted a relatively permissive attitude toward what were often hostile external events and policy moves by trading partners. This relaxed attitude was facilitated by the dominant competitive position of US producers in the world economy and by the relatively small role international trade played in the economy.

In recent years, however, as foreign competitive presence has risen in industries once dominated by US firms and as the end of the Cold War has dissolved strategic arguments, economic considerations have reasserted themselves. A major contributing factor, as Destler (1995), Krueger (1995) and others have noted, has been the sharp deterioration of the US current account. Although this erosion has been the result mainly of macroeconomic conditions within the United States, represented in particular by the budget deficit and a large shortfall of private saving relative to investment, the enormous size of the current account deficit has made it an easy political target and opponents of a more open economy have been quick to place the blame on 'unfair' foreign trade practices.

As noted, in the first few decades after World War II, multilateral approaches played a dominant role in US trade policy. The motivation was provided in part by the US objective of developing and sustaining coherent and coordinated policies among its allies in the context of the Cold War. More recently, as the US position in multilateral organizations has become weaker, Washington has looked more toward regional approaches and has become a primary practitioner of unilateral trade policy. In the process, as Krueger (1995) has observed, protection in the USA has taken on an 'administered' look, with trade policy relying more and more on bilateral bargaining – over dumping, subsidies, escape-clause issues and other unfair-trade provisions of US law.

This approach has been criticized by the country's trading partners, but the USA has rejected such complaints and has rebuffed calls to subject these policies to multilateral surveillance and regulation. This stance has served protectionist interests and has given the executive branch a way of dealing with interventionist sentiments in the Congress, but as other countries have become frustrated with what they perceived as US abuses in this policy area, they have started to employ similar practices. As a result, US exporters are now increasingly harassed by contingent protectionism abroad. In the future, US trade negotiators will have to devote a rising share of their time to bilateral bargaining over 'administered protection.' When this burden becomes sufficiently onerous, the USA will bring the issue to the global negotiating table for resolution. Until that happens, however, conflicts over administered protection will become an increasingly costly and potentially disruptive element in the country's trade relations.[4]

In addition to systemic external influences on US trade policy, relations with Japan have been a major source of challenges and frictions for policy-makers. In their efforts to open up the Japanese economy, US policy-makers have employed the gamut of approaches from sector-specific, market-opening negotiations to initiatives aimed at changing the structure of the Japanese economy and society. Whatever may be said about the intrinsic value of such efforts, they were often justified politically by reference to Japan's large and sustained trade surplus with the world generally and with the USA in particular.

Bilateral disputes of a similar nature, but less severe and sustained, have arisen in US relations with China. Here, the United States has pursued its efforts to pry open China's market and to press China to adopt certain practices and policies by linking them to negotiations over Chinese membership in the World Trade Organization (WTO). These bilateral engagements are likely to continue, even after China gains admission.

From time to time, the European Union (EU) has caused problems for US trade policy, less on overall grounds and more with respect to specific issues, including the EU's Common Agricultural Policy (CAP). US policy objectives have been more focused on resolving specific issues rather than restructuring a trading partner's internal economy. Bilateral frictions between the two partners will continue and possibly intensify as the introduction of monetary union in Europe (EMU) comes to challenge US hegemony in world financial markets.[5]

EXTERNAL ORIENTATION OF US MANUFACTURING

In much of the post-war period, the dominant orientation of US manufacturers has been to serve the domestic market. Unlike producers in countries with small domestic markets, US manufacturers can focus on developing products for the internal market. That market is large enough to support exploitation of scale and scope economies, while leaving plenty of room for the benefits that flow from product variety.

When US manufacturers turned to offshore production in the post-war period, it was the first-generation multinationals who led the way. Makers of automobiles and computers, among others, set up production operations in a foreign country to serve the local market. Often, an important motivation was to jump tariff barriers, especially the discriminatory kind of barriers levied by preference areas like the EEC and EFTA. In the early years, goods produced abroad were very similar to those made for the US market, but model types and other details were increasingly tailored to respond to local tastes, practices and regulatory requirements.

Local production typically required some direct investment outlays and so capital flows were closely linked to the global production decisions of multinational firms. This created pressures on US trade policy to push for the elimination of barriers on capital flows and the opening of foreign capital markets and financial sectors.

The current phase of globalization also contains an element of offshore production and, once again, multinational firms are playing an important role. But this time it is not necessarily production of entire products but rather of parts and components that is moved offshore. Production is becoming increasingly decentralized and globally 'fragmented'[6] as the various phases of the manufacture of a product or the provision of a service are spread across national borders. Components made abroad may or may not be produced by affiliates of a US company. Offshore sourcing of components is playing a growing role in industries whose final products are exportables as well as industries who compete with imports in final product markets.[7]

In some cases, US firms export components for assembly abroad and then import the final product. Well-known examples of this type of arrangement are US–Canada linkages in the auto industry and the maquiladora operations in Mexico. In other cases, US manufacturers, including aircraft and computer makers, import components for domestic assembly and then export the final product. In this way, a significant portion of the value-added of US imports of final products may be represented by US-made components, while the value-added of US exports of final products may include component imports from abroad. As production becomes increasingly decentralized and scattered across borders, products take on an increasingly multinational character.

This new form of specialization pushes the global division of labour beyond products into the realm of parts and components. For the world as a whole, the chemicals and machinery and equipment industries have led the rush to 'vertical specialization,' according to Hummels et al. (1998). Overall, 'increases in vertical-specialization-based trade ... account for more than 25 per cent of the increase in total trade in a group of ten OECD countries' (p. 81). In particular regions and settings, offshore production has been important in the automobile industry and in textiles and apparel. But even aircraft producers like Boeing and Airbus routinely use offshore production and procurement in order to stay competitive.

The Costs and Benefits of Offshore Sourcing by US Industries

Offshore sourcing by US firms has raised concerns among some observers. During the NAFTA debate, for example, Ross Perot warned that it would contribute to the 'great sucking sound' of jobs lost by US workers. Patrick Buchanan wants to levy special tariffs on component imports. Boeing workers have protested against offshore activities by their company. In Europe, critics see offshore procurement as a source of their continent's high unemployment.

What makes this issue a particularly volatile topic is that offshore sourcing often involves low-wage countries. The perception is widespread that trade with such countries destroys jobs in high-wage economies and depresses wages there. It turns out, however, that at least some of these fears are misplaced, because offshore procurement of labour-intensive parts and components often raises employment, output and wages in industries which undertake it. This section lays out the basic intuition in support of this conclusion, while the appendix provides a more formal and rigorous development of the argument.

If specialization according to comparative advantage is beneficial at the level of finished products, why would it not bring further benefits if it were applied to trade in components? Such specialization obviously works within nations, where it has been practised for years. Until recently, however, outsourcing across national borders has been limited by a variety of barriers, including high transport and coordination costs.

If the various components of a product are subject to different resource- or factor-intensities, then comparative advantage in component production will be systematically related to resource or factor endowments. Then, if each country produces and exports those components which use its plentiful resources, while importing components using scarce resources, all will gain.

The 'resources' in which we have a special interest are labour and capital. In the making of the typical product, some components will use more capital relative to labour than others at any given ratio of labour to capital costs. We may thus rank components in terms of their capital/labour ratios. At one end of the spectrum will be components with relatively high ratios of capital to labour, the so-called capital-intensive components, while the other end will track components with relatively low capital–labour ratios. Those will be the labour-intensive elements of a production process.

All other things being equal, the relative price of labour should be lower in labour-rich countries and the relative price of capital should be lower in capital-rich countries. For any common technology, then, labour-intensive components should be relatively cheaper to produce in labour-rich countries, while capital-rich countries should have a cost advantage in producing capital-intensive components. Hence, capital-rich countries should export capital-intensive components and import labour-intensive components and vice versa for labour-rich countries. A capital-rich country can reduce the cost of producing a final product by importing labour-intensive components from labour-rich countries. As production costs fall relative to prices, profitability rises, allowing the industry to expand.

This principle applies to product assembly as well. When assembly is relatively labour-intensive, it will be cheaper in labour-rich countries, while capital-intensive assembly will be cheaper in capital-rich countries. We see this principle in action in the maquiladora system in Mexico, where capital-intensive components of consumer electronics products are imported from the United States to be combined with labour-intensive components made in Mexico and assembled in labour-intensive assembly operations into final products, which are then shipped to the United States. At the other end, we see the Boeing Company importing less capital- and skill-intensive components, which are combined with relatively more capital- and skill-intensive US-made components in a US-based, relatively capital- and skill-intensive assembly process.

Component Specialization in the Import-Competing Industry

Given the logic of component specialization, how does its implementation affect employment, output and wages? Specifically, what are the consequences of its implementation in an industry which competes with imports in the markets for its final product? In advanced, capital-rich, high-wage countries, this type of industry tends to be the relatively labour-intensive industry which thus has most to fear from foreign competition.

The effect on employment and output depends on the movement of costs relative to prices. If offshore procurement of a component reduces costs relative to product price, then output expands as firms pursue the new profit opportunities. They will either sell more of the product at given world prices or sell more by undercutting the competition with lower prices.

Whether employment increases with output depends on whether the jobs created by the rise in total output are greater in number than the jobs lost when production of the labour-intensive component is shifted abroad. The appendix develops the precise conditions under which employment of both labour and capital in the industry will rise along with output.

The effect on wages, on the other hand, is determined by the growth in demand for both labour and capital as the industry expands and by the conditions under which resources are shifted from the rest of the economy into the expanding industry. When, as in the present case, it is the labour-intensive industry that expands, wages rise relative to capital rentals as well as absolutely.

These results are clearly at odds with the predictions of some opponents of component specialization. While these findings need to be empirically tested, they are compatible with studies of the effects of protection (Corden, 1972), where tariffs on imports of intermediate goods were shown to reduce the effective rate of protection provided by tariffs on imports of final goods by reducing domestic value added. In the present case, the cost reduction generated by component imports increases domestic value added at given world prices.

Component Specialization in the Export Sector

As noted earlier, export industries, which tend in advanced countries to be capital- and skill-intensive, are also making use of offshore component sourcing. As before, the object is to reduce costs by obtaining relatively labour-intensive components from their cheapest source. Cost reduction makes firms more competitive and thus increases their share of world markets. As sales rise, output and employment rise.

The effect on wages depends on the interaction of several influences. If the domestic industry is small relative to world markets, output can expand without depressing world prices. If it is large, additional output can only be sold at lower prices. Price cuts offset the effect on profit opportunities opened up by cost reductions. Output expands, however, as long as the price effect is smaller and when the capital-intensive industry expands in an economy, the wage–rental ratio must fall.

THE GLOBALIZATION OF FINANCE

While the globalization literature has tended to focus on integration of goods markets, financial turmoil in Asia, Latin America and elsewhere has drawn attention to financial markets generally and those in emerging market economies in particular. Liberalization of exchange and capital controls and of domestic financial markets around the globe has enabled capital to flow ever more freely across national frontiers. An important benefit has been the enhanced ability of countries with low saving rates to mobilize external resources. A disadvantage has been the disruption caused by large and rapid reversals of capital flows.

A very important lesson to be learned from recent financial upheavals is the danger of viewing exchange rates too much in terms of the trade balance or the current account. While such a view was appropriate in an earlier age of capital controls, in today's environment exchange rate determination and macroeconomic stability are crucially linked to capital movements. The ease with which capital crosses borders changes the character of exchange rate regimes and of macroeconomic adjustment in open economies. While goods market responses still play an important role, far more attention will have to be paid in the future to capital flows, asset market adjustment and associated wealth effects.

To a significant extent, the internationalization of production discussed in earlier sections depends on foreign investment. NAFTA was a pact to liberalize foreign investment as much as trade, as the growing flow of US and foreign capital into the maquiladora sector illustrates. But although capital moves more easily across national boundaries today, its flow is still hampered by considerable obstacles, particularly in areas such as right of establishment, national treatment of foreign investment, discriminatory performance requirements, restrictions on income remittance, interventions via incentives and disincentives, as well as threats of expropriation.

US policy continues to pursue greater openness with respect to capital flows. While this objective still enjoys broad and bipartisan political support, it is not universally accepted. There are some who believe that capital outflows, particularly of the direct investment type, are detrimental to US well-being. It is a view, expressed by candidate Ross Perot during the NAFTA debate, for example, which treats foreign direct investment as a zero–sum game, so that an outflow of investment capital from the US to Mexico necessarily implies a reduction in US domestic investment.

The role of foreign investment in promoting the globalization of production and the impact of financial capital flows on exchange rates and macro stability raise important questions about their supervision and regulation. National governments have an important responsibility in this area, but policies run at national levels are likely to raise disputes over differences in standards and treatment. Thus, mechanisms will be needed for harmonization and coordination of policies and for dispute settlement. This raises important questions about the level – bilateral, regional, multilateral – at which to pursue this objective. The international institutions also have responsibilities here, although it is unclear whether their current structures are adequate for the purpose. Development and implementation of the future 'architecture' of the global economy will place heavy demands on US policy-makers.

DEEPER INTEGRATION: COMPETITION POLICY

While there remains considerable unfinished business in the area of trade liberalization, including agriculture and services, there is a growing consensus that future negotiations at multilateral and subsidiary levels will have to pay more attention to barriers other than those that occur at national borders.[8] While negotiations under the General Agreement on Tariffs and Trade (GATT) took up the anticompetitive features of subsidies, procurement and standards, more needs to be done in those areas, as well as in the regulation of antitrust policies, the treatment of cross-border mergers and acquisitions, and with respect to other aspects of economic relations that go beyond the mere movement of products.[9]

In their study of competition policy, Graham and Richardson (1997, p. 3) distinguish between border barriers, which have been the main focus of trade negotiations in the past, and entry barriers, such as monopoly and national competition policies, which limit the ability of foreign firms to gain entry into a country's markets. As the importance of trade barriers has been reduced by successive rounds of trade negotiations, the protectionist implications of these barriers to market entry have become more urgent. The economic benefits to be obtained from the reduction of these entry barriers are likely to be larger, perhaps much larger, than the gains associated with further reductions in traditional constraints on trade.

The task is to make markets more contestable. The question is how? Ensuring market access is not always enough to enable foreign suppliers to contest a market.[10] While trade liberalization continues to be an important means of raising market contestability, it may need to be supported with other policies, in areas like government procurement, contingent protection, antidumping intervention, regulation of standards and antitrust policy.

At the multilateral level, the World Trade Organization (WTO) has established a Working Group on the Interaction between Trade and Competition Policy. Among the specific sectors or industries in which competition policy has been an issue of contention between countries are airlines, telecommunications, insurance and financial services. The USA has strong policy interests in each of them. Differences in regulatory practices, entrenched state or private monopolies and variations in cultural attitudes toward markets and competition, present major challenges to those wishing to lower barriers to entry and to facilitate the harmonization of policy approaches.

As Graham and Richardson note (1997, p. 5), competition policy determines the institutional mix of competition and cooperation that gives rise to a market system. But the regulations encompassed by competition policy differ widely and those differences can become the cause of frictions when globalization brings countries closer together. When confronted with such differences, it is easy for policy-makers to take the attitude that theirs is the better and fairer system and that it is up to other countries to conform. US policy-makers have been far from immune to the siren call of such self-serving 'solutions' of disputes. They have been aggressive not only in pushing the US view but in the extraterritorial extension of US laws to other nations.

In their dealings with Japan, US policy-makers have talked openly about remaking Japanese society. That experience makes an eloquent case for shifting some of these disputes to the multilateral level. It suggests that global standards of competition policy cannot be developed solely through bilateral bargaining. This does not mean, however, that all competition policy issues must be addressed at the multilateral level. Mutual recognition of national standards, for example, offers a broadly applicable approach for dealing with a variety of competition policy issues at sub-global levels. This applies especially to the multitude of cases where disputes over competition policy and market access involve particular activities. Mergers and acquisitions are a case in point.

THE POLITICAL ECONOMY OF GLOBALIZATION

It is clear that globalization creates winners and losers. As economies become more open and domestic goods, factor and capital markets are drawn more completely into the world system and as production itself becomes more globalized, larger numbers of a country's citizens are directly exposed to external shocks, but their control and regulation seem to lie beyond the reach of national policy-makers. Unfairness is not only perceived, but is perceived to be irremediable as far as the purview of national policy is concerned. Accountability appears to have been eroded. As this perception spreads, it leads many observers to join Rodrik (1997) in asking whether globalization may have gone too far.

While economists can show how globalization may increase overall welfare, they cannot guarantee that the costs and benefits will be distributed 'fairly'. They typically assume that the political process will take care of the distributional issues. Global economic integration will lose political support if it moves too far ahead of the ability of political processes and social structures to deal with its consequences.

The increasing role of low-wage countries in international trade has added a new dimension and urgency to these considerations. While economists are still arguing over the relative roles of trade and technological change in explaining rising income inequality in the United States and high unemployment in Europe, the public debate is already altering the political economy of trade policy.[11] In the United States, trade with low-wage countries is perceived by many to have contributed to rising income inequality and wage-disparity among workers. In Europe, it shares the blame for high and persistent unemployment.

The case against trade has been made with reasoning that draws from the standard Heckscher–Ohlin, Stolper–Samuelson (HOSS) model and its prediction that trade with low-wage countries has a dampening effect on wages. While the HOSS model develops the argument in terms of trade in final products, opponents of global integration have extrapolated its conclusions to trade in components. Thus, the prediction that trade liberalization on the part of high-wage countries will cause the import-competing industry to shrink and wages to fall has been used to conclude that competition from imported components will have identical effects on the industry. As the preceding analysis makes clear, however, the two forms of competition should have exactly opposite effects on the competitiveness of the domestic import-competing industry. The inflow of cheaper imports of final goods hurts the domestic industry, while the inflow of cheaper components strengthens it.

Apart from these issues, trade policy in the USA will continue to be haunted by the huge current account deficit. Liberal trade policies and the openness of the US economy will be blamed for the deficit and trade intervention will be advocated as a way of solving it. Such efforts will, of course, fail to eliminate the problem, because it is essentially a macroeconomic phenomenon. But protectionists will not fail to see the deficit as a useful policy wedge.

The political economy of trade policy will be further influenced by efforts to 'capture' trade policy as an instrument for the achievement of other objectives and purposes, including the imposition of tougher environmental protection and labour standards and improved human rights in other countries. If these efforts succeed in influencing US trade policy, the result is likely to be protectionist and welfare-reducing.

The Future of Sovereignty

The onrush of globalization has led some observers to conclude that this latest industrial revolution will make the nation state obsolete, in the sense that significant powers now residing with the nation state will pass to multilateral institutions or into the hands of regional entities like the European Union.[12] Others are more agnostic about the net effect of globalization on the role of the state. They suggest that globalization's tendency to touch the lives of more and more citizens will rouse political demands for governmental protection through improvements in safety nets and the like. Such developments would strengthen rather than weaken the nation state.[13]

CONCLUSION

The US economy is passing through another phase of globalization. On all fronts – goods and services, factors and finance – domestic markets are becoming more integrated into the world economy. While there is some debate over whether the economy is more open and global today than it ever was, it clearly is more so now than at the end of World War II.

The process of globalization brings challenges and opportunities for market participants and policy-makers alike. The opportunities flow importantly from the more efficient use of productive resources and the welfare gains implied by it. The challenge is to ensure rough balance between the distribution of welfare gains and the incidence of adjustment costs. Some critics of globalization believe that this challenge is not being met. Others worry that globalization is eroding national sovereignty, diminishing not only the effectiveness of domestic economic policies but reducing the relevance of national governments and institutions, very much like the rise of national governments eroded the sovereignty of states and provinces in an earlier age. The issues are joined, but the answers are far from clear.

With the passage of time, the sources of US trade policy have changed. Whereas import-competing industries dominated the formation of trade policy earlier in the modern period, exporters and their need for open foreign economies have become a more organized and forceful influence in the recent past.

The instruments of US trade policy have also changed with time and with the changing nature of the global trading system. Once a staunch exponent of multilateral approaches to trade liberalization, the United States has gradually become frustrated and disenchanted. It has sought refuge in a variety of alternative approaches, including preferential trade liberalization and 'aggressive unilateralism'.

While the present phase of globalization shares many features with past episodes, it also differs in important respects. One of these is the increasing role of offshore sourcing of parts and components. Innovations in communications and transportation technologies have drastically reduced the cost of cross-border coordination and have thereby enabled production to be globalized. Thus, the integration of economies into the global market is being accomplished by the disintegration and cross-border fragmentation of production as the international division of labour spreads beyond products into the realm of parts and components.

When integrated production is replaced with processes that are dispersed across borders, prices, employment and output are affected – sometimes in ways that are at odds with the predictions of globalization's critics. This is true for component trade with low-wage countries which has the capacity to raise rather than reduce wages in high-wage countries, to raise rather than lower employment there and to boost output and welfare: No 'sucking sound' of jobs lost or convergence of wages to the 'lowest common denominator'.

APPENDIX

Offshore Component Sourcing by the Import-Competing Industry

Consider the simplest of trade models, the 2x2x2 Heckscher–Ohlin model, and assume that the country in question is small and thus does not affect world prices.[14] In Figure 3.1, X_0 and Y_0 are the unit-value isoquants, respectively, for final goods X and Y, while (w/r) represents the isocost line. This is the standard set-up for the analysis of trade in final goods under conditions of integrated production.

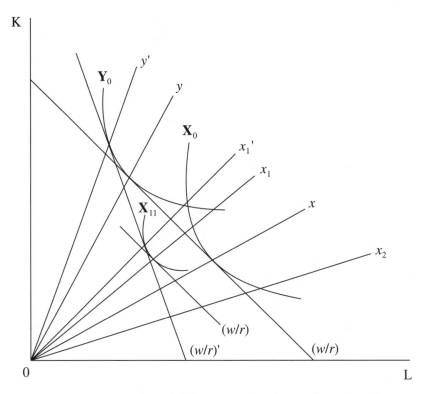

*Figure 3.1   Offshore component production in the labour-intensive import-
competing industry*

In order to examine the implications of component specialization, assume
that commodity **X** is made up of components x_1 and x_2, with the former more
capital intensive than the commodity overall and the latter less capital intensive. These conditions are reflected by the expansion paths for x_1 and x_2 in the
figure. Thus, the amounts of the two factors used in producing X_0 units of **X**
are obtained by vector addition of the amounts given for the two components
along their respective expansion paths. We assume, further, that these components are dedicated components of product **X** and cannot be used elsewhere.
There are thus no stand-alone markets for them.[15]

Starting with full home production of good **X**, suppose that there exists a
second country, which is capable of producing component x_2 at lower cost and
that reductions in cross-border coordination costs allow the industry to manufacture component x_2 abroad. Assume that the industry pays for imports of x_2
with exports of x_1. Then, the cost of producing a unit of **X** will be smaller if the
factor cost of x_1-exports is lower than the factor cost of producing x_2 directly.

With x_2 made abroad and **X**-assembly assumed to be part of x_1-production, x_1 isoquants now fully reflect input–output relationships in the **X**-industry. Suppose that at the initial factor–price ratio (w/r), isoquant $\mathbf{X}_{11}$ now represents the factor cost of producing $\mathbf{X}_0$ units of **X**. In other words, the factor inputs given by isoquant $\mathbf{X}_{11}$ produce the same value of **X**-output as the factor inputs given by isoquant $\mathbf{X}_0$. The difference in costs results from the resource savings inherent in offshore sourcing of component x_2.

With prices of final goods given in world markets, **X**-production now generates excess profits. Resources will be drawn into the industry and output and employment will expand until the excess profits are driven to zero. In the process, the factor–price ratio will rotate in a clockwise direction until it is tangent to the new **X**-isoquant and the original **Y**-isoquant. That new factor–price ratio is given by $(w/r)'$. It is clear that, in this instance, extending the international division of labour into the realm of parts and components raises wages and increases employment and output in the industry. Output and employment decrease in the **Y**-industry. The effect on trade is to reduce both imports and exports of final products.[16] National welfare increases unambiguously, as shown by Arndt (1998b).

This result suggests that import-competing, final-goods producers in high-wage, labour-poor countries can strengthen their international competitive positions by sloughing off production of the labour-intensive components of those products.[17]

Offshore Component Sourcing by Exportables Industries

In the US context, the foregoing would apply to a variety of products in the textiles and apparel, furniture, automobile, consumer appliances and electronics industries. Offshore sourcing, however, takes place among exportables producers as well. An obvious example is the Boeing company and various computer producers. In this section, we examine the implications of offshore procurement in the export industry.[18]

In Figure 3.2, it is now the **Y**-industry which is assumed to be capable of fragmented production. When the industry drops domestic production of the labour-intensive component y_2 in favour of cheaper imports, the relevant isoquant $\mathbf{Y}_{11}$ reflects the new unit value of **Y**-production. Again, that cost will be lower than before, provided that the amount of labour and capital embodied in the quantity of y_1 which is exported to pay for imports of y_2 is less than the resource cost of producing y_2 at home.

As before, with commodity prices given in world markets, factor prices must adjust to eliminate the profit opportunities created by the decline in production costs. The new factor–price ratio is assumed to be given by $(w/r)'$. In this instance, wages have fallen as a result of the intensification of

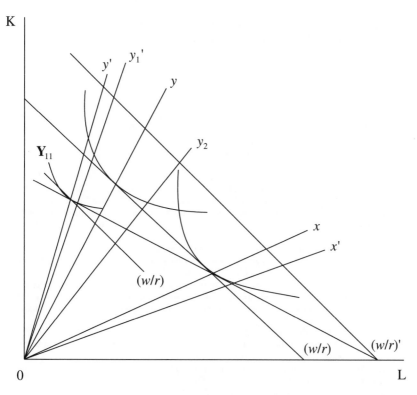

Figure 3.2   Offshore component production in the capital-intensive industry

international specialization. **X**-production has become more labour intensive, while the outcome is ambiguous for the **Y**-industry. In the case shown in Figure 3.2, **Y**-production is more capital intensive than before, but less capital intensive than production of component y_1. In general, output and employment in the **Y**-industry may rise or fall as a result of intra-product specialization.[19]

Terms-of-Trade Effects

When the countries in question are large, the shift to intra-product specialization will change the terms of trade. In the first case examined above, intra-product specialization in the import-competing industry (**X**) increases output in that sector while reducing output in the **Y**-sector. In general, these volume changes should reduce the price of **X** and raise the price of **Y** in world markets. This improvement in the terms of trade is welfare enhancing. In Figure 3.1, these price changes will shift the **X**-isoquants out and the

Y-isoquants in, thereby tending to offset the effects on wages, output and employment brought about by intra-product specialization.[20]

NOTES

1. See Feenstra (1998) and Hummels et al. (1998) for some recent ratios. Both Irwin (1996) and Krugman (1995) have argued that integration of the USA into the world economy is probably no greater today than it was at the end of the 19th century.
2. For a discussion of this well-known point, see for example, Rodrik (1997). See also Arndt (1997b) for a collection of views on globalization and its implications.
3. For a broad overview of US policy history, see Committee for Economic Development (1991). For an analysis of global trade policy issues, see Hoekman and Kostecki (1995).
4. On antidumping policies, see Hindley and Messerlin (1996). See also Mastel (1998).
5. For a general examination of trans-Atlantic economic relations, see Eichengreen (1998).
6. Application of the term 'fragmentation' in this context is due to Jones and Kierzkowski (1990).
7. See Campa and Goldberg (1997) for some recent evidence.
8. See, for example, Feketekuty and Rogowsky (1996), Graham and Richardson (1997) and the symposium on competition policy in *The World Economy* (1998).
9. Inclusion of competition policy in future trade rounds should not be seen as a casual or trivial expansion of the agenda of trade negotiations. It raises a host of issues associated with 'deeper integration' of national economies into the global system. For an analysis, see Lawrence et al. (1996).
10. See Lloyd (1998) for a detailed discussion.
11. For a recent review of the evidence regarding the respective shares of trade and technology in income disparities, see Sachs and Shatz (1996). See also Feenstra and Hanson (1996), Jones and Engerman (1996) and Leamer (1997).
12. See, for example, Feketekuty in Arndt (1997b).
13. See, for example, Ethier and Jones in Arndt (1997b).
14. This section draws on Arndt (1997a, 1998a,b). See also Deardorff (1998) and Jones and Kierzkowski (1999).
15. Deardorff (1998) and Jones and Kierzkowski (1999), on the other hand, assume that components have free-standing markets.
16. This form of specialization, which has also been called intra-product specialization (Arndt, 1997a) and super-specialization (Arndt, 1998b), thus increases intra-industry trade while reducing inter-industry trade.
17. It can be shown that analogous gains accrue to the low-wage, capital-poor country if it sloughs off production of the capital-intensive component of product **X** (Arndt, 1997a). Thus, if both countries continue to assemble the final product, but each specializes in the component in which it has a comparative advantage, wages will rise in both countries, output and employment will increase in both industries, and national welfare will rise in both countries. Price effect!
18. This section draws on Arndt (1998a).
19. These ambiguities are analogous to those found in the context of technological change. Indeed, although technological change has not taken place in the industry, the results of intra-product specialization have much in common with those long familiar from the literature on technological change. See, for example, Johnson (1971).
20. See Arndt (1998b).

REFERENCES

Arndt, S.W. (1997a), 'Globalization and the open economy', *North American Journal of Economics and Finance*, **8** (1), 71–9.

Arndt, S.W. (1997b), 'Globalization and trade: a symposium', *The World Economy*, **20** (5), 695–707.

Arndt, S.W. (1998a), 'Globalization and the Gains from Trade', in K.-J. Koch and K. Jaeger (eds), *Trade, Growth, and Economic Policy in Open Economies*, New York: Springer, pp. 3–12.

Arndt, S.W. (1998b), 'Super-specialization and the gains from trade', *Contemporary Economic Policy*, **XVI** (4), 480–5.

Campa, J. and L.S. Goldberg (1997), 'The evolving external orientation of manufacturing: a profile of four countries', *Economic Policy Review*, New York: Federal Reserve Bank of New York, **3** (2), 53–81.

Committee for Economic Development (1991), *Breaking New Ground in U.S. Trade Policy*, Washington, DC: Westview.

Corden, M.W. (1971), *The Theory of Protection*, Oxford: Clarendon Press.

Deardorff, A.V. (1998), 'Fragmentation in simple trade models', Research Seminar in International Economics Working Paper No. 422, Ann Arbor: University of Michigan, January.

Destler, I.M. (1995), *American Trade Politics* (3rd edition), Washington, DC: Institute for International Economics.

Eichengreen, B. (ed.) (1998), *Transatlantic Economic Relations in the Post-Cold War Era*, New York: Council on Foreign Relations.

Feenstra, R.C. (1998), 'Integration of trade and disintegration of production in the global economy', *Journal of Economic Perspectives*, **12** (4), 31–50.

Feenstra, R.C. and G.H. Hanson (1996), 'Globalization, outsourcing, and wage inequality', *American Economic Review*, **86** (2), 240–45.

Feketekuty, G. and R.A. Rogowsky (1996), 'The Scope, Implication and Economic Rationale of a Competition-Oriented Approach to Future Trade Negotiations', in S. Arndt and C. Milner (eds), *The World Economy: Global Trade Policy 1996*, Oxford: Blackwell.

Graham, E.M. and J.D. Richardson (eds) (1997), *Global Competition Policy*, Washington, DC: Institute for International Economics.

Hindley, B. and P.A. Messerlin (1996), *Antidumping Industrial Policy*, Washington, DC: AEI Press.

Hoekman, B.M. and M.M. Kostecki (1995), *The Political Economy of the World Trading System: From GATT to WTO*, Oxford: Oxford University Press.

Hummels, D., D. Rapoport and K.-M. Yi (1998), 'Vertical specialization and the changing nature of world trade', *Economic Policy Review*, New York: Federal Reserve Bank of New York, **4** (2), 79–99.

Irwin, D.A. (1996), 'The United States in a new global economy? A century's perspective', *American Economic Review*, **86** (2), 41–6.

Johnson, H.G. (1971), *Two-Sector Model of General Equilibrium*, Chicago: Aldine Atherton.

Jones, R.W. and S.L. Engerman (1996), 'Trade, technology, and wages: a tale of two countries', *American Economic Review*, **86** (2), 35–40.

Jones, R.W. and H. Kierzkowski (1990), 'The Role of Services in Production and International Trade: A Theoretical Framework', in R.W. Jones and A.O. Krueger (eds), *The Political Economy of International Trade*, Oxford: Blackwell.

Jones, R.W. and H. Kierzkowski (1999), 'Globalization and the Consequences of International Fragmentation', in R. Dornbusch, G. Calvo and M. Obstfeld (eds), Festschrift in honour of Robert A. Mundell (forthcoming).

Krueger, A.O. (1995), *American Trade Policy: A Tragedy in the Making*, Washington, DC: AEI Press.

Krugman, P.R. (1995), 'Growing world trade: causes and consequences', *Brookings Papers on Economic Activity*, (1), Washington, DC: Brookings Institution.

Lawrence, R.Z., A. Bressand and T. Ito (1996), *A Vision for the World Economy: Openness, Diversity, and Cohesion*, Washington, DC: Brookings Institution.

Leamer, E.E. (1997), 'In Search of Stolper–Samuelson Linkages between International Trade and Lower Wages', in S.M. Collins (ed.) (1998), *Imports, Exports, and the American Worker*, Washington, DC: Brookings Institution, pp. 141–203.

Lloyd, P.J. (1998), 'Multilateral rules for international competition law?', *The World Economy*, **21** (8), 1129–49.

Mastel, G. (1998), *Antidumping Laws and the U.S. Economy*, Washington, DC: M.E. Sharpe.

Rodrik, D. (1997), *Has Globalization Gone Too Far?*, Washington, DC: Institute for International Economics.

Sachs, J.D and H.J. Shatz (1996), 'U.S. trade with developing countries and wage inequality', *American Economic Review*, **86** (2), 234–9.

Schott, J.J. (ed.) (1996), *The World Trading System: Challenges Ahead*, Washington, DC: Institute for International Economics.

The World Economy (1998), **21** (8).

4. A public choice perspective on the globalizing of America

Willem Thorbecke

INTRODUCTION

Traditional international economic models assume that the government promotes the public interest. In such a framework free trade will usually be the policy of choice. Comparative advantage and economies of scale will produce gains from trade, increasing aggregate welfare. Agents profiting from liberalization can compensate those losing and still retain net benefits.

A caveat to this analysis concerns optimum tariffs and strategic protection. The optimum tariff argument holds that if a country is large enough to influence its terms of trade, it can employ a tariff to increase welfare. The strategic protection argument holds that in the presence of increasing returns, government subsidies could enable domestic firms to produce at lower average costs and drive foreign rivals out of the market. Both optimum tariffs and strategic protection imply that one country can increase its welfare at the expense of other countries.

International relations scholars of the Realist school have viewed trade protection as the attempt of one nation to gain at the expense of others. As Milner (1997) discusses, Realists hold that the state can be represented as a unitary actor. The executive is assumed to add up the gains and losses from any policy into a single ranking. He or she then makes decisions to maximize economic welfare and the national interest. Protectionism in this perspective is viewed as an attempt by a unified rational actor to benefit the home country at the expense of the rest of the world (see Goldstein and Krasner, 1984).

Public choice takes a fundamentally different tack in explaining protectionism and other international economic policies. It focuses on distributional conflicts within a country. In the case of changes in trade policy, compensation is rarely paid by those benefiting to those harmed. Thus, changes in trade policy produce both gainers and losers. Rather than assuming that the state is a unified actor unaffected by distributional considerations, public choice views distributional issues as central to the policy formation process. As

Willett (1995) emphasizes, the hallmark of the public choice approach is the assumption that politicians, voters, bureaucrats, interest groups and others in the political process act as rational utility maximizers subject to the constraints they face.[1]

While public choice analysis sheds light on the formulation of all types of international economic policies, it is especially useful in explaining trade policy due to the intense interest group pressure often accompanying trade policy debates. In the public choice perspective, the quantity of trade protection provided is assumed to be determined in the political market-place. Voters and special interests who gain from protection demand these policies. They offer politicians votes and campaign contributions to obtain the benefits. Congress and the president broker trade protection. Voters and special interests who lose from protection supply the benefits. They are unwilling or unable to muster sufficient votes or contributions to resist the transfers.

An early voting model was developed by Downs (1957). It indicated that the policy equilibrium is determined by the preferences of the median voter. Political parties wanting to remain in power have no choice but to satisfy the desires of the median voter. Proponents of majoritarian voting claimed vindication in this theorem.

More recent research, however, has pointed to several factors attenuating the link between voters' preferences and policy outcomes (see Rowley, 1984). For the median voter theorem to obtain the election must have only two political parties. In the United States, Southern Democrats have often behaved like a third party. For Downs's result to hold political parties must be able to move freely across policy space. As Enelow and Hinich (1984) argue, for credibility reasons parties often cannot move very far from their initial position. Finally, for the vote motive to control political markets voters must be well informed about the policy positions of the parties. However, the chance that an individual's vote will decide an election is minuscule, implying that voters have an incentive to be rationally ignorant about parties' policy positions.

The weakness of the vote motive opens the door for interest groups to exert a disproportionate influence on the policy process. Special interests pursue issues that generate large benefits to a small number of constituents while imposing small costs on a large number of constituents (see Gwartney and Wagner, 1988). To obtain benefits they employ campaign contributions, blocks of votes and persuasive advertising. They tend to be most effective when they represent small, geographically concentrated segments of society. When they represent large, diffuse interests such as those of consumers they tend to be ineffective because of the free-rider problem (Olson, 1965).

Members of Congress are assumed to seek re-election. To do this, they need to broker benefits to both their geographic constituents and to the interest groups that bankroll their campaigns. To secure passage of bills containing particularist benefits, members of Congress often must engage in logrolling trades. They are more likely to broker benefits either when the benefits are hidden or when those demanding transfers provide arguments that the redistribution is in the national interest. In the latter case, members of Congress can argue, in Bhagwati's (1989, p. 445) words, that they are 'not ... politicians responding to narrow sectional interests but statesmen safeguarding the national interest'. However, since voters are rationally ignorant, members of Congress can accept these arguments without detailed empirical justification.

A first-term president is assumed to seek re-election and a second-term president a dynasty and a place in history. Since the president has a larger constituency than members of Congress, he often must avoid protectionism because of the damage it does to the aggregate economy. However, as with members of Congress, the president will be more willing to broker protection when he can do it in a hidden way or with national interest justifications. He also must avoid trade protection because of the strong ideology favouring free trade.

Economists generally believe that ideology has an important impact on the policy process. Mises (1957, p. 138) stated that, 'Ideas tell a man where his interests are.' Keynes (1936, p. 383) argued that, 'The ideas of economists and political philosophers, both when they are right and when they are wrong, are more powerful than is commonly understood. Indeed, the world is ruled by little else. Practical men, who believe themselves to be exempt from any intellectual influence, are usually the slaves of some defunct economist.' Cooper (1989, p. 181) discussed the need for 'international consensus about practical knowledge' in order to agree on policies between countries. When the prevailing ideology indicates that constituents' self-interest lies in one direction, it becomes more costly for politicians to broker policies in the opposite direction.

Along with ideology, the public choice approach emphasizes the importance of the institutional structure within which policies are implemented. As Milner (1997) discusses, institutions are the rules of the game within a society. The way the polity is organized affects the constraints facing actors in the political market-place. For instance, on the issue of trade policy, one would expect substantially more protection if Congress is the major player than if the president is. As discussed above, members of Congress have narrower constituencies, and thus are more likely to be receptive to demands by constituents for particularist benefits.

Finally, in a public choice perspective macroeconomic conditions should influence international economic policies (see Rowley et al., 1995). If output declines, firms facing declining profits and possible layoffs are likely to demand more protectionism. Rationally ignorant voters, susceptible to special interest advertising and unlikely to understand the costs of protectionism, are likely to supply the benefits. Similarly, if the dollar appreciates and damages trade-sensitive sectors, these industries are likely to demand more protection. Again, rationally ignorant voters, influenced by politically salient measures such as the trade deficit, are likely to supply the additional protectionism. If inflation increases, it is possible that voters will become better informed of the costs of trade protection and reduce the supply.

The following sections employ historical evidence to demonstrate the ability of the public choice model to shed light on America's forays into the global economy; the first examines the evolution of trade policy through the lens of public choice analysis. The second attempts to explain changes in international monetary policy using a political economy framework.

A BRIEF HISTORY OF TRADE PROTECTION IN THE USA

To demonstrate the usefulness of the public choice model a brief history of trade protection in the United States is presented. The historical overview will also shed light on how America has become increasingly integrated into the global economy.

As Gardner (1980) discusses, before 1930 American foreign policy, for several reasons, was characterized by economic isolation and economic nationalism. Tariffs were continually raised, repayment on World War I debts was demanded and membership in the League of Nations was declined. Gardner ascribes America's attitude partly to the fact that it was a large continental land mass that was nearly self-sufficient in many types of production. In addition, he argues that many in the USA favoured *laissez-faire* and were uncomfortable with the high degree of government intervention in the international economy. Finally, he argued that the political system, by giving power to local units, made it difficult for the country to agree on a united foreign economic policy.

The tendency towards economic nationalism over this period is well illustrated by the Smoot–Hawley Tariff Act of 1930. Schattschneider (1935) reports that well-organized interest groups testified before the House seeking tariff increases, whereas many other producers were unaware of the hearings. Taussig (1931, p. 495) states that lobbyists, 'pretty much got what they wanted'. Schattschneider also documents the extensive logrolling that Congress engaged in to secure passage of the bill. Rowley et al. (1995) discuss the opposition to the bill by women who complained that dresses would become more expensive. Speaking of the latter group, the *New York Times* (23 May 1929, p. 28) argued that these consumers did not receive any benefits from the bill because they had no organized lobbies to testify before Congress. The final act revised tariffs on 20 000 items, producing the highest tariff rates in US history.

The Smoot–Hawley Act is a showcase for public choice theory. Well-organized special interests lobbied Congress for particularist benefits. Members of Congress brokered these transfers. To get the legislation passed they engaged in massive logrolling. More diffuse interests such as consumers were either unaware of the legislation or unable to influence it.

Shortly after passage of the Smoot–Hawley Act of 1930, the USA experienced an economic disaster. Real US net national product fell by 30 per cent from 1929 to 1933. Several countries retaliated, raising tariff walls against US products. US exports fell from \$5.2 billion to \$1.7 billion and imports from \$4.4 billion to \$1.5 billion.

Rightly or wrongly, people attributed these economic difficulties partly to Smoot–Hawley. Newspapers throughout the country argued that high barriers to imports were a grave economic mistake.[2] One estimate indicated that 75 per cent of the people wanted lower import duties.[3] The Republican president (Hoover) and Republican Congress, who together had produced Smoot–Hawley, were voted out of office by landslides in 1932. The experience of a depression following passage of a major tariff-raising bill strengthened the ideology, developed by Adam Smith and David Ricardo, that free trade rather than protectionism leads to prosperity.

In this atmosphere President Roosevelt and his secretary of state, Cordell Hull, began in 1933 seeking to wrest tariff-setting authority from Congress. According to the US Constitution, Congress has the power to 'regulate commerce with foreign nations'. However, the logrolling and tariff-raising that accompanied Smoot–Hawley convinced many that Congress could not resist narrow sectional interests. Thus the Roosevelt Administration sought, under the executive branch's treaty-negotiation authority, the right to engage in reciprocal tariff cuts with other countries. Exporters such as the auto industry lobbied in favour of the bill. The Democratic Congress, in the Reciprocal Trade Agreements Act (RTAA) of 1934, authorized the president to negotiate tariff cuts of up to 50 per cent in exchange for similar concessions by trading partners.

Public choice analysis, as outlined above, would predict for several reasons that a large decline in tariffs would ensue. First, the ideological change triggered by the Smoot–Hawley debacle should shift the policy equilibrium in the direction of free trade. Second, the institutional change shifting power from Congress to the president should make commercial policy less vulnerable to narrow, sectional interests. Third, the harnessing of export interests such as the automobile industry should offset the demand by import-competing interests for protectionism.

Tariffs did indeed fall shortly after passage of the RTAA, and for several reasons continued falling after World War II (see Baldwin, 1985). One reason was the hegemonic position of the USA. The US economy in the late 1940s was so powerful relative to its trading partners that it could afford to lower tariffs even if trading partners did not. The cost to US firms of industries in other countries free-riding in this way was small compared to the benefits that US firms stood to gain from an open trading system. A second reason was the strong export position of the USA. Up to 1952, the US export share to the 10 largest industrial countries was 35 per cent, up from 26 per cent in 1938. In manufacturing, the US export share was also 35 per cent, up from 21 per cent in 1938. Every major sector was running an export surplus. In such an environment, lobbying pressure in the USA for open international markets far exceeded pressure for protectionism. A third reason was national security. Trade liberalization was viewed as a way to strengthen the free world against communism.

As Willett (1995) argues, the 1940s and 1950s can be viewed as a time when the unified rational actor model of the state helps explain US trade policy, with the twist that it helps explain trade liberalization rather than protectionism. He argues that the institutional changes following the RTAA strengthened the hand of the executive branch relative to Congress. These changes were reinforced by the participation of the USA in the General Agreement on Tariffs and Trade (GATT) beginning in the late 1940s. The executive branch pursued free trade not only because of the ideology indicating that it would produce prosperity but also because, during the Cold War, it was considered necessary for national security reasons. This combination of institutions and ideology allowed the executive branch to deflect distributional demands for protectionism and pursue the national interest by liberalizing trade.

The GATT (supplanted by the World Trade Organization in 1995) has provided an international institutional structure conducive to freer trade. It pitted exporting firms, interested in open markets abroad, against import-competing firms, interested in closing domestic markets. As Jackson (1998) discusses, it evolved into a rule-based system to resolve trade disputes rather than a results-oriented system employing conciliation and negotiation. GATT rules emphasized the use of tariffs (because of their greater transparency) and the principle of non-discriminatory most favoured nation relations between countries. Under the aegis of the GATT, weighted average tariff rates in the USA fell from above 50 per cent in 1947 to below 5 per cent in 1980. Tariff rates also fell to 6 per cent by 1980 in the European Economic Community and to 5.4 per cent in Japan (see Bhagwati, 1988).

However, these large tariff reductions and the recovery of trading partners led to pressure for protectionism. As Baldwin (1985) discusses, following the

Trade Liberalization Act of 1962 imports of automobiles, footwear, electrical goods, steel and textiles soared. These industries lobbied Congress for relief.

Several factors limited the ability of Congress to provide protection. The ascendency of the executive branch in trade policy decisions reduced the influence of narrow sectional interests in the political market place. The GATT-based approach, emphasizing fixing rules and letting the chips fall where they may, reduced the options to respond *ex-post* to increased import penetration.[4] The ideology that free trade produced prosperity and protectionism led to immiseration militated against an increase in tariffs.

Members of Congress circumvented these obstacles by employing fair trade policies such as antidumping (AD) and countervailing duty (CVD) laws to provide relief. Antidumping duties are designed to offset the effect of foreigners selling products in US markets below the prices they charge in their home markets, and countervailing duties are intended to offset the effects of government subsidies on the production of exported goods. As Baldwin (1985) and Destler (1986) document, members of Congress in the 1960s and 1970s wrested control of the AD and CVD laws from the executive branch.[5] These laws were legal under GATT rules. They also did not violate ideological strictures because they were framed in terms of fairness, a concept that Americans value. As Destler (1986) discusses, by the 1980s many more AD and CVD petitions were filed, and much more relief was granted.

However, much of this relief has been protectionist. Bhagwati (1988) has argued that since these laws have no penalties for frivolous complaints, domestic rivals have used them to file complaints and keep competitors mired in expensive litigation. Palmeter (1989) has argued that the practice of determining dumping by comparing a weighted average of the exporter's price with each individual price in the USA is unfair. For instance, if the exporter sells a good for $200 in his country and the USA one week and $150 in his country and the USA the next week, the average price in the USA would be $175. Since this is less than the price of $200 that was charged at one time in the USA, the foreign firm would be guilty of dumping. Finger et al. (1982) have argued that since AD and CVD rulings are issued based on narrow, technical criteria away from the media's eye, protection can be granted without displeasing voters. Further, fear of positive AD and CVD rulings have caused foreign firms in almost half of the cases considered during the 1980s to agree to voluntary export restraints (VERs).

VERs, 'voluntary' agreements between the USA and foreign firms to limit imports, are undesirable economically but desirable politically. Economists argue that VERs not only distort prices but also transfer quota rents abroad. It has been estimated that VERs cost society $169 000 for each job paying $12 600 in clothing, $105 000 for each job paying $38 000 in automobiles and $750 000 for each job paying $50 000 in steel (see Blinder, 1990).

Politicians often choose VERs because they benefit US firms seeking protection, benefit foreign firms involved in negotiations and are unlikely to be understood by the rationally ignorant voters who supply the benefits. Thus VERs multiplied in the USA in the 1970s and 1980s, despite the damage they inflict on the aggregate economy.

A good example of how the political system produces VERs came in the early 1980s. Unemployment in the USA in 1982 reached a post-war high of over 10 per cent. Much of the economic dislocation was borne by trade-sensitive sectors. The dollar had appreciated 26 per cent between the first quarter of 1981 and the end of 1982, hurting US import-competing and export firms. By 1985 the dollar had appreciated 50 per cent. The current account deficit grew and by 1984 exceeded $100 billion. Many sectional interests lobbied Congress for protection. Congress turned to protectionism as the solution to the problems of unemployment and the current account imbalance.[6] In 1982 it passed the blatantly protectionist Domestic Content Bill, requiring companies such as Toyota to use 75 per cent domestic parts and labour. In 1984 it passed the Omnibus Trade Bill, which the *Washington Post* called the 'Anti-Trade Bill' and a 'classic of special interest politics'.[7] The Reagan administration worked assiduously to remove protectionist elements, and the *Washington Post* described the bill President Reagan finally signed as 'pretty respectable legislation'.[8] However, to convince Congress to drop protectionist provisions, President Reagan agreed to negotiate a VER with foreign steel producers limiting imports to 20 per cent of the market.

This experience in the early 1980s demonstrates the usefulness of public choice theory. Macroeconomic imbalances such as unemployment and the appreciation of the dollar increased pressure for protectionism. Members of Congress were responsive to sectional demands for protection. They used national interest arguments such as the need to fight unemployment to rationalize protectionist bills. The president, representing a broader constituency, opposed outright protectionism. The benefits he did broker, VERs on foreign steel, were in a form that rationally ignorant consumers were unlikely to understand and complain against.

The Reagan administration during its second term embraced fair trade more forcefully.[9] As the *Wall Street Journal* reports, the first draft of President Reagan's autumn 1987 trade speech emphasized free trade, but Reagan advisers rewrote it to emphasize fair trade.[10] Finger (1991) discusses how bald-faced protectionism is a loser politically – witness Walter Mondale, John Connolly, Richard Gephardt and Ross Perot – while fair trade is a winner. It allows politicians to avow support for free trade and still broker benefits. However, assuming politicians pursue re-election by benefiting constituents and special interests maximize utility by seeking particularist transfers, there is no reason that the behaviour of foreign traders actually be unfair. It is enough if a superficially plausible case can be made to mollify rationally ignorant voters. The Reagan administration, according to Treasury Secretary James Baker, used the fair trade laws to broker more import relief than any administration over the past 50 years.

The ethos of fairness, combined with export interests and new economic theories, led to unilateral demands by the USA in recent years for greater opening of markets abroad. As large trade deficits emerged in the 1980s and persisted in the 1990s, many Americans began arguing that trading partners were cheating. They argued that foreign markets were much more closed to US exports than US markets were to foreign exports. Export interests in the USA embraced this proposition, seeking greater openness of foreign markets without needing to reciprocate by opening US markets more. These demands were reinforced by economic models developed by economists such as Krugman (1990). These models emphasize that much trade takes place in industries facing increasing returns to scale. In this situation, a government subsidy can enable an industry to increase production and produce at lower average cost, driving foreign rivals out of the market. This rationale, combined with lobbying by export interests and arguments for fairness, led to passage of the 'Super-301' clause of the Omnibus Trade and Competitiveness Act of 1988. This clause authorizes the United States Trade Representative to identify unfair practices abroad and to impose sanctions if these practices are not removed.

The way the political market-place implements this market opening approach is well illustrated by recent attempts by the Clinton administration to open up Japan's market for motor cars and parts (see Thorbecke, 1997b, for a detailed narrative). When President Clinton ran for election in 1992, he used arguments based on the work of Krugman and others to advocate a tough approach on trade issues with Japan. In 1993, he employed this get-tough strategy by seeking to raise tariffs on Japanese minivans by 1000 per cent. As the *New York Times* notes, this policy could not be justified by new trade policies but was rather 'rank protectionism'.[11] Later in 1993, the Clinton administration demanded that Japan increase its imports of car parts by $21 billion. When Japan baulked, Clinton invoked the Super-301 clause. This would impose punitive tariffs if consultation with Japan did not remove the 'unfair' practices. In these negotiations, the USA demanded specific numerical targets for the number of US car parts that Japanese car makers would purchase. This idea came from the motor car industry,[12] which spent months 'building support in Washington with administration officials and government leaders'.[13] Japan argued that such targets represented managed trade and thus violated WTO rules. The USA responded by threatening to impose 100 per cent punitive tariffs on Japanese luxury cars if their demands were not met. The *Wall Street Journal* argues that the Clinton administration was attempting to reward constituent groups that had supported him in 1992 and might do so again.[14] Finally, hours before the tariffs were scheduled to take effect, a compromise was reached.

This episode displays the usefulness of the public choice model. US car makers invested time and money lobbying Washington. President Clinton responded to these constituents by seeking protection. He was able to offer protection partly because the concepts of fairness and Japanese firms trying to capture US markets helped satisfy many rationally ignorant voters that the policy was in the national interest. However, as the *New York Times* and *Wall Street Journal* reported, his policies were often pure protectionism aimed at rewarding constituents.

While President Clinton was brokering protectionism under the cover of national interest arguments such as the need to oppose unfair foreign practices, he also pursued free trade by securing congressional ratification of NAFTA and negotiating an agreement on the Uruguay Round of GATT negotiations. In pursuing free trade in these ways, he was representing the interests of his larger constituency over narrow, sectional interests. By simultaneously pursuing fair trade and free trade the president is able, to quote Finger (1991), to have his cake and eat it too. He can broker benefits to narrow constituents using national interest arguments such as fairness but still claim to be a free trader.

The debate and final House vote on NAFTA illustrates the deep divisions that have arisen in the USA over globalization. In the final vote 156 members of the president's party opposed the bill that he endorsed. Thorbecke (1997a) presents empirical evidence indicating that representatives with more low-skilled workers in their districts were more likely to oppose the bill, representatives with greater contributions from labour unions were more likely to oppose the bill and representatives with greater contributions from management groups were more likely to favour the bill. This division mirrors the recent cleavage in America between low-skilled workers (and labour in general) opposing greater trade with low-wage nations and management groups supporting greater liberalization.

A recent manifestation of this division has been the debate over labour standards. Labour unions in the USA are arguing that low-wage countries violate workers' rights. They are demanding that these countries accept a set of labour standards as a precondition to trade. Such standards would increase the costs of production in poor countries and reduce their comparative advantage in producing goods requiring unskilled labour. Developing countries, and free traders in developed countries, suspect that these demands are driven partly by protectionist lobbies seeking advantage. In any case, concerns such as these and those of environmentalists were responsible for the recent failure of President Clinton to obtain 'fast-track' authority to negotiate new trade treaties.

A BRIEF OVERVIEW OF EXCHANGE RATE AND INTERNATIONAL MONETARY POLICY IN THE USA

While trade policy provides a fertile field to demonstrate the usefulness of public choice analysis, exchange rate policy is more barren. As Gowa (1988) argues, trade policy differs fundamentally from exchange rate policy in that trade policy offers excludable goods while exchange rate policy offers non-excludable goods. A non-excludable good is one that it is very hard to prevent an agent from consuming whether he has paid for it or not. Trade policy is replete with particularist benefits for individual industries. Exchange rate policy, as in the depreciation of an overvalued dollar, extends automatically to many who do not lobby for it. Thus, according to Olson's (1965) analysis, it would be difficult to organize for collective action on exchange rate policy.

Willett's experience at the Council of Economic Advisors and the Treasury confirms Gowa's insight. He states:

> It did not take many months working in government for me to learn that the factors influencing international trade policy formulation were very different from the factors influencing international monetary policy formulation. Inter-agency meetings on international monetary policy came very close to conforming to a unified rational actor model. ... There was little concern about the effects of policies on specific industries or congressional districts. Most of the analysis would be on how a policy would likely work in the aggregate. ... In contrast, trade policy issues prompted negotiations within the government before we began any international negotiations. ... It was a completely different environment from the monetary one.[15]

Thus, much of modern exchange rate policy in the USA can be explained not by responsiveness to interest group pressure but by government agencies such as the Federal Reserve and the Treasury pursuing the national interest. The post-war Bretton Woods system of fixed exchange rates, as Willett (1995) relates, was designed by economists such as John Maynard Keynes based on economic rather than political considerations. Similarly, the switch by the USA to a flexible exchange rate system in the early 1970s was motivated by a desire to seek first domestic macroeconomic objectives.

As Henning (1994) discusses, one period when political factors did influence exchange rate policy was during the 1980s, when the dollar was significantly overvalued. The combination of contractionary monetary policy and expansionary fiscal policy led to a 67 per cent appreciation in the trade-weighted value of the dollar between 1980 and 1985. Henning discusses the large costs this appreciation imposed on US export and import-competing industries. Big firms (such as Caterpillar, Chrysler, General Motors and Kodak), business groups and organized labour began lobbying the administration and Congress to depreciate the dollar. The Treasury Department, led by Secretary Regan, believed the exchange rate was a market-determined price and should not be a target of government policy. Members of Congress were more sympathetic but controlled trade policy and not exchange rate policy. As Henning relates, Congress used the threat of protection to motivate the administration on exchange rate policy. James Baker took this threat seriously, and on becoming Treasury Secretary in 1985 orchestrated a depreciation of the dollar. His success at lowering the dollar's value helped relieve special interest lobbying and reduce the protectionist content of the Omnibus Trade Act of 1988.

Another aspect of international monetary policy that has been susceptible to lobbying concerns capital mobility. Henning (1994) and Wade (1998) relate how bankers and Wall Street firms opposed capital controls that limited their access to foreign markets. Kristoff and Sanger (1998) discuss how the US Treasury responded to demands from Wall Street by pressing for free mobility of capital into foreign countries. Bhagwati (1998) has coined the term 'Wall Street–Treasury Complex' to describe this link between lobbying by Wall Street firms and US demands for financial liberalization abroad. Thus the American financial services industry has led the US government to seek unfettered capital mobility.

CONCLUSION

This chapter has employed a public choice perspective to explain the international economic policies of the USA. In this framework, special interests will lobby the president and Congress for particularist benefits. Congress will tend to be more responsive to narrow, sectional interests while the president will tend to be more responsive to broader interests. Institutions, ideology and macroeconomic conditions all influence the ability of politicians to provide benefits. This chapter has provided numerous examples of the ability of special interests to receive benefits (for example, import-competing firms following the Smoot–Hawley Act), the greater responsiveness of Congress to sectional interests (for example, the protectionist bills passed during the 1980s), the importance of institutions (for example, the decline in protection when the president took over primary control of tariff-making policy from Congress in the 1930s), the influence of ideology (the impact of concepts such as free trade or fairness on the amount of protectionism provided) and the relevance of macroeconomic conditions (for example, the greater demand for protectionism during the recessions of the 1980s). The chapter has also argued that interest groups should have greater influence on trade policy, where free-riders can be excluded from receiving benefits, than on exchange rate policy where excludability is difficult.

Interest groups, politicians and bureaucrats have often produced dysfunctional trade policies, and an important question concerns how better outcomes can be achieved. In a public choice perspective, one solution involves developing and promulgating correct ideologies. When the prevailing ideology indicates that certain policies are beneficial to citizens, it moves the political equilibrium towards those policies. An important role for scholars is thus to investigate and document the functioning of the US economy under alternative types of international economic policies. Clear evidence of the aggregate costs imposed by voluntary export restraints, antidumping duties and aggressive unilateral demands for foreign liberalization will make it more difficult for politicians to broker these policies. Bhagwati (1988, p. 85) has labelled this process of using correct information to limit dysfunctional policies the Dracula Effect: 'exposing evil to sunlight helps to destroy it'.

This chapter has presented evidence that America's international economic policies are often implemented not to maximize aggregate efficiency but rather to satisfy the demands of special interests. Resulting policies such as the Smoot–Hawley Act in the 1930s or the antidumping laws in the 1990s have imposed substantial costs on the overall economy while benefiting pressure groups. International political economy scholars can constrain the political market-place from producing such harmful policies by demonstrating and publicizing that the outcomes are contrary to the self-interest of the great mass of voters.

NOTES

* I thank Gavin Boyd and participants at the Workshop on Globalizing America at Rutgers University for helpful comments. Parts of this paper draw on previous work cited in the references. I acknowledge my intellectual debt to Jagdish Bhagwati and Charles Rowley. Any errors are my own responsibility.
1. These political actors do operate in social environments, accepting diverse kinds of informal accountability, contributing to and experiencing diverse forms of socialization and profiting from learning experiences regarding the public goods as well as the individually centred concerns that motivate them. I am indebted to Gavin Boyd for this point.
2. These newspapers include the *Saint Louis Globe Democrat*, the *Kansas City Star* and the *New York Times*. For references to these newspapers, see the *New York Times*, 6 May 1934, p. 4.
3. *New York Times*, 16 December 1933, p. 6.
4. Bhagwati (1988) makes this point.
5. Before 1967 more than half the commissioners appointed to the International Trade Commission (ITC), which adjudicates the injury portion of the AD and CVD laws, were from the executive branch or academia and less than 10 per cent had Congressional backgrounds. After 1967, less than 10 per cent of the appointees were from the executive branch or academia and more than 50 per cent had congressional backgrounds. In 1974 Congress gained exclusive control of the budget of the ITC. In 1979, Congress shortened the time limits in which AD and CVD rulings could be made. They also transferred authority for AD and CVD determinations to the Commerce Department, which was

thought to be more responsive to the demands of business, and away from the Treasury Department, which was thought to be concerned about broader issues.

6. See, e.g. *The Wall Street Journal*, 8 February 1982, p. 1 and 24 March 1982, p. 12.
7. *The Washington Post*, 28 September 1984, p. A21.
8. *The Washington Post*, 18 October 1984, p. A1.
9. This section draws on Finger (1991).
10. *The Wall Street Journal*, 24 September 1987, p. 7.
11. *The New York Times*, 3 May 1993, p. A14.
12. *The Wall Street Journal*, 10 May 1995, p. A14.
13. *The Wall Street Journal*, 28 June 1995, p. A2.
14. *The Wall Street Journal*, 10 May 1995, p. A14.
15. Willett (1995) pp. 9–10.

REFERENCES

Baldwin, Robert (1985), *The Political Economy of U.S. Import Policy*, Cambridge, MA: The MIT Press.

Bhagwati, Jagdish (1988), *Protectionism*, Cambridge, MA: The MIT Press.

Bhagwati, Jagdish (1998), 'Free trade: why the AFL–CIO, the Sierra Club, and Congressman Gephardt should like it', unpublished manuscript, Columbia University.

Bhagwati, Jagdish (1989), 'United States trade policy at the crossroads', *World Economy*, **12**, 439–79.

Blinder, Alan (1990), *Hard Heads, Soft Hearts*, New York: Macmillan.

Cooper, R. (1989), 'International Cooperation in Public Health as a Prologue to Macroeconomic Cooperation', in R. Cooper et al., (eds) *Can Nations Agree*, Washington, DC: Brookings Institution, pp. 178–254.

Destler, I.M. (1986), *American Trade Politics: System Under Stress*, Washington, DC: Institute for International Economics.

Downs, Anthony (1957), *An Economic Theory of Democracy*, New York: Harper and Row.

Enelow, J.M. and M.J. Hinich (1984), *The Spatial Theory of Voting*, Cambridge: Cambridge University Press.

Finger, J.M. (1991), 'The meaning of unfair in U.S. import policy', World Bank Policy, Research, and External Affairs Working Paper no. 745, Washington, DC.

Finger, J.M., C.K. Hall, and D.R. Nelson (1982), 'The political economy of administered protection', *American Economic Review*, **79**, 452–6.

Gardner, Richard (1980), *Sterling-Dollar Diplomacy in Current Perspective*, New York: Columbia University Press.

Goldstein, Judith and Stephen Krasner (1984), 'Unfair trade practices: the case for a differential response', *American Economic Review*, **74**, 282–7.

Gowa, Joanne (1988), 'Public Goods and Political Institutions: Trade and Monetary Policy Process in the United States', in G. Ikenberry, D. Lake and M. Mastanduno, (eds), *The State and American Foreign Economic Policy*, Ithaca: Cornell University Press, pp. 15–32.

Gwartney, J. and R.E. Wagner (1988), *Public Choice and Constitutional Economics*, Greenwich, CT: JAI Press.

Henning, C.R. (1994), *Currencies and Politics in the United States, Germany, and Japan*, Washington, DC: Institute for International Economics.

Jackson, John H. (1998), *The World Trading System*, 2nd edition, Cambridge, MA: MIT Press.

Keynes, J.M. (1936), *The General Theory of Employment, Interest, and Money*, New York: Harcourt, Brace.

Kristoff, N.D. and D.E. Sanger (1998), 'How U.S. wooed Asia to let the cash flow in', *The New York Times*, 16 February.

Krugman, Paul (1990), *The Age of Diminished Expectations*, Cambridge, MA: The MIT Press.

Leamer, Edward (1993), 'Wage effects of a U.S.–Mexico Free Trade Agreement', in P. Garber (ed.), *Mexico–U.S. Free Trade Agreement*, Cambridge, MA: The MIT Press.

Milner, Helen (1997), *Interests, Institutions, and Information*, Princeton, NJ: Princeton University Press.

Mises, L. von (1957), *Theory and History*, New Haven: Yale University Press.

Olson, Mancur (1965), *The Logic of Collective Action*, Cambridge, MA: Harvard University Press.

Palmeter, D. (1989), 'The capture of the antidumping laws', *Yale Journal of International Law*, **14** (1), 182–98.

Rowley, Charles (1984), 'The relevance of the median voter theorem', *Journal of Institutional and Theoretical Economics*, **140**, 104–35.

Rowley, Charles, Willem Thorbecke and R.E. Wagner (1995), *Trade Protection in the United States*, Aldershot, UK: Edward Elgar.

Schattschneider, E.E. (1935), *Policies, Pressures, and the Tariff*, New York: Prentice Hall.

Taussig, Frank (1931), *The Tariff History of the United States*, New York: G.P. Putnam.

Thorbecke, Willem (1997a), 'Explaining House voting on the North American Free Trade Agreement', *Public Choice*, **92**, 231–42.

Thorbecke, Willem (1997b), 'Choosing free trade without amending the U.S. Constitution', *Public Choice*, **90**, 185–200.

Wade, Robert (1998), 'The coming fight over capital flows', *Foreign Policy*, **113**, Winter 1998/9, 41–54.

Willett, Thomas (1995), 'The public choice approach to international economic relations', Eleventh Annual Virginia Political Economy Lecture, Public Choice Center, Fairfax, Virginia.

5. The globalization of US industries*

Mona Makhija and Sandra Williamson

In this chapter, our basic purpose is to consider the industry level of analysis in the overall discussion regarding globalization in the USA. In order to accomplish this, we begin by defining a global industry, and differentiating it from other levels of analysis also relevant to globalization, such as the firm, the economy or the role of international institutions. While the globalization of an industry has direct relevance and significant consequences for each of these other levels of analysis, we leave this discussion for other chapters. From our perspective, a global industry is one that is vertically linked to those industries of other countries. Vertical linkage stems from a type of international production that requires industries in different countries to specialize in particular stages of a good's production. In such a case, a sequential mode of production arises in which one country imports a raw or intermediate good from another country, uses that good in the production of its own good and then exports its own good to another country. This process continues until the good in its final form reaches its final destination. In this respect, a global industry is 'a series of linked domestic industries in which the rivals compete against each other on a truly worldwide basis' (Porter, 1986, p. 18). None the less, a central role is played by domestic or national industries in a global industry. This is due to the fact that specific national industries are likely to vary in the extent and manner in which they are linked to other national industries, due to domestic forces (political, economic, social and other institutional) that may facilitate or hamper globalization (e.g. Chandler, 1990; North, 1990; Porter, 1990).

In this chapter, we provide evidence on the historical movement towards globalization of industries in the USA, and attempt to explain future directions of these industries. We accomplish this by providing a comparative analysis of US industries in the manufacturing and chemical sectors in relation to those of other developed economies. Although the issue of industry-level globalization is conceptually well developed, it has received limited empirical treatment due to difficulties in its systematic measurement. This study addresses this issue by developing a measure of industry globalization based on the level of an industry's international linkages (LIT) and level of integration of value-added activities (IIT) which jointly assesses important aspects of the extent of globalization. This procedure has also allowed us to identify industries along the lines of widely cited international industry definitions (Bartlett and Ghoshal, 1989; Porter, 1986), thereby differentiating between multiple levels of globalization (Prahalad and Doz, 1987; Yip, 1992), and to assess globalization across countries and time. Our historical analysis indicates that industries in different countries do exhibit highly differing globalization levels. In particular, we found the USA to be far less global in comparison to European industries, and less so in manufacturing compared to Japan. This overwhelming domestic orientation of US industries in comparison to other major industrial countries has not previously been recognized. Moreover, it appears that, despite positive change, the lag in US globalization relative to other major economies has continued to the present (Hummels et al., 1998). None the less, the US economy is expected to continue in the direction of globalization, as are other industrialized nations.

We argue that differences in US industry globalization stem from highly significant institutional factors, including the role of governmental policy, the national technology structure (Ostry and Nelson, 1995), macroeconomic factors such as exchange rates, trade barriers and interest rates (Campa and Goldberg, 1997), as well as the size of the domestic market (Hummels et al., 1998). These institutional factors are enduring, and will continue to provide differing pressures for globalization. At the same time, global competitive pressures, such as the rapid transfer of technology and knowledge across national borders, will also play a role in homogenizing the extent of globalization.

This chapter is organized as follows. The first section outlines the notion of industry globalization as it exists in this literature, and discusses the importance of the institutional context in providing pressures both towards and away from globalization. Broad institutional features relevant for US globalization are identified. In the third section, our measure of industry globalization is presented, while the fourth contains our sample and methodology. This is followed by a discussion of our findings on 27 US industries during the period 1970 to 1986. We broadly compare these findings for a similar group of industries in Japan, the former West Germany, France and Great Britain. In the final section, conclusions are presented.

INDUSTRY GLOBALIZATION AND THE INSTITUTIONAL CONTEXT

Porter (1986) has noted that the unique combination of economic, technological and competitive pressures characterizing each industry causes the pattern of international competition to differ markedly from one industry to another. Some of these pressures create the need for firms to distribute and coordinate the various value-added activities they perform across multiple countries; this is commonly termed 'global integration' (Bartlett and Ghoshal, 1989; Dunning, 1980). These value-adding activities comprise both tangible assets (for example, raw materials, goods-in-process or components and end products) and intangible assets (for example, the application of firm-specific knowledge such as proprietary technologies, management and marketing skills, brand equity and production know-how). Generally, competitive conditions requiring cost rationalization and scale economies, high technological intensity, access to raw materials, as well as standardized market needs and tastes, impel firms to globally integrate the relevant value-added activities. Other pressures create a need in the opposite direction, towards 'customizing' value-added activities to a given environment. This is generally referred to as local responsiveness (Prahalad and Doz, 1987). Industry conditions, such as differences in distribution channels and market structures, unique local tastes and host government demands, push firms towards adapting relevant value-added activities to a given environment. The extent to which industry conditions require firms to globally integrate their value-added activities determines the industry's level of, and propensity for, globalization. Industries are rarely identical on each and every characteristic related to globalization. Rather, these pressures differentially characterize industries and result in significant variation in the nature and extent to which they are globalized (Yip, 1992).

In line with the above, globalization may be conceptualized in terms of a continuum from low to high, along which different industries fall (Porter, 1986). At one extreme is the type of industry, most often referred to as multidomestic, in which virtually all of the firms' value-added activities are located in a single country. For this reason, competition is limited to the domain of one country, and is essentially unrelated to competition in other countries (Prahalad and Doz, 1987). Such an industry is at the lowest end of globalization, with few opportunities within the value chain to build global-scale efficiencies and linkages with industries in other countries. Somewhat more global is an industry that has some but limited external linkages. These linkages may stem primarily from firms' knowledge flows from headquarters in the home country (Bartlett and Ghoshal, 1989), or from uncoordinated or sporadic marketing of end products to other countries (Porter, 1986), but with the primary focus still on the domestic market. Even higher in the continuum is the industry in which a few, usually downstream, value-added activities of firms are significantly driven by the need for global scale, and are relatively unimpeded by national differences (i.e. they are standardized). The focus of firms in such an industry is predominantly on external end markets; therefore, the international linkages in this case are more significant and of an outward flowing nature (Bartlett and Ghoshal, 1989). The type of industry that is highest in terms of globalization is one which is competitively linked to similar industries in other countries through the integration of most or all of firms' value-added activities (Yip, 1992). In such an industry, firms must simultaneously accomplish global-scale efficiency, local responsiveness and world-wide learning (Bartlett and Ghoshal, 1989). It therefore is characterized by the highest number of international linkages, in the form of inward as well as outward flows.

Each country has unique institutional features which form the environment in which local firms compete (Chandler, 1986, 1990; Porter, 1990). These features include the extensive range of political, social and economic institutions that shape interaction within a given environment (North, 1990).[1] These determine firms' operating environment and make performing a particular value-added activity in one location more or less preferable to another. Firms seek environments in which laws and regulations are favourable for performing a given activity, and where appropriate skills, infrastructure, resources, demand and competition, etc. exist. In this regard, certain countries may be better 'global platforms' than other countries, if they provide an environment yielding firms domiciled there an advantage in competing globally in that particular industry (Porter, 1986, p. 39). The specific composition of a nation's environmental attributes determines the pressures on firms and creates the incentives (or disincentives) for globalization. Due to these variations in institutional environments, we would not automatically expect industries to be similar in their globalization levels across countries.

As Hummels et al. (1998, p. 81) state, 'the story of globalization is a story about specialization'. By this they mean that firms pursue production strategies that use country platforms in a narrow and specialized way. Rather than specializing in all the activities associated with a particular product, however, this type of specialization is related to each of the specific value chain activities. A national context is seen as desirable for one or more of these activities, but not all. A given country context is likely to be optimal in terms of conditions for certain activities, but not for others.

What specific attributes of the US institutional environment reflect on industry globalization? It has often been noted that large countries are less likely to be involved with globally integrated activities. Such countries will have adequate demand within their borders to achieve scale economies in virtually all of the value-added activities. Therefore, there is more incentive to retain production of every stage of the production process. A rapidly expanding economy of a small or medium-sized country, perhaps as evidenced by growing GNP, will also have the same effect. This explanation suggests that the USA, being a considerably larger economy than other developed economies, may globalize less rapidly than other countries.

Decreases in tariff and non-tariff trade barriers also create incentives that favour international trade and, by association, globally integrated activities. Generally, the reduction of trade barriers reduces the costs of overseas production and procurement, and facilitates the process of globalization. A country such as the USA, that has relatively low trade barriers in comparison to other countries, is therefore likely to see a positive effect on globalization. On the other hand, regional trading arrangements like the European Union, that lower or eliminate tariff and non-tariff barriers among members, promote globalization even further. For this reason, the USA is likely to appear less global than the European nations. The USA–Canada Free Trade Agreement, and later the North American Free Trade Agreement, which includes Mexico, has lowered trade barriers between the USA, Canada and Mexico. This has led to increasing integration of the North American market.

Governments provide research funding, credits and export incentives. They can also protect local markets from import competition, especially during an industry's infancy. This allows the industry to quickly reap economies of scale in the protected local market and to seek outlets in foreign markets. Unlike many other countries, the USA does not have explicit industrial or strategic trade policies. Nevertheless, the USA has a clear policy of supporting industries that are important militarily, such as aircraft and computers, particularly by providing funding for basic research and a market for the product.[2] In addition, the USA has also used trade negotiations to open foreign markets for US goods, such as agricultural products, semiconductors and car parts.

Countries that have invested in improvements in communication costs, transportation and other features associated with the infrastructure are likely to be seen as attractive from a global platform point of view. These features reduce costs of production and increase the efficiency of engaging in vertically specialized production. In this respect as well, the USA is likely to fare well in relation to globalization, due to its highly developed infrastructure. On the other hand, transportation costs associated with trade and foreign direct investment are likely to be higher due to the USA's distance from the European and Asian continents, thus having a dampening effect. A highly skilled workforce and worker mobility is likely to have a positive effect on globalization. On the other hand, the high cost of US labour (though not higher than those of Japan, Germany, France or Great Britain) is likely to have a negative effect.

The sources of innovation related to a country context are also important to its desirability as a production site for globally integrated activity. Ostry and Nelson (1995) note that a nation's overall innovation structure tends to be highly complex and specific to particular industries:

This structure consists of a diverse array of public policies and programs whose instruments and objectives vary from industry to industry and country to country. All the countries with a strong pharmaceuticals or fine chemical products industry also have a strong university research system supported by the government, but there is little direct government involvement in the development of new pharmaceuticals or direct subsidization of firms. On the other hand, in virtually all countries that have tried to support the development of electronics industries or aircraft industries, government funds flow directly to the companies, and some form of protection or preferred procurement is also provided. (Ostry and Nelson, 1995, p. 48)

For most of the post-World War II era, the USA has been the world's preeminent technological power, backed by a strong university research system. Japan has been close behind since the late 1970s and even in the lead in some areas in recent years, due to government-backed research programmes instead of university research. In contrast, European countries are sometimes characterized as being left behind. Those industries that can benefit from state of the art research and development activity taking place in a country will receive the impetus for globalization, while those that do not experience such a connection will be less likely to globalize. Some of the most dynamic areas of research in the USA include computers and software, machinery and equipment, and chemicals (including pharmaceuticals).

In sum, numerous institutional factors affect the development of globalization, many more than those listed above. A national context such as the USA is likely to have differing influences on the globalization of industries. We believe that the large size of the US economy, its geographical distance and lack of strategic trade policy will have a negative impact on the globalization of industries. However, industries associated with US technological areas of excellence, and those that benefit from very good US infrastructure and generally low tariffs, are likely to be higher in the globalization scale.

INDUSTRY-LEVEL MEASURE OF GLOBALIZATION

In this section we discuss the nature of our measure of industry globalization. This measure incorporates the whole range of activities performed by industry participants that contributes to overall industry globalization. This two-pronged measure provides a quantitative and systematic assessment of industries, ranging from those that are multidomestic to highly (integrated) global (Bartlett and Ghoshal, 1989; Porter, 1986; Prahalad and Doz, 1987; Yip, 1992).

We had noted earlier that an industry at the very low end of globalization is highly independent of industries in other countries, while one at the very high end is significantly linked to similar industries in other countries. Such link-

ages are most readily captured by the extent of international trade characterizing the industry in relation to the market. We agree with Kobrin (1991) that
tangible flows (exports and imports) also embody intangible asset flows such
as technology transfers and management skills. Thus, *the level of international linkages* is measured by *LIT* (level of international trade). A low *LIT*
indicates that international linkages in the form of imports and exports are
not a pivotal aspect of this industry. In contrast, a high *LIT* suggests that
international linkages play an integral part in the industry. The following
equation captures this relationship:

$$LIT_{it} = (X_{it} + M_{it})/(P_{it} + M_{it} - X_{it})$$

where for an industry i in year t, LIT_{it} is the extent of international linkages
for this industry, X_{it} is exports, M_{it} is imports and P_{it} is the level of production.

LIT alone is not adequate in measuring industry globalization, since it
cannot capture the type of international linkages involved. For example, an
industry's international linkages would primarily be comprised of end product exports when most of firms' value chain activities are located in the home
country but a substantial portion of their final product is sold in other countries. In contrast, an industry's international linkages would show a large
amount of primary, intermediate and end product imports and exports when
firms engage in vertically specialized activities in many countries. These
different types of linkages are indicative of different levels of integration of
value-added activity.

In order to measure the compositional nature of international trade linkages described above, we use intra-industry trade (*IIT*), defined as trade that
takes the form of a simultaneous exchange of goods (both components and
end products) within an industry category (Greenaway and Milner, 1986;
Tharakan, 1983). The validity of this measure is confirmed by empirical
evidence that shows that it is a function of precisely those factors that characterize globalization, including 'taste overlap', or similarity in demand across
markets in different countries for specific products, scale economies, high
product differentiation, technological factors including intensity, a competitive market structure and lower tariff and non-tariff barriers. *IIT* has also been
found to be related to FDI, presumably related to the network of exports and
imports created by the subsidiaries of multinational firms (Norman and Dunning, 1984). A large proportion of *IIT* has in fact been shown to be comprised
of intra-firm trade (MacCharles, 1987; Swamidass, 1993). In order to capture
the extent to which an industry's various value-added activities are globally
integrated, we employ the standard Grubel and Lloyd Index of Intra-industry
Trade (Greenaway and Milner, 1986; Grubel and Lloyd, 1975; Hassan, 1987).

This index measures the extent of the absolute amount of exports in a particular industry which is offset by imports in the same industry, and expresses this intra-industry trade as a proportion of the total trade in this industry. IIT is defined as:

$$IIT_{it} = |1 - X_{it} - M_{it}|/(X_{it} + M_{it})$$

where for an industry i in year t, IIT_{it} is intra-industry trade, X_{it} is exports and M_{it} is imports. $|X_{it} - M_{it}|$ refers to the absolute value of the net of exports minus imports. By definition, IIT lies between zero and one, with zero indicating no intra-industry trade (trade consists only of either exports or imports) and one indicating 'complete' intra-industry trade (exports equal to imports within the industry).

Measurement of Different International Industries

The two measures discussed above, *LIT* and *IIT*, together help to distinguish between four types of international industries discussed in Porter (1986) and Bartlett and Ghoshal (1989) and shown in Figure 5.1. These include: a *multidomestic industry*, in which competition in one country is largely independent of that in other countries. In such a case, the vast majority of firms' value-added activities are performed within a single country. International firms derive competitive advantage through largely separate and unlinked foreign direct investments in multiple countries. Thus, a low *LIT* (indicating low international linkages), along with an *IIT* indicating that neither exports nor imports dominate, reflects such a multidomestic industry. The *LIT* and *IIT* together reflect the fact that imports and exports, although balanced, are a small proportion of the overall domestic market (Box A in Figure 5.1). The relatively lower levels of trade do not provide much opportunity for significant integration of value-added activities.

Box B shows a *multidomestic transitional industry*, indicating a primary focus on the domestic industry along with a significant, although uncoordinated, export orientation. Decentralized marketing of end products to a relatively few countries would be characteristic of such an industry. In this case, a low *LIT* (indicating low international linkages) along with a low export-led *IIT* (indicating a preponderance of exports) captures the increase in exports in an otherwise multidomestic industry. It reflects a higher stage of globalization.

Box C shows a *simple global industry*, in which the scope of competition transcends domestic borders. Such an industry involves the use of the home country as an export platform to reach international markets, usually in the form of end and close-to-end products (suggesting that firms have a geo-

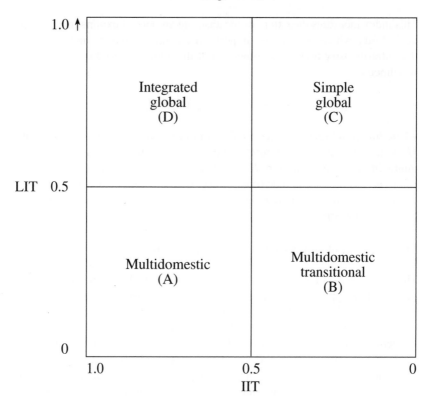

Figure 5.1   Types of international industries

graphically concentrated configuration). The level of product standardization would be high, with far less adaptation of products to specific markets. This scenario is indicated by a high *LIT* (indicating high international linkages) with a low export-led *IIT* (suggesting that exports dominate trade). Despite the importance of trade in this industry, imports do not play a significant role.

   The final category is Box D, an *integrated global industry*, which also indicates a high level of international competition, but suggests that in this industry competitive advantage is derived by firms from high coordination of geographically dispersed value-added activities. In contrast to the simple global industry, a single country serving as an export platform would not be adequate for attaining efficiencies in all the value-added activities. While some of these activities may be highly standardized, others are customized for specific markets. This type of industry is therefore characterized as the most complex, due to the need of firms to manage intricate linkages among the overseas operations; it is also the most global. A high *LIT* with a high *IIT* suggests such an integrated global industry in which international trade dominates the domestic industry and includes high levels of both imports and exports. Note that the four categories represent points of increasing globalization, with the integrated global industry as the most advanced.

In all, four types of industries can be distinguished, representing varying levels of globalization. The industries, ranked in descending order from least to most global, are: (1) multidomestic, (2) multidomestic transitional, (3) simple global and (4) integrated global.

The *LIT* and *IIT* data used to analyse industry globalization are continuous, and as Kobrin (1991) also notes, it is difficult precisely to delineate where one industry category ends and another begins. Since the appropriate cut-off points for differentiating among the categories are not obvious, we rely on precedents already established by previous research. In the case of *LIT*, the cut-off point of 0.50 has been used by Cvar (1984) and Morrison and Roth (1992) and will also be used here. For *IIT* as well, a cut-off point of 0.50 is deemed to be appropriate for distinguishing low and high *IIT* levels since it is at the midpoint of the possible range of *IIT* (0–1). While it is necessary to use cut-off points in order to categorize the industries according to the classification discussed earlier, the actual *LIT* and *IIT* scores for each industry are in themselves highly informative, and provide depth in understanding the exact position of the industry relative to any other. Utilizing these actual scores circumvents the problem of determining the precise level at which an industry makes the transition from low to high internationalization, from simple global to integrated global and so on.

SAMPLE AND METHODOLOGY

Twenty-seven 4-digit ISIC industries in the manufacturing and chemical sectors are examined (these are listed in the appendix). The OECD Compatible Trade and Production (COMTAP) database provided the necessary import and export trade data between OECD countries and other countries in the world, as well as production data, for the years from 1970 to 1986, constituting a 17-year period. In addition to the USA, data for four other developed economies are analysed for comparative purposes (Japan, Germany, France and the UK). We took the mean of the last four years of *LIT* and *IIT* scores in our database in order to calculate the level of industry globalization for the period as close to the present as possible, and to avoid possible undue variation in the data for just the last year.[3] For determining the trend of industry globalization, *LIT* and *IIT* for all 17 years of the database were regressed against time using ordinary least squares regression (OLS). This estimation was accepted when there was no indication of significant autocorrelation as indicated by the Durbin–Watson d-statistic (Kelejian and Oates, 1981). Next, when significant first-order autocorrelation was detected, an autoregressive procedure in the generalized least squares regression (GLS) was used to correct for it. Higher-order autocorrelation was not found to be a problem in our data. The statistical package used was SAS AUTOREG, a procedure of SAS which specializes in solving autocorrelation problems.

EVIDENCE ON THE GLOBALIZATION OF US INDUSTRIES

The results of the analysis are presented in Tables 5.1 through 5.4, located in the appendix. Tables 5.1 and 5.2 contain estimates of *LIT* and *IIT* across the 27 industries for five countries which are then used to classify industries according to the four industry categories discussed earlier.[4] Tables 5.3 and 5.4 contain the *LIT* and *IIT* trends for both sets of industries using all 17 years of data. Figure 5.2 indicates the location of the 27 chemical and manufacturing industries relative to the globalization categories depicted in Figure 5.1, for each of the five countries. The graphical representation of these results in Figure 5.2 allows for comparison of relative positions and trends of industries in each country, as well as their position within the four categories.

A comparison of the five countries highlights some dramatic differences in globalization patterns, particularly in the manufacturing industries. As can be seen in Figure 5.2, as well as Tables 5.1 and 5.2, considerable diversity exists among the five countries. In the United States, both the chemical and manufacturing industries are overwhelmingly multidomestic during the period under study. This indicates that US industries are oriented primarily towards supplying the US market. This is accomplished by using domestic production facilities and inputs largely produced in the United States. Of the 27 industries we examined, all but eight were identified as multidomestic. As indicated in our discussion of US institutional factors at the beginning of this chapter, it appears that the large size of the US economy, and high transportation and coordination costs associated with its location, is largely responsible for this finding.

Of the eight outliers, four US industries (fertilizers and pesticides, engines and turbines, specialized industrial machinery and office machines) are classified as integrated global. Four other US industries (petroleum refining, tyres and tubes, motorcycles and watches and clocks) are import driven. In addition, the civilian portion of the US aircraft industry, if considered on its own, would also be classified as integrated global. In the discussion below, we consider the nature of these particular industries and the features differentiating them from those industries found to be multidomestic.[5] We also include a discussion of the motor car industry, which is classified as multidomestic, which is in part a result of US trade policy.

Interestingly, fertilizers and pesticides is the only segment of chemicals that we categorize as global (integrated global), in contrast to many others who have identified chemicals as a whole as global. As an example, the US Commerce Department states that 'the chemical industry is truly global in nature'.[6] The publication then goes on to detail the substantial inward and outward investments that are its criterion for defining the global nature of the chemicals industry. However, foreign investments can be in industries that are oriented toward serving the local market and therefore are multidomestic in orientation. Using our criteria, only the fertilizer and pesticides segment of the US chemicals industries is global, with a relatively high level of international trade and of intra-industry trade. The large, government-supported agricultural sector in the USA has been a fast-growing and demanding home market for agricultural chemicals. Usage of these inputs has increased sevenfold in the USA in the post-war period. Agricultural chemicals have three main segments, phosphatic and nitrogenous fertilizers and pesticides. The USA is a large consumer of a fourth segment, potash, but most of this is imported from resource-rich Canada. We believe that the key institutional factors here are the availability of low-cost raw materials, a high level of technology and a demanding domestic market for both fertilizers and pesticides. The USA has the second largest reserves of phosphates in the world, after Morocco. Based on its rich resources and sophisticated process technology, the USA remains the world's largest producer, as well as the largest consumer and exporter, of phosphatic fertilizers.[7] It was also the leading producer of nitrogenous fertilizers until the 1970s, based on its abundant and cheap natural gas.[8] Since this period, the USA has been losing market share in nitrogenous fertilizers to countries such as Russia, Canada and Mexico, all of whom have cheaper natural gas. Consequently, the USA has become a net importer of nitrogenous fertilizer. In the case of pesticides, the USA remains the largest producer in the world, followed by Germany and Japan, and is a substantial net exporter. The high R&D expenditures by this industry, necessitated in part by tough US environmental requirements regarding pesticides, suggest that the USA will remain an important global player in this high-tech industry.

In manufacturing, three industries are found to be globally integrated. The first of these, *engines and turbines*, includes steam engines and turbines and internal combustion engines, excluding those used by the marine and aircraft industries. The USA historically has been a leader in research and development associated with these and other machinery products. This is an industry

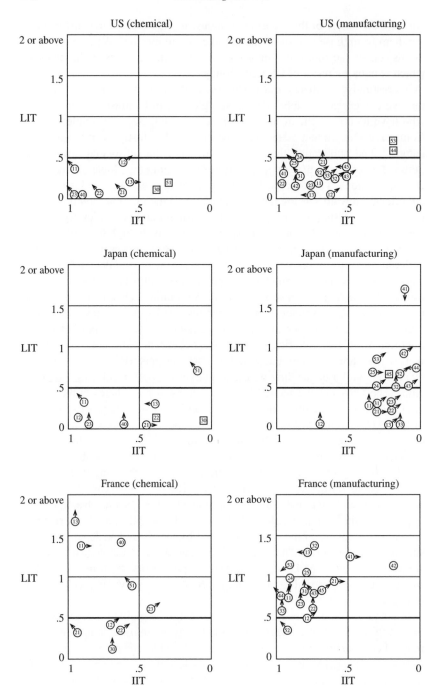

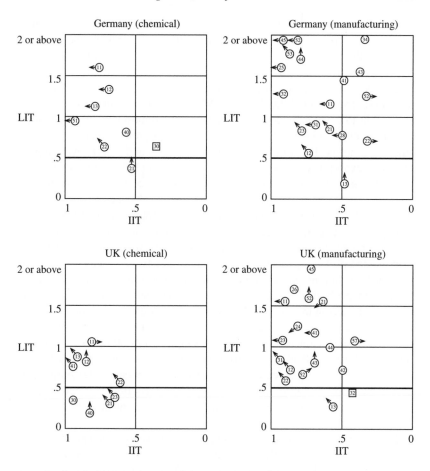

Legend: O indicates the position of an industry, which is designated by the last two digits of its ISIC code shown in the appendix

□ indicates the position of an industry in which imports dominate international trade

➤ indicates the general direction of the industry's trend, significant to the level of *alpha* 0.10 (no arrow indicates an insignificant trend)

Note: * Figure 5.2 depicts the level and trend of globalization of chemical and manufacturing industries in five countries, based on the *LIT–IIT* framework shown in Figure 5.1. The lower left-hand box in Figure 5.2 represents a multidomestic industry; the lower right-hand box, and a multidomestic transitional industry; the upper right-hand box, a simple global industry; the upper left-hand box, an integrated global industry.

*Figure 5.2   The level and trend of globalization of chemical and manufacturing industries in five countries**

that is also heavily influenced by government industrial and procurement policies. Electric utilities are the primary users of turbines and in many countries these utilities are state owned (although in the USA the industry is largely privately owned). US power generating equipment is relatively expensive, especially when the dollar is high, but is generally thought to be of higher quality and reliability.[9] The USA has been successful at exporting this equipment to developing countries, but markets in most developed countries have been closed to US exports, as these countries protect what they see as a strategic industry. In addition, foreign governments in the past have provided attractive export incentives to their manufacturers to help them capture overseas sales, including in the United States. With few competitors in the nuclear area, the export share of US nuclear generators has been consistently higher than that of conventional generators in the period from 1970 to 1985.

Key segments in *specialized industrial machinery* are construction and oil field machinery, with smaller roles played by paper, food, mining, textile and printing and packaging machinery. The important export-oriented sectors are construction, mining and oil field machinery. The food, paper and printing trades and packaging machinery segments saw traditional trade surpluses turn into deficits in the early 1980s as the strong dollar eroded their competitiveness. The textile machinery segment is traditionally import driven. But even in textile machinery, where imports supplied over 60 per cent of the US market, US firms remain competitive in certain niches (e.g. in the application of sophisticated computer controls),[10] with over 40 per cent of US output sold abroad in 1992. The largest markets for US exports from this industry are Canada and Mexico. Canada is the third largest source of imports, following Japan and Germany.

The international competitiveness of US *construction equipment* was adversely affected by the strong dollar in the first half of the 1980s, as the US industry had no technological advantages to offset its high-cost labour and raw materials, especially steel. The traditionally large trade surplus in construction equipment shrank from $5 billion in 1980 to some $500 million in 1985. Exports declined from an average of 30–40 plus per cent of industry shipments in the 1970s and early 1980s, to just above 20 per cent in 1985. Imports from US foreign subsidiaries and other suppliers rose, especially of small and medium-sized equipment in which US-based manufacturing was less competitive. To enhance competitiveness, US firms consolidated, outsourced components and met foreign sales demand from overseas manufacturing facilities. These efforts, coupled with a weakening of the dollar from early 1985 and the industry's ability to compete on non-price factors, such as a world-wide distribution and service network and high quality products, helped to restore the US industry's world-wide competitiveness. Major competitors are Japanese, German and, more recently, Korean construction equipment manufacturers.

The USA has traditionally accounted for half of all oil drilling in the free world, giving US *oil field equipment* manufacturers the largest domestic market in the world. But with the number of active drilling rigs in the USA peaking in 1982, foreign markets became increasingly attractive to US equipment manufacturers. In response, the export share of US-manufactured oil field equipment rose to 75 per cent in the late 1980s and early 1990s, up from 40–60 per cent in the 1970s. US imports of oil field equipment continue to be a minor share of consumption, making this industry segment simple global. The greater focus on drilling outside the USA has led to the expansion of oil field equipment manufacturing in Europe and Asia. None the less, US firms have been able to remain internationally competitive because of their technological lead in producing high quality equipment for deep-well drilling and for drilling offshore and in hostile environments. A high level of R&D has been critical to maintaining US competitiveness in this industry.

The much smaller *mining equipment* segment primarily served the domestic market from 1970 to 1986, exporting some 20 per cent of its output while imports provided less than 10 per cent of consumption. The declining competitiveness of the US mining industry and the strong dollar in the first half of the 1980s adversely affected mining equipment manufacturers, whose shipments in 1985 were half the level of a decade earlier in real terms. The strong dollar helped erode this segment's traditional trade surplus, which declined from a peak $449 million in 1981 to less than $150 million on average in the mid-1980s. The dollar decline from early 1985 enhanced the competitiveness of US exports, which are concentrated in the high end, while the expansion of mining outside the USA made foreign markets more attractive to US manufacturers of mining equipment. By 1992, US manufacturers were exporting over 40 per cent of their output, while the import share of consumption reached 17 per cent, making this segment simple global.

The *office, computing and accounting machinery* industry is also classified as integrated global. Although this industry includes typewriters, calculators and accounting machines, computers are the dominant segment of this industry. The electronic computer industry grew out of a research programme funded by the US Defense Department during World War II, attesting to the early and ongoing influence of government policy, both at home and abroad, on this strategic industry. Although government funding accounts for only a small share of industry R&D spending, it was a catalyst both in the USA and abroad. In the USA, government-funded R&D has focused on basic computer research, which has been key to the industry's long-run prospects. Firm R&D has increasingly focused on applied research and product development, with less than 1.5 per cent of firm R&D spent on basic research in 1994.

Foreign governments have supported development of local computer industries, favoured local procurement and restricted computer imports. These policies encouraged US foreign investment to serve local markets and the transfer of US computer technology abroad, enhancing foreign technological capability. However, as late as 1971, 'the US was preeminent' in the semiconductor/computer industry.[11] But efforts to develop indigenous computer industries by Japan (for example, the $415 million, fifth-generation computer project, begun in the early 1980s and followed by the $450 million Real World Computing Project) and Europe (for example, the ESPRIT project, begun in 1984) eroded US leadership in many areas of the computer industry. Coupled with the strong dollar in the first half of the 1980s, these efforts increased competition. To lower costs, US computer firms stepped up their overseas investment, sourced parts and equipment offshore and automated their facilities. For its part, the US government continued to provide vital funding for basic computer research ($249 million in 1984, but much less than the $6 billion spent by computer manufacturers on R&D that same year) and relaxed its antitrust laws to permit cooperative research efforts like those abroad.[12] By 1991, federal funding of computer research had climbed to $681 million while R&D spending by 92 US computer firms rose to $14 billion.[13]

Even so, US leadership in this industry continues to be eroded, particularly by Japanese competitors, even in supercomputers, the most sophisticated and fastest computers. By the 1990s, the traditional US trade surplus in computers, $6.6 billion in 1986, had given way to a fast-growing deficit, which topped $20 billion in 1995. The USA had a trade surplus in computer systems but a deficit in peripheral equipment, such as printers, and parts. Demonstrating the integrated nature of the US computer industry, the Commerce Department reported in 1993 that two-way trade in computer parts exceeded two-way trade in computers and peripheral equipment.[14] Unlike this industry in the USA, Germany, France and the UK, where trade flows are very much two-way, the Japanese industry during our time period is classified as simple global, with trade flows that are overwhelmingly outward. The USA has pressured Japan to open its computer market to imports, especially of semiconductor chips and supercomputers, and to end what the USA has considered Japanese dumping of these products in the USA and other markets. In further support of the strategically important semiconductor industry, the US government provided substantial funding for Sematech, a consortium of US firms. This multi-year effort, begun in 1987, to make US semiconductors more competitive has met with some success.

The *petroleum refining* industry in the USA was found to be multidomestic transitional but import driven, with imports of refined petroleum products substantially outweighing exports. Trade plays a very small role in this industry, with some 90 per cent of local consumption of refined petroleum products supplied by local refineries and less than 5 per cent of output exported. The USA is the largest market in the world for refined petroleum products, with consumption topping 16 million barrels a day in 1987, so economies of scale at home are more than adequate. Imports and exports generally occur because of regional shortages or excesses of refined product within the USA and high land transportation costs, which make moving refined products from one region to another prohibitive. Most refined petroleum products are imported from Venezuela and Canada for East Coast markets. Most US exports originate in the Gulf Coast and California and go to Canada, Mexico, Latin America and the Far East. Thus, economies of scale, regional imbalances and high land transportation costs help to explain why this industry is multidomestic transitional, but import oriented.

The US *tyre* industry is now largely foreign owned, but it remains heavily oriented toward the large domestic market, in part because high transportation costs make local production desirable.[15] However, the level of international trade within the industry has risen substantially during the period, with exports and imports representing only 5 per cent of the US industry's shipments in 1970 versus 22 per cent in 1985 and over 30 per cent by 1990. The USA imports significantly more tyres than it exports and, hence, the industry is categorized as import-driven multidomestic transitional. In 1971, US-owned firms dominated the world market, with a near 60 per cent share of world tyre production and four of the top five world producers. However, the delayed transition to longer-lasting radial tyres, pioneered by Michelin in 1948 but opposed by US car manufacturers until the 1970s, left the US companies playing technology catch-up during a time of weak markets for automobiles, and therefore, original tyres. Meanwhile, mergers among major US tyre makers, which would have enabled efficiencies in production and increased economies of scale in R&D and advertising, were, in principle, opposed by the car manufacturers companies, who strived to maintain competition among their tyre suppliers. Added to this were the competitive pressures created by the increasing globalization of the world car industry (particularly the need for foreign tyre makers to have a presence in the US market). The openness of the USA to foreign investment in non-strategic industries made foreign takeovers easy, and most American tyre companies were acquired by foreign tyre makers in the 1980s. Impediments to foreign takeovers in Europe and Japan inhibited US tyre manufacturers from making foreign acquisitions. Today, the tyre industry in the USA and world-wide is dominated by a few European and Japanese firms, with only Goodyear remaining a significant American player in the top five.

The US *motorcycle* industry is simple global, but was import driven from 1970 to 1986, with imports accounting for two-thirds of consumption in 1985, over 90 per cent of which came from Japan. Indeed, Japan accounted for 82 per cent of all world motorcycle exports in that year.[16] Harley-Davidson, the only American-owned motorcycle manufacturer, has focused on producing large motorcycles. In 1973, it had a 75 per cent share of the US market for 'super-heavyweight' motorcycles. The Japanese manufacturers concentrated initially on small and later medium-sized motorcycles, exporting them to the USA from Japan. In the late 1970s, Kawasaki and Honda established assembly facilities in the USA, using parts imported from Japan. The Japanese producers continued to move upscale and, by 1981, the Japanese producers had nearly 70 per cent of the US market for super-heavyweight motorcycles, in comparison to under 30 per cent for Harley and less than 2 per cent for BMW. The Japanese manufacturers were able to produce a higher quality, more technologically advanced motorcycle at a significantly lower price, aided at least in part by the strong US dollar in the early 1980s. With Harley's very existence threatened, the US government intervened, imposing a temporary tariff on Japanese motorcycles in 1983 to give Harley some relief from the Japanese import competition. The temporary tariff allowed Harley to regain its competitive edge, helped by the weakening of the dollar in 1985. Harley regained market share and has exported about 30 per cent of its output since 1990. The tariff also encouraged the Japanese manufacturers to increase production at their plants in the USA. Although imports of heavyweight motorcycles declined from $473 million in 1982 to $229 million in 1983, imports of motorcycle parts from Japan more than doubled to $87 million. Despite Harley's recovery, Japanese manufacturers still dominate the US market for motorcycles. US production, by both Harley and the Japanese manufacturers, remains concentrated on heavyweight motorcycles. US exports of motorcycles have grown dramatically since 1987, aided by the weaker dollar and increasing demand in overseas markets for larger motorcycles, a demand shift in favour of US-based manufacturers. By 1992, US exports totalled $528 million, compared to US imports of $658 million. As a result of the rapid US export growth, intra-industry trade had become much more closely balanced between exports and imports, shifting the US motorcycle industry from import driven, simple global to globally integrated.

The US *aircraft* industry is classified as 'multidomestic', a characterization that contradicts the prevalent notion that this is a highly global industry in the USA. The explanation for this can be found in the fact that the industry includes the production of both civil and military aircraft. From 1970 to 1986, over 50 per cent of all complete US aircraft went to the US military, the most important customer of the US aerospace industry. Looking only at the civil aircraft component, over half of all US civil aircraft shipments went to overseas customers during 1978 to 1985, which, combined with the relatively high level of intra-industry trade for the whole industry, would qualify the US civil aircraft sector to be classified as integrated global. The US aircraft industry has benefited from commercial spillovers from military R&D, first mover benefits and economies of scale and scope. US technological leadership in the aircraft industry during our period was supported by the high level of industry R&D, which reached $18 billion in 1985, higher than any other US industry. The lion's share of R&D was government funded, with only one-quarter funded by firms. The US government has also used antitrust legislation to maintain competition in the US industry. The US had large trade surpluses in 1985 in finished aircraft ($7 billion), in aircraft engines and engine parts ($1.9 billion) and in other parts ($3.6 billion). Engines and other parts comprised half of US exports of aircraft and parts, and two-thirds of imports, indicating the integrated nature of this global industry. The high level of trade in parts reflects increasing demand for US engines and other components for foreign manufactured aircraft while shared production projects, offsets and outsourcing increased US parts imports. The USA has continued to run large trade surpluses in aircraft and parts in the 1990s. But competition from Airbus, Europe's largest aircraft manufacturer, has intensified, with Airbus now enjoying technological parity with Boeing according to some experts.[17] Without European government intervention, the US aircraft industry would be unchallenged in the world market today. An additional challenge facing the US industry is the decline in US military spending and government-funded support for the aerospace industry in the 1990s.

Airbus Industrie, now the second largest world-wide aircraft supplier after Boeing, is a consortium of Europe's four largest aircraft manufacturers. These include Aerospatiale of France, Daimler-Benz Aerospace Airbus (originally Deutsche Airbus), British Aerospace and CASA of Spain. Airbus planes are assembled in Toulouse, France and, since 1992, in Hamburg, Germany from components provided by the four participating companies and other suppliers. The consortium was created in 1970, with the encouragement and support of the governments of the participating firms, to create a world-scale 'European' competitor to the American aircraft companies, who dominated the world-wide aircraft industry. The governments provided 'close to 100%' of the launch aid for the development of the A300 and were still providing some 60 per cent of launch costs for the A330 and A340.[18] Without this aid, Airbus would never have got off the ground, given the very high development costs and commercial risks associated with launching new aircraft. The integration of the manufacturing and assembly operations of the four partners of Airbus help account for the integrated global designation of the aircraft industries of France, Germany and the UK.

Unlike the European aircraft industries and unlike most Japanese manufacturing industries, the aircraft industry in Japan is classified as import driven, simple global, with imports providing a large share of total consumption and exports playing a minor role. This is the only Japanese manufacturing industry that is import driven. The growth of the Japanese aircraft industry in the post-World War II period has been hindered by a number of critical factors:

first, aircraft manufacturing was prohibited during the US occupation (1945–52), and, consequently, Japan 'missed the start of the jet engine technology age and has been behind ever since'.[19] Second, the Japanese industry has heavily concentrated on the production of military aircraft. And third, Japanese government policy prohibits the export of military equipment, including aircraft. This policy has largely confined Japan's aircraft industry to the small domestic market for military aircraft and prevented the industry from reaping the significant economies of scale and scope characteristic of aircraft production.

Another noteworthy industry is that of motor car manufacture. The US *auto* industry is classified as multidomestic during the period from 1970 to 1986. Two factors help explain the domestic orientation of this industry: (1) US automotive demand favours larger, more powerful and more accessorized vehicles than other markets; and (2) US trade policy. The first trade initiative, the 1965 US–Canada Auto Agreement, removed tariffs on car trade between the two countries. At the same time, the agreement specified that output in Canada had to be more or less equivalent to sales in Canada, and required domestic content of 60 per cent.[20] Within these constraints, car manufacturers tended to view the United States and Canada as one market, resulting in consolidated production.[21] US–Canada car trade exploded after the agreement. However, because of the relatively small size of the car market in Canada compared to the USA, the bilateral car trade was far more important in the Canadian market than the US market. In 1996, Canada was the largest market for the US automotive industry, absorbing over half of all US exports of finished vehicles and of parts. Canada was also the largest source of US imports of finished vehicles and the second largest source, after Japan, of parts that year.

The next impetus for globalization of the US *auto* industry resulted from the oil shocks of the 1970s which increased US demand for small, fuel-efficient cars. The poor quality and high cost of US-made cars added to the demand for imported cars. As the import share of the US car market rose in the early 1980s, strong protectionist sentiment in the USA led the Japanese, who held some three-fourths of the import market, to impose 'voluntary' export restraints (VERs) beginning in 1981. In addition to restricting exports to the USA, the VERs encouraged the major Japanese car manufacturers to establish joint ventures in the USA (for example, GM and Toyota) and stand-alone transplants (such as Honda). As a result, the import share of the US car market coming from outside North America declined from a peak of 30 per cent in 1987 to about 15 per cent in 1996. However, the growing presence of Japanese transplants in the USA increased imports of car parts from their traditional Japanese suppliers (although ultimately Japanese parts suppliers would begin to build transplants in the USA as well). US car manufacturers also began outsourcing car parts from abroad in their efforts to cut costs, further increasing US imports of car parts in the mid-1980s, and turning the traditional US trade surplus in car parts into a deficit in 1984. The USA didn't register a trade surplus in car parts again until the early 1990s. In 1996, car parts and accessories accounted for over one-third of all US automotive trade.

The North American Free Trade Agreement, which includes Canada, Mexico and the USA, has led to further integration of the North American automotive market since it became effective in 1994. By 1996, Mexico was the largest market, after Canada, for US exports of finished vehicles and of parts and the third largest source of US imports of finished vehicles and of parts, after Canada and Japan.

THE GLOBALIZATION OF JAPANESE AND EUROPEAN INDUSTRY

In the case of Japan, globalization levels for the chemical industries do not appear to be significantly different from the USA. All of Japan's chemical industries are either multidomestic or multidomestic transitional, with the exception of tyres and tubes (simple global). Japan stands out, however, in the manufacturing industries, showing a great disposition towards multidomestic transitional and simple global. Generally, the much lower *IIT* levels and significant negative trends for *IIT* across the manufacturing industries for Japan indicate that export orientation is extremely dominant and growing during the period under study. Only one manufacturing industry is found to be multidomestic (metal furniture and fixtures), while nine of the 18 are simple global (specialized industrial machinery, office and computing machinery, radio and telecommunications, shipbuilding, railroad, motor vehicles, motorcycles, photographic and optical goods and watches). The petroleum refining, pharmaceutical and aircraft industries are import oriented. In all, these findings are consistent with the export platform strategies known to have been pursued by Japanese manufacturers during this time.

In contrast to both the USA and Japan, an overwhelming majority of Germany's industries are integrated global for both chemical and manufacturing industries. Germany stands out as being the most globally oriented in chemicals, with only one that is multidomestic (paints). In terms of manufacturing industries as well, the majority (13) are integrated global, while four are simple global (agricultural machinery, specialized industrial machinery, railways, motor vehicles). Only the structural metal products industry is multidomestic, while petroleum refining is found to be import oriented. France exhibits the most diversity of all the countries with respect to chemical industries: five are integrated global, one is simple global and three are multidomestic. For the manufacturing industries, the great majority are integrated global (16 out of 18). Only one is simple global (railways) and one is multidomestic (electrical appliances and housewares). Interestingly, none of France's industries are found to be import oriented. Similar to those in France and Germany, UK industries are also found to be highly global. Five of the chemical industries are integrated global (basic industrial chemicals, fertilizers and pesticides, plastics, drugs and medicines, and tyres), while the rest are multidomestic. The great majority (16) of UK manufacturing industries are integrated global, with only one that is multidomestic (structural metal products). The one remaining industry is import driven (watches).

We created aggregated industry estimates by country for both chemical and manufacturing industries. When we compare them, these differences are again borne out. The aggregate weighted *LIT* and *IIT* at the country level indicate that, for the chemical industries as a group, the United States and Japan are both multidomestic, while France, Germany and the United Kingdom are all integrated global. For the manufacturing industries as a group, these measures indicate that the United States is multidomestic, Japan is simple global, while the three European countries again are integrated global.

At the same time, Japan is unique in terms of the strong domination of a simple global strategy pursued by firms in manufacturing industries; its extremely low *IIT*s with negative trends suggest an increasing export orientation over this time period. Interestingly, however, Japanese chemical industries behave much more like those of the other countries (excluding Germany). Germany, on the other hand, is found to be overwhelmingly globally integrated for both chemical and manufacturing. This country is in fact unique in the extent to which it exhibits an integrated global strategy in the chemical industry. This finding is not surprising due to Germany's historical competitive advantage in chemical industries (Chandler, 1986). France and the United Kingdom show a mix of integrated global and multidomestic strategies in their chemical industries, yet they are similar to Germany in their globally integrated manufacturing industries. In all, the three European countries exhibit higher levels of integrated globalization in their industries as compared to the United States and Japan.

Composite industry estimates for both *LIT* and *IIT* across all five countries helped to proxy the globalization of different world-wide industries. These estimates suggest that the chemical industries (ISIC 35) overall are low in their globalization levels across the five countries (six out of the nine world-wide industries). This conclusion is reinforced by the overall industry composite estimate (located in the lower right-hand corner of Tables 5.1 and 5.2), which suggests that the world-wide chemical sector may be multidomestic for this time period. Three world-wide industries in the chemical sector are multidomestic (paint and lacquers, soaps and cosmetics, and miscellaneous petroleum and coal products), while two are multidomestic transitional (drugs and medicines, tyres and tubes) and one is import oriented (petroleum refineries). Only three world-wide chemical industries (industrial chemicals, fertilizers and pesticides, and resins and plastics) are found to be global (integrated). We find a different picture for the world-wide manufacturing industries. A majority (11 out of the 18 industries) are found to be either integrated global (engines and turbines, specialized industrial machinery, office and computing machinery, radio and telecommunications equipment, shipbuilding, railways, aircraft, and photographic and optical goods) or simple global (motor cars, motorcycles and watches). Only six of the world-wide industries are multidomestic (cutlery and hand tools, furniture, structural metal products, agricultural machinery, metal and woodworking machinery, electrical industrial machinery) and one is multidomestic transitional (electrical appliances and housewares). The highly global orientation of the world-wide manufacturing industries is confirmed by the overall industry composite estimate. In total, one-third of the world-wide industries in the chemical sector can be classified as global (either simple or integrated) in comparison to almost two-thirds in the manufacturing sector. A similar conclusion can be reached if one makes a comparison of the chemical and manufacturing industries on a country-by-country basis. In all the countries, the proportion of simple and integrated global (multidomestic and multidomestic transitional) industries is comparatively higher in manufacturing industries.

The European nations appear to be much more global in chemicals than the USA and Japan; this reflects the fact that European firms on the whole are the largest producers and exporters of chemicals, led by Germany and France. As is consistent with our results, a large percentage of these are industrial and agricultural chemicals (OECD, 1992). In contrast, Japan's chemical industry is much smaller as compared to the other countries, with Japanese chemical firms one-fifth to one-tenth the size of their Western counterparts.

We also find that the overwhelming majority of the industries across the five countries are globalizing over time. In Figure 5.2, these trends are depicted. The existence of significance (at a .05 level) in the trend is indicated by the presence of an arrow; the direction of the arrow is determined by jointly taking into account significant trends of *LIT* and *IIT*. The generally upward direction of the arrows indicates a tendency towards increasing globalization, either simple or integrated. There is only one case of a clearly downward trend; this is for France's specialized industrial machinery industry. Three industries appear to be moving laterally in a multidomestic direction; these include Japan's plastics industry, the US structural metal products industry and the overall aircraft industries. Despite these exceptions, it is generally the case that trends are upwards towards increasing globalization and almost never downwards away from globalization. These results suggest that both chemical and manufacturing industries are indeed globalizing over time for all five countries.

CONCLUSIONS

Our findings that US industries are mostly multidomestic, particularly in comparison to other nations, are consistent with those of a number of other researchers. Although both use different and more indirect methods at arriving at their conclusions, Hummels et al. (1998) and Campa and Gold (1997) find that the USA continues to have a less external orientation vertical specialization than other OECD countries. In addition, Johann and Yip (1994) find that US firms tend to use fewer global strategies their Japanese counterparts. It may be that two fundamental features institutional environment in the USA, both of which are not shared by other developed nations to any great degree, play a major role in influencing US industry globalization. These include the size of the domestic market and country distance. On the other hand, those industries that showed higher levels of globalization are characterized by US technological know-how and historical R&D leadership (e.g. machinery and equipment, engines and agricultural chemicals). The USA possesses significant innovative capability in these areas, which may explain why in these cases, the USA is able to overcome the effects of market size and distance. We had noted that the civilian aircraft industry appears to be integrated global as well (after exempting from consideration the military sales of planes). This industry has also been characterized by US technological superiority in a number of areas associated with aircraft development and manufacturing.

APPENDIX

Description of Industries

Chemical (ISIC 35)

3511:   Basic industrial chemicals except fertilizers
3512:   Fertilizers and pesticides (agricultural chemicals)
3513:   Synthetic resins, plastic materials, manmade fibres
3521:   Paints, varnishes and lacquers
3522:   Drugs and medicines
3523:   Soap, cleansing preparations, perfumes, cosmetics
3530:   Petroleum refineries

3540:   Miscellaneous products of petroleum and coal
3551:   Tyre and tube industries

Manufacturing (ISIC 38)

3811:   Cutlery, hand tools and general hardware
3812:   Furniture and fixtures primarily of metal
3813:   Structural metal products
3821:   Engines and turbines
3822:   Agricultural machinery and equipment
3823:   Metal and woodworking machinery
3824:   Specialized industrial machinery and equipment
3825:   Office, computing and accounting machinery
3831:   Electrical industrial machinery and apparatus
3832:   Radio, telecommunications equipment and apparatus
3833:   Electrical appliances and housewares
3841:   Shipbuilding and equipment
3842:   Railroad equipment
3843:   Motor vehicles
3844:   Motorcycles and bicycles
3845:   Aircraft
3852:   Photographic and optical goods
3853:   Watches and clocks

Table 5.1 Relative globalization levels of chemical industries across five countries

ISIC	LIT/IIT	USA Mean	USA Ind	Japan Mean	Japan Ind	France Mean	France Ind	Germany Mean	Germany Ind	UK Mean	UK Ind	LIT(WI)/IIT(WI)	Ind
3511	LIT	.29	MD	.29	MD	1.45	IG	1.58	IG	1.05	IG	.59	IG
	IIT	.95		.91		.93		.74		.86		.91	
3512	LIT	.46[ns]	IG	.15	MD	.48[ns]	IG	1.36	IG	.76	IG	.51[ns]	IG
	IIT	.64		.93		.74		.67		.84		.73	
3513	LIT	.20	MD	.25	MT	1.72	IG	1.18	IG	.87	IG	.48[ns]	IG
	IIT	.59		.45		.95		.75		.92		.62	
3521	LIT	.04	MD	.05	MD	.38	MD	.34	MD	.28	MD	.12	MD
	IIT	.61		.45[ns]		.96		.51		.69		.59	
3522	LIT	.15	MD	.10	(MT)	.35	MD	.57	IG	.59	IG	.19	MT[a]
	IIT	.75		.45		.68		.73		.62		.42	
3523	LIT	.05	MD	.05	MD	.58	SG	.49[ns]	IG	.45[ns]	MD	.18	MD
	IIT	.87		.86		.46		.67		.69		.79	
3530	LIT	.10	(MT)	.10	(MT)	.22	MD	.60	(SG)	.40	MD	-.06	(MT)[a]
	IIT	.38		.10		.72		.37		.91		-.14	
3540	LIT	.09	MD	.07	MD	1.49	IG	.80	IG	.21	MD	.17	MD
	IIT	.82		.69		.64		.57[ns]		.85		.76	
3551	LIT	.18	(MT)	.68	SG	.92	IG	1.00	IG	.79	IG	.27	MT[a]
	IIT	.30		.17		.55		.99		.99		.06	
Country Composite	LIT	.04	MD	.06	MD	.55	IG	.75	IG	.61	IG	.29	MD[b]
	IIT	.15		.26		.74		.48		.85		.58	

Notes:

MD: multidomestic; MT: multidomestic transitional; SG: simple global; IG: integrated global; ( ): import driven.

All of the mean estimates are significant at the 5% level, unless otherwise noted.

[ns] not significant at the 5% level.

[a] the industry composite in this case takes into account import-driven industries by utilizing the negative of their *LIT* and *IIT* estimates.

[b] overall industry and country composite estimates of *LIT* and *IIT*.

Table 5.2 *Relative globalization levels of manufacturing industries across five countries*

ISIC	LIT/IIT	USA Mean	USA Ind	Japan Mean	Japan Ind	France Mean	France Ind	Germany Mean	Germany Ind	UK Mean	UK Ind	Industry composite LIT(WI)/IIT(WI)	Industry composite Ind
3811	LIT	.21	MD	.27	MT	.75	IG	1.23	IG	1.55	IG	.44	MD
	IIT	.73		.27		.93		.58		.95		.62	
3812	LIT	.05	MD	.09	MD	$.49^{ns}$	IG	.57	IG	.66	IG	.16	MD
	IIT	.68		.68		.82		.73		.90		.70	
3813	LIT	.05	MD	.06	MT	1.38	IG	.21	MD	.28	MD	.19	MD
	IIT	.73		.15		.82		$.49^{ns}$		.58		.49	
3821	LIT	$.48^{ns}$	IG	.26	MT	.96	IG	.90	IG	1.53	IG	.57	IG
	IIT	.68		.28		.59		.58		.69		.54	
3822	LIT	.20	MD	.30	MT	.56	IG	.76	SG	.55	IG	.35	MD
	IIT	.94		.16		.76		.40		.92		.74	
3823	LIT	.20	MD	.32	MT	.72	IG	.85	IG	1.16	IG	.40	MD
	IIT	.75		.20		.85		$.52^{ns}$		.95		.56	
3824	LIT	$.50^{ns}$	IG	$.50^{ns}$	SG	1.08	IG	3.82	SG	1.29	IG	1.12	IG
	IIT	.85		.24		.92		.35		.86		.63	
3825	LIT	$.49^{ns}$	IG	.61	SG	1.34	IG	1.68	IG	1.71	IG	.69	IG
	IIT	.84		.30		.80		.96		.86		.72	
3831	LIT	.25	MD	.27	MT	.80	IG	.93	IG	.79	IG	.41	MD
	IIT	.82		.28		.89		.70		.93		.64	
3832	LIT	.31	MD	$.52^{ns}$	SG	.58	IG	1.39	IG	.68	IG	$.47^{ns}$	IG
	IIT	.61		.14		.97		.94		.79		$.47^{ns}$	
3833	LIT	.28	MD	.09	MT	.41	MD	.92	IG	$.46^{ns}$	IG	.23	MT
	IIT	.63		.12		.93		.78		$.44^{ns}$		.36	
3841	LIT	.26	MD	1.73	SG	1.29	IG	1.44	IG	1.20	IG	.96	IG
	IIT	.91		.10		$.52^{ns}$		$.50^{ns}$		.70		.57	
3842	LIT	.25	MD	.89	SG	1.22	SG	1.28	SG	.72	IG	.66	IG
	IIT	.82		.07		.20		.31		$.51^{ns}$		.51	

Table 5.2 *continued*

ISIC	LIT/IIT	USA Mean	USA Ind	Japan Mean	Japan Ind	France Mean	France Ind	Germany Mean	Germany Ind	UK Mean	UK Ind	Industry composite LIT(WI)/IIT(WI)	Industry composite Ind
3843	LIT	.32	MD	.50[ns]	SG	.80	IG	1.58	SG	.82	IG	.57	SG
	IIT	.52[ns]		.05		.84		.44		.73		.40	
3844	LIT	.55	(SG)	.65	SG	.76	IG	.77	IG	1.02	IG	.50	SG[a]
	IIT	.14		.02		.95		.82		.57[ns]		.11	
3845	LIT	.35	MD	.57	(SG)	.93	IG	2.28	IG	2.09	IG	.57	IG[a]
	IIT	.50[ns]		.16		.71		.92		.78		.52	
3852	LIT	.32	MD	.63	SG	1.41	IG	2.28	IG	1.62	IG	.60	IG
	IIT	.69		.13		.78		.89		.78		.46	
3853	LIT	.56[ns]	(SG)	.81	SG	1.23	IG	1.81	IG	1.05	(SG)	.60	SG[a]
	IIT	.12		.26		.89		.89		.42		.25	
Country Composite	LIT	.31	MD	.48	SG	.84	IG	1.50	IG	1.00	IG	.54	IG[b]
	IIT	.65		.14		.83		.56		.77		.51	

Notes:
MD: multidomestic; MT: multidomestic transitional; SG: simple global; IG: integrated global; ( ): import driven.
All of the mean estimates are significant at the 5% level, unless otherwise noted.
[ns]   not significant at the 5% level.
[a]   the industry composite in this case takes into account import-driven industries by utilizing the negative of their *LIT* and *IIT* estimates.
[b]   overall industry and country composite estimates of *LIT* and *IIT*.

Table 5.3   Globalization trends of chemical industries across five countries

ISIC	*LIT/IIT*	USA	Japan	France	Germany	UK
				Trends		
3511	*LIT*	.0078***	.0026*	−.0221	−.0212	−.0162
	IIT	.0202**	.0098***	−.0002***	.0043***	−.0092***
3512	*LIT*	.0167***	−.0041	.0121***	−.0245	.0311***
	IIT	−.0127***	.0009	−.0067*	.0243***	−.0064
3513	*LIT*	.0034	.0018	.0293***	−.0414	.0419***
	IIT	.0170*	.0151***	−.0019	.0065***	.0059*
3521	*LIT*	.0010***	.0004	.0146***	.0132***	.0124***
	IIT	.0430***	−.0340***	.0116***	−.0001	.0171***
3522	*LIT*	.0061***	.0001	.0117**	.0093*	.0077***
	IIT	.0251***	−.0015	−.0105***	.0134***	.0149***
3523	*LIT*	.0021***	.0012***	.0251***	.0239***	.0234***
	IIT	.0327***	−.0020	−.0024**	.0107***	.0220***
3530	*LIT*	−.0004	−.0028**	.0117***	.0259***	.0036
	IIT	.0006	−.0059	.0054	−.0124***	.0037
3540	*LIT*	−.006	.0015**	.0014	.0223	.0094***
	IIT	.0318*	.0005	.0087	.0075	.0045
3551	*LIT*	.0077***	.0285***	.0304***	.0015	.0389***
	IIT	−.0139**	.0098***	.0105*	.0074***	.0340***

Note: * significant at .10; ** significant at .05; *** significant at .01.

*Table 5.4   Globalization trends of manufacturing industries across five
            countries*

ISIC	*LIT/IIT*	Trends				
		USA	Japan	France	Germany	UK
3811	*LIT*	.0072***	.0054***	.0244***	−.0233	−.0139
	IIT	−.0182*	−.0005	−.0030	.0099***	.0218***
3812	*LIT*	.0016*	.0043***	.0195***	.0143***	.0362***
	IIT	−.0261**	.0233	−.0154***	.0153***	.0213**
3813	*LIT*	.0015	.0023***	−.0121	.0082***	.0180***
	IIT	.0352**	−.0125***	.0209**	−.0101	.0222**
3821	*LIT*	.0205***	.0085**	−.0014	.0376***	−.0258**
	IIT	−.0103	−.0153**	−.0112***	.0120***	.0201***
3822	*LIT*	.0008	.0143***	.0135***	.0080	.0056***
	IIT	.0119	−.0375***	−.0009	−.0037*	.0401***
3823	*LIT*	.0068***	.0183***	.0167***	.0265	.0080***
	IIT	.0073	−.0453***	.0033	.0112*	.0119***
3824	*LIT*	.0166***	.0271***	−.0649***	−.0185	−.0330*
	IIT	.0264***	−.0335***	−.0007	.0007	.0187***
3825	*LIT*	.0093***	.0216	−.0030	−.0055	−.0009
	IIT	.0255**	−.0440***	−.0018	.0077*	−.0032
3831	*LIT*	.0109***	.0117***	.0286***	.0134	.0359***
	IIT	.0068**	−.0128***	−.0013	.0054**	.0056*
3832	*LIT*	.0109***	.0177***	.0150***	−.0185	.0289***
	IIT	−.0184	−.0026**	−.0027	.0149***	−.0067*
3833	*LIT*	.0167***	.0040**	.0209***	.0379***	.0199***
	IIT	−.0275**	−.0067	.0101***	.0089***	−.0219*
3841	*LIT*	.0061***	.0267*	−.0142	.0182	.0008
	IIT	.0134	.0036	−.0211***	−.0037	.0151*
3842	*LIT*	.0107***	.0201*	.0133	.0078	.0122***
	IIT	.0481***	−.0062***	−.0023	−.0119***	.0066
3843	*LIT*	.0113***	.0257***	.0147***	−.0146	.0251***
	IIT	−.0238***	−.0043***	.0139***	−.0001	.0205
3844	*LIT*	.0019	.0047	.0207***	.0341**	−.0123
	IIT	.0094***	.0015***	.0165***	.0061	.0064
3845	*LIT*	.0099	−.0012	.0083**	−.0044	−.0319**
	IIT	.0244***	.0016	−.0146***	.0206***	−.0007
3852	*LIT*	.0096***	.0149**	−.0403	.0055	.0308**
	IIT	−.0208***	−.0062***	−.0018	.0163***	−.0046
3853	*LIT*	.0230***	.0346***	−.0462**	.0352**	.0075
	IIT	−.0076	−.0113**	.0001**	.0174**	−.0179***

Note: * significant at .10; ** significant at .05; *** significant at .01.

NOTES

* This chapter draws from and extends our study on industry globalization, entitled 'Measuring globalization of industries using a national industry approach: empirical evidence across five countries and over time', co-authored with Kwangsoo Kim, and published in the *Journal of International Business Studies*, **28** (4), 679–710.

1. Institutions, as defined by North (1990), can be differentiated into two categories, formal and informal. Formal institutions are the formal laws, regulations and property rights established in a society for regulating behaviour, including that associated with business and commerce. Informal institutions include codes of conduct, cultural norms of behaviour and other societal conventions. The broad nature of this definition allows us to capture the range of unique forces that characterizes the operating environment of a given country.

2. US government support for both the aircraft and computer industries played a key role in their global status today. To maintain domestic production capacity, the USA has also protected defence-related industries such as flat-panel computer screens from import competition, thereby limiting globalization. Although the goal was to maintain computer screen production at home, this effort proved futile.

3. Since using only the last four years will yield a very small sample on which to calculate the standard deviation, it was decided that the full 17 years of the data set would be utilized for this purpose. Although doing so has the disadvantage that the past variation in *LIT* and *IIT* may not be completely representative of the observed current variation, it allows for a mote rigorous statistical examination of these values.

4. Correlation coefficients between *LIT* and *IIT*:

	US	Japan	France	Germany	UK
Chemical	0.46565	−0.42312	0.08531	0.20941	0.35293
Manufacturing	−0.43184	−0.41316	−0.2916	−0.03664	0.28985

5. The discussion below draws heavily upon Department of Commerce data.
6. *U.S. Industrial Outlook 1993*, p. 11-2.
7. *U.S. Industrial Outlook 1993*, p. 11-12.
8. *U.S. Industrial Outlook 1986*, p. 13-1.
9. *U.S. Industrial Outlook 1986*, p. 25-2.
10. *U.S. Industrial Outlook 1993*, p. 17-19.
11. Porter, 1990, p. 289.7-19.
12. *U.S. Industrial Outlook 1986*, p. 28-2.
13. *U.S. Industrial Outlook 1993*, p. 26-2 to 26-3.
14. *U.S. Industrial Outlook 1993*, p. 26-4.
15. This paragraph is based largely on Rajan et al. (forthcoming).
16. Porter, 1990, p. 385.
17. Tyson, 1992, p. 155.
18. AIRBUS News & Information, 1998, pp. 2–3.
19. Friedman and Samuels, 1993, p. 267.
20. Wonnacott and Wonnacott, 1967, as cited in Hummels et al., endnote 9, p. 97.
21. Hummels et al., p. 83.

REFERENCES

Airbus News & Information (1998), (http:\\www.airbus.com/news_faq.html), 4 November.

Balassa, Bela (1986), 'The determinants of intra-industry specialization in United States trade', *Oxford Economic Papers*, **38**, 220–33.

Balassa, Bela (1988), 'The determinants of intra-European trade in manufactured goods', *European Economic Review*, **32**, 1421–37.

Bartlett, C. and S. Ghoshal (1989), *Managing Across Borders: The Transnational Solution*, Boston: Harvard Business School Press.

Birkinshaw, J., A. Morrison and J. Hulland (1995), 'Structural and competitive determinants of a global integration strategy', *Strategic Management Journal*, **16**, 637–55.

Campa, J. and L. Goldberg (1997), 'The evolving external orientation of manufacturing: a profile of four countries', *Federal Reserve Bank of New York Economic Policy Review*, July, 53–82.

Carr, C. (1993), 'Global, national and resource-based strategies: an examination of strategic choice and performance in the vehicle components industry', *Strategic Management Journal*, **14**, 551–68.

Casson, M. (1986), *Multinationals and World Trade: Vertical Integration and the Division of Labor in World Industries*, Boston: Allen & Unwin.

Caves, R. (1981), 'Intra-industry trade and market structure in the industrial countries', *Oxford Economic Papers*, **33**, 203–323.

Chandler, A. (1986), 'The Evolution of Modern Global Competition', in M. Porter (ed.), *Competition in Global Industries*, Boston: Harvard Business School Press.

Chandler, A. (1990), *Scale and Scope: The Dynamics of Industrial Capitalism*, Cambridge: The Belknap Press of Harvard University Press.

Cho, K.R. (1990), 'The role of product-specific factors in intra-firm trade of U.S. manufacturing multinational corporations', *Journal of International Business Studies*, Second Quarter, 319–30.

Collis, D.J. (1991), 'A resource-based analysis of global competition: the case of the bearings industry', *Strategic Management Journal*, **12**, 49–68.

Contractor, F. (1990), 'Ownership patterns of U.S. joint ventures abroad and the liberation of foreign government regulations in the 1980s: evidence from the benchmark surveys', *Journal of International Business Studies*, **21** (1), 55–73.

Cvar, M. (1984), 'Competitive strategies in global industries', PhD Dissertation, Harvard Business School.

Dunning, J. (1980), 'Toward an eclectic theory of international production: some empirical tests', *Journal of International Business Studies,* Spring/Summer, 9–31.

Encarnation, D. and L. Wells (1986), 'Competitive Strategies in Global Industries: A View from Host Governments', in M. Porter (ed.), *Competition in Global Industries*, Boston: Harvard Business School Press.

Flaherty, M. (1986), 'Coordinating international manufacturing and technology', in M. Porter (ed.), *Competition in Global Industries*, Boston: Harvard Business School Press.

Franke, R.H., G. Hofstede and M.H. Bond (1991), 'Cultural roots of economic performance: a research note', *Strategic Management Journal*, **12**, 165–75.

Friedman, David B. and Richard J. Samuels (1993), 'How to Succeed without Really Flying: The Japanese Aircraft Industry and Japan's Technology Ideology', in Jeffrey A. Frankel and Miles Kahler (eds), *Regionalism and Rivalry: Japan and the United States in Pacific Asia*, Chicago: University of Chicago Press.

Greenaway, David and Chris Milner (1986), *The Economics of Intra-industry Trade*, Boston: Basil Blackwell.

Grubel, H.G. and P.J. Lloyd (1975), *Intra Industry Trade*, London: Macmillan.

Hassan, F.M.A. (1987), 'Intra-industry trade: theory and evidence', PhD Dissertation, University of Pittsburgh.

Hipple, F.S. (1990), 'Multinational companies and international trade: the impact of intrafirm shipments on U.S. foreign trade, 1977–1982', *Journal of International Business Studies*, Third Quarter, 495–504.

Hollingsworth, J. Rogers and Robert Boyer (eds) (1997), *Contemporary Capitalism: The Embeddedness of Institutions*, Cambridge: Cambridge University Press.

Hummels, D., D. Rapoport and K. Yi. (1998), 'Vertical specialization and the changing nature of world trade', *Federal Reserve Bank of New York Economic Policy Review*, (June), 79–99.

Jarillo, J.C. and J.I. Martinez (1990), 'Different roles for subsidiaries: the case of multinational corporations in Spain', *Strategic Management Journal*, **11** (7), 501–12.

Johansson, J.J. and G.S. Yip (1994), 'Exploiting globalization potential: U.S. and Japanese strategies', *Strategic Management Journal*, **15**, 579–601.

Kelejian, H. and W. Oates (1981), *Introduction to Econometrics: Principles and Applications*, New York: Harper and Row.

Kimura, Y. (1989), 'Firm-specific strategic advantages and foreign direct investment behavior of firms: the case of Japanese semiconductor firms', *Journal of International Business Studies*, Summer, 297–314.

Kobrin, S. (1991), 'An empirical analysis of the determinants of global integration', *Strategic Management Journal*, **12**, 17–31.

Kogut, B. (1991), 'Country capabilities and the permeability of borders', *Strategic Management Journal*, **12**, 33–47.

Kotabe, M. (1990), 'The relationship between offshore sourcing and innovativeness of U.S. multinational firms: an empirical investigation', *Journal of International Business Studies*, Fourth Quarter, 623–38.

Kotabe, M. and J.Y. Murray (1990), 'Linking product and process innovations and modes of international sourcing in global competition: a case of foreign multinational firms', *Journal of International Business Studies*, Third Quarter, 383–408.

Kotabe, M. and G.S. Omura (1989), 'Sourcing strategies of European and Japanese multinationals: a comparison', *Journal of International Business Studies*, Spring, 113–29.

Lee, Y.S. (1989), 'A study of the determinants of intra-industry trade among the Pacific Basin countries', *Weltwirtschaftliches Archiv*, **125**, 346–58.

Levitt, T. (1983), 'The globalization of markets', *Harvard Business Review*, **61**, 92–102.

Loertscher, R. and F. Wolter (1980), 'Determinants of intra-industry trade: among countries and across industries', *Weltwirtschaftliches Archiv*, **116**, 280–92.

Lundberg, M. (1982), 'Intra-industry trade: the case of Sweden', *Weltwirtschaftliches Archiv*, **118**, 302–16.

MacCharles, D. (1987), *Trade Among Multinationals: Intra-Industry Trade and National Competitiveness*, London: Croom Helm.

Makhija, Mona V., Kwangsoo Kim and Sandra D. Williamson (1997), 'Measuring globalization of industries using a national industry approach: empirical evidence across five countries and over time', *The Journal of International Business Studies*, **28** (4), 679–710.

Mitchell, W., J.M. Shaver and B. Yeung (1992), 'Getting there in a global industry: impacts on performance of changing international presence', *Strategic Management Journal*, **13**, 419–32.

Morrison, A.J. (1990), *Strategies in Global Industries: How U.S. Businesses Compete*, New York: Quorum Books.

Morrison, A.J. and K. Roth. (1992), 'A taxonomy of business-level strategies in global industries', *Strategic Management Journal*, **13**, 399–418.

Nohria, N. and C. Garcia-Pont (1991), 'Global strategic linkages and industry structure', *Strategic Management Journal*, **12**, 105–24.

Norman, G. and J. Dunning (1984), 'Intra-industry foreign direct investment: its rationale and trade effects', *Weltwirtschaftliches Archiv*, **120**, 522–40.

North, D. (1990), *Institutions, Institutional Change, and Economic Performance*, Cambridge: Cambridge University Press.

Organization for Economic Cooperation and Development (1992), *Globalization of Industrial Activities: Four Case Studies (Auto Parts, Chemicals, Construction and Semiconductors)*, Paris: OECD.

Ostry, S. and R. Nelson (1995), *Techno-Nationalism and Techno-Globalization*, Washington, DC: The Brookings Institution.

Pagoulatos, E. and R. Sorensen (1975), 'Two-way international trade: an econometric analysis', *Weltwirtschaftliches Archiv*, **111**, 454–65.

Pauly, Louis W. and Simon Reich (1997), 'National structures and multinational corporate behavior: enduring differences in the age of globalization', *International Organization*, **51** (1), 1–30.

Porter, Michael E. (1986), 'Competition in Global Industries: A Conceptual Framework', in M. Porter (ed.), *Competition in Global Industries*, Boston: Harvard Business School Press.

Porter, Michael E. (1990), *The Competitive Advantage of Nations*, New York: The Free Press.

Prahalad, C.K. and Y.L. Doz (1987), *The Multinational Mission: Balancing Local Demands and Global Vision*, New York: The Free Press.

Rajan, Raghuram, Paolo Volpin and Luigi Zingales (forthcoming), 'The Eclipse of the U.S. Tire Industry', in Steve Kaplan (ed.), *Mergers and Productivity*, Chicago: University of Chicago Press.

Roth, K. and D. Ricks (1994), 'Goal configuration in a global industry context', *Strategic Management Journal*, **15**, 103–20.

Swamidass, P.M. (1993), 'Import sourcing dynamics: an integrative perspective', *Journal of International Business Studies*, Fourth Quarter, 671–91.

Swamidass, P.M. and Masaaki Kotabe (1993), 'Component sourcing strategies of multinationals: an empirical study of European and Japanese multinationals', *Journal of International Business Studies*, First Quarter, 81–99.

Tallman, S.B. (1991), 'Strategic management models and resource-based strategies among MNEs in a host market', *Strategic Management Journal*, **12**, 69–82.

Tharakan, P.K.M. (1983), *Intra-Industry Trade: Empirical and Methodological Aspects*, Amsterdam: North-Holland.

Toh, K. (1982), 'A cross-section analysis of intra-industry trade in U.S. manufacturing industries', *Weltwirtschaftliches Archiv*, **118**, 281–300.

Tyson, Laura D'Andrea (1992), 'Industrial Policy and Trade Management in the Commercial Aircraft Industry', in *Who's Bashing Whom?: Trade Conflict in High-Technology Industries*, Washington, DC: Institute for International Economics.

US Department of Commerce (1970–93) (selected years), *Industrial Outlook 1970–1993*, Washington, DC.

US Department of Commerce/International Trade Administration (1998), *U.S. Industry and Trade Outlook '98*, Washington, DC: DRI/McGraw-Hill, Standard & Poor's.

Vachani, S. (1991), 'Distinguishing between related and unrelated international geographic diversification: a comprehensive measure of global diversification', *Journal of International Business Studies*, Second Quarter, 307–22.

Yip, G. (1992), *Total Global Strategy: Managing for Worldwide Competitive Advantage*, Englewood Cliffs: Prentice-Hall.

Yoshino, M. (1986), 'Global Competition in a Salient Industry: The Case of Civil Aircraft', in M. Porter (ed.), *Competition in Global Industries*. Boston: Harvard Business School Press.

6. Technology in the globalization of the USA

Maria Papadakis

INTRODUCTION

In the first chapter of this volume, Frederic Pryor made the useful distinction between 'old' and 'new' globalization. The difference between these two international dynamics is an important one, especially for understanding how technology figures in the global economic presence of the United States. Prior to the US competitiveness crisis of the mid-1980s, US interactions with the world economy largely involved what Pryor refers to as 'old' globalization: the volume of international trade exploded; economic, political, and communication linkages between nations expanded and tightened; and the international trade regime experienced a dramatic liberalization. Old globalization represents the growing internationalization of the world political economy, a period in which system interdependence increased by several orders of magnitude.

For the United States, technological considerations were not primary ones during old globalization. The emphasis was on free trade and improving American access to foreign markets; no real notion of international business competition existed. Conventional perceptions of comparative advantage – as determined by the underlying productivity structures of the American economy – influenced policy approaches to international competitiveness, and American industry itself appeared woefully naive about the emerging character of global competition (Zysman and Tyson, 1983). Trade liberalization was pursued by government and business as an end in itself, with no real appreciation of technology as a strategic element of international trade and global markets. Trade liberalization was instead intended to allow US comparative advantage to more clearly manifest itself in international trade flows.

Such a *laissez-faire* attitude toward technology changed suddenly and dramatically with the American 'competitiveness crisis' of the mid-1980s. Until this time, the USA enjoyed a steady balance of trade and modest trade surpluses in manufactured goods. But from 1982 to 1987, the US manufactures trade balance plunged from surplus to an historically unprecedented deficit of $125 billion. A pervasive erosion in the export strength of all the US high-tech industries except aerospace gave the distinct impression that the United States could no longer take for granted its assumed comparative advantage in technology-based industries.

The competitiveness crisis itself did not really exist, but was instead largely the by-product of several macroeconomic imbalances (Papadakis, 1994; Blecker, 1992), but the perception of one created a watershed in public and private sector attitudes toward technology and its role in international comparative and competitive advantage. The ensuing decade of change very much reflects Pryor's 'new globalization'. Whereas the previous era passively encouraged technological advantage via trade liberalization, the new era regarded technology as a strategic weapon – one that could be manipulated, promoted and protected. The shift was toward an active and deliberate creation of competitive advantage via technology. At the federal level, dozens of policies were passed to increase technology transfer, strengthen intellectual property protection both domestically and internationally and intensify research and development in strategic industries and technology sectors such as flat panel displays, high temperature superconductivity, supercomputers and so on. Manufacturing extension services – akin to those of the Department of Agriculture – sprang up across the nation to stimulate renewal in the American manufacturing infrastructure.[1] In the private sector, R&D and technology-based competition strategies emerged as a distinctive form of business strategy (Roussel et al., 1991; Betz, 1987; Kash, 1989; Hamel and Prahalad, 1994), and corporate technology strategies distinctly internationalized (Hagedoorn, 1998).

The outward orientation of US high-technology industries intensified after the depreciation of the US dollar in the later 1980s. The share of domestic production for export in several key sectors (industrial machinery and equipment, electronic and other electric equipment, transportation equipment and instruments and related products) rose from about 15 per cent to 22 per cent between 1985 and 1995. Shares of domestic consumption accounted for by imports in these sectors however rose more than proportionally (Campa and Goldberg, 1997), reflecting a continued decline in the US share of world high-technology trade (Guerrieri and Milana, 1997) and the effects of a decline in the USA's international technological leadership (Nelson and Wright, 1992).

The main international challenges for US high-technology sectors are presented by Japanese industries (Mowery and Teece, 1993). Japanese strengths include a superior capacity for progress in applied technology based on higher levels of corporate investment in research and development and intensive intercorporate technology sharing, but depend at a fundamental level on access to US institutions engaged in basic research. Japanese high technology competition has activated vigorous US corporate responses, notably in the development of semiconductor consortia (Ham et al., 1998).

Secondary challenges for US high-technology industries are presented by European firms, principally German enterprises. A technological lag in the European Union has been largely attributable to the restricting effects of market separation on the development of European firms before the establishment of the Single Market in 1992. The German system of corporate governance, it has been argued, is conducive to incremental rather than radical innovation, while the American system is more effective in generating radical innovations (Soskice, 1998).[2]

A TECHNOLOGICAL PROFILE OF US INDUSTRY

Because of widespread attention given to the competitiveness crisis, technology and innovation over the past decade, most people have an intuitive impression that technical change is an important determinant of US global economic stature. This is true to some extent, but the relationship is complex and indirect. It is important to keep the role of technology in perspective, neither over- nor underestimating its significance for competitive advantage. For high-technology sectors, it is obviously crucial. But for other industries, more traditional competitive dynamics are at play – such as price advantages, product features, channels of distribution and so on.

There is thus an important duality to the technological basis of the American economy. The high tech sectors – the ones for whom technology is most central to their survival and vitality – are not the 'bread and butter' American industries in terms of their share of employment and output. However, the high-tech sectors are high-skill, high-wage sectors; employment in them is increasing at a faster rate than others (particularly in information technologies); they return the highest profit ratios and value added; they grow at faster rates than other types of industries; they produce the innovations that have the greatest spillover effects for the manufacturing sector; and they have the strongest export performance.

For example, The National Science Board reports that four high-tech industries (aircraft, drugs and medicine, office and computing machines, and communications equipment) accounted for only 15 per cent of total manufacturing output in 1995, but 27.5 per cent of manufactured exports. The domestic value added[3] of these four industries combined is 43 per cent compared to 35 per cent for other manufactured goods, and in communications equipment and drugs and medicine the proportion is more than half of total production value (National Science Board, 1998). If high tech is expanded into a more inclusive set of products that involve scientific and technological research,[4] high tech accounts for about one-third of US manufactured goods exports.

THE TECHNOLOGICAL ACTIVITY OF US INDUSTRIES

In 1996, the most current year for which data are available, US industry – including manufacturing and non-manufacturing sectors – spent $145 billion on research and development (R&D). R&D expenditures are a conventional measure of technological activity, and serve as a useful proxy for the role of technology in an industry in terms of both creating the technology and adopting technologies generated in other sectors.

For the United States, this $145 billion represents about 3.5 per cent of the domestic net sales of all US industries, a ratio comparable to that of the other industrialized nations (National Science Board, 1998; National Science Foundation, 1998). However, the United States is the world's largest performer of industrial R&D in terms of the dollar magnitude of its spending: not only does it expend more on research and development than any other country, but US industrial R&D expenditures exceed that of all 15 members of the European Union combined.

US industrial research and development is concentrated in a few firms and industries. Throughout the 1990s, the hundred largest industrial R&D performers consistently represented about 62 per cent of all research and development conducted by the private sector. And for the manufacturing sector, these R&D performers are corporate giants. Just over half of all manufacturing R&D is conducted in businesses with more than 25 000 employees. Small manufacturing enterprises – those with fewer than 500 employees and which also comprise more than 90 per cent of all US manufacturing establishment – account for less than 10 per cent of total US manufacturing R&D (National Science Foundation, 1998). Thus of the hundreds of thousands of enterprises that operate in the United States, only a handful account for the technological activity of industry. The vast majority of businesses conduct no research and development of their own.

R&D is similarly not essential to the innovativeness of all industrial sectors. Tables 6.1 and 6.2 present two dimensions of the role of R&D in different industries. Several aspects are striking. First, as seen in Table 6.1, high-tech manufacturing industries devote considerably more of their resources to research and development than either R&D-intensive or low-tech sectors. The classification system in Table 6.1, which is that of the Organization for Economic Cooperation and Development, reveals that high-technology industries spend up to 13 per cent of their net sales on research and develop-

Table 6.1   R&D-to-sales ratios for major US industrial sectors

Industry status	R&D-to-sales ratio (in per cent)
High-technology manufacturing sectors	
Aerospace	12.9
Drugs & medicine	10.1
Electrical machinery & equipment	na
Electronic equipment & components	7.5
Office machines & computing equipment	7.9
Professional & scientific instruments	11.5
R&D-intensive manufacturing sectors	
Industrial chemicals	4.6
Motor vehicles	na
Non-electrical machinery	2.4
Rubber & plastic products	na
Low-tech manufacturing sectors	
Fabricated metal products	1.1
Primary metals	0.5
Food, beverages, & tobacco	0.4
Paper & printing	1.1
Petroleum refining	0.7
Stone, clay, & glass products	1.3
Textiles, footwear, & leather	0.6
Wood, cork, & furniture	na
Service sectors	
Transportation, utilities, & communications	1.2
Retail trade	2.3
Computer & data processing	11.8
Health services	5.2
Engineering & management services	9.7
Other services[1]	0.6

Notes:
[1]   For example, the hospitality and personal care industries.
na = not available. R&D-to-sales ratio is that most currently available between the years 1991 and 1996.

Source: National Science Foundation (1998), Table A-17a.

Table 6.2   Industrial shares of total manufacturing R&D, 1996

Industry	Share of total manufacturing R&D (in per cent)
Transportation	29.6
Electrical machinery & equipment	20.6
Chemicals	16.0
Non-electrical machinery	12.3
Professional & scientific instruments	11.8
Paper & printing	1.7
Petroleum refining	1.5
Fabricated metals	1.3
Rubber & plastic products	1.2
Wood & furniture	0.6
Primary metals	0.6
Stone, clay, & glass products	0.5
Textiles, clothing, footwear, & leather	0.4
Miscellaneous manufactures	0.4
Food, beverages, & tobacco	na

Notes: na = not available.

Source: Estimated by the author from National Science Foundation (1998), Table A-2a.

ment, in contrast to between 2 to 5 per cent for R&D-intensive sectors and roughly 1 per cent or less for low-tech industries.

Quite simply, technological innovation is not equally important to all manufacturing industries, a fact even more forcefully brought home by the figures in Table 6.2. Of the roughly $111 billion spent on R&D by the US manufacturing sector in 1996, 90 per cent is accounted for by five industries alone: transportation, electrical equipment, chemicals, non-electrical machinery and professional and scientific instruments. These five industries also reflect the high-tech sectors of the economy, since the majority of R&D contained in these broad two-digit industry classifications is composed of narrower high-technology sectors within it. Thus transportation R&D is composed principally of aerospace research; electrical equipment of electronic components; chemicals of drugs and medicines; and machinery of office and computing machines.

The service sector likewise shows variation in the significance of technological innovativeness to different industries. Although R&D data for services were not collected until 1995, the data shown in Table 6.1 reflect low-tech and high-tech service sectors. For example, computer and data processing services are as high tech as that of manufacturing, with an R&D-to-sales ratio of 12 per cent. Health services are R&D intensive with a ratio of about 5 per cent; and 'other' services are low tech with a ratio under 1 per cent. Unlike the manufacturing sector, however, small businesses are far more technologically dynamic in services: they account for more than one-third of service sector R&D, in contrast to less than 10 per cent of manufacturing R&D (National Science Foundation, 1998).

Do these R&D figures indicate that industries and sectors with relatively low levels of R&D spending are not technologically active? The answer is no, in one particular respect. What R&D data cannot account for is technical innovation in an industry that is captured by its production processes. For example, fabrication and assembly-based industries rely heavily on computer-numerically-controlled machine tools and statistical process control, techniques involving equipment that is generally regarded as being technologically advanced. Similarly, service industries are increasingly dependent on information technologies, which undergo constant and rapid technological change.

We are therefore not able easily to represent the 'spillover' effects of research and development from one industry to another or even within a single industry. To illustrate, while R&D activity in the banking industry is comparatively low, the accumulated capital stock of information technology in the banking sector increased eightfold from 1980 to 1989. Information technology is directly credited for rapid product diversification, transactions growth and recent productivity gains in banking, a link between technology and competitiveness that is otherwise missed by R&D figures (National Science Board, 1998). The precise competitive effects of these 'infra-structure' technologies are thus difficult to measure, and are often reflected in comparative advantage indicators for international trade. They will be discussed in a later section of this chapter.

TECHNOLOGY AND STRUCTURAL ADVANTAGE

Structural competitiveness refers to the competitive advantage engendered by a country's productive structure and national innovation system – the long term, slow-to-change institutions and relationships that comprise an economy. Labour skills; efficiencies deriving from long-standing capital–labour intensities; the nature of financial investments; R&D laboratories; university research; engineering capacity; the machinery base; know-how and tacit skills that pass from generation to generation in industrial centres; and government policies are all examples of structural factors that affect competitive performance in the global arena (see Porter (1990) for more detail).

While short-run factors like advertising, pricing practices, incremental product changes and management strategies affect the immediate competitive success of a firm, the idea behind structural competitiveness is that there are more fundamental determinants of the competitive potential of a country's businesses in the international market-place. For example, the capital–labour relationship in an industry is the primary determinant of productivity and the cost structure in that sector, and therefore substantially limits what firms can and cannot do in their pricing practices. Similarly, a highly educated workforce is a prerequisite for R&D-intensive industries, which require substantial scientific and engineering inputs. The structural attributes of competitiveness evolve uniquely in each nation subject to historical circumstance, geographic location, political ideologies, government policies, resources available for production and so on.

Structural competitiveness expresses itself in one primary way in the international economy, as that of 'comparative advantage'. Comparative advantage is posited by the classical Ricardian model of international trade, in which the relative capital–labour intensities of industries determine how and when nations should specialize in both domestic production and international trade. The result is that countries will sell to one another the goods each is more efficient at producing. Structural advantage is therefore expressed as trade specialization, or what is otherwise known as the 'export structure' of a nation. Such specialization is also present when a country has a global monopoly position in a particular resource or good – for example, bauxite, bananas or commercial aircraft. Both sources of competitive structural advantage (monopoly position and relative productivity) are more conventionally known as the 'factor endowments' of a nation.

Technology plays a significant role in international structural competitive advantage. First and foremost, technology mediates the capital–labour relationship in an industry, and is consequently an important determinant of productivity. As Jorgenson and Kuroda (1992) have found (among others), differences in total factor productivity explain many of the bilateral trade patterns between Japan and the United States. And because wage rates among the industrialized nations have converged to a remarkable degree, divergence in their total factor productivity can be attributed in large part to the technology that forms the foundation of their industrial production systems.

Second, technology can engender monopoly positions in international trade and markets. The sole producer of a good or service is, by definition, going to be the hegemonic presence in that market. Thus, Boeing Aircraft dominated the world commercial airframe market for decades, as did IBM with mainframe computers. Very simply, ongoing leadership in a technology field is likely to create a structural competitive advantage internationally. The complication for the United States now is that the substantial technology gaps that contributed to US market hegemony in the immediate post-World War II period are no longer present. Technological convergence between the USA, Japan and Western Europe in the industrial production base occurred in the early 1970s, and concerted governmental efforts can create viable global competitors where none previously existed, as is the case with the European Airbus Consortium and the Japanese presence in supercomputer markets.

Finally, by carefully managing the product cycle dynamics of their business lines, corporations can minimize what may be inevitable foreign competition in their markets. Global product cycle theory[5] reflects the idea that firms should relocate their manufacturing offshore once they no longer have a monopoly position in their technology/product and they lose productivity advantages in domestic production because of high wage rates and the standardized nature of their goods. By moving offshore, corporations can maintain ownership and control of manufacturing and production, and perpetuate their competitive presence in international markets.

TECHNOLOGY, TRADE AND COMPARATIVE ADVANTAGE

Empirical research on three basic types of international trade flows – endowments based, intra-industry and intra-corporate – suggests the growing influence of technology (for a review, see Grant et al., 1993). Because of the intensive R&D investments required for radical technological change, technology gaps can be systematically created and maintained through aggressive innovation strategies and government policies. Such thinking is what lies behind national efforts in biotechnology, advanced robotics, specialized materials, microelectronics and so forth, and research-driven technological leads are a form of endowments-based trade. The result is sustained inter-industry specialization and trade flows between countries, a classic manifestation of comparative advantage. And as illustrated in Papadakis (1995), the United States demonstrates substantial global comparative advantage in several high-tech industries, including electronics, instrumentation, computing machines, aerospace and pharmaceuticals.

The growing role of technology is likewise found in intra-industry trade, a form of international trade that takes place within the same industrial classification (for example, a significant volume of both imports and exports in personal computers for a single country). In (neo)classical trade theory, such intra-industry trade should not exist, because in principle nations specialize in trade. Since the volume of intra-industry trade expanded considerably in the 1980s, alternative explanations for this counter-theoretical behaviour were sought. The answer was found in more market-based explanations:

Explanations of monopolistic competition and product differentiation soon provided a theoretical basis for measured intraindustry trade. Products were recognized as differing in quality, durability, serviceability, proximity, and fashionability, [all] dimensions that matter to buyers as well as price, and ways that sellers could compete with each other in addition to price competition. It should then be no surprise to see simultaneous exports and imports of goods that differ in quality and durability, for instance, even when their factor requirements, commodity classification, and price were the same. (Grant et al., 1993, p. 31)

In this respect, then, an important determinant of intra-industry trade is technology because of the way technology (manifested as either product or process) creates highly differentiated varieties of the same products. In turn, highly differentiated products (whether in terms of quality or product features) can result in monopolistic competition even when there are numerous competitors in the same general product classification. Unfortunately, empirical work on the causes of intra-industry trade is scant, so it is difficult to weigh the importance of technology and innovation against other potential explanations of intra-industry trade, such as trade of parts and components between products at various stages of assembly and fabrication.

Finally, intra-corporate trade reflects the influence of technological factors somewhat. As demonstrated in Lipsey (1991) and Lipsey and Kravis (1987), US multinationals have the strongest trade performance in high-technology manufactures – US multinational firms' share of world exports is largest in this category, and US MNCs account for about one-third of all global high-tech exports. Notably, about one-third of all MNC exports are to their affiliates which suggests a relatively substantial amount of global high-tech, intra-firm trade. This trade pattern is a bit puzzling, since it cannot be accounted for by technology gap or global product cycle explanations. One possibility is the greater globalization of production itself, where various stages of the manufacturing process are spread out across the world regardless of the technological status of the industry. Another is that US corporations are availing themselves of strategic technology alliances or specialized scientific and technological resources abroad. In any event, this characteristic of multinational trade suggests that US high-technology leadership is not necessarily derived from resources within US national boundaries. The implications of this are not clear.

NECESSARY, BUT NOT SUFFICIENT

The problem with looking only at trade flows as an indicator of global competitiveness is that we miss the perspective most relevant to business competition – that of markets, market share and market presence. And from this vantage point, it is clear that technology may be a necessary, but not sufficient, condition of competitive strength. Although the United States demonstrates solid comparative advantage in several technology-based industries (such as electronics, pharmaceuticals and aerospace), and high-tech goods figure prominently in US exports (accounting for roughly one-third of all US exports), the USA simply does not dominate markets in which it has strong technological leadership or trade advantage. For example, Papadakis (1994) demonstrates that three critical industries that had very high comparative advantage indexes in international trade and represented substantial shares of US exports – electronics, electrical machinery and office and computing machines – were simply uncompetitive when conventional measures such as domestic market share and trends in market share were analysed. Likewise, in a detailed assessment of US and Japanese bilateral competitiveness, Papadakis (1995) found that industrial R&D expenditures and technology intensity proved to be a poor predictor of relative competitive strength. Instead, total factor productivity better differentiated competitive strengths of US and Japanese industries relative to one another.

Long-term global market share data for high-technology industries indicate that US global competitive strength in these industries is variable (National Science Board, 1998). For example, US competitive strength declined in both computer and communications equipment throughout the 1980s, but began increasing again in the 1990s. American aerospace companies still dominate global markets, but their market share has been steadily eroding for over 15 years. Only the pharmaceutical industry has been able to steadily increase its share of world markets.

In sum, international trade and world market share data indicate several aspects of the role of technology in the globalization of US industry. First, high-tech and technology-intensive sectors are significant contributors to US export strength (measured as both export share and comparative advantage), suggesting that relative to other sectors, US technology-based goods are more attractive than other American products in global markets. Second, having advantages in global trade does not necessarily equate to market strength: the US share of various technology markets has been respectable, but it is not unusual to observe rapid declines and reversals of market strength in some areas (particularly in electronics and some kinds of machinery and equipment). Successful globalization (e.g. competitive strength) of US technology-based industries is therefore crucially dependent on other factors, including the strategies and skills of individual firms as well as public policy.

TECHNOLOGY, POLICY AND GLOBAL COMPETITIVENESS

Technological excellence alone is clearly not enough to prevail in the marketplace. A number of factors mediate the competitive impacts of technology, including, as previously discussed, the strategy and behaviours of firms. But public policy also plays a significant role in both fostering the development of new technologies and in eliminating obstacles to successful commercialization and competitive success. This section overviews the key areas of policy-making and their importance to the globalization and competitive strength of American technology-based industries. Several areas of public and corporate policy are addressed: (1) science and technology policy, (2) corporate governance, (3) competition policy and (4) trade policy.

Science and Technology Policy

US science and technology policy has historically been 'supply sided.' That is, it concentrates on the supply of scientific research as a primary source of new technologies. Supply-sided policies rely on the undirected support of scientific research in fields of primary national importance, such as medicine and health, solid state physics and so on. Such science and technology policies are based explicitly on market failure theory: the idea is that some areas of research are so risky, uncertain and long term that the private sector lacks sufficient market incentive to conduct the research. With rare exceptions (such as AT&T, Bell's labs and other corporate research centres), few industries and firms do in fact conduct the basic scientific research that is widely regarded as necessary for both the public interest and industrial vitality.

The United States government has traditionally been a significant source of money for fundamental scientific and technological research, currently funding about one-third[6] of all research and development conducted in the United States. For the most part, federal spending has been associated with the particular mission roles of different government agencies, e.g. defence, agriculture, space and health. Notably, defence, health and space research have dominated the federal R&D budget for decades (National Science Foundation, 1996). Only recently has there been a systematic effort to identify and target key technology sectors specifically for their commercial role and significance to the US economy. A primary example of such strategic activity is the creation of the Department of Commerce's Advanced Technology Program, which has funded over $1 billion for such key technologies as biotechnology, new materials and integrated circuits.

A relative new emphasis in US science and technology policy – particularly because of competitiveness issues emerging in the late 1970s – is that of technology transfer. The federal government has made a concerted policy effort to enhance the movement of research knowledge and technology between the public and private sector, particularly from government research laboratories to firms. For example, the Bayh–Dole Act and the Stevenson–Wydler Act provide explicit incentives to public laboratories to increase their effectiveness at technology transfer (for example, in granting more generous property rights to labs and inventors) and to eliminate barriers between the public and private sector for transfer (for example, the creation of a specific class of contracts, cooperative research and development agreements). In sum, the primary significance of US science and technology policy for US global competitiveness has been, and will continue to be, in the support and encouragement of the nation's research infrastructure.

Corporate Governance

A major problem for US technology enhancement initiatives has been the dominance of short-term financial management objectives in the operations of many US firms. Managements under shareholder pressures to demonstrate high earnings have neglected long-term investments in new technology and investment in workforce skills that are important elements in the tacit knowledge that has to accumulate for the development of substantial innovative potential (Lazonick and West, 1998). The financial pressures on management have been strong, especially because of an active market for corporate control and high levels of speculation in US stock markets as these have become more closely linked with international financial markets. The effects of the emphasis on financial management have raised questions about the efficiencies of the institutional frameworks of US firms that have been considered especially appropriate for radical innovations (Soskice, 1998).

A further difficulty for US technology policy has been a low level of cooperation between US firms, because of distrust associated with intense competition and with the inhibiting effects of antitrust enforcement. This lack of cooperation has mirrored larger problems – inadequate collaboration between government science and technology agencies, and conflicted legislative involvement in technology policy (Ham and Mowery, 1995). A degree of liberalization in antitrust enforcement has opened the way for waves of mergers and acquisitions in recent years that have been associated with high levels of stock market speculation. A general effect appears to have been an increase in shareholder pressures for high short-term yields in high and mature technology stocks.

Management in low-technology sectors, facing more and more intense import competition from foreign lower-cost areas, have been under very severe pressures to raise returns on investments, and thus have had strong incentives to lobby for protection while making increased use of antidumping remedies. These sectors have become more exposed to international competition because of the depreciation of East Asian currencies. Felt imperatives for higher performance in financial management through reliance on protectionist measures have evidently been encouraged by general increases in demand for import restraints as sectors and communities have experienced the costs of globalization (Rodrik, 1997).

Shareholder pressures on management across all sectors in effect give impetus to the international mobility of US capital as the costs of sheltering and compensating industries disadvantaged by globalization remain substantial and threaten to increase. The outward movement of industrial capacity does not necessarily reduce innovative endeavours at home, but brings US international firms into complementary as well as competitive relations with foreign enterprises. Technology-based alliances with such firms tend to become more extensive, and tend to have increasing significance because of the widening range of advances in frontier technology that have to be continually surveyed for assessment of their potentials in commercial application.

The scope for technology-based alliances is especially important in Germany, in part because the German system of corporate governance restricts opportunities for foreign involvement in mergers and acquisitions. High-technology sectors have been lagging behind those in the USA because the form of alliance capitalism that has evolved under the system of corporate governance does appear to have been more suited for incremental rather than radical innovation (Soskice, 1998). Germany's centres of innovation however have been the most active in Europe, and the scale of fundamental research has a breadth which indicates potentials for frontier breakthroughs. Tapping the results of any breakthroughs as well as incremental advances can assist US high-technology firms to maintain a strong presence in Europe, where continued advantages are in prospect because most of the region's enterprises have to contend with high labour costs, high taxation and weak demand. US firms, with larger international operations, have generally superior resources to cope with the weaknesses of the area's economies and to exploit increases in demand as the Union absorbs new East European members.

Competition Policy

Antitrust enforcement has inhibiting effects on cooperation between US firms. Collaboration for the development of new technology is virtually restricted to precompetitive research, and corporate interests in this tend to be discouraged because proceeding to collaborative production and marketing would risk severe penalties. An important consequence is that incentives for technology-based mergers and acquisitions are strong in the home economy. A concentration trend can thus threaten to reduce the spread of innovative capabilities in the intercorporate system; this may happen because of bureaucratic deficiencies in the emerging large enterprises and increased emphasis by their management on strategies designed for high short-term profits.

Change in antitrust enforcement through guidelines from the Department of Justice has led to increased acceptance of mergers and acquisitions at the policy level and in public attitudes (Destler, 1998), but the restraints on intercorporate cooperation remain potent. The basic problem is that legislative change is extremely difficult, because of the dynamics of congressional operations. While legislative action remains unlikely, multiple court rulings complicate the entire process of antitrust enforcement, while in effect encouraging litigation by firms alleging injury to their interests (White, 1993).

Legislative, interest group and popular reluctance to support change in antitrust legislation is attributable in varying degrees to awareness that anticompetitive behaviour by firms has to be restricted in the public interest. There are fears that collusive activities can enable firms to extract large benefits from market strengths, at costs to consumers; vigorous competition is seen as a protection against this danger.

Concerns with enhancing the USA's structural competitiveness cause reconsideration of the restrictions on intercorporate cooperation because of awareness, in technology policy communities, that the widening range of advances in frontier research with potential industrial applications indicates requirements for broadening knowledge-intensive exchanges between firms that can facilitate complementary specializations. Explicit agreements on production sharing and market sharing are actionable under antitrust legislation, and accordingly the scope for cooperation between firms in the commercial development of new technology has to be limited to tacit collaboration. Low levels of intercorporate trust, however, it must be stressed, restrict what can be achieved through tacit alignment of entrepreneurial strategies. It has to be reiterated, accordingly, that the incentives to proceed through mergers and acquisitions for the exploitation of new technology are quite strong.

Trade Policy

The relaxation of antitrust enforcement, allowing more scope for mergers and acquisitions over the past two decades, has been intended to assist the emergence of large US firms with superior international competitiveness. This objective has had increased significance since the phasing in of trade liberalization measures adopted in the Uruguay Round agreements, but the openness of the US economy has been limited by forms of protectionism, including especially the operation of antidumping procedures. These, although biased in favour of domestic producers, (Destler, 1998), have not significantly affected import penetration in high technology sectors by Japanese firms, which have been advantaged by investment in production within the USA, but appear to have increased risks for exporters of high-technology products from newly industrializing countries, especially in east Asia.

Protection of the domestic market strengths of US high-technology firms can enable them to devote more resources to the penetration of foreign markets and thus recover shares of world high-technology trade. Market-opening leverage directed against major trading partners meanwhile can assist recoveries of those world trade shares. Both forms of trade policy activism have been justified in policy literature that has stressed the unfair advantages derived by Japanese and European firms from their governments' subsidies programmes, protectionist measures and liberal competition policies (Tyson, 1992). The persistence of very large trade deficits has made the rationales for trade policy activism rather persuasive but more with reference to the fortunes of low-technology sectors affected by substantial import penetration.

Problems of aggregating corporate interests and preferences affect the degrees of coherence and thrust in US trade policy activism devoted to protection of the domestic market and the opening of foreign markets, (Destler, 1998). Because of the resultant uncertainties about outcomes, managerial willingness to commit resources to lobbying is often at low levels. Energetic efforts by trade policy officials can mobilize interest group and legislative support for specific ventures in trade policy activism but with results that do not endure when administrations change. Issues of technology enhancement for the upgrading of US structural competitiveness tend to be obscured in the complex pluralism of trade policy processes, especially because of the prominence of import penetration problems attributed to foreign unfair trading rather than to foreign technological achievements.

Highly self-reliant strategies thus appear to be appropriate for US high-technology firms seeking to maintain their domestic positions and penetrate foreign markets. Expansion at home through mergers and acquisitions is all the more rational with this perspective, and such expansion can support wider involvement in world markets, especially the European Union, which, it must be stressed, deserves high priority because of its size and the weaknesses of its firms. Japanese corporate competition, although very active, has become a more manageable problem for US enterprises operating in Europe, while facilitating more advantageous interaction with European firms. At the same time, US corporate dealings with Japanese enterprises can exploit favourable shifts in bargaining strengths, in a context in which Japanese trade policy objectives have become more dependent on access to the US market.

PROSPECTS

Structural and policy trends interact as technology factors evolve in the globalization of the American economy. The scope for corporate operations in pursuit of world trade shares is widening, primarily on the basis of shares already won that sustain reinvestments of profits: national economic structures are thus being altered on a very extensive scale and are becoming more closely linked through trade and transnational production in which US enterprises are especially prominent. The American administration endeavours to provide a market-friendly environment at home, to enhance structural competitiveness, and it is being challenged to give increasing attention to the promotion of technological progress. This is difficult because of the pluralistic dynamics of the political process, and because of issues of deindustrialization associated with continuing globalization. Corporate interests and preferences are not sufficiently aggregated, in the US system of divided government, to support a technology policy that would be coherent and relatively comprehensive (Ham and Mowery, 1995), or to cope with the larger issues of macromanagement posed by the costs of globalization.

The range of ongoing and anticipated advances in frontier technology with potential commercial applications, however, is becoming more extensive. The areas of progress identified in research literature include advanced materials, linkages between atomic and molecular engineering and electronics, microelectronics, photonics involving microelectronics and microoptics, and the broad field of information engineering (Welfens et al., 1997). Surveillance of the entrepreneurial possibilities discernible in the frontier advances is necessary for management in US high-technology firms, and for their international alliance partners, but the potential advantages of collaboration for this purpose tend to be neglected, because of the persistence of intensely competitive intercorporate relations. At the same time, the political difficulties of evolving a technology policy in broadening alignment with the expanding entrepreneurial opportunities of frontier research advances remain serious.

Dangers of technology-based imbalances in the development of the USA's structural interdependencies demand recognition because of coordination problems, although these imbalances have been and are likely to remain overshadowed by import penetration volumes attributable simply to low-cost foreign production and to reliance on such production by US enterprises serving external markets. Coordination problems between US high-technology firms, in the development of their international production and marketing systems, tend to result in sub-optimal evolution of complementary approaches to the use of frontier innovations, despite incentives to realize efficiencies through collaboration as those innovations multiply. Coordination problems at the policy level meanwhile persist while diversified frontier innovations become more numerous, raising issues about the further development of technology policy.

Public choice perspectives can direct attention to all the conflicts of incentive-based motivations at the corporate and policy levels that hinder systemic development logic. The problems of market failure, however, and problems in the marketing of policies, have to be viewed, in the public interest, as leadership challenges. Institutional weaknesses in responding to aggressive competing representations of interests have to be overcome through leadership. Achieving a functional balance between competition and cooperation in the US intercorporate system, as it develops new technology and becomes more international, will also require leadership. Ideally this, and the policy leadership, should be collegial, with consensus about the priority of the real economy which can be adversely affected by managerial zeal for high short-term financial yields.

NOTES

1. For a detailed overview of the extent and performance of such manufacturing extension services, see the special issue on industrial modernization in the *Journal of Technology Transfer*, **23** (1), Spring 1998 edited by Philip Shapira and Jan Youtie.
2. For an alternative perspective, see Pepper D. Culpepper, 'The future of the high-skill equilibrium in Germany', *Oxford Review of Economic Policy*, **15** (1), 43–59.
3. Domestic value added reflects the amount of the final output value of a good that is represented solely by the domestic content of production – foreign inputs into the production process are excluded.
4. Drugs and medicine, computers, aerospace, communications equipment, biotechnology and life science products, flexible manufacturing systems, advanced materials, software technology and weapons and nuclear technology.
5. Extensive treatments of technology gap and global product cycle theories can be found in Posner (1961), Hirsch (1965), Hufbauer (1966) and Vernon (1966).
6. This is a notable shift in the role of the federal government. Up to (and including) the late 1980s, the US government provided roughly one-half of all R&D funds in the United States. The decline is attributable largely to decreasing amounts of defence-related R&D spending.

REFERENCES

Betz, Frederick (1987), *Managing Technology: Competing Through New Ventures, Innovation, and Corporate Research*, Englewood Cliffs, NJ: Prentice-Hall.

Blecker, Robert (1992), *Beyond the Twin Deficits. A Trade Strategy for the 1990s*, New York: M.E. Sharpe.

Campa, Jose and Linda S. Goldberg (1997), 'The evolving external orientation of manufacturing: a profile of four countries', *Economic Policy Review*, Federal Reserve Board of New York, **3** (2), 53–82.

Destler, I.M. (1998), 'US Approach to International Competition Policy', in Robert Z. Lawrence (ed.), *Brookings Trade Forum, 1998*, Washington, DC: Brookings Institution.

Grant, Richard, Maria Papadakis and J. David Richardson (1993), 'Global Trade Flows: Old Structures, New Issues, Empirical Evidence', in C. Fred Bergsten and Marcus Noland (eds), *Pacific Dynamism and the International Economic System*, Washington, DC: Institute for International Economics.

Guerrieri, Paolo and Carlo Milana (1997), 'High Technology Industries and International Competition', in Daniele Archibugi and Jonathan Michie (eds), *Trade, Growth and Technical Change*, Cambridge: Cambridge University Press, pp. 188–207.

Hagedoorn, John (1998), 'Atlantic Strategic Technology Alliances', in Gavin Boyd (ed.), *The Struggle for World Markets*, Cheltenham: Edward Elgar, pp. 177–91.

Ham, Rose Marie and David C. Mowery (1995), 'Enduring dilemmas in US technology policy', *California Management Review*, **37** (4), 89–107.

Ham, Rose Marie, Greg Linden and Melissa M. Appleyard (1998), 'The evolving role of semiconductor consortia in the US and Japan', *California Management Review*, **41** (1), 137–63.

Hamel, Gary and C.K. Prahalad (1994), *Competing for the Future*, Boston: Harvard Business School Press.

Hirsch, S. (1965), 'The United States electronics industry in international trade', *National Institute Economic Review*, November.

Hufbauer, G.C. (1966), *Synthetic Materials and the Theory of International Trade*, London: Duckworth.

Jorgenson, Dale and Masahiro Kuroda (1992), 'Productivity and international competitiveness in Japan and the United States, 1960–1985', *Economic Studies Quarterly*, **43**, 313–25.

Kash, Don E. (1989), *Perpetual Innovation: The New World of Competition*, New York: Basic Books.

Lazonick, William and Jonathan West (1998), 'Organizational Integration and Competitive Advantage: Explaining Strategy and Performance in American Industry', in Giovanni Dosi, David J. Teece and Josef Chytry (eds), *Technology, Organization, and Competitiveness: Perspectives on Industrial and Corporate Change*, Oxford: Oxford University Press, pp. 247–88.

Lipsey, Robert E. (1991), 'Foreign direct investment in the United States and U.S. trade', *The Annals of the American Academy of Political and Social Science*, July, 76–90.

Lipsey, Robert E. and Irving Kravis (1987), 'The competitiveness and comparative advantage of U.S. multinationals', *Banca Nazionale del Lavoro Quarterly Review*, **161**, 147–65.

Mowery, David C. and David J. Teece (1993), 'Japan's growing capabilities in industrial technology: implications for US managers and policymakers', *California Management Review*, **35** (2), 9–34.

National Science Board (1998), *Science and Engineering Indicators 1998*, Washington, DC: US GPO.

National Science Foundation (1996), *National Patterns of R&D Resources: 1996*, Washington, DC: National Science Foundation.

National Science Foundation (1998), *Research and Development in Industry: 1995–96*, Washington, DC: National Science Foundation.

Nelson, Richard R. and Gavin Wright (1992), 'The rise and fall of American technological leadership: the postwar era in historical perspective', *Journal of Economic Literature*, **XXX** (4), 1931–64.

Papadakis, Maria (1994), 'Did or does the United States have a competitiveness crisis?', *Journal of Public Policy Analysis and Management*, **13** (1), 1–20.

Papadakis, Maria (1995), 'The delicate task of linking industrial R&D to national competitiveness', *Technovation*, **15** (9), 569–83.

Porter, Michael (1990), *The Competitive Advantage of Nations*, New York: The Free Press.

Posner, M.V. (1961), 'International trade and technological change', *Oxford Economic Papers*, **13** (3).

Rodrik, Dani (1997), *Has Globalization Gone Too Far?*, Washington, DC: Institute for International Economics.

Roussel, Philip, Kamal N. Saad and Tamara J. Erickson (1991), *Third Generation R&D: Managing the Link to Corporate Strategy*, Boston: Harvard Business School Press.

Soskice, David (1998), 'Openness and Diversity in TransAtlantic Economic Relations', in Barry Eichengreen (ed.), *TransAtlantic Economic Relations in the Post-Cold War Era*, New York: Council on Foreign Relations.

Tyson, Laura D'Andrea (1992), *Who's Bashing Whom? Trade Conflict in High Technology Industries*, Washington, DC: Institute for International Economics.

Vernon, R. (1966), 'International investment and international trade in the product cycle', *Quarterly Journal of Economics*, May, 190–207.

Welfens, Paul J.J., David Audretsch, John T. Addison and Hariolf Grupp (1997), *Technological Competition, Employment and Innovation Policies in OECD Countries*, Berlin: Springer-Verlag.

White, Lawrence J. (1993), 'Competition policy in the United States: an overview', *Oxford Review of Economic Policy*, **9** (2) 133–51.

Zysman, John and Laura Tyson (1983), *American Industry in International Competition: Government Policies and Corporate Strategies*, Ithaca: Cornell University Press.

7. The United States and global capital markets

Joseph P. Daniels

INTRODUCTION

During the Bretton Woods period, central banks were responsible for maintaining pegged exchange values thereby reducing exchange rate risk and currency arbitrage opportunities. The existence of significant capital controls made sovereign governments and international agencies the primary source of official development financing. The *ad hoc* system of flexible exchange rates that emerged in 1973 through 1976 resulted in a transfer of exchange rate risk, and arbitrage opportunities, from government agencies to the private sector. The dismantling of capital controls and deregulation of domestic financial sectors signalled a willingness of governments to substitute private sector financing for official financing by domestic governments and international agencies.

Liberalization of capital markets, along with increased international transactions in the real sector, have spurred dramatic growth in the international money and capital markets. (See Williamson and Mahar (1998) for an excellent essay on financial liberalization.) Daily foreign exchange transactions, for example, have grown to nearly $1.4 trillion. This growth highlights the importance of today's capital markets in allocating savings worldwide. By channelling savings to borrowers, capital market institutions help finance domestic investment and direct savings, whether it be domestically and globally, to their most efficient use, allowing savers to achieve higher risk adjusted rates of return. Access to global capital markets allows borrowers to pursue investment projects in times of domestic downturns, thus reducing domestic business cycles (Eichengreen et al., 1999). In light of recent financial crises, however, many observers have come to question the benefits of uninhibited international capital flows and its contribution to real sector investment.

Eatwell and Taylor (1998) argue that the performance of the financial sector must ultimately be judged on its contribution to the real sector in terms of long-run trends in employment and growth. In this regard they make two important observations. First, trend growth of the G7 economies has slowed to two-thirds of the rate posted in the 1960s. Second, there is disagreement as to whether the performance of financial institutions affects medium or long-term trend performance of the real sector or if it is determined solely by structural aspects of the real sector.

It is assumed here that the performance of capital markets and financial institutions is important for real sector outcomes as it affects public and private sector behaviour. Hence, a solvent and sound system of financial institutions may promote continued domestic growth and prosperity. Under unstable conditions, however, intermediaries may channel capital flows in a way that 'undermine domestic policies' (Crockett, 1997, p. 7), triggering a financial crisis.

The potential costs of these financial crises is abundant. For example, it is believed that the costs of the 1980s banking crises in Argentina equalled one-half of the nation's GDP while the United States' bailout of banks during the early 1990s totalled at least $200 billion. The 1995 real estate collapse in Japan resulted in the non-performance of more than $250 billion in bank loans. In South Korea more than 10 per cent of all bank loans are non-performing. For India and China non-performing loans are estimated to be nearly 20 per cent of outstanding loans. Since 1980, the IMF estimates that 133 of 181 IMF member nations have suffered banking problems it considers to be 'significant' (Lindgren et al., 1996).

Further, as has been seen in recent financial crises, banking solvency is critical to the operation and stability of the global economy as well. How should sovereign governments and international organizations respond to this issue? One view is that financial intermediation is inherently an unstable business the fortunes of which rise and fail with the business cycle. Hence, government regulation and safety nets are required to prevent periodic banking collapses. Another view is that safety nets themselves create a moral hazard problem and may actually be responsible for recent banking crises. Regardless of the view taken, it is important to ensure that global capital markets operate as efficiently as possible. As capital markets become more integrated internationally, therefore, the need for stability, solvency and regulation becomes paramount as financial crises can be magnified.

This chapter considers these issues, focusing on institutions, market structure and growth, and risk. The next section considers the basic rationales for, and characteristics of, financial intermediation with attention given to the unique characteristics of the United States in financing capital investment projects. The section after that highlights recent developments in world financial markets, distinguishing between the money and capital markets, and examines the most important development, the increase in capital flows to developing markets. The next section explores various sources of risks and examines opposing views on regulation, presents recent attempts and proposals for global regulation and questions whether new or old institutions are best suited to supervise intermediation. The final section offers a conclusion.

RATIONALES FOR, AND CHARACTERISTICS OF, FINANCIAL INTERMEDIATION

Financial transactions can be direct or indirect. For example, households may allocate wealth to the purchase of a bond issued by a company, effectively making a direct loan to that business. In this way, households assist in the direct finance of domestic capital investment projects. It is also possible that a household may obtain a long-term time deposit at a banking firm. In turn, the bank may allocate these funds, together with those of other deposit holders, to holdings of bonds issued by the same company as before. In this instance, the household would indirectly finance domestic capital investment. The bank, in turn, intermediates the financing of the domestic investment. The process of indirect finance, or financial intermediation, is the most common way in which funds are channelled from saving to investment and the financial institutions that fulfil this role are called financial intermediaries.

The Rationales for Domestic and International Financial Intermediation

One rationale for the use of intermediaries is the existence of asymmetric information. Often lenders are not privy to all of the pertinent information about the borrower and the investment project, particularly information about risk. The existence of asymmetric information can lead to adverse selection, or the potential for those who desire funds for unworthy projects to be the most likely to want to borrow or to issue debt instruments. A result of adverse selection is that the issuance of poor-quality instruments can make savers less willing to lend to or hold debt instruments issued by those seeking to finance high-quality projects. Also, poor market information or uncertainty about the competence of the financial intermediaries' market may result in herding behaviour; that is, when savers follow the behaviour of someone they feel is better informed, leading to self-fulfilling outcomes. High-quality banking institutions may minimize herding behaviour by depositors.

A third problem that financial market participants face is moral hazard. Moral hazard is the potential that, after they have access to funding, a borrower might engage in behaviour that increases risk – or, in other words, the 'immoral' behaviour, from the lender's perspective, that the borrower would thereby have exhibited. Moral hazard is the primary argument used against the recent financial support arrangements offered by the IMF and G7 nations, and used to argue in favour of debt restructuring schemes that involve private sector bondholders. Another important reason for agents to use financial intermediaries is economies of scale. Financial intermediaries make it possible for individuals to pool funds together, increasing the scale of possible opportunities. In addition, this centralization of management can reduce the average fund management costs below the level an individual would incur.

Financial intermediaries, therefore, exist to save holders of financial instruments from incurring risks and allow them to enjoy reduced costs as described above. While these institutions cannot eliminate adverse selection, herding behaviour and moral hazard problems, they can collect information, at a lower marginal cost, about the underlying riskiness of financial instruments and monitor the continuing performance of those who issue such instruments, thereby reducing the extent of adverse selection and moral hazard problems in the market for these bonds.

The rationales for international financial intermediation are the same as for domestic intermediation. For example, asymmetric-information problems are likely to be at least as severe when evaluating the riskiness of foreign financial instruments as compared to domestic instruments, and therefore the need for international financial intermediation is greater. Banks located in various countries take part in the process of international financial intermediation by using some of the funds of domestic deposit holders to finance loans to individuals and companies based in other nations. Most of this international banking activity takes place in the Eurocurrency markets. Today, very few nations' capital investment projects are purely domestically financed. Even bank-financed investment in the United States increasingly stems from loans by non-US banks, with the largest US corporations on average using the services of more foreign banks as compared with the average number of domestic institutions whose services they utilize.

As shown in Table 7.1, the world's largest banking institutions, sometimes referred to as 'megabanks', tend to be located outside of the United States. By increasing their asset portfolios through regional or world-wide expansion, megabanks may reduce average operating costs, gaining efficiency. The evidence for economies of scale in banking is more mixed for US banks than for their European counterparts, even though US bank managers themselves commonly offer economies of scale as a key rationale for large-scale mergers in the United States.

National Characteristics of Intermediation

There are several ways in which countries' banking systems and the use of banks and market finance differ. The first is the extent to which domestic firms use foreign banks relative to domestic banks. US multinationals tend to rely on foreign banking institutions to intermediate investment projects to a

Table 7.1   The largest banks

Bank	Country	Assets (US$ billions)
Tokyo Mitsubishi Bank	Japan	692
Deutsche Bank AG	Germany	580
Sumitomo	Japan	484
Credit Suisse Group	Switzerland	474
HSBC Holdings	United Kingdom	471
Dai-Ichi Kangyo Bank	Japan	433
Sanwa Bank	Japan	428
Credit Agricole Mutuel	France	420
Fuji Bank	Japan	414
ABN Amro Holdings	The Netherlands	412

Note: Based on total assets held on 31 December 1997.

Source: *American Banker*, 6 August 1998.

much higher degree than multinationals of other nations. By the 1990s, for example, a typical multinational US firm had accounts with at least as many banks abroad as they maintained with US-based banking institutions.

Another aspect in which national banking systems differ concerns the extent to which banks are the predominant means by which firms finance their working capital needs. For instance, British, German and Japanese businesses use bank loans to finance significantly larger shares of their investment as compared with businesses located in the United States. In the United Kingdom, nearly 70 per cent of funds raised by businesses typically stem from bank borrowings. The proportions for Germany and Japan were of the order of 50 per cent and 65 per cent, respectively. In contrast, US businesses normally raise fewer than 30 per cent of their funds through bank loans. This difference helps to explain why German and Japanese banks more than doubled their size between the 1970s and the 1990s. Though British banks grew by less in relative terms, their importance in British business finance permitted them to grow faster than US banks, whose overall size, adjusted for inflation, failed to change significantly in the two decades following the 1970s.

There also are differences in market structures across nations. In particular, the extent of potential rivalry, often measured by the portion of total deposits concentrated within a nation's largest banks, can vary considerably. The top five banks in Belgium, Denmark, France, Italy, Luxembourg, Portugal, Spain and the United Kingdom have over 30 per cent of the deposits of their nations' residents. In Greece and the Netherlands, this figure is over 80 per cent. In contrast, the top five US banks account for fewer than 15 per cent of the deposit holdings of US residents. With regard to total bank assets, the US banking system also appears to exhibit more potential for rivalry among its banks, as less than a third of total bank assets are concentrated among the top ten US banks. In Germany, Japan and the United Kingdom, this figure is about two-thirds.

The degree of banking competition within a nation also depends on how open the nation's borders are to rivalry from foreign-based banking operations. By the early 1990s, foreign banks made many loans to US individuals and firms, but foreign banks had barely penetrated the German and Japanese loan markets. This undoubtedly has played a role in producing the high levels of bank asset concentration in Europe and Japan, as shown in Table 7.1.

Another feature that distinguishes national banking systems is the extent to which they permit universal banking, under which there are few if any limits on the ability of banks to offer full ranges of financial services and to own equity shares in corporations. In Germany and the United Kingdom, as well as in several other European nations, banks face few such restrictions. Japanese banks face greater restrictions on their activities, but many Japanese banks have the authority to underwrite stocks and bonds. By contrast, in the United States universal banking has been prohibited since 1933, when the US Congress passed the Glass–Steagall Act. There has been little evidence that banks in nations with universal banking are significantly more risky than their US counterparts; one of the common arguments against universal banking. The purchase of Bankers Trust by Deutsche Bank in 1998 highlights how disadvantaged US banks are internationally and helped put the removal of the Glass–Steagall Act back on the congressional agenda in 1999.

The legal environment, the level of diversification and the degree of competition are characteristics which are highly interdependent, making it difficult to delineate the cause and effect of market outcomes. The result for the United States is that US firms rely on foreign banks to a greater extent than do their foreign counterparts, yet rely on bank financing to a significantly lesser degree overall. Some nations protect their banking industries to a higher degree while allowing them to compete in a broader range of services. The German and Japanese systems of banks, therefore, tend to have fewer institutions, each with a much larger degree of market concentration.

Some key observations can be made at this point. First, soundness of domestic banking systems is important for the efficient channelling of savings to productive investment projects, and for the heavy costs that banking crises can entail. Second, because US firms rely on foreign banking institutions to such a high degree, the soundness and solvency of foreign banks is important to US business managers and policy-makers. Finally, because of the extent to which US firms rely on direct intermediation to finance investment projects, managers and policy-makers must be concerned with the reliability and stability of domestic and global capital markets.

In regard to the first observation, the questions faced by US policy-makers are: to what extent should concentration be allowed, at the risk of reduced domestic competition; what services should banks be allowed to compete in; and what, if anything, should be done to enhance the global competitiveness of US banking institutions. To some degree these have been answered, as technological advancements, deregulation efforts in the 1980s and increased willingness for mergers and acquisitions have slowly eroded the restrictions placed on US banks through dual-system regulations and the Glass–Steagall Act. Now that these important financial institutions have been considered, we next examine how global financial markets have evolved.

WORLD FINANCIAL MARKETS

Following the end of World War II, the industrialized nations pursued a goal of greater trade liberalization. Not until the 1970s, however, did most industrialized nations begin to liberalize financial markets. Changes in communications technology combined with the introduction of innovative new financial instruments has moved even reluctant nations to liberalize and deregulate their financial markets. The advent of instant and low-cost communications and information innovations allows a wider range of firms and individuals to participate in international financial markets and to manage their risk exposure more effectively. As a result, since the 1970s the growth of international financial markets has far outpaced the growth of international trade in goods and services. Savers, as discussed below, have yet to take full advantage of these new opportunities. This stylized fact, combined with the usual econometric evidence on parity conditions, indicates that though capital markets have become more integrated, they are far from perfectly integrated.

International Capital Markets

International capital markets are the markets for cross-border exchange of financial instruments which have a maturity of a year or more, or with no distinct maturity. Table 7.2 presents evidence on the dramatic growth of issues in the international capital markets. Between 1986 and 1996 total financing activity that took place on the international capital markets increased by $526.7 billion, or 219.6 per cent.

Table 7.2 separates the data into two of its most important components: international bonds and international equities. A third component of the

Table 7.2   Growth of the international capital market (US$ billions)

	1986	1997	Change	Percentage change
Total	389.5	1769.3	1379.8	354.2
Securities	195.5	916.7	721.2	368.9
Loans	88.5	390.4	301.9	341.1

Source: Organization for Economic Cooperation and Development, *Financial Market Trends*.

international capital markets is foreign direct investment. The international bond market, which represents 92 per cent of the international capital markets, experienced the greatest absolute growth, with an increase of $480.7 billion. The international equities market, on the other hand, experienced the most rapid rate of growth with a fivefold increase over the 10-year period.

The impact of increased participation of institutional investors has been given much attention of late. Deregulation, liberalization and the technological advances described earlier create a wider range of savings opportunities for individuals through institutional investors. A recent study by the OECD (1997) details the size and growth of financial instruments managed by institutional investors. Table 7.3 presents the OECD's data for the six nations with the largest institutional investor activity. As shown, the United States and the United Kingdom are two of the nations with the greatest amount of institutional investor activity. The table also shows that between 1990 and 1995 the financial assets of institutional investors increased by one-third to one-half for the United States, the United Kingdom and Canada.

Even though the development and growth of the international capital market allows individuals and businesses greater opportunities to manage risk and increase potential returns, savers do not utilize the international capital

Table 7.3   Financial assets of institutional investors (%GDP)

	1995	Percentage change 1990–95
Canada	87.9	50.0
Luxembourg	2132.8	0
Netherlands	158.4	18.7
Sweden	114.8	34.4
United Kingdom	162.3	41.7
United States	170.8	34.1

Source: Organization for Economic Cooperation and Development, *Financial Market Trends*.

market to the extent we might expect. French and Poterba (1991) find that savers demonstrate a low level of international diversification in their portfolios and that most corporate equity is held by domestic residents.

Table 7.4 provides estimates of equity portfolio weights for US, Japanese and UK savers. French and Poterba also estimate the additional return that savers must expect in order to justify the low level of international diversification. As the table shows, US savers hold almost 94 per cent of their portfolios in domestic equities. The estimates of the return on an internationally diversified portfolio are compared with estimated returns on portfolios with distributions comparable to British, Japanese and US investors. To justify the low level of international diversification, US savers must anticipate a return on their domestic equity holdings that exceeds the actual return by almost 1 per cent. UK savers, due to a smaller overall equity market, have the most internationally diversified portfolios of the three nations. To justify 82 per cent of their portfolio in UK equities, however, UK savers must anticipate a return on their domestic holdings that exceeds the actual return by more than 4 per cent.

Table 7.4   Equity portfolio diversification (%)

	United States	Japan	United Kingdom
United States	93.8	1.3	5.9
Japan	3.1	98.1	4.8
United Kingdom	1.1	0.2	82.0
France	0.5	0.1	3.2
Germany	0.5	0.1	3.5
Canada	1.0	0.1	0.6
Excess returns required to justify domestic share of equity portfolio (as per cent)	0.9	2.5	4.4

Source: French and Poterba (1991).

French and Poterba conclude that these low levels of international diversification are not due to any national or institutional constraints. The three countries in their study have few if any capital controls in place today, and tax differences and transaction costs are also very small for these nations. The authors conclude, therefore, that the low levels of diversification are due to savers' tastes. They speculate that savers perceive a greater degree of risk in foreign equity markets because they are less familiar with those markets than they are with domestic equity markets.

International Money Markets

International money markets are markets for cross-border exchange of financial instruments with a maturity of less than one year. Although traders exchange a number of different types of instruments in international money markets, foreign exchange instruments are most actively traded. As noted earlier, the international capital markets have experienced considerable growth since the early 1970s. The international money markets, however, have experienced astounding growth. Economists periodically estimate the volume of transactions in the foreign exchange markets based on surveys of the largest banks and foreign exchange trading firms. Current estimates of the daily activity on the foreign exchange markets indicate that the daily turnover is approximately $1.25 billion. On average, the daily volume of the foreign exchange market approximates two months of activity that occurs in the New York stock exchange market.

The international money markets are comprised of a number of financial instruments other than spot and forward exchange contracts. These instruments include short-term international bank, government and corporate notes, and international commercial paper. Because transactions among large banks constitute the bulk of international money market exchanges, we can use reports of these banks' cross-border asset and liability positions to estimate the size of the market. Table 7.5 provides data on the cross-border positions for December 1997 and the change in cross-border positions for the year 1997. As shown, reporting banks had over $8 trillion in both outstanding assets and liabilities. The change in these positions for the year 1997 was approximately $0.5 trillion.

Table 7.5 also shows the dominance of the industrialized countries' banks in international money markets. Cross-border positions of the industrialized countries represents over 78 per cent of the total. The dominance of the US dollar, as discussed by Daniels and Davis in Chapter 9, is also apparent with the dollar denominating over one-third of outstanding positions.

Capital Flows and Developing Economies

Arguably the most important feature of the international financial markets is the increased volume of financial flows between nations. Indeed, the most striking feature of the 1990s is the increased volume of flows to the emerging countries. Figure 7.1 illustrates the rise in total net private capital flows for the emerging economies, distinguishing between official net direct investment flows and portfolio flows. As shown in the figure, net private capital flows to the emerging economies have risen a dramatic 415 per cent.

Table 7.5   *Reporting banks' cross-border positions, December 1997 (US$ billions)*

	December 1997	Estimated change
Assets		
Industrial countries	7123.6	1019.4
US dollar	3178.1	461.3
Other currencies	3945.5	558.1
All other countries	1914.7	137.3
Total	9038.3	1156.7
Liabilities		
Industrial countries	6948.7	963.6
US dollar	3215.7	419.3
Other currencies	3733.0	544.3
All other countries	1892.2	183.2
Total	8840.9	1146.9

Source: Bank for International Settlements.

As learned from the 1994–95 Mexican financial crisis, it is important to recognize the proportion of net private capital flows that are portfolio investment. Portfolio investment, often referred to as 'hot money', can reverse direction quickly, leaving a nation's financial sector in an illiquid position. (See Chang and Velasco (1998) for an excellent review of the Asian liquidity problem.) Figure 7.1 shows that for the emerging economies, the proportion of net portfolio investment increased from 1990 through 1994, representing a sizable overall proportion in 1993 and 1994. Much of this is reflected in portfolio flows to the Western Hemisphere, or countries such as Mexico, Brazil and Argentina. The sizable decline in portfolio flows in 1995 is also reflected in the Western Hemisphere data as these flows reversed following the Mexican financial crisis, resulting in a drop of $68.3 million in 1995 alone, representing a 112 per cent decline and overall negative net portfolio flows for the region.

Figure 7.1 also illustrates that the proportion of net portfolio flows to total private capital flows differs widely across the various regions. For the Middle East and Europe, net portfolio flows account for 42 per cent of total private flows, while it is a mere 8 per cent for the transitional economies. Net direct foreign investment flows as a percentage of total net private flows range from 58 per cent for the transitional economies to a scant 7 per cent for the Middle East and European economies.

RISK AND REGULATION

As described above, the growth and globalization of financial markets and institutions has brought about a vast number of new opportunities for savers and borrowers. It has, however, also generated new risks and magnified existing risk potential. The four types of risk considered here, in the context of globalization and technological advance in financial instruments, are: Herstatt risk, legal risk, operational risk and systemic risk. There are a number of other types of risk that could be explored, such as liquidity risk and settlement risk, but these would be beyond the confines of this chapter. Hence, only the most obvious sources are discussed, in brief.

Risk

More than two decades ago the impact of Herstatt Risk, or settlement risk that spans time zones or systemic risk, was felt. In 1974, German banking regulators closed the failed Herstatt Bank at 3.30 p.m., after the bank had received European foreign exchange payments but before it made required payments to US banks. Because the US banks did not receive their anticipated payments, they were, in many cases, unable to fulfil their own obligations. By the time the entire event unwound, US banks had lost as much as $200 million dollars.

Systemic risk, settlement or credit risk that spills over and effects third parties, has been a significant concern following the Mexican crisis of 1994 and the 1997 East Asian financial crisis. An important aspect of increased globalization is the transmission of shocks and the potential for contagion. As financial markets become more integrated, the transmission of shocks becomes possible and can even be magnified. Such was the case in the US stock market crash of the 1980s. Because of intertwined markets, the crash spilled into exchanges across the globe.

As demonstrated in the previous section, there has been a dramatic increase in short-term portfolio flows, particularly to the emerging economies. Many of these emerging nations have financial and banking sectors that are underdeveloped, not regulated and not properly supervised. When positive, these net inflows can put upward pressure on a nation's currency and on domestic inflation. On the other hand, they also represent a lower-cost form of financing, hence lower interest rates, and stimulate a nation's economy.

Portfolio flows can, however, reverse direction at rates that quickly exhaust the cumulative buildup of years of inflows. In an economy with an underdeveloped financial sector, these outflows may result in an illiquid banking system and put downward pressure on the nation's currency. Under a fixed exchange rate regime, the government is faced with opposing problems: the banking system needs additional liquidity while the exchange rate regime

Emerging economies

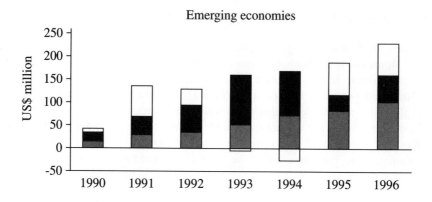

Asia

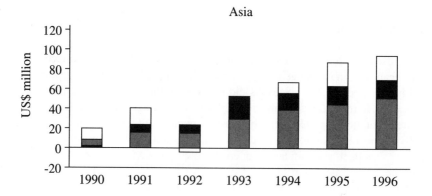

Transitional

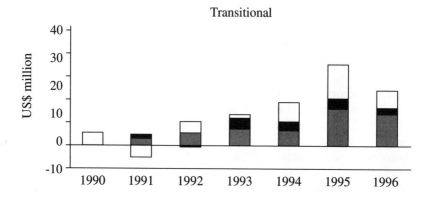

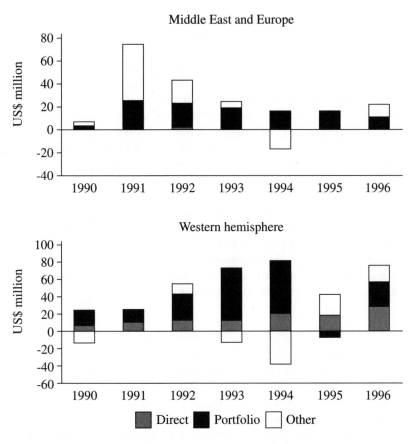

Source: *Developments and Prospects In Emerging Markets*, International Monetary Fund, 1998. IMF country classification groups can be found in the introduction to the statistical annex of the *World Economic Outlook*.

Figure 7.1   Net private capital flows to emerging economies, 1990–96

requires higher interest rates. These hot money flows appear to occur regionally as opposed to nationally, with one country serving as the trigger for a regional crisis (Mexico and Thailand, for example). This is the type of problem seen in the recent financial and currency crises (see Glick (1998) for a survey of the literature in this area). Empirical work by Glick and Rose (1998) indicates that currency crises affect regions or 'clusters' of nations through international trade channels.

As the financial markets have evolved, new and highly sophisticated financial instruments have been introduced. The use of these instruments often becomes widespread before appropriate domestic regulators and corporate managers fully understand their risks and benefits, thereby increasing operational, or management risk, and legal risk, the risk that the contract cannot be enforced by a legal body. The 1995 collapse of Barings Bank illustrates operational risk. The same day that Peter Baring had to ask the Bank of England to intervene, and the day after the trader involved in the derivatives fiasco, Nick Leeson, faxed in his resignation, Barings was to announce and award company bonuses, including a bonus to Leeson in the amount of £450,000. The total losses to Barings is estimated to be £927 million. (See Kuprianov (1995) for case studies on Barings PLC and Metallgesellschaft AG.)

A final aspect considered here is the impact of increased globalization, competition and technological advances on bank structure. Regulatory arbitrage, the practice of establishing foreign offices to avoid domestic regulation, has increased dramatically due in part to technological advances in banking. Globalization and competition have led to increased merger activity and the creation of 'mega' banks. Both activities undermine the attempts of sovereign governments to regulate and supervise national banking institutions.

Global Regulation

How should sovereign governments and international organizations respond to the risks of increasing financial integration? It is important first to distinguish between international financial liberalization and financial regulation. Liberalization is the opening up of the financial market to foreign participants, increasing competition and opportunities for domestic banks. Regulation is the governing of the financial sector in order to improve its operation of financial intermediation. Obviously, and as evident in the recent financial crises, appropriate regulation and supervision is important for the domestic financial system to absorb and channel in an economically efficient way the inflows and outflows of capital that result from financial liberalization.

Views of government intervention

One view of government intervention in the financial sector is that financial intermediation is inherently an unstable business the fortunes of which rise and fall with the business cycle and that financial markets may have inherent imperfections. Hence, government regulation and safety nets are required to prevent periodic banking collapses.

In line with this view, Von Hagen and Fratianni (1998) identify three main reasons for financial regulation. The first is that small depositors find it too costly to continuously monitor the activities of intermediaries. Hence, small depositors need protection from the risk of bank failure. The second is that regulation is required to prevent large withdrawals from one bank that might affect the entire industry, or to prevent contagion. The final reason is to preserve the integrity of the payments system. The authors assert that these types of banking regulation involve the reallocation of risk and therefore wealth among market participants. In a global setting this reallocation can become quite complex as sovereign governments wish to protect domestic residents over foreign residents.

Another view is that regulation that eliminates competition, and the existence of safety nets, creates a moral hazard problem and may actually be responsible for recent banking crises. This second view has been used extensively to build a critical case against the necessity for international organizations such as the IMF. It has played particularly well on the floor of the US Congress which begrudgingly approved new funds to the IMF.

Regulation and supervision: new or old institutions?
In spite of recent criticism, there have been a number of well-placed initiatives and actions taken in response to the risks described above. Examples are the Lamfalussy Report, a 1990 G10 initiative that outlined the legal responsibilities of any intermediary undertaking a large volume wire transfer; the Basle Capital Accord for capital adequacy standards; cross-border banking principles for consolidated supervision; risk management guidelines for derivatives trading and core principles for effective banking supervision.

Many of these initiatives resulted from G7 directives. The Halifax and Lyon Summits, in particular, addressed the global financial situation. (See the excellent volume by Kenen (1996) and the summary by the BIS (1999). Directives to the IMF included a request to the IMF to develop procedures to provide faster access to IMF credit with strengthened conditionality, to develop standards for data availability and to intensify surveillance beyond Article IV policy reviews. The response was an emergency financing mechanism, the Special Data Dissemination Standards, and publication of Article IV reviews for those countries wishing the reviews to be public.

The G10 was asked to double the credit facilities available to the IMF and to review procedures that might prevent or resolve financial crises. The G10 responded with a new arrangement that doubled available IMF credit and, as a first-step, conducted a survey of market participants and domestic regulations in numerous countries. Based on the results of the survey, the G10 emphasized market-based governance and that countries should not expect bailouts the 'size of Mexico'.

Arguably most important, in regard to government intervention, is the problem of IMF bailouts. As is frequently argued, unlimited IMF bailouts increase the moral hazard of lending and borrowing activities. Jeffery Sachs (1998, p. 24) argues that the IMF worked 'mightily and wrongheadedly' to make the world safe for 'naive 25-year-old investment bankers who do not know much about world politics'. Bailouts such as that in East Asia should cease.

Recent words of the G8, particularly at the Birmingham Summit, indicate that nations should not expect unlimited bailouts. It appears, however, that the IMF is continuing to approach problems as it has in the past, and thus IMF actions say otherwise. It is vital that the G7/G8 formulate a coherent and consistent approach to bailouts in future financial crises. The G7/G8 and the IMF must break the expectations they helped create. It is disappointing that the strongest statement the leaders could offer at the Birmingham Summit was that, 'It is also important to ensure that the private sector plays a timely and appropriate role in crises resolution.' US influence is strong in these organizations and US officials need to play an activist role in setting the agenda.

In the long term, policy-makers should rethink completely the role of and even the necessity for the IMF and the World Bank. They must first realize that the IMF is not technically equipped to deal with the types of financial crises that occur in the post-Bretton Woods era. Due to the increased integration of capital markets, the current crises have been fast developing, financial in nature and beyond the capacity of the fund and other existing international organizations. As an example, the current IMF *Manual For Country Economists* states: 'A country will require IMF assistance when it is having balance of payments difficulties or, in other words, when the normal inflow of external savings is not sufficient to finance its resource gap, which is defined as the difference between domestic savings and domestic investment.'

In addition, the current approach to fund conditionality is counterproductive. Sachs (1998, p. 25), states that:

> This process [conditionality] is out of hand. It has undermined political legitimacy in dozens of developing countries, especially since the IMF is often happy to conspire with governments to make end runs around parliaments in the interests of 'reform'. The contents of IMF programmes are too flawed to be a standard of good or poor performance. Markets realize this, so IMF programmes do less and less to rally them.

Finally there must be further discussions on supervisory coordination. Primarily an initiative of Canadian Finance Minister Paul Martin, the issue should be expanded to include regulatory coordination in order to reduce regulatory arbitrage. In contrast to the Martin initiative, however, this should not lead to a new supranational body composed of governmental agents. It should be delegated to an agency with the greatest comparative advantage, perhaps the London Club or the Bank for International Settlements. None the less it should be a market-based approach as has been pursued thus far, since in today's financial environment, operational risk is greater than market risk. Bank management must therefore be involved.

CONCLUSION

Financial intermediaries play an extremely import role as they channel savings to borrowers and help finance domestic investment. The solvency of a nation's system of banks is critical for the stable flow of capital and continued growth and prosperity. Unfortunately, history has shown that financial systems and intermediaries are quite fragile. As one might suspect, given the increase in international capital flows, very few national capital investment projects are financed purely by domestic intermediaries. Given the heightened level of integration, a nation's system of intermediaries is now exposed to new sources of risk. These risks must be measured and managed in a global context, presenting challenges for financial managers and regulatory authorities and creating a need for coordinated efforts. US policy-makers should take an active role in ensuring that a market-based approach continues to be pursued in addressing these challenges.

REFERENCES

Altunbas, Yener and Philip Molyneux (1996), 'Cost economies in EU banking systems', *Journal of Economics and Business*, **48**, 217–30.

Caiola, M. (1995), *A Manual For Country Economists, Training Series Number 1, Volume 1*, Washington, DC: International Monetary Fund.

Chang, R. and A. Velasco (1998), 'The Asian liquidity crises', Federal Reserve Bank of Atlanta Working Paper 98-11.

Crockett, Andrew (1997), 'Why is Financial Stability a Goal of Public Policy?', in *Maintaining Financial Stability in a Global Economy: A Symposium Sponsored by the Federal Reserve Bank of Kansas City*, Jackson Hole, Wyoming: Federal Reserve Bank of Kansas City, pp. 7–36.

Daniels, Joseph and David Van Hoose (1999), *International Monetary and Financial Economics*, Cincinnati: SouthWestern Publishing.

Eatwell, J. and L. Taylor (1998), 'International capital markets and the future of economic policy', Working Papers Series III, Centre for Economic Policy Analysis, New School for Social Research, New York.

The Economist, (1998), 'Capital Controversies', 23 May, p. 72.

Eichengreen, Barry, Michael Mussa, Giovanni Dell'Ariccia, Enrica Detragiache, Gian Maria Milesi-Ferretti and Andrew Tweedie (1999), 'Liberalizing capital movements', International Monetary Fund, *Economic Issues*, **17**.

French, Kenneth and James Poterba (1991), 'Investor diversification and international equity markets', *American Economic Review Papers and Proceedings*, **81** (2), 222–6.

Glick, R. (1998), 'Capital flows and exchange rates in the Pacific Basin', *Federal Reserve Bank of San Francisco Economic Letter*, 98-22.

Glick R. and A. Rose (1998), 'How do currency crises spread?', *Federal Reserve Bank of San Francisco Economic Letter*, 98-25.

Kenen, P. (ed.) (1996), *From Halifax to Lyons: What Has Been Done about Crisis Management?* Essays in International Finance, 200, International Finance Section, Princeton University.

Kuprianov, Anatoli (1995), 'Derivatives debacles: case studies of large losses in derivatives markets', Federal Reserve Bank of Richmond, *Economic Quarterly*, **8** (4), 1–39.

Lindgren, C., G. Gillian and M. Saal (1996), *Bank Soundness and Macroeconomic Policy*, Washington, DC: International Monetary Fund.

Organization for Economic Cooperation and Development (1997), *Financial Trends*, Paris: OECD.

Sachs, J. (1998), 'Global capitalism: making it work', *The Economist*, 23–5.

Von Hagen, J. and M. Fratianni (1998), 'Banking Regulation with Variable Geometry', in B. Eichengreen and J. Frieden (eds), *Forging an Integrated Europe*, Ann Arbor: The University of Michigan Press, pp. 159–84.

Williamson, John, and Molly Mahar (1998), 'A survey of financial liberalization', International Finance Section, Princeton University, *Essays in International Finance*, 211.

8. American corporate planning and international economic disputes*

Thomas L. Brewer and Stephen Young

INTRODUCTION

Purpose

The purpose of this chapter is to analyse the implications for American corporate strategic planning of the new rules concerning trade, investment and intellectual property and the associated dispute resolution process of the World Trade Organization (WTO). The chapter discusses how the World Trade Organization, as an institutionalized mechanism of global rules and procedures for settling disputes, requires companies to respond to an important new public policy regime in their global strategic and operational environment.

The chapter presents statistical data concerning the 155 dispute cases that had entered the WTO dispute settlement process during its first four years (1995–98), and it highlights selected cases that illustrate the implications of the globalization of international economic dispute resolution processes through a multilateral organization. In particular, the chapter uses several key WTO dispute cases to illustrate the theme that the new rules and dispute settlement processes tend to globalize key issues faced by American corporations in their strategic planning process.

Globalization

The analysis of the chapter is consistent with an encompassing notion of 'globalization', which can be conceived as a process that occurs in several related spheres – economic, political and cultural.[1] Within the economic sphere in particular, there are both quantitative and qualitative aspects to each of two dimensions at the macro level. One dimension concerns the countries that are involved in international economic relationships in which the quantitative aspect is the number of countries and the qualitative aspect is the diversity of the countries. This dimension is the geographic dimension. The second dimension is the economic relationship among countries in which the quantitative aspect is the number of interactions among countries and the qualitative aspect is the variety of the interactions.

According to this notion of globalization at the macro level, therefore, there are four sets of indicators for a complex concept: the quantitative and qualitative aspects of each of the two dimensions:

- number and diversity of countries for the geographic dimension;
- volume and variety of interactions for the relationship dimension.[2]

As parallels to these macro-level dimensions, there are micro-level dimensions concerning corporations' strategies and operations. Indeed, many of the macro-level aspects of economic globalization are aggregations of corporate-level international interactions – in terms of the quantity and diversity of their interactions as well as the number and diversity of the countries involved. Thus, a corporation that is headquartered in one country, with foreign affiliates and other business interests in most countries and in all regions and that carries out an enormous volume of transactions of many types with them everyday, can be reasonably called a 'global' corporation.

At the same time, there is often an additional element of globalization at the corporate level – a strategic element – that is used as the basis of identifying a corporation as 'global'.[3] That is, a global corporate strategy takes into account the interdependencies and similarities of its markets and other interests in all countries in an integrative way. Such a strategy is often contrasted with a 'multi-domestic' strategy, according to which each national market and national production system is treated more or less independently. To the extent, then, that a corporation's marketing, production, government relations, financial and other functions are globally integrated, the firm has a 'global' strategy; to the extent that these functions are focused on individual countries separately, the firm has a 'multi-domestic' strategy.

Use of these corporate, strategy-based conceptualizations of globalization, however, needs to take into account two complicating factors. First, just as with the macro-level conceptualization, the micro-level concept has several dimensions: for instance, the marketing, production, government relations and finance functions. Within any one corporation, some management functions are more globalized than others. Second, there is a tendency for corporations to declare themselves as having global strategies, when, in fact, they do not have such strategies by an explicit definition of the term; the tendency is both cause and consequence of the term having acquired a certain degree of faddishness.[4]

Focus of the Chapter

The substantive content of this chapter is consistent with all of these notions and dimensions of economic globalization, and uses them either explicitly or implicitly. It does so, however, within the context of several specific focuses. At the corporate level, the chapter focuses on the government relations function. At the macroeconomic level, it focuses on foreign direct investment, trade and intellectual property transactions, but does not include portfolio investment, money market transactions, other types of funds transfers or the foreign exchange aspects of transactions. The reason for this delimitation is that it is specifically concerned with the World Trade Organization as an institution and its implications for corporate strategic planning. Since many types of financial transactions are only marginally within the mandate of the WTO but are generally within the purview of the International Monetary Fund and other international organizations, they are omitted here.

The macro-level and micro-level processes of economic globalization discussed above of course occur within a broader context, and in particular they interact with globalization processes concerning politics and culture. The globalization processes within each of the political and cultural spheres themselves are complex, and they interact with economic globalization processes in a variety of ways. In this chapter, we focus on a specific, tangible institutional element of political globalization, namely the emergence of global rules and dispute settlement procedures at the World Trade Organization. Thus, we are concerned with a narrow, but important and increasingly salient, set of interactions between economic and political globalization processes.

THE WTO AS A GLOBAL INSTITUTION: MEMBERSHIP AND RULES

The evolving multilateral trade-investment system centred in the World Trade Organization (WTO) creates important new issues concerning strategic planning and government relations for firms in nearly all industries. In addition to the wide-ranging rules covering investment and intellectual property as well as trade, there is a dispute settlement process, which has attracted much interest among firms and industry associations. During its first four years, 1995–98, there were 155 dispute cases that were initiated through the formal consultation process, which is often a first stage leading to the establishment of formal dispute panels.

Literature

Among the dispute cases to date, the Kodak–Fuji case is the subject of an analysis by Baron (1997) in the context of a discussion of a conceptual framework for analysing firms' 'non-market' strategies.[5] There is also a business school teaching case about the implications of the Uruguay Round agreement on agriculture for the sugar industry (Weston and Koehn, 1996). Otherwise, the literature about WTO cases is thus far quite limited, except for the rapidly increasing legal scholarship on the dispute settlement process.[6] There has been some analysis of related international organization–corporate strategy issues by Rugman and Verbecke (1998), though without a specific focus on dispute settlement processes.

Two introductory surveys prepared soon after the completion of the Uruguay Round (EIU, 1995; and International Trade Centre UNCTAD/WTO and Commonwealth Secretariat, 1996) provide useful overviews of the importance to business of the agreements. However, neither study contains detailed or conceptual analyses of issues of business strategy or business–government relations. Furthermore, the legal scholarship quite naturally focuses on the details of provisions in the agreements, including their logical structure and their application in cases, as well as other institutional procedures (Petersmann, 1997; *International Lawyer*, 1998). Nor do more broadly based studies (Hoekman and Kostecki, 1995; Krueger, 1998) of the political and economic context and implications of the WTO system address issues of business strategy or business–government relations. Other studies have addressed only very broad strategic issues from a normative standpoint and in terms of criteria for evaluating public policies. This literature includes analyses of: 'market contestability' (Graham and Lawrence, 1996; Sauve, 1994); 'modal neutrality' (Julius, 1994); and 'policy coherence' (UNCTAD, 1997).

In sum, there has been a lack of explicit and detailed attention to the implications for firms' strategies and the political behaviour of the WTO in studies by scholars of business strategy and business–government relations.[7]

Membership

The membership of the WTO had already expanded to 133 by the end of 1998, slightly more than the 128 in the GATT at the end of 1994, as it was merged into the WTO. These membership numbers compare, for instance, with a GATT membership of 90 in 1989 during the early phase of the Uruguay Round of negotiations. In addition, there are 31 countries (including China, Russia and other former Soviet Union countries) that have applied for accession – a process that can take several years. If/when all of these applicants gain membership, WTO rules will apply to 164 countries accounting for approximately 99 per cent of the world's total international trade and investment (Brewer and Young, 1998, p. 469). In that sense, it is appropriate to speak of the WTO as a 'global', or perhaps 'virtually global', institution at the time of this writing.

Agreements/Rules

One way to summarize most of the 50-some Uruguay Round agreements being implemented at the WTO is to classify them as concerning goods, services and intellectual property. (In technical legal terms, these represent three 'annexes' to the Marrakesh Agreement Establishing the World Trade Organization, i.e. annexes 1A, 1B and IC. There are also technically three separate councils – on goods, services and intellectual property – which implement the agreements along with the biannual ministerial conference and the continually meeting General Council.)[8]

As for goods, the modification of the existing GATT through an agreement called GATT 1994 further lowered tariffs on trade in goods; expanded restrictions on a variety of non-tariff barriers; and addressed a series of traditional GATT issues such as safeguards, balance of payments provisions, antidumping, subsidies and countervailing measures (SCMs), and rules of origin. In addition, it included the agreement on Trade-Related Investment Measures (TRIMs.) This expanded GATT is technically embedded in the new WTO framework, so that the GATT as an agreement continues, though the GATT as an informal organization has been superceded by the WTO.

As for services, the new General Agreement on Trade in Services (GATS) establishes a variety of 'general obligations' such as transparency and MFN non-discrimination in a framework of rules for trade and investment in potentially all service sectors (with government services being exempted). In addition, however, in complex multi-tiered 'schedules of specific commitments' that total over a thousand pages in three volumes, each signatory lists – in 'positive list' form – those sectors for which it is making market access, national treatment and other liberalization commitments. Each signatory also lists – in 'negative list' form – each of the exceptions to those commitments that it is making for each of four different modes of supply. The modes of supply are: cross-border trade, consumption abroad by consumers, commercial presence (approximately equivalent to foreign direct investment) and the movement of suppliers. These specific commitments, then, represent analogues of the bindings of national tariff schedules in agreements on trade in goods. However, the liberalization commitments concerning services pertain to the four modes of supply, including investment, and they are expressed in terms of a combination of positive commitments to liberalize in specified sectors and negative exceptions to those commitments for market access and/or national treatment. The original lists of industry-specific commitments which were agreed by the time of the entry into force of the WTO on 1 January 1995 have since been amended by agreements on basic telecommunications services and financial services. Both of these agreements represent significant expansions of WTO rules into obviously major service sectors in the global economy and in the national and regional economies of each member of the WTO. At the same time, efforts to include maritime transportation services have thus far failed. In any case, the GATS commitments are to be subjected to 'progressive liberalization', according to the agreement, and in fact a new round of negotiations towards further reductions to barriers to trade and investment may well commence by the end of 1999, depending on the outcome of the next ministerial meeting in November 1999.

As for intellectual property, the agreement on Trade-Related Aspects of Intellectual Property Rights (TRIPs) includes new rules that standardize protection standards across countries and obligate their governments to provide transparent and non-discriminatory processes to enforce them.

There is also a dispute settlement process where inter-governmental conflicts about the implementation of these agreements can be addressed.

DISPUTE SETTLEMENT PROCESS AND CASES

The International Trade Organization (ITO) charter of the late 1940s would have established a rigorous dispute settlement procedure as part of its comprehensive framework of trade and investment rules. After the defeat of the ITO charter by the USA, however, dispute settlement was given much less emphasis in the GATT regime. The WTO brought dispute settlement back to centre stage as a linchpin of the multilateral trade system. It is no exaggeration to say that the success or failure of the dispute settlement understanding (DSU) at the WTO will be a key determinant of the credibility and success of the organization. Jackson (1998, pp. 175–6), for example, suggests that the dispute settlement mechanism 'is likely to be seen in the future as one of the most important, and perhaps even watershed, developments of international economic relations in the twentieth century'. Experience with the new process in its first few years has been marked by a positive contribution to the resolution of disputes between members and much controversy about a few cases (Jackson, 1998; Shoyer, 1998). In comparison with its predecessor in the GATT, the WTO dispute settlement system is regarded as a less political and 'unified system with much broader jurisdiction and less scope for "rule shopping" and "forum shopping"' (Petersmann, 1997, p. 178). Of course, many interpretative issues need to be settled on a case-by-case basis for the new agreements such as TRIMs, TRIPs and especially the GATS, given the range and also the ambiguity of some of their provisions.

A number of concerns about the operation of the new process have already emerged. In the former GATT system, various countries had a record of non-compliance (especially the EU in respect of its common agricultural policy). This led to repeated use of the GATT dispute settlement system, especially by the USA, against the same import restrictions. In principle, this should be avoided in the WTO process, with fixed, closed-ended time periods being set for implementation. Current evidence from some high profile disputes, such as the case against the EU concerning its import regime for bananas (*Financial Times*, 13 November 1998, p. 13), suggests, however, that somewhat similar problems will occur. There have been concerns too about the number of 'copycat' complaints (Shoyer, 1998), where complaints have been brought by more than one member, either by a joint request for consultations or as separate requests submitted more or less in parallel. The involvement of multiple complaints in a single dispute is not necessarily problematic: in relation to complaints by developing nations, for example, it may increase their leverage with developed country respondents. But a series of similar complaints runs the danger of clogging up a system that is overloaded already.

From the perspective of multilateral trade and investment liberalization, the key issue concerns the nature and significance of the cases brought to the WTO, and the mechanisms for bringing such cases. As Petersmann (1997, p. 244) has pointed out, 'broad trade policy discretion in domestic laws often operates as an incentive for "rent-seeking" and power politics by import-competing producers interested in influencing the application of discretionary trade rules in a manner generating "protection rents" for the benefit of powerful lobbies'. This criticism has commonly been applied to the operation of antidumping rules, which are operated in a way that generates 'protection rents' for powerful, vocal domestic lobbies using 'shelter-based strategies' (Rugman and Verbeke, 1990); and antidumping affords the same opportunities for this behaviour in the WTO as it did in the GATT. To date, however, only limited consideration has been given to such issues.

Whatever the fate of the WTO's new dispute settlement process and whatever legal and political issues it poses, the very existence of the process and the outcomes of particular cases that are brought to it have important implications for corporations' strategic planning and international operations. The relatively frequent use of the new process, as compared with the use of its predecessor GATT process, is suggestive of its increasing importance (see Table 8.1).

Outcomes of particular dispute cases have important implications for corporations' overall strategic positions, including in particular their access to

Table 8.1   Number of GATT and WTO dispute cases, 1948–59 to 1998

Years	Mean number per year	Mean number per year per member[a]
GATT 1948–59	5.2	0.208
GATT 1960–69	2.2	0.042
GATT 1970–79	4.1	0.054
GATT 1980–89	13.5	0.157
GATT 1990–94	6.5	0.059
WTO 1995	25	0.189
WTO 1996	38	0.288
WTO 1997	51	0.386
WTO 1998	41	0.308

Note: [a] Number of members for each period was computed as the mean of the numbers for the beginning and end of each period.

markets, the location of their production and the structure of their industries. These broad implications are in addition to more specific implications for a variety of strategic and operational issues in each functional area: e.g. finance, marketing and of course government affairs.[9]

Illustrative Dispute Cases

Tangible and specific implications for corporations and industries can be illustrated by a variety of dispute settlement cases. Despite the fact that WTO disputes are formally and officially legal disputes between governments, their origins often lie in the political as well as the economic activities of corporations.[10] In this section, we use these cases to illustrate strategic issues for corporations as well as various aspects of the globalization process concerning both the dispute settlement mechanism and firms' strategies. The cases selected for illustrative purposes cover diverse industries, diverse types of international economic transactions and all three of the principal categories of agreements noted above (goods, services, intellectual property). The cases are grouped as follows:

- Trade-Related Investment Measures in Brazil and Indonesia in the motor vehicle industry.
- Importation and distribution of bananas in the European Union.
- Intellectual property protection for pharmaceutical and agricultural

chemical products in India, and quantitative restrictions on imports of agricultural, textile and industrial products by India.

Additional factual details about these cases are presented in the annex to the chapter. Here we shall highlight features of direct relevance to the analytic themes of the chapter.[11]

In the Brazilian and Indonesian cases concerning trade-related investment measures (TRIMs) affecting the automobile industry, there were separate but similar complaints by Japan, the EU and the USA. From 1993 Indonesia granted tax and tariff benefits to producers of cars based on the local content of the finished vehicle. In 1996 the Indonesian government established the 'National Car Program' which granted 'pioneer' companies similar benefits. The effect was that PT Timor Putra Nasional, a pioneer company, was given the right to import 45 000 finished cars from its Korean partner, Kia Motor Corporation. A WTO dispute panel found these Indonesian policies to be in violation of the GATT 1994, the TRIMs and Subsidies agreements.[12] A similar set of cases involving Brazilian TRIMs in the form of domestic content requirements in the car industry was settled among the disputants without a formal dispute panel ruling.

Together, these cases established that TRIMs, which have been so prevalent in the motor vehicle industry around the world and which have affected many corporations' international production and sourcing strategies, would have to be reduced or even eliminated. In that respect, the cases facilitate the adoption of more nearly global strategies and the concomitant discontinuance of multi-domestic strategies.[13]

In the European Union case concerning the regime for the importation, sale and distribution of bananas, the complaints by Ecuador, Guatemala, Honduras, Mexico and the USA highlight a different globalization story. The EU's banana regime, which provided preferential access for ACP (Africa, Caribbean and Pacific) country bananas over those from Latin America, was deemed to be illegal. The major publicized issue in this case has concerned the EU–US confrontation over alleged non-compliance by the European Union. From a developing country perspective, by contrast, the main question concerns the implication of the dispute panel ruling that the case evaluation process does not include economic development components.

In terms of the particular themes and context of this chapter, however, there is another important aspect to the case: a case was brought by the US government even though there are, of course, no bananas exported from the USA to the EU. Rather, the US government's interest in the issue stems from the combination of the fact that a US-based firm, Chiquita, would like to export more to the EU from its plantations in Central American countries and the fact that the owners of the firm have been major contributors to candidates of both major parties for the Congress and the presidency for the past several elections. Thus, foreign direct investment in the agricultural sector by a US-based firm has transformed a Central American–European trade dispute into a Transatlantic (investment-related) dispute as well. A globalization aspect of that case therefore is that foreign direct investment in combination with trade has significantly broadened the geographic scope of the conflict.

In the Indian cases concerning patent protection for pharmaceutical and agricultural chemical products, complaints by the United States and separately by the EU alleged that the Indian government had not met its obligations under the TRIPs. The WTO ruled that India must establish a 'mailbox' system for filing patent applications and provide exclusive marketing rights for pharmaceuticals and agricultural chemicals – as had been required by the TRIPs agreement by 1 January 1995 – even though the developing countries such as India would have 10 years to phase in their new patent protection regimes in full. In the Indian cases concerning quantitative restrictions on imports of agricultural, textile and industrial products, a complaint by the United States and separate complaints by Australia, Canada and New Zealand focused on India's import quotas on over 2700 agricultural and industrial products. These quotas had been maintained for a lengthy period of time under the balance of payments exceptions of GATT (Article XVIII and other articles and agreements). From the US perspective, the aim was to show that these restrictions were unnecessary, and also to pre-empt widespread use of this exception in the wake of the Asian financial crisis. The decisions in both sets of cases against the Indian government demonstrate the extent to which developing countries, which had often been exempted from the application of liberalization rules in the GATT system, are now expected to comply with WTO rules more fully. In the respect that this represents a significant geographic expansion of the effective scope of the trade-investment regime, it also illustrates a globalization dimension of the system.

In short, these three sets of dispute cases indicate that the WTO system of rules is being applied in ways that reflect several dimensions of the globalization of an international public policy regime and that have important implications for corporations' strategies and government relations. In each instance, several governments from different parts of the world filed complaints against a government in yet another part of the world and in that sense globalized the dispute along the geographic dimension. In each instance, furthermore, corporations from many parts of the world had direct interests and involvement in their governments' cases, and in that respect also globalized the cases along the geographic diversity dimension. The implications of the WTO dispute cases and rules are discussed further in the next section.

CONCLUSION

There has been a 'globalization' of the international trade-investment–intellectual property regime as a result of the significant increases in the number of countries, the industry sectors, the types of international transactions and the types of government policies that have been covered by the WTO since 1995, as compared with the GATT. This globalization is manifest not only in the extent of the rules themselves, but in the dispute cases that have arisen in their application. This chapter has briefly highlighted the nature of the new rules, including their coverage of trade and investment in services, as well as the enforcement of intellectual property rights associated with international technology transfers – in addition to the traditional GATT coverage of traded goods in the manufacturing and agricultural sectors. The chapter has also used dispute cases to illustrate the significance of their implications for the strategies and operations of corporations.

Yet, while the global public policy regime for international trade, investment and technology transfer has become much more highly developed and much more significant for corporations, the corporations' strategic planning and government affairs functions seem not to have adjusted to these new realities. Indeed, the government affairs offices are generally being downsized and their capacity to follow WTO matters accordingly downgraded at precisely the time when the global trade-investment regime is becoming more complex and more important to corporations than at any time during the past half-century.[14]

ANNEX   SYNOPSES OF SELECTED WTO DISPUTE CASES

Brazilian and Indonesian Auto TRIMs Cases

Brazil – Certain Automotive Investment Measures, complaint by Japan (WT/DS51). This request, dated 30 July 1996, concerns certain automotive investment measures taken by the Brazilian government. Violations of the TRIMs Agreement Article 2, GATT Articles I:1, III:4 and XI:1 as well as the Subsidies Agreement Articles 3, 27.2 and 27.4 are alleged. In addition, Japan makes a non-violation claim under GATT Article XXIIII:1(b).

Brazil – Certain Measures Affecting Trade and Investment in the Automotive Sector, complaint by the United States (WT/DS52). This request, dated 9 August 1996, concerns the same measures as identified in Japan's request above. Violations of the TRIMs Agreement Article 2, GATT Articles I:1

and III:4 as well as the Subsidies Agreement Articles 3 and 27.4 are alleged. In addition, the United States also makes a non-violation claim under GATT Article XXIII:1(b).

Brazil – Certain Measures Affecting Trade and Investment in the Automotive Sector, complaint by the United States (WT/DS65). This request, dated 10 January 1997, concerns more or less the same measures as in WT/DS52 above. However, this request also includes measures adopted by Brazil subsequent to consultations held with the United States pursuant to the request under WT/DS52, which measures confer benefits to certain companies located in Japan, the Republic of Korea, and the European Communities. The United States alleges violations under Articles I:1 and III:4 of GATT 1994, Article 2 of the TRIMs Agreement, and Articles 3 and 27.4 of the SCM Agreement. The United States has also made a nullification and impairment of benefits claim under Article XXIII:1 (b) of GATT 1994.

Brazil – Measures Affecting Trade and Investment in the Automotive Sector, complaint by the European Communities (WT/DS81/1). This request, dated 7 May 1997, is in respect of certain measures in the trade and investment sector implemented by Brazil, including in particular, Law No. 9440 of 14 March 1997, Law No. 9449 of 14 March 1997, and Decree No. 1987 of 20 August 1996. The EC contends that these measures violate Articles I:1 and III:4 of GATT 1994, Articles 3, 5 and 27.4 of the Subsidies Agreement, and Article 2 of the TRIMs Agreement. The EC also makes a claim for nullification and impairment of benefits under both GATT 1994 and the Subsidies Agreement. See also DS51, 52 and 65.

Indonesia – Certain Measures Affecting the Automobile Industry, complaint by Japan (WT/DS55). This request, dated 4 October 1996, concerns Indonesia's National Car Programme – basically the same measures as in WT/DS54. Japan contends that these measures are in violation of Indonesia's obligations under Articles I:1, III:2, III:4 and X:3(a) of GATT 1994, as well as Articles 2 and 5.4 of the TRIMs Agreement. On 17 April 1997, Japan requested the establishment of a panel. At its meeting on 12 June 1997, the DSB established a panel. In accordance with Article 9.1 of the DSU, the DSB decided that a single panel will examine this dispute together with DS54 and DS64. The Panel found that Indonesia was in violation of Articles I and II:2 of GATT 1994, Article 2 of the TRIMs Agreement, Article 5(c) of the SCM Agreement, but was not in violation of Article 28.2 of the SCM Agreement. The Panel, however, found that the complainants had not demonstrated that Indonesia was in violation of Articles 3 and 65.5 of the TRIPS Agreement. The report of the Panel was circulated to Members on 2 July 1998. In view of the fact that a single Panel examined the disputes in DS55, DS64, DS54, and DS59, pursuant to Article 9.1 of the DSU, a single Panel report was issued which covers this dispute, as well as those listed below. At its meeting on 23 July 1998, the DSB adopted the Panel report.

Also see three related cases:

Indonesia – Certain Measures Affecting the Automobile Industry, complaint by Japan (WT/DS64).

Indonesia – Certain Measures Affecting the Automobile Industry, complaint by the European Communities (WT/DS54).

Indonesia – Certain Measures Affecting the Automobile Industry, complaint by the United States (WT/DS59).

EU Bananas Case

European Communities – Regime for the Importation, Sale and Distribution of Bananas, complaints by Ecuador, Guatemala, Honduras, Mexico and the United States (WT/DS27). The period for implementation was set by arbitration at 15 months and 1 week from the date of the adoption of the reports, i.e. it expires on 1 January 1999. The EC has undertaken to comply with the recommendations of the DSB within the implementation period. On 18 August 1998, the complainants requested consultations with the EC (without prejudice to their rights under Article 21.5), for the resolution of the disagreement between them over the WTO-consistency of measures being proposed by the EC in purported compliance with the recommendations and rulings of the Panel and Appellate Body. At the DSB meeting on 25 November 1998, the EC announced that it had adopted the second Regulation to implement the recommendations of the DSB, and that the new system will be fully operational from 1 January 1999. The complainants have expressed their dissatisfaction with the WTO consistency of the new system and consultations are continuing between the two sides to this dispute.

Indian Cases

India – Patent Protection for Pharmaceutical and Agricultural Chemical Products, complaint by the United States (WT/DS50). The period of implementation was agreed by the parties to be 15 months from the date of the adoption of the reports, i.e. it expires on 16 April 1999. India has undertaken to comply with the recommendations of the DSB within the implementation period.

India – Patent Protection for Pharmaceutical and Agricultural Chemical Products, complaint by the European Communities (WT/DS79/1). This request, dated 28 April 1997, is in respect of the alleged absence in India of patent protection for pharmaceutical and agricultural chemical products, and the absence of formal systems that permit the filing of patent applications of and provide exclusive marketing rights for such products. The EC contends that this is inconsistent with India's obligations under Article 70, paragraphs 8 and 9, of the TRIPS Agreement (see similar US complaint in DS50, where the Panel and Appellate Body reports were adopted on 16 January 1998). On 9 September 1997, the EC requested the establishment of a panel. At its meeting on 16 October 1997, the DSB established a panel. The US reserved its third-party rights. The Panel found that India has not complied with its obligations under Article 70.8(a) of the TRIPS Agreement by failing to establish a legal basis that adequately preserves novelty and priority in respect of applications for product patents for pharmaceutical and agricultural chemical inventions, and was also not in compliance with Article 70.9 of the TRIPS Agreement by failing to establish a system for the grant of exclusive marketing rights. The report of the Panel was circulated to Members on 24 August 1998. At its meeting on 2 September 1998, the DSB adopted the Panel Report.

India – Quantitative Restrictions on Imports of Agricultural, Textile and Industrial Products complaint by the United States (WT/DS90/1). This request, dated 15 July 1997, is in respect of quantitative restrictions maintained by India on importation of a large number of agricultural, textile and industrial products. The US contends that these quantitative restrictions, including the more than 2,700 agricultural and industrial product tariff lines notified to the WTO, are inconsistent with India's obligations under Articles XI:1 and XVIII:11 of GATT 1994, Article 4.2 of the Agreement on Agriculture, and Article 3 of the Agreement on Import Licensing Procedures. On 3 October 1997, the US requested the establishment of a panel. The DSB established a panel on 18 November 1997.

Source: WTO web site, http://www.wto.org/dispute/bulletin.htm, with update as of 9 December 1998.

NOTES

* This chapter is one of a series by the authors on investment-related issues and dispute settlement at the World Trade Organization and their implications for corporate strategy and public policy. Portions of the research were undertaken while Stephen Young was an EU-Fulbright Scholar-in-Residence at Georgetown University.

1. For extensive discussions on the nature of globalization and its implications for corporations and governments, see, for instance, Dunning (1997) and Hood and Young (forthcoming).

2. Furthermore, each set of indicators uses different data, and each therefore has its own distinctive methodological issues concerning reliability and validity. On measurement issues at the industry level, see, for instance, Makhija et al. (1997). On issues concerning labour and national sovereignty at the macro level, see, for instance, Burtless et al. (1998).

3. There is a large and proliferating literature on global strategy. See, for instance, the analyses by Doz (1986) and Yip (1989).

4. See, for instance, materials on the Ford Motor Company in *The Economist* (1994), *The Financial Times* (1995) and *Business Week* (1995).

5. However, that analysis treats the case as a US 301 case, which it originally was, and does not include information about subsequent developments as a WTO dispute case.

6. See, for instance, the article by Shoyer (1998) and the collection of articles in *The International Lawyer* (1998).

7. In addition to the studies by Young and Brewer represented by this chapter, other studies in progress include: a study of the implications for technology transfer to developing countries, with an emphasis on the telecommunications industry in India, by Nollen and Brewer (in progress); a study of the implications of the General Agreement on Trade in Services (GATS) for financial services and firms in other service sectors in the three Nordic- EU countries by Oxelheim and Brewer (in progress).

8. There are also some plurilateral agreements administered by the WTO, even though their signatories include relatively small subsets of the WTO membership. There are four such agreements: government procurement, civil aircraft, dairy and bovine meat.

9. It should also be noted that it is not only the dispute cases of the WTO system that have important strategic implications for corporations. Other aspects of the system, which are outside the scope of this chapter, are also important in this respect.

10. It is nevertheless important to note that WTO dispute cases do differ fundamentally from the disputes between corporations as investors and host governments, i.e. the types of disputes that are familiar in international law concerning the treatment and protection of investors. These disputes may involve such public institutional arrangements as the Centre for the Settlement of International Investment Disputes (ICSID) at the World Bank, or private arbitration organizations such as the International Chamber of Commerce (ICC), or London Court of International Arbitration (LCIA), and involve rules such as those of the United Nations Commission on International Trade Arbitration Law (UNCITRAL). However, those disputes are between investors and governments about particular corporate international investment projects, while the WTO disputes are between governments about government policies concerning trade and/or investment and/or intellectual property – disputes which may or may not stem from corporation specific cases.

11. The authors are developing and updating periodically a data set of more than a hundred variables on all WTO dispute cases.

12. This and other cases established that TRIMs violated already existing GATT national treatment provisions and that the TRIMs agreement is in that sense superfluous.

13. There were significantly different implications for General Motors and Ford, on the one hand, and Chrysler, on the other, because of differences in their strategies for serving the Brazilian market. Whereas the former already had engaged in direct investment in Brazil, the latter was serving the market by exporting from the USA. Because the former had already met the Brazilian TRIMs' requirements and thus were granted relatively low tariff levels for the parts and additional vehicles that they imported, the latter faced much higher tariffs because it did not have facilities in Brazil.

14. These trends are at least apparent among the US-based corporations whose Washington, DC offices were interviewed for a companion study (Young and Brewer, in progress).

REFERENCES

Baron, David P. (1997), 'Integrated strategy, trade policy, and global competition', *California Management Review*, **39**, 145–69.

Brewer, Thomas L. and Stephen Young (1998), *The Multilateral Investment System and Multinational Enterprises*, Oxford: Oxford University Press.

Burtless, Gary, Robert Z. Lawrence, Robert E. Litan and Robert J. Shapiro (1998), *Globaphobia: Confronting Fears about Open Trade*, Washington, DC: Brookings Institution.

Croome, John (1995), *Reshaping the World Trading System*, Geneva: World Trade Organization.

Dunning, John H. (ed.) (1997), *Governments, Globalization and International Business*, Oxford: Oxford University Press.

Economist Intelligence Unit (EIU) (1995), *The EIU Guide to the New GATT*, London: EIU.

Doz, Yves (1986), *Strategic Management in Multinational Companies*, Oxford: Pergamon.

Graham, Edward M. and Robert Z. Lawrence (1996), 'Measuring the international contestability of markets', *Journal of World Trade*, **30** (5), 5–20.

Hoekman, Bernard M. and Michael M. Kostecki (1995), *The Political Economy of the World Trading System*, New York: Oxford University Press.

Hood, Neil and Stephen Young (eds) (1999), *The Globalization of Multinational Enterprise Activity and Economic Development*, London: Macmillan and New York: St. Martin's Press.

The International Lawyer (1998), Special Issue, 'First three years of the WTO dispute settlement system', fall.

International Trade Centre UNCTAD/WTO and Commonwealth Secretariat (1996), *Business Guide to the Uruguay Round*, Geneva: ITC/CS.

Jackson, John H. (1998), 'Designing and Implementing Effective Dispute Settlement Procedures: WTO Dispute Settlement, Appraisal and Prospects', in Anne O. Krueger, (ed.), *The WTO as an International Organization*, Chicago: The University of Chicago Press, pp. 161–80.

Julius, DeAnne (1994), 'International Direct Investment: Strengthening the Policy Regime', in Peter B. Kenen (ed.), *Managing the World Economy*, Washington, DC: Institute for International Economics, pp. 269–86.

Krueger, Anne O. (ed.) (1998), *The WTO as an International Organization*, Chicago and London: University of Chicago Press.

Makhija, Mona V., Kwansoo Kim and Sandra D. Williamson (1997), 'Measuring globalization of industries using a national industry approach: empirical evidence across five countries and over time', Journal of International Business Studies, **28** (4), 679–710.

Nollen, Stanley D. and Thomas L. Brewer (in progress), 'Knowledge Transfer by International Firms: Responses to Government Policy Liberalizations'.

Oxelheim, Lars and Thomas L. Brewer (in progress), 'Implications of the WTO General Agreement on Trade in Services for the Nordic-EU Economies'.

Petersmann, E.-U. (1997), *The GATT/WTO Dispute Settlement System*, London: Kluwer Law International.

Rugman, Alan M. and Alain Verbeke (1998), *Global Corporate Strategy and Trade Policy*, London: Routledge.

Sauve, Pierre (1994), 'A first look at investment in the final act of the Uruguay Round', *Journal of World Trade*, **28** (5), 5–16.

Shoyer, Andrew W. (1998), 'The first three years of WTO dispute settlement: observations and suggestions', *Journal of International Economic Law*, **1**, 277–302.

United Nations Conference on Trade and Development (1995), *World Investment Report 1995: Transnational Corporations and Competitiveness*, New York and Geneva: UNCTAD.

United Nations Conference on Trade and Development (1996), *World Investment Report 1996: Investment, Trade and International Policy Arrangements*, New York and Geneva: UNCTAD.

United Nations Conference on Trade and Development (1998), *World Investment Report 1998: Trends and Determinants*, New York and Geneva: UNCTAD.

United States Trade Representative (1998), *1998 Trade Policy Agenda and 1997 Annual Report*, Washington, DC: US Government Printing Office.

Yip, George S. (1989), 'Global strategy in a world of nations', *Sloan Management Review*, **31** (1), 29–41.

Young, Stephen and Thomas L. Brewer (in progress), 'Global Corporate Strategies and the Evolving Trade and Investment Regime at the WTO'.

Weston, Max and Nancy F. Koehn (1996), 'The world sugar industry and Tate & Lyle', Harvard Business School, Case 9-794-119.

World Trade Organization (1996), *Annual Report 1996*, Geneva: WTO.

9. American macromanagement issues and policy

Joseph P. Daniels and John B. Davis

INTRODUCTION

Technological gains, advances in communications, and lower transportation costs, combined with trade liberalization efforts of post-war multilateral institutions, such as the General Agreement on Tariffs and Trade (GATT), the World Trade Organization (WTO) and the International Monetary Fund (IMF), as well as regional and unilateral actions, have increasingly opened nations to trade and capital flows creating a dynamic global market-place. Though liberalization has faced numerous obstacles and advanced at an uneven pace, it has advanced. As illustrated in Figure 9.1, over the last two decades world trade in goods and services has grown in excess of an annual average rate of 5

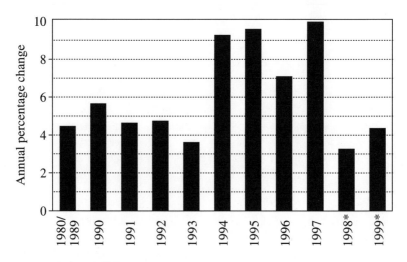

Note: * Projected, IMF.

Figure 9.1   Volume of world trade: goods and services, 1980/89–99

per cent. In the early 1990s, in spite of a US economy in recession and stagnant European economies, the volume of world trade increased at a rate of 3 per cent or more each year, and by the middle 1990s it approached double digits. Due to the Asian financial crises of 1997, projections for growth of world trade are much smaller than the actual rates of the middle 1990s, yet they still are positive and in excess of 3 per cent a year.

Even the United States, the largest individual economy, has become more dependent on and integrated with foreign markets. As pointed out by John Kirton in Chapter 2, this has occurred even though most Americans, 56 per cent versus 37 per cent according to a recent poll conducted by the Angus Reid Group (*The Economist*, 1999, and as cited by Kirton, Chapter 2), view protectionism over free trade as best for US prosperity. In Chapter 1, Figure 1.1, Pryor examines the extent of globalization of the US real sector using exports and imports as a per cent of GDP. Focusing on the evidence for the last two decades we see that, following the depreciation of the US dollar from its historic high valuation in 1985, imports relative to GDP have increased from approximately 10 per cent to over 13 per cent and exports relative to GDP have increased from approximately 7.25 per cent to 12 per cent. As we point out later in this chapter, however, this type of measure is likely to underestimate the extent of globalization as it masks the increased trade in intermediate goods and inputs that reflects companies' decisions to outsource increasing amounts of their production processes.

The increasing integration of the United States economy into the world economy at the end of the 20th century none the less needs to be understood in part within the context of US domestic economic policy issues. The USA, like Japan, combines a large domestic economy with a ratio of trade to GDP that is small compared to other OECD countries. This means that domestic economic issues are generally the primary concern of policy-makers, and that trade policy questions are often formulated in terms of domestic issues. This focus is sometimes overlooked on account of the strong commitment on the part of the USA since World War II to a liberal international trading order. But most individuals who come to play a role in US policy-making towards the international economy first spend years being involved in debates over domestic economic questions, and this later plays a role in framing their thinking about international economic policy.

In this chapter, we describe some of the macroeconomic challenges facing the American economy at the end of the 20th century that result from increasing globalization. We focus on issues that tend to reflect the special position of the USA in the world economy today, rather than issues shared with other OECD countries, in order to specifically describe how the American macroeconomy may differ from other countries and, therefore, how US macromanagement strategies differ. In particular, this chapter offers an examination of a specific concern in the issue areas of balance of payments and exchange rate management, monetary policy, fiscal policy and trade policy. Hence, the first of these issues are by nature macroeconomic in the usual sense of the term, while others are more microeconomic in nature. Our main example of the former concerns the inconsistent attention given to the exchange value of the dollar. Because the US government is able to finance deficit spending solely in dollars, US budget policy has often been carried out without attention to the consequences of changes in the dollar's value. We also consider the euro's challenge to US dollar hegemony and the spillover effects of US monetary policy.

Our main example of the latter concerns the relatively high degree of decentralization and flexible character of US labour markets. Though changes in US labour markets, specifically in regard to wage dispersion and inequality, may be largely caused by forces independent of globalization, they are none the less perceived by many people in the USA as being related to the integration of the USA into the world economy. Here, in contrast to a past policy of neglect towards the value of the dollar at the macro level, there may be a tendency for policy-makers to become preoccupied with the connection between trade and income. The intensity of the debate over NAFTA is an illustration of this. To the extent that falling wages for low-skilled workers requires trade adjustment assistance, there are implications for fiscal policy. Hence, fiscal solutions are necessary in order to avoid pressure to use second-best commercial policies.

In this chapter we thus examine four important economic challenges faced by US policy-makers that fit in the issue areas of balance-of-payment, exchange rate, monetary policy and fiscal policy management, and that result from globalization of the US economy. We begin in the next section by considering the implications of exchange rate movements for US industries and US balance-of-payments performance and then turn to the question of whether the USA ought to adopt a unified policy toward exchange rate management. The next section considers the issue of spill-over effects of US monetary policies on foreign economies, concentrating on the case of Mexico. The section after that examines the fiscal challenges that result from reduced seigniorage revenues due to the birth of the euro. The penultimate section turns from macro to micro, and considers the distribution of welfare gains from increased trade liberalization and the inequality of income resulting. The final section offers conclusions regarding the overall character and direction of American macromanagement in a period of increasing globalization.

CURRENT ACCOUNT AND THE VALUE OF THE DOLLAR

Randall Henning (1994) describes US exchange rate policy, in contrast to German and Japanese policy, as having been less consistent over time – evolving through cycles of neglect and activism – and less conscious of the competitive ramifications of currency valuation. Recently, US Secretary Robert Rubin's approach to exchange rate policy was described as 'intervening in currency markets rarely, but like a ton of bricks when he does' (Hirsh, 1997). Henning argues that in the United States, the private sector is 'fractionalized' and therefore is unable to communicate a clear preference for external monetary and exchange rate policy. If the private sector could demonstrate a clear preference on exchange rate policy, then that preference could anchor policy and lend it continuity.

Figure 9.2 illustrates the nominal and real effective exchange values (trade weighted) of the US dollar for the past two decades, and thus reveals the currency instability that results from inconsistent policies. From 1981 to 1985, the dollar made a remarkable run, reaching unprecedented highs in both nominal and real value. The cause of the rise was primarily a mismatch of domestic monetary and fiscal policies and a mismatch of US policies with its major trading partners. Monetary policy was tight in order to stamp out inflation and fiscal policy was loose, with tax cuts combined with structural deficits resulting from increased defence spending. Both actions caused nominal and real US interest rates to skyrocket, attracting foreign capital inflows and causing the dollar to appreciate.

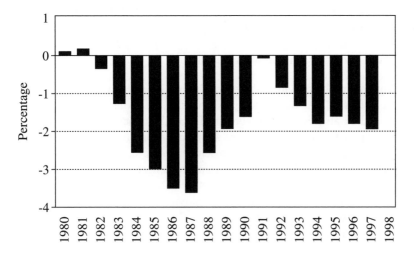

Figure 9.2   US current account balance, 1980–98 (% GDP)

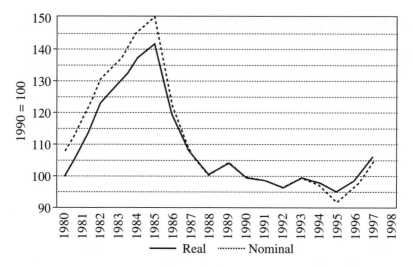

Figure 9.3   US dollar effective exchange value: nominal and real, 1980–98

As shown in Figure 9.3 the dollar appreciation reversed a modest surplus at the beginning of the 1980s and the current account deficit eventually widened to over 3.5 per cent of GDP in 1987 before declining following the depreciation of the dollar in 1987. The late 1980s to the mid-1990s was a period of general depreciation of the dollar and a decline of the US current account deficit, until 1992 when the deficit began to widen again.[1] With a strengthening US economy, the dollar began to appreciate again in the mid-1990s. The current account deficit widened as well, and was magnified by the collapse of the East Asian economies in late 1997.

Interpreting the Current Account Deficit

The principal problem with an appreciating dollar and a widening current account deficit is that they often lead to cries for protection from cheap imports and unfair pricing from abroad. Hence, the deficit provides political 'cover' for policy-makers who choose to pursue second-best policies of trade protection as opposed to less popular macroeconomic strategies. Higgins and Klitgaard (1998) argue, however, that from a macroeconomic perspective the mounting current account deficit need not necessarily mean lower employment levels overall. Lower domestic employment in specific sectors may indeed result from higher end-use imports. This, however, can be offset by the employment generated by the inflow of job-creating foreign capital into the United States. The evidence summarized by the authors indicates that US multinationals produce more than $500 billion in goods and services abroad annually rather than producing them in the United States. On the other hand, in 1997 alone the United States was the recipient of $255 billion in net investment inflows. In addition, the use of imported inputs may allow firms to shift their capacity from low profit margin operations at the front of the production process to higher profit margin operation nearer the end of the production process, thereby raising wages. This is evident in the steel industry where, during the 1980s, US firms reduced their capacity for manufacturing slab steel and increased their capacity for rolled finished steel products by relying on imported slab steel.

The relationship between a current account deficit and capital inflows can be better understood in terms of the national income and production accounts. By definition, the current account *CA* equals the sum of the gap between domestic private saving *S* and private domestic investment *I* and the gap between taxes *T* and government spending *G* – the fiscal balance $(T - G)$ – expressed as

$$CA = (S - I) + (T - G). \tag{9.1}$$

Additionally, domestic private saving is equivalent to the sum of private domestic investment spending, the fiscal balance, and the accumulation of foreign financial assets *FA*,

$$S = I + (G - T) + FA. \tag{9.2}$$

Combining the two equations, it is shown that the current account balance – which equals the difference between private and public savings and private investment spending – is equal to the accumulation of foreign assets,

$$CA = S + (T - G) - I = FA. \tag{9.3}$$

Hence, if private saving exceeds the sum of private investment spending and the fiscal deficit, a current account surplus results and the nation is accumulating foreign assets. If, on the other hand, domestic private saving does not match private domestic investment and the fiscal deficit, a current account deficit results and the nation borrows from abroad.

Currently, US private saving is not sufficient to meet desired domestic private investment, which is job creating. The fall in private saving and the rise in domestic private investment necessitates the inflow of foreign capital. As argued by Higgins and Klitgaard (1998, p. 4), therefore, the current account deficit can be viewed as 'a reflection of the need for foreign capital to sustain the economy'. By viewing the current account deficit as a macroeconomic outcome, we can conclude that, in general terms, policy-makers have two options in reducing the need for foreign capital inflows (other than reducing domestic private investment which would be undesirable): stimulate private saving and/or reduce the fiscal deficit. In the United States actions have been taken in both areas. The deficit has been reduced and it appears a true surplus may result for the next fiscal year. Policy actions to increase domestic saving, however, have been unsuccessful. For the third quarter of 1998, the US personal saving rate turned negative for the first time since the 1930s and, according to calculations by J.P. Morgan, the private saving rate has declined to its lowest level ever, with investment and consumption spending exceeding income by more than 4 per cent of GDP (*The Economist*, 1998). Obviously further attention by economists and policy-makers is needed in this area.

Because the current account deficit is large and persistent, it implies very large levels of debt. Large levels of foreign debt may affect the creditworthiness of a nation and impinge on its ability to finance investment via international capital markets. According to Humpage (1998, p. 2) 'the mere existence of these debts indicates neither profligacy nor an unstable situation'. What is important is whether a nation can service its debt. By the mid-1990s, the level of net international debt as a share of GDP for the United States was the third largest of all the G7 economies, yet US international debt only amounts to 16 per cent of GDP. Humpage concludes, therefore, that under current circumstances the United states could remain a net debtor forever.

In addition to the creditworthiness issues, large levels of foreign debt, in the long run, may mean either a reduced standard of living for future generations who have to repay the debt, or an increased standard of living if the capital inflows are invested in a manner that spurs future productivity gains. What is important here is whether the foreign capital inflows finance current consumption or investment. One way of determining this is to see if investment spending has increased with the capital inflows. In an early study of this issue, Faust (1989) claims that investment spending was unchanged during the 1980s. Based on more recent data though, Hakkio (1995) argues that US investment spending actually declined after 1992. Hence, the impact of the large and persistent current account deficits on future living standards remains somewhat unclear and yet the employment consequences appear to be less than desirable.

Industry Level Effects of Exchange Rate Movements

Henning's hypothesis on the fractionalization of American businesses in regard to currency valuation is perhaps best explained by the uneven effects of currency movements on profit and performance across industries and firms. The effects of currency movements on profitability and performance depend upon the degree of globalization of a particular industry. The typical measure of the extent of industry openness is the total of import and export sales as a per cent of domestic production (import plus export revenue divided by domestic production revenues). This particular measure, however, only considers the revenue and market share aspects of currency movements. As argued by Campa and Goldberg (1997), foreign shocks that impinge upon a domestic industry because of that industry's dependence on export sales and exposure to import competition can be offset in part by the use of imported inputs in the domestic production process. In other words, the effect on revenues may be offset by lower costs of imported inputs. The importance of intra-industry trade is incorporated in the creative approach to measuring globalization by Makhija and Williamson, Chapter 5 in this volume.

Campa and Goldberg calculate four different measures to determine the extent of globalization and 'external orientation' of an industry, that is, the degree to which an industry may be affected by foreign shocks, such as a dramatic currency swing. The authors' four measures, provided in Table 9.1, are: export share, the ratio of industry export revenues to industry shipments; import share, the ratio of imports to consumption; imported input share, imported inputs as a share of the value of production; and net external orientation, the difference between industry export share and imported input share. The measures, provided for 20 industry classifications, show that some industries, such as industrial machinery and instruments and related products, can be adversely affected by a dollar appreciation as they rely heavily on export revenues as indicated by a high export share. Industries such as leather products, petroleum products and printing and publishing are likely to benefit from a dollar appreciation as their export share is low relative to their use of imported inputs. Still others yet, such as transportation equipment and primary metal products, are likely to be little affected even though their export share is relatively high. This is because their imported input share is high as well and a dollar appreciation will lower the cost of imported inputs and offset the lower export revenues.

Subsequent empirical work by Goldberg and Crockett (1998) shows that producer profits and investment spending are likely to be hurt by a dollar appreciation in industries where the measure of external orientation is high. In regard to wages, the 1995 dollar appreciation constrained wages considerably in the chemicals, industrial machinery, electronic equipment and instruments industries: four of five industries with the highest net external orientation measures. The authors also find that in the mid-1980s – when the net orientation for US manufacturing was less than 2 per cent – a 10 per cent rise in the value of the dollar resulted in a 2.4 per cent average decline in the investment rate of manufacturing industries while in 1995 – when the net

Table 9.1 *External orientation*

Category	Export share	Import share	Imported input share	External orientation	Industry integration
Food and kindred products	5.9	4.2	4.2	1.7	10.1
Tobacco products	14.9	0.6	2.1	12.8	17
Textile mill products	7.6	9.1	7.3	0.3	14.9
Apparel and other textiles	7.4	31.4	3.2	4.2	10.6
Lumber and wood products	7.6	10.3	4.3	3.3	11.9
Furniture and fixtures	5.5	14.1	5.7	-0.2	11.2
Paper and allied products	9	10	6.3	2.7	15.3
Printing and publishing	2.4	1.6	3.5	-1.1	5.9
Chemicals and allied products	15.8	11	6.3	9.5	22.1
Petroleum and coal products	3.9	5.7	5.3	-1.4	9.2
Rubber and miscellaneous products	9.2	12.8	5.3	3.9	14.5
Leather and leather products	14.4	59.5	20.5	-6.1	34.9
Stone, clay and glass products	5.6	9.5	4.7	0.9	10.3
Primary metal products	11.2	17.4	10.6	0.6	21.8
Fabricated metal products	7.9	8.5	8.7	-0.8	16.6
Industrial machinery and equipment	25.8	27.8	11	14.8	36.8
Electronic and other electric equipment	24.2	32.5	11.6	12.6	35.8
Transportation equipment	17.8	24.3	15.7	2.1	33.5
Instruments and related products	21.3	20.1	6.3	15	27.6
Other manufacturing	13.5	41.1	9.9	3.6	23.4
Total manufacturing	13.4	16.3	8.2	5.2	21.6

Source: Campa and Goldberg (1997).

orientation rate exceeded 5 per cent – the same appreciation resulted in a 6 per cent drop in investment spending.

The measures of Campa and Goldberg can also be used to show the increasing dependence of US industries on the foreign markets. Figure 9.4 charts the changes in the four measures and a measure of our own, which we label *industry integration*. This last measure adds the export share and imported input share to show the overall, as opposed to net, orientation of US manufacturing industries. Hence, it intends to show the extent of globalization of US manufacturers. Over the three sample periods the measure of industry integration rose 73 per cent, from 12.5 per cent to 21.6 per cent. For all of the measures, the only decline over the entire period is the decline in the export share during the dramatic dollar appreciation of 1985. None the less, the export share has increased by 60 per cent over the last three decades.

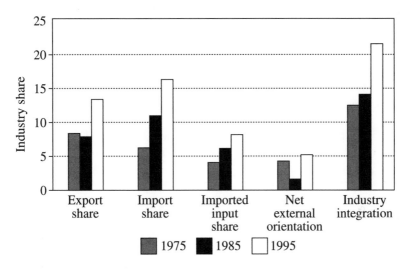

Figure 9.4   Globalization of US industries

As is also shown in Figure 9.4, the large increase in the export share over the last three decades generated a 21 per cent increase in the net external orientation measure. This is of importance because it means that US manufacturing industries are becoming more sensitive to dollar appreciations. This implies that for most industries when the dollar appreciates, export revenue losses will exceed input cost savings. Hence, exchange rate policy has become more important and US industries should express their concerns and preferences for a stable dollar policy.

SPILLOVER EFFECTS OF US MONETARY POLICY

The previous section concluded with evidence of the increasing globalization of US industries. As the US economy becomes increasingly more integrated with foreign economies, and as developing and emerging economies continue to manage their currency values relative to the US dollar, channels for spillover effects of US exchange rate and monetary policies on foreign economies are strengthened. Monetary policy actions, therefore, can affect the exchange and interest rates of trading partners and investor attitudes towards these economies. Hence, the macroeconomic and financial situations of strategically important partners must be considered.

It is reported that the Federal Reserve was inclined to increase interest rates in late 1997, but decided against it because of the fear that it would further destabilize international markets (Obstfeld, 1998). More recently Argentina has floated the notion of dollarization of their economy. In regard to this, the *Wall Street Journal* (18 January 1999, p. A1) reported that it 'doesn't much matter to the Fed, given that it already has to worry about the international ramifications of anything it does'. It does not appear, however, that the Federal Reserve was as cognizant of the international dimensions of its actions in 1994. In this section we consider an example of the importance of these international dimensions: the 1994 collapse of the Mexican peso.

From 1992 through the first quarter of 1994, Mexico enjoyed rather robust international investment flows to its economy. During 1994, however, Mexico endured a political assassination, the Chiapas uprising and a burgeoning deficit. As if that were not enough, as investors became nervous about the political and economic environment the US Federal Reserve acted to pre-empt domestic inflation by raising interest rates. To the surprise of many market participants (Federal Reserve Bank of New York *Annual Report*, p. 16), the Fed increased the Fed Funds Rate by 2.5 percentage points and the discount rate by 1.75 percentage points over the course of the year. As capital flows reversed, Mexican authorities acted to maintain the crawling peg exchange rate arrangement that was in place at the time. Reserves were quickly drawn down and a devaluation was attempted in December 1994. A complete loss of confidence in the peso caused the arrangement to be abandoned in favour of a floating rate system.

A number of empirical studies have concluded that US interest rates have a significant, perhaps even greater than one-to-one, impact on emerging markets (see Frankel and Okongwu, 1995, for a summary of the evidence). Figure 9.5 attempts to illustrate the impact of US interest rate increases on the Mexican exchange rate arrangement. (It is impossible to separate the political assassination with the second interest rate increase as they differ by

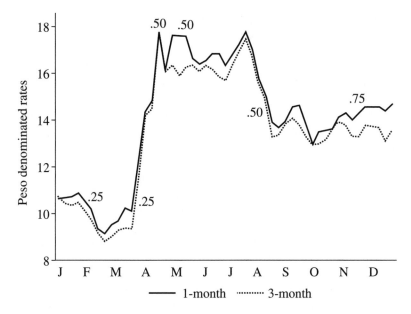

Figure 9.5   1-month and 3-month interest rates: Mexico, 1994

a single day.) Figure 9.5 plots the one-month and three-month rates on peso-denominated government debt and marks the date and size of increases in the Federal Funds Rate. As seen in the figure, there is, in general, an associated increase in Mexican interest rates or sustained high rates following an increase in the Federal Funds rate.

Given the political and economic costs associated with the bail-out monies provided to Mexico in 1995, the Fed and the Treasury have become much more aware of the international dimensions of their actions. The question then becomes: what does this additional responsibility mean for policy-making? Surely it must bring greater stability to the deliberative policy process, not less stability. Further, the potential for policy cooperation and coordination must be considered. Currently the views of the Federal Reserve and the US Treasury revealed in responses to a proposed target zone arrangement for the euro, dollar and yen, and the consideration of dollarizing developing economies, indicate that the United States will encourage cooperation and consultation but not coordination of policies.

THE EURO: CHALLENGE TO US DOLLAR HEGEMONY
AND SEIGNIORAGE REVENUES

Another linkage between US fiscal policy and the unique position of the dollar is that of seigniorage. Along with the launch of the euro in January 1999, much speculation has been offered in regard to the challenge to the US dollar hegemony. To be sure, many of the wishes for euro supremacy are political in nature. If the euro does challenge the international use of the dollar, there are economic ramifications as well. In particular, a government that issues fiat money earns seigniorage revenues: that is, the government profits on the difference between the market value of the currency and the cost of actually issuing the currency. There are two principle ways that a government can generate seigniorage revenues: by printing money and by inflating the economy. For the United States, only the first is relevant today.

It is indeed true that seigniorage revenues are a small portion – approximately 3 per cent of overall federal government revenues. None the less, the US Treasury estimates that annual seigniorage revenues for the United States are between \$13 and \$16 billion a year. A currency that could challenge dollar hegemony could therefore reduce these sizable seigniorage revenues.

Tavlas (1998) provides the most recent survey data on the international uses of currencies. The data, as shown in Table 9.2, compares the US economy and uses of the dollar with all 15 EU members in aggregate. Though the two economies are relatively the same in terms of share of world GDP and share of world exports, the dollar is dominant in terms of its use as a vehicle currency (use in world trade), in developing country debt and as a reserve currency. Though the European currencies represent three times the turnover of the dollar in foreign exchange markets, the dollar is still the dominant single currency and turns over more than twice that of the next currency, the Deutsche Mark.

If the euro were to replace all EU member country currencies overnight, it still would not be a considerable rival to the dollar in international markets. Tavlas argues, however, that with time the euro will be more stable than any individual European currency as it will denominate all inter-EU trade, European financial markets will deepen and more euro-denominated assets will be issued and the European Central Bank will likely establish its own anti-inflation credentials. Hence, the euro will be needed to properly diversify portfolios and may offer an alternative safe-haven currency. In a static environment, it is likely, therefore, that the euro will challenge dollar hegemony in time. As the proposed dollarization of Argentina shows, however, the world is dynamic and not static, and the importance of the dollar is growing in other areas of the world, not shrinking.

Table 9.2   United States and European Union: relative size and use of currencies (%)

	United States	European Union
Economic size		
Share of World GDP, 1996	20.7	20.4
Share of World Exports, 1996	15.2	14.7
Use of currencies		
World Trade, 1995	51.0	31.0
International Bond Offerings, Sept. 1997	45.1	41.9
Developing Country Debt, year-end 1996	50.2	15.8
Global Foreign Exchange Reserves, year-end 1996	63.7	19.5
Foreign Exchange Transactions, April 1995	11.5	35.0

Source: Tavlas (1998).

GLOBALIZATION AND WAGE INEQUALITY

A domestic economic issue particularly central to US experience that has gained greater attention in the 1990s is the issue of income inequality and globalization. The central question is whether increasing trade integration causes or is exacerbating income inequality in the USA. That real income – or wage – inequality has increased since the 1970s and especially the 1980s is clear (Gottschalk, 1997). Increased income inequality in the USA is currently understood largely in terms of increased wage inequality, since it is difficult to model the processes leading to changes in the distribution of family income, and since labour economists have well-developed tools with which to analyse changes in the relative demand and supply of low and less skilled labour. Thus among the results of recent research is that changes in mean wage differences between education groups, as reflected in the high school–college premium, and between experience groups explain much of recent increased inequality. The standard interpretation is that labour market forces are driving up the price of skills, adversely affecting high school graduates and those individuals less insulated from market forces by seniority or union coverage. This consequent relative decline in the demand for low and less skilled labour relative to skilled labour has undermined both employment and wages of the former.

Note that this issue particularly confronts the USA on account of generally greater wage flexibility in its labour markets as compared to most other

OECD countries – with the possible exception of Canada and the UK (Gottschalk and Smeeding, 1997). Most OECD countries have more central-ized wage-setting institutions that have permitted them to escape or moderate worldwide trends toward greater income inequality. In addition, they have also relied in recent years more than the USA on tax and transfer systems to offset changes in labour market outcomes where these did tend to produce substantial increases in earnings inequality. This difference indicates that the issue of wage and income inequality not only places special burdens on the USA *vis-à-vis* its primary trading partners, but especially does so if an impor-tant source of this inequality is understood by the public to be the increased global integration of the American economy.

Globalization and Wage Inequality: the Evidence

In fact, it is probably not the case that the principal cause of this development is increased integration of the US economy through trade. Most research indicates that technological change in the USA since the 1980s has been biased against low-skilled workers, boosting the productivity and wages of the better educated, and that trade has been at best a secondary cause of increased wage inequality (see, for example, Johnson, 1997). Thus in ad-dressing the possible impact of trade on wage and income inequality the research of Lawrence and Slaughter (1993) and Berman et al. (1994) pro-ceeds on the assumption that declines in employment and wages for low-skilled workers are due to within-industry shifts in labour demand due to changes in technology, and that trade operates on inequality only indirectly through between-industry shifts in labour demand. This view that trade plays a lesser role is consistent with the fact that the level of merchandise trade relative to GDP is not high for the USA relative to other industrialized countries.

There are good reasons, however, for thinking that this measure of trade integration may not fully explain the effects of globalization on US employ-ment and wages. First, the rising share of services in GDP and in trade suggests the need for caution in relying on the merchandise share, particu-larly since trade in services seems to favour higher skilled workers. Second, focusing on the final goods share masks increased trade in intermediate goods and inputs which reflects companies' decisions to outsource increasing amounts of their production processes to take advantage of low-wage labour in other countries. In this case, international trade not only affects labour demand through inter-industry shifts, but trade also affects demand for labour within industries as well, so that globalization arguably plays a more impor-tant role than previously thought. We emphasize this latter issue here, since most critics of the idea that increased openness of the US economy is respon-sible for increased income inequality cite the size of the tradeable goods sector as simply being too small to have an impact (for example, Johnson, 1997).[2]

Outsourcing may be generally understood as the disintegration of the traditional vertically integrated production process, such as characterized Fordist development of manufacturing in the USA in the 20th century, through an increased outsourcing that combines manufacturing or service activities done abroad with those done domestically. In response to opportunities for low-cost production across countries, intermediate inputs may cross borders multiple times before they are marketed as final goods. An important dimension of this process is that independent firms may produce, sell and resell intermediate inputs before final goods emerge under corporate brand names sold in the USA. Thus while the final goods producer with consumer brand name identification and developed marketing structures ends up being responsible for a lengthy, cross-nation, cross-firm 'value chain', it does so by relying on contractual arrangements with independent firms in production locations around the world to increase its flexibility and enhance profitability.

One problem with gaining a better understanding of trade in intermediate inputs is in finding a measure of outsourcing. The strategy of Lawrence (1994) and Krugman (1995) is to focus on multinational firms, the former using imports of US multinationals as a measure of outsourcing, and the latter arguing in terms of flows of foreign direct investment through multinational firms. But a focus on the internal operations of multinational firms alone is not likely to provide a broad enough perspective on outsourcing to be representative of the general situation for the American economy, since outsourcing may involve independent companies selling and reselling semi-finished goods in a larger overall 'value chain'. Feenstra (1998, p. 36) consequently adopts a more general definition of outsourcing that 'in addition to imports specifically by US multinationals, includes all imported intermediate or final goods that are used in the production of an American firm, or sold under its brand name'.

To construct a data series that reflects the full range of industries and activities included within outsourcing, Feenstra (1998) follows Irwin (1996) in examining what has happened to the composition of US trade using Bureau of Economic Analysis 'end-use' categories that assign goods by purchasers rather than production processes, and this is provided in Table 9.3 below. As shown in Table 9.3, across five major categories in which the bulk of trade has historically occurred, the record shows the USA shifting away from agriculture and raw materials and toward manufactured goods. Particularly significant is the fact that the share of capital plus consumer goods together have increased from 10 per cent of imports and 15 per cent of exports in 1925 to over 50 per cent in 1990. This suggests that what may be termed processed manufactured goods (some of which are sold directly to consumers and some

Table 9.3   Shares of US exports and imports by end-use categories (%)

Category		1925	1950	1965	1980	1995
Foods, feeds and	Imports	21.9	30.0	19.1	11.3	5.0
beverages	Exports	18.7	15.5	19.2	16.9	9.2
Industrial supplies and	Imports	68.2	62.4	53.3	31.3	18.2
materials	Exports	59.8	45.5	34.8	32.2	25.6
Capital goods (except	Imports	0.4	1.3	7.1	19.0	33.6
autos)	Exports	8.7	22.4	31.4	35.0	42.4
Consumer goods	Imports	9.4	6.1	16.0	21.5	24.3
(except autos)	Exports	6.0	8.9	7.0	7.8	11.7
Automotive vehicles	Imports	0.02	0.3	4.5	16.9	18.9
and parts	Exports	6.8	7.8	7.5	8.1	11.2

Source: Feenstra (1998).

of which will receive additional value added by American firms) now play an increasingly important role in US trade, and that more products are being imported into the USA at various stages of processing.

To further investigate this hypothesis, Feenstra and Hanson (1997) consider the ratio of imported to domestic intermediate inputs for US manufacturing industries, and find that imported inputs have increased from 5.7 per cent of total intermediate purchases in 1972 to 13.9 per cent in 1990. Similar calculations by Campa and Goldberg (1997) for Canada, Japan, the UK and the USA show a doubling of the share of imported inputs for the USA between 1975 and 1995 for all manufacturing. Hummels et al. (1997), who use the term 'vertical specialization' to describe a country's specialization in particular segments of the value chain, also find the USA to have higher values of vertical specialization in 1990 as compared to 1970.

Policy Implications

Further research on the impact of outsourcing on wages still needs to be done, but there is enough evidence to suggest that outsourcing may contribute to a reduction in relative demand for low-skilled labour in developed countries beyond what trade in final goods contributes. How important, then, is this connection between globalization and wage inequality? Perhaps representative of the general view on the effects of trade *per se* is Richardson (1995, p. 51): 'My own reading of this research is that trade is a moderate contributing source of income inequality trends; it may not overshadow other sources, but it cannot be shrugged away.' Taken together with the additional impact of outsourcing, this suggests that Americans are likely to place pressure on policy-makers to somehow protect those affected adversely by increasing integration. But the situation is more complicated. Recognizing that those production activities lost by more developed countries are typically gained by less developed countries, and that outsourced activities are low skilled, labour intensive for developed countries and high skilled, labour intensive for developing countries, we see that outsourcing raises the average skill-intensity of production in both locations, and assists the general tendency toward factor price equalization with respect to wages between developed and developing countries that trade in final goods involves. Thus, lying in the balance for policy-makers with increasing US wage inequality is the prospect of increasing wage equality in low-income US trading partners. Were this to help move developing economies towards the size of developed economies, according to the arguments of Hummels and Levinsohn (1995), we might expect an even faster growth of world trade with the prospect of rapidly increasing gains from trade. These possibilities suggest that policy-makers will be disinclined to adopt second-best initiatives that attempt to 'tame trade', and will rather favour 'first-best' strategies for compensating those possibly affected by the economy's greater openness.[3]

In welfare and efficiency terms, this might first be formulated in terms of Corden's (1997) 'conservative social welfare function' that precludes significant reductions in real income of important sections of the community through trade adjustment assistance directly targeted on those adversely affected by increasing trade integration. Using a labour economics perspective, a long-run strategy to offset the reduction in demand for low-skilled workers through a parallel reduction in their supply is for government action to improve education and training. In the short run, subsidies to boost living standards of workers who take low-paying jobs may take the form of tax cuts, cash supplements to wages, improved public services and subsidies to employers to hire workers in non-traded services (Wood, 1994). An important problem is that in either case these policies in the USA would impose fiscal burdens at the federal level precisely at a time when federal budgets are being reduced rather than expanded, and when the majority of citizens are most concerned about anticipated funding shortfalls for social security and medicare. Indeed, from an intergenerational perspective on budgets rather than the traditional annual one normally taken, the fiscal liability for future social security and medicare benefits place the budget in deficit through the current 10 year projections.[4] Thus, the USA appears to be operating with a federal 'budget constraint' that makes significant trade adjustment assistance unlikely, and one cannot consequently rule out the possibility that political pressures may build for protection.

But might trade adjustment assistance somehow pay for itself? Phelps (1997) has recently argued that a wage subsidy directed at low-skilled workers might pay for itself through savings on social expenditures and increased tax revenues. Rather than revenue-neutral, such subsidies might be 'revenue-positive', and actually help the USA address its future fiscal imbalance. More research needs to be done to demonstrate the viability of this strategy if the USA is to resist popular demands for protecting low-skilled workers.

CONCLUSIONS

Here we offer three broad conclusions about the nature and direction of American macromanagement in a period of globalization. First, it is important to be aware of how the size and relative autonomy of the American economy tends to narrow the focus of policy-makers on domestic concerns. With respect to exchange rate and monetary policy, this is manifest in a not-always benign neglect toward the impact of managing the value of the dollar on both domestic business and foreign economies. At the opposite extreme is a perhaps too strong concern with addressing wage inequality. In a society accustomed to thinking in domestic terms, the tendency to focus strictly on the American side of trade in the form of increasing wage dispersion pushes the experience in developing economies, their decreasing wage dispersion and possible increased gain from trade, out of view.

Second, it is important to remember that the policy-making process always reflects a political balancing of competing interests, so that what may be the most rational policy in any given circumstance is less the point than what reconciling competing interests may achieve. Our argument in this connection is that having a unified exchange rate and monetary policy has been hobbled by the inability of competing interests to reach agreement about the value of the dollar. But the fractionalization of business interests, together with an increasing awareness of the effects on other countries of US policy, may now lead the USA toward a more consistent strategy towards the dollar, and one, moreover, that attempts to stabilize its value along with stabilizing prices.

Third, our view is that first-best, non-protectionist policy that targets particular problems directly, as would wage subsidies for low-skilled workers, remains a consensus view among US policy-makers. This is not to say that protectionist thinking does not represent a danger in the USA. Rather it is to say that protectionist thinking is largely confined to industries, firms and sectors of the population interested in their own case alone, and does not constitute a view of the best interest of the country as a whole. Of course, enough voices adversely affected by trade in some circumstances can together constitute a majority. Whether this is prevented from happening may depend in part on the success of trade adjustment policies that pay for themselves in a period of constrained fiscal budgets.

NOTES

1. The relatively small current account deficit of 1991 reflects a surplus in the unilateral transfers category that resulted from receipts from Gulf War allies.
2. Another approach for estimating the effects of trade on labour markets, and thus showing a link between globalization and wage inequality, is the factor content approach used by Wood (1994). See Leamer (1994) for a critique of Wood's results.
3. For a minority view favouring protection and trade barriers see Batra (1993). For an intermediate view recommending moderating the pace of globalization, see Rodrik (1997).
4. In particular, it has been estimated that social security benefits promised to the working population today may exceed the taxes this population will pay for these benefits by seven to ten trillion dollars in present value terms (Feldstein, 1998).

REFERENCES

Batra, Ravi (1993), *The Myth of Free Trade*, New York: Scribner.

Berman, Eli, John Bound and Zvi Griliches (1994), 'Changes in the demand for skilled labor within U.S. manufacturing: evidence from the annual survey of manufacturers', *Quarterly Journal of Economics*, **109** (2), 367–98.

Campa, José and Linda Goldberg (1997), 'The evolving external orientation of manufacturing: a profile of four countries', Federal Reserve Bank of New York, *Economic Policy Review*, July, 53–81.

Corden, Max (1997), *Trade Policy and Economic Welfare*, 2nd edition, Oxford: Clarendon Press.

The Economist (1998), 'Saving disgrace', 14 November, 80.

The Economist (1999), 'Liberalism lives', 2 January, 59–60.

Faust, Jon (1989), 'U.S. foreign indebtedness: are we investing what we borrow?', Federal Reserve Bank of Kansas City, *Economic Review*, July, 3–20.

Federal Reserve Bank of New York (1994), *Annual Review*.

Feenstra, Ronald (1998), 'Integration of trade and disintegration of production in the global economy', *Journal of Economic Perspectives*, **12** (4), 31–50.

Feenstra, Ronald and Gordon Hanson (1997), 'Foreign Investment, Outsourcing and Relative Wages', in R.C. Feenstra, G.M. Grossman and D.A. Irwin (eds), *The Political Economy of Trade Policy: Papers in Honor of Jagdish Bhagwati*, Cambridge, MA: MIT Press.

Feldstein, Martin (1998), *Privatizing Social Security*, Chicago: University of Chicago Press.

Frankel, Jeffrey and Chudozie Okongwu (1995), 'Liberalized portfolio capital inflows in emerging markets: sterilization, expectations, and the incompleteness of interest rate convergence', *International Journal of Finance and Economics*, VI, 1–23.

Goldberg, Linda and Keith Crockett (1998), 'The dollar and U.S. manufacturing', Federal Reserve Bank of New York, *Current Issues in Economics and Finance*, **4** (12).

Gottschalk, Peter (1997), 'Inequality, income growth, and mobility: the basic facts', *Journal of Economic Perspectives*, **11** (2), 21–40.

Gottschalk, Peter and Timothy M. Smeeding (1997), 'Cross-national comparisons of earnings and income inequality', *Journal of Economic Literature*, **35** (2), 633–87.

Hakkio, Craig (1995), 'The U.S. current account: the other deficit', Federal Reserve Bank of Kansas City, *Economic Review*, Third Quarter, 11–24.

Henning, Randall (1994), *Currencies and Politics in the United States, Germany, and Japan*, Washington, DC: Institute for International Economics.

Higgins, Matthew and Thomas Klitgaard (1998), 'Viewing the current account deficit as a capital inflow', *Current Issues in Economics and Finance*, Federal Reserve Bank of New York, **4** (13), December.

Hirsh, Michael (1997), 'Looking Upward', *Newsweek*, 23 June, 12–16.

Hummels, David and James A. Levinsohn (1995), 'Monopolistic competition and international trade: reconsidering the evidence', *Quarterly Journal of Economics*, **110** (3), 799–836.

Hummels, David, Dana Rapoport and Kei-Mu Yi (1997), 'Globalization and the Changing Nature of World Trade', University of Chicago, Federal Reserve Bank of New York and Rice University.

Humpage, Owen (1998), 'Is the current account deficit sustainable?', *Economic Commentary*, Federal Reserve Bank of Cleveland, 15 October.

Irwin, Douglas (1996), 'The United States in a new world economy? A century's perspective', *American Economic Review*, **86** (2), 41–51.

Johnson, George E. (1997), 'Changes in earnings inequality: the role of demand shifts', *Journal of Economic Perspectives*, **11** (2), 41–54.

Krugman, Paul (1995), 'Growing world trade: causes and consequences', *Brookings Papers on Economic Activity*, **1**, 327–62.

Lawrence, Robert (1994), 'Trade, Multinationals and Labour', in Philip Lowe and Jacqueline Dwyer (eds), *International Integration of the Australian Economy*, Sydney: Reserve Bank of Australia, pp. 23–65.

Lawrence, Robert Z. and Matthew J. Slaughter (1993), 'International Trade and American Wages in the 1980s: Giant Sucking Sound or Small Hiccup?', *Brookings Papers on Economic Activity: Microeconomics*, pp. 161–226.

Learner, Edward E. (1994), 'Trade, Wages and Revolving-Door Ideas', NBER Working Paper no. 4716.

Obstfeld, Maurice (1998), 'The Global Capital Market: Benefactor or Menace?', *Journal of Economic Perspectives*, **12** (4), 9–30.

Phelps, Edmund (1997), *Rewarding Work*, Cambridge, MA: Harvard University Press.

Richardson, J. David (1995), 'Income inequality and trade: how to think, what to conclude', *Journal of Economic Perspectives*, **9** (3), 33–55.

Rodrik, Dani (1997), *Has Globalization Gone Too Far?*, Washington, DC: Institute for International Economics.

Tavlas, George (1998), 'The international use of currencies: the U.S. dollar and the euro', *Finance and Development*, **35** (2), June.

The Wall Street Journal (1999), 'Argentina considers a radical peso defense: use dollars instead', 18 January, p. A1.

Wood, Adrian (1994), *North–South Trade, Employment and Inequality: Changing Fortunes in a Skill-Driven World*, Oxford: Clarendon Press.

10. Regional trade agreements[1]

Ronald J. Wonnacott

INTRODUCTION

Following World War II, US trade policy was based on a single-track commitment to multilateral liberalization in the GATT (General Agreement on Tariffs and Trade). With all countries participating in the reduction in trade barriers, this was quite different from the Europeans' two-track commitment – not only to GATT liberalization but also to regional liberalization in their Common Market (now the EU, the European Union). However, since the 1989 Canada–US Free Trade Area, US policy has also been set on a two-track course of both multilateral liberalization in the GATT – now the World Trade Organization (WTO) – and regional initiatives covering a narrower subset of countries.[2] The North American Free Trade Agreement (NAFTA) defines the extent to date of this initiative although the US administration has been attempting – so far unsuccessfully – to extend this to a Free Trade Area of the Americas (FTAA).

This chapter sets out the simple economic theory of regional agreements: what a policy-maker should know before embarking on such an initiative. As such agreements multiply, it is essential to have a clear background frame of reference for what a regional FTA (Free Trade Agreement) does and does not do. What are the benefits and costs to its members and outsiders? How should any FTA, such as the intended FTAA, be designed to act as a building block rather than stumbling block in multilateral WTO liberalization? What economic complications arise if a second major regional initiative – APEC, covering nations on both sides of the Pacific – eventually develops into a concrete FTA?

In focusing on the possible role in US trade policy of regional agreements and the various forms these may take, it must be emphasized how essential it is to keep in mind the superiority of full multilateral free trade (synonymously referred to here as WTO liberalization). To clarify this superiority, and indeed demonstrate the fundamental gains from trade, the next section reviews the economics of WTO liberalization. The two sections which then follow analyse a regional FTA, in the process clarifying why it is the less attractive option. Succeeding sections then demonstrate why regional FTAs may be better than supposed – or worse – and how any regional agreement should be designed. Finally, this analysis is brought to bear on what may develop into one of the most substantial future challenges in US trade policy: the attempt to negotiate both an FTAA and APEC.

This chapter is in response to a request to set out simply and apply the theoretical trade concepts that I have come to view as important in analysing any such regional agreement. While many of the effects included here – such as removal of a country's trade barriers against its imports – have been long accepted, others (e.g. the effect of removing partners' barriers against that country's exports) have still not been fully recognized. Finally, space limitations rule out an analysis of non-trade provisions that may or may not be included in a trade agreement – in particular, the liberalization of foreign investment. Hence this chapter refers only to some important effects on foreign investment of trade liberalization alone.

THE ECONOMICS OF MULTILATERAL FREE TRADE (MFT)

To begin with the simplest possible case, suppose A (America) and B (Europe) are the only two 'countries' in the world. When each removes its tariffs against the other in WTO liberalization, (1) the prices of their tradeable goods change, inducing (2) an increase in their trade flows. Box 1 describes just the price effects, while we now turn in the text to the changes in trade flows, reflecting the reallocation of resources.

BOX 1   TERMS-OF-TRADE EFFECTS OF TRADE LIBERALIZATION: HOW DOES TARIFF REMOVAL AFFECT THE RELATIVE PRICE OF A COUNTRY'S EXPORTS AND IMPORTS?

To analyse tariff *removal*, first consider the effects that existing tariffs have had in the past.

A past tariff by A can be viewed as a tax on its imports; like any tax, this has been typically borne, directly or indirectly, by both sellers (exporters in B who have received a lower price) and buyers (importers in A who have paid a higher price), with the difference or 'wedge' between these two prices being the tariff collected by the treasury of A. A has benefited because its treasury has received all of this tariff, while its importers have only borne some of it. B has lost because its exporters have borne the other part of this tariff. Technically, B has suffered a terms-of-trade loss (i.e. a reduction in the price it receives for its exports divided by the price it pays for its imports). At the same time, A has acquired a terms-of-trade gain. When this tariff is *removed*, the effects are, of course, reversed:

When importing country A removes its tariff, it suffers a terms-of-trade loss, while its exporting partner realizes a terms-of-trade gain.

If a country is unilaterally removing its own tariff (with its partner's tariff left in place) then that country suffers a terms-of-trade loss. But if both countries are removing their tariffs, i.e. if each is suffering a terms-of-trade loss from removing its own tariff but acquiring a terms-of-trade gain because the tariff on its exports is also being removed by its partner, it is not clear how these negative and positive effects on each country will offset each other. Thus the terms-of-trade effect on an individual country is not clear. However, because one country's loss is its partner's gain, there is no collective gain or loss to both countries taken together. To find any collective gains, one must examine the increase in trade flows reflecting the reallocation of resources, as described in the main text.

Now let's consider the special case so far neglected, in which the terms-of-trade effect on each country *is* clear – namely, the case where one country is relatively so large and the other so small that the large country determines the price of tradeables, i.e. the terms of trade, while the small country has no influence. Because the small country lacks such influence, any change in its policy, i.e. the removal of its tariff, does not affect the terms of trade. At the same time, because the large country determines the terms of trade, these do change when it changes its policy, i.e. reduces its tariff. Moreover, this terms-of-trade change is in favour of the small country.[3] Thus when both countries remove their tariff, there is a change in the terms of trade, and it is paradoxically in favour of the small country that has no terms-of-trade influence – except in so far as it can negotiate down its large partner's tariff. This simply illustrates a familiar principle: with free trade, the large country allows the small country to trade with it for the first time at the more favourable domestic terms of trade of that large partner.

How Do Increased Trade Flows Affect Each Country?

Any country, say A, benefits from its increased imports. Just one of the reasons for this is that A now acquires these products from B for less than it previously cost A to produce them domestically.

Any country A benefits from its increased exports. Just one of the reasons for this is that A now receives a higher price for its increased exports than the cost it incurs in expanding its production of these goods. (Technically, these two benefits to A are two of the Harberger triangles of efficiency gain, with the triangle on the export side less well recognized, though also potentially important.)[4]

Summary of the benefits to each partner from increased trade flows.[5] Like A, B also gets import and export benefits from increased trade flows. Note that each country benefits by buying relatively inexpensive imports from its partner. Each also benefits on its exports since, for those products of its *comparative advantage* in which it specializes, it acquires a price that exceeds its relatively low cost of production. Thus both partners benefit on both the import (buying) and export (selling) side. This is just a special case of the general principle that in any market transaction – in the absence of special circumstances – both buyers and sellers benefit.

All these benefits follow in the standard classical case where costs of production rise with increased output. Do they still follow in the economies-of-scale case where production costs fall?

Economies of Scale Augment Collective Gains from Increased Trade

With economies of scale, there are even larger possibilities (slices rather than triangles) of efficiency gain because expanded production for export brings with it reductions in costs not only of increased output, but also of all units originally produced – with such cost reductions, under standard conditions, increasing income. Just as in the increasing-cost case, it is such efficiency gains that guarantee a collective gain to the two countries. In a nutshell: with expanded output for export specialization, rising costs put a brake on gains from trade; but with economies of scale, falling costs add to gains from trade. If there are economies of scale, the greater expected gains from trade make it more likely that each country will individually benefit. (This isn't absolutely guaranteed because one country may be unusually damaged by a change in its terms of trade.)

A Downside? Does Increased Trade Reduce the Number of Jobs?

While an FTA does reduce jobs in import-competing activities, it increases them in expanding export industries. There is no guarantee that job openings will completely offset losses; after all, by increasing labour productivity, trade liberalization – like technological change – makes it possible for the same national output to be produced by fewer workers, and there is no guarantee against job loss unless output rises with productivity. (This is a question of macroeconomic policy.) Thus the point of trade liberalization is not 'jobs, jobs, jobs' as politicians claim. Instead, as with technological change, it is to increase productivity and income, and thus, arguably, opportunities for jobs with high productivity and income in the future. There is one big difference between trade liberalization and technological change: the offsetting new jobs created by a trade agreement are more obvious because they are in export industries that are expanding precisely because of explicit provisions in the agreement that reduce partners' trade barriers.

Similar Effects of MFT Tend to Hold in a World of Many Countries

In particular, in the three-country world to which we now turn, all countries will benefit collectively from multilateral free trade; and, as in the two-country world, each will benefit individually (in the absence of sufficiently large terms-of-trade changes, a special case which – unless otherwise specified – is hereafter assumed away).

ECONOMICS OF A REGIONAL FTA:[6] WHY MFT (OR WTO LIBERALIZATION) IS SUPERIOR

Now suppose in the three-country world of America (A), Europe (B) and the rest of the world (C), all three 'countries' do not agree to full trade liberalization; instead A and B form an FTA that removes their tariffs against each other but not against outsider C. How does this FTA compare to MFT, with all countries participating – from the point of view of the two FTA insiders, and the outsider?

For Any FTA Partner, MFT is Likely to be Superior

The starting point in analysing any FTA is to recognize that, in removing their barriers against each other, partners A and B each get the same sorts of benefits on the export and import side in the trade between themselves that they would enjoy under three-country MFT. However for any partner, say A, the expected effects will be less beneficial under an FTA for two reasons. First, an FTA would provide A with fewer free-trade partners and therefore less scope for specialization based on comparative advantage or economies of scale. Specifically, with only one free-trade partner (B), A has less opportunity for *trade creation*: i.e. the expansion of its previous trade with its partner in products where that partner is the world's lowest-cost source. Second, there are also products where outsider C is the world's lowest-cost source. Here the FTA imposes a *trade diversion* cost on A whenever its importers switch their original purchases from C to higher-cost partner B. (They do this because they can now acquire B's – but not C's – goods duty free). This additional FTA cost from more expensive imports is not incurred under MFT because, with all imports duty-free, all countries continue to buy from the lowest-cost source: i.e. there can be no trade diversion because there are no outsiders from which trade can be diverted.

For these two reasons, the conclusion so far is that MFT is likely to be more beneficial for a member than an FTA.[7] Moreover, for the world as a whole, MFT superiority is even more strongly assured: because the trade diversion that occurs in an FTA does not occur under MFT, MFT alone leaves production in the lowest-cost world location. This superiority of MFT becomes clearer when one also takes into account the point of view of C, the country excluded from the FTA between A and B.

For Any Outside Country C, the Margin of MFT Superiority is Even Greater

For any outsider C, MFT is superior to an FTA between A and B not only because the FTA leaves C without any of the free trade relationships available under MFT, but also because whenever an FTA member A or B diverts its trade, C is damaged by the loss of this export market.

Finally, as an aside, the cost to outsider C of trade diversion by the FTA not only guarantees that C will be worse off than under MFT, it also suggests that the FTA may leave C worse off than under the original status quo (SQ), in other words, C will be damaged overall if an FTA is created in which it does not participate. This may well be true, but not necessarily. Outsider C could still benefit if the damage to its exports to the FTA from trade diversion by A and B is more than offset by a stimulus to its exports because the FTA has sufficiently increased the growth of its internal market, and hence its demand for imports from all sources, including C. This argument has in fact been used by FTA members in defending themselves from outsiders' criticism; the Europeans used this in defending the creation of their Common Market.

In assessing the importance of this 'export-stimulus', all that can theoretically be stated is that (1) barring increased growth in FTA markets, outsiders are damaged; or (2), if there is such growth and it is sufficient to more than compensate outsiders for their trade diversion losses, those outsiders benefit despite the discrimination they now face, and by less than the FTA members that are discriminating. One cannot expect outsiders to welcome the creation of an FTA – unless the door is open for them to join.

GIVEN THE ECONOMIC SUPERIORITY OF MFT, WHY DO COUNTRIES FORM AN FTA?

While there may, as in the European case, be all sorts of political reasons, the economic reason for a group of countries to negotiate an FTA is that they view this as a second-best option for achieving free trade benefits among themselves when the first-best option of MFT is uncertain, or at best may involve substantial delay. The 1989 Canada–US FTA provides an example: it was negotiated much more quickly than the Uruguay Round of GATT negotiations, and provided a more open border between Canada and the USA than would have existed had there been only GATT/WTO liberalization. The same supporting argument applies to non-regional agreements such as the long-standing 'GATT-plus' proposal to get deeper trade liberalization among a subset of WTO countries than is now possible in any 'lowest-common-denominator' WTO negotiation.

Some have argued that an FTA isn't even a second-best – or for that matter, even an nth-best option – i.e. 'it is worse than nothing'.[8] While in any specific case this is possible, it is difficult to argue that this is true – or even likely – in general. This pessimistic conclusion has typically been based on one or more of the following: first, the view that any FTA will deter, rather than speed up, the move to MFT; (each of these possibilities is so important that they are considered in detail later). Second, there can be an understatement of the gains from an FTA by implicitly assuming that they come on the import side, with gains on the export side left largely unrecognized. Third, there may be the expectation of large costs of trade diversion, without adequate recognition that such diversion may, in certain circumstances, be beneficial rather than costly.

AN FTA MAY BE BETTER THAN PRESUMED: A RECONSIDERATION OF TRADE DIVERSION AND CREATION

Both trade creation and diversion may have effects opposite to the one expected. Specifically, creation may, in some situations, damage – rather than benefit – an FTA member. Bhagwati et al. (1998) provide an example when there are 'voluntary' export restraints on partners and other forms of administered protection. But in a world with VERs, an example of almost any welfare effect can be found, depending on what happens to rents. Let's now consider (as in Wonnacott, 1996a) how, under broad circumstances of either adminis- tered or tariff protection, trade diversion may increase – rather than decrease – welfare for both the diverting country and, more remarkably, *the world as a whole*.[9] The first three points below look beyond diversion's traditional supply-switching effect to recognize that it also triggers a process of trade liberalization between partners in which standard effects of increased compe- tition, specialization and trade over the FTA domain may reduce partner B's costs enough to make it A's lowest-cost source, and thus increase A's and world welfare by lowering the cost of producing the good.

1. *Economies of scale*   Corden (1972) and others, including even Viner (1950), recognized how economies of scale can reduce costs in an FTA. The point here goes beyond this: when member A diverts its import purchases to partner B, increased production in B may, for economies-of-scale reasons, not only lower its costs, but may do so enough to make B the lowest-cost world source.[10]
2. *Technical efficiency gains and reduced profit margins*   Greater competi- tion – even in a heavily diverting FTA – may put pressure on profit margins and reduce inefficiency in B sufficient to make it the lowest-cost source.
3. *Cost reductions from greater investment within the FTA*   B's costs may be reduced by increased foreign investment at a lower supply price as B becomes a more attractive location because of, e.g. its new preferential access to FTA-wide markets, the FTA's discipline over B's domestic policies or an announcement effect eliminating any unjustified past dis- advantage of B in attracting foreign investment. Moreover such investment may bring world class technology that further reduces B's costs. (These possible benefits follow, even if there is liberalization only of trade, but not investment. If the FTA does include provisions to liberalize invest- ment, as for example in NAFTA, then this opens up a whole set of additional possible benefits.)
4. *The effects of an FTA in also reducing costs in diverting country A* Increased FTA competition facing A's import-competing industries may reduce their size, political influence and hence ability to resist erosion of their MFN tariffs against outsiders (Richardson, 1993). If this erosion is sufficient, A may switch its import purchases – and more – back from partner B to the low-cost outside country. Thus A's initial diversion may be transformed into welfare-increasing trade creation with original out- side source C.
5. *Some apparently damaging diversion may instead be beneficial diversion reversal*   Before considering how this phenomenon may occur in a new

FTA, consider how it may arise in the more transparent case where an existing FTA is being expanded. For example, with the 1994 expansion of the Canada–US FTA to include Mexico in NAFTA, there will be a reversal of some past diversion of US import purchases from Mexico to higher-cost Canada that resulted from the earlier 1989 Canada–US FTA. With the production of this good shifted back to lower-cost Mexico, this diversion reversal increases US and world welfare.[11]

To illustrate beneficial diversion reversal when a new two-country FTA is first created, eliminate away Canada and suppose the USA and Mexico alone had formed an FTA. Then, some past US diversion from low-cost Mexico to the Caribbean under the preferential CBI (Caribbean Basin Initiative) would now be reversed back to Mexico. This illustrates how diversion reversal must be explicitly recognized to warn of any cases in which an FTA member has given preferential treatment in the past to an FTA outsider. The warning in the CBI case – that trade flows that seem to indicate trade diversion, may instead be, at least partly, welfare-increasing diversion reversal,[12] – also applies to GSP, Lomé and other preferential systems.

6. *Have FTAs been underrated for other reasons as well?* Another reason for being less pessimistic about diversion and FTAs is that any diverting country A is also a divertee in other products, acquiring export benefits when its partner(s) divert their purchases to it. A further reason is that, in the important, 'any-outcome is possible' world of quotas, trade diversion may not even occur, in which case it can have no negative welfare effects.[13]

FURTHER REASONS WHY AN FTA MAY BE BETTER THAN PRESUMED: EFFECTS THAT CHALLENGE ESTIMATION

The consequence of FTA tariff reduction is far easier to estimate than the FTA's effects in reducing antidumping action or other forms of administered protection. It is thus very difficult for policy-makers to give such non-quantifiable effects appropriate weight in analysing, e.g. NAFTA. The same is true for the following other effects of NAFTA.

NAFTA Opens Up Negotiating Opportunities Not Available Otherwise

In hemispheric liberalization, Mexico was a gatekeeper. Had NAFTA been rejected, there would now be essentially no chance of extending the Canada–US FTA into the hemisphere beyond. In this sense, NAFTA has been almost a necessary condition for the FTAA. Doesn't this mean that, in assessing the effects of NAFTA one should ideally also include the benefits from the FTAA multiplied by how much NAFTA has, roughly speaking, increased the probability of negotiating the FTAA?

Reducing the Risk of Damage to Existing Trade

In the rapidly changing international economy, the status quo is not an option: a nation cannot freeze in the conditions it faces today. If these are liable to deteriorate if it doesn't join an FTA, then it may get substantial benefits from participating in an FTA that reduces this risk. For example, the major benefit – at least in the eyes of Canadian business – of the Canada–US FTA was not the improvement that it would bring to the status quo, but was instead the reduced risk of damage from increasing US protection to Canada's status quo exports. A second example: when other countries are forming an FTA, an outside country may have little choice but to seek entry since this is the only way of avoiding the costly FTA discrimination against its exports if it does not join (Baldwin, 1992). Finally, expanding NAFTA into an FTAA would pre-empt possible developments damaging to NAFTA members, such as the deepening and/or extension of Mercosur or other Latin American unions, or a possible closer Mercosur–EU association (with the discriminatory damage to NAFTA exports that any of these imply).

AN FTA MAY BE LESS BENEFICIAL THAN PRESUMED IF IT IS PART OF A HUB-AND-SPOKE SYSTEM (H&S)

What is an H&S?

The answer (Wonnacott, 1996b) is a system in which a hub country has a separate FTA with each spoke, with no liberalized trade between spokes. See Figure 10.1 for the H&S system that would have been created in 1994 had the USA signed a bilateral FTA with Mexico rather than including Canada in NAFTA, the full three-country FTA. Note that, in considering only the classic case of a single stand-alone regional FTA, we have so far avoided this H&S issue.

Is an H&S Beneficial?

One cannot answer this (i.e. compare an H&S to the status quo) in general, but only in each specific case. For example, while there may be examples of net damage to participants in recent H&S developments in Latin America, it

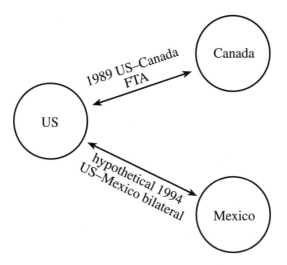

Figure 10.1   A hypothetical North-American hub-and-spoke system

seems likely that the current European H&S in Figure 10.2 is, on balance, beneficial – even to the eastern spokes because of their large, albeit heavily compromised, gains from their bilateral FTAs with the EU hub.[14]

The only comparison that is theoretically possible is between an H&S and the full FTA covering all the same countries.

How Does an H&S Compare to the Corresponding FTA?

An H&S will generate less collective income for the participants than the corresponding FTA covering the same countries because, for example: (1) trade barriers remain within the H&S but not the FTA; (2) more protective barriers create greater rent-seeking waste; and (3) there will be a whole additional set of inefficiencies if H&S bilaterals are inconsistent. The one country that may benefit more from an H&S than an FTA is the hub because of the preferences it gets in each spoke market in competition with all other spokes, and because of its advantage in attracting investment since it is the only location with duty-free access to all participating countries. But despite this, an H&S may still be judged inferior by the hub; despite its larger relative slice, it is out of a smaller income pie.[15]

Compared to the corresponding full FTA, an H&S will be the inferior option for spokes because of their smaller share of a smaller income pie and relatively less attractive investment locations. In more detail, spoke-to-spoke trade suffers not only because of the foregone benefits from liberalizing that trade in a full FTA, but also because even existing spoke–spoke trade is

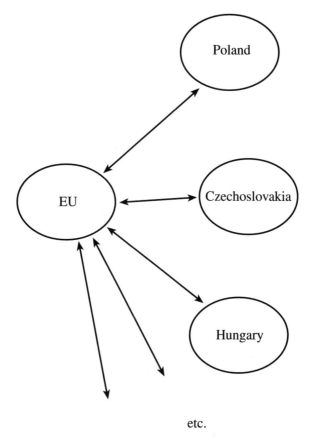

etc.

Figure 10.2   The EU-centred hub-and-spoke system

damaged from the new discrimination each spoke faces in all other spoke markets in competition with the hub. A spoke can't even expect lower adjustment costs when an H&S is created even though less of its trade is liberalized, because of its greater problems in competing everywhere with the hub's firms that alone get not only duty-free market access, but also duty-free inputs from all spokes.[16]

Spokes will face discrimination not only in each others' markets, but perhaps even in the hub's market if, beyond their control, the hub negotiates more favorable bilaterals with new spokes. Even the hub may lose control, if spokes sign bilateral deals with outsiders that damage the hub by reducing it to spoke status in new H&S systems. In that event, the result would be a example of the even more complex 'spaghetti bowls' that have evolved, e.g. in Latin America (Bhagwati et al., pp. 1138–40).

Why is the H&S Issue Important?

1. Intentionally or inadvertently, an H&S – along with its more complicated spaghetti versions – has now become by far the most common format for liberalizing trade.
2. It's not the (possibly small) size of initial spoke–spoke trade that's important, but its future potential – especially among Central and Eastern European spokes where past trade has already been so distorted for other reasons. The obvious way for these countries to escape from the H&S is to enter the EU or create a full new FTA with the EU.
3. If the EU's framework agreements with Mercosur and/or Russia become substantially more than an indication of intent, the result will be new, more complex H&S systems with their even broader domains of discrimination against NAFTA exports.
4. While the H&S issue, just like the traditional 'CU issue' (Viner, 1950), has been based on margins of preference and these have been reduced by GATT/WTO tariff reductions, substantial margins still exist because of restrictive NTBs and remaining tariffs in certain sectors.

   Some day WTO liberalization may so reduce margins of preference that H&S issues will disappear. But on that day, all other preference-based issues such as CUs, regional FTAs, trade diversion etc., will also disappear. That day – the end of CU and H&S history – is still distant.

Concluding Observations on an H&S

Each spoke thinks it is participating in regional trade liberalization – and it is, but only with the hub. At the same time it is simultaneously moving further away from free trade with the other spokes – for example, because of the discrimination it faces in other spokes' markets. Thus, an H&S combines regional integration with the hub and disintegration among the spokes. When the hub looks out over an H&S region, it sees nothing but free trade, with special preferences to boot – albeit in a lower-income system. But when a spoke looks out over this region, it sees free trade with the hub combined with a byzantine maze of discriminatory trade barriers everywhere else (Figure 10.2). Nor can a spoke escape, as has been suggested, by unilaterally liberalizing its trade with other spokes – for the same reason that a country excluded from a simple FTA can't escape this way since it would solve one major problem (acquiring duty-free imports) but not the other (discriminatory damage to its exports). This leaves us with an important overall principle in liberalizing regional trade: rather than creating an H&S system, negotiate the corresponding full FTA instead.

DESIGN GUIDELINES (1): CRITERIA FOR SELECTING PARTNERS

In defining guidelines for FTA design, we return to the case of a simple free-standing FTA, free of H&S complications. How should a country select its partners? Often – and especially in the case of a regional FTA – partners are determined by political or geographical factors, as in the case of the FTAA or the EU. But even here it is important to recognize the characteristics to be sought in a partner; at a minimum this will be useful in evaluating how beneficial the trade agreement may – or may not – be.

A Partner With a Rich Market

The larger the partner's market, the greater the opportunity for a country to specialize and capture gains from trade, especially if there are economies of scale; this is based on roughly the same argument as 'the more-partners-the-better' case. At the same time, the larger the partner, the greater the opportunity for the home country to ensure a terms-of-trade benefit: as noted in Box 1, when a small country forms an FTA with a country large enough to determine prices of their tradeables, the small country benefits from being allowed for the first time to trade at the more favourable domestic terms of trade of its large partner.[17]

To keep this in perspective, it must be recognized that having a large trading partner raises special problems for a small country, whether or not they have an FTA. Indeed, the larger the partner, the stronger its negotiating position, and the more likely it is that the small country will be at a substantial disadvantage in resolving their trade disputes. Thus if there is not already an FTA between these two countries, the small country will have a strong incentive to seek one in order to create, in so far as possible, a rules-based system that reduces the risk of such disputes and ensures a reasonably equitable resolution of those that do arise. However, even an FTA doesn't allow the small country to escape entirely from its relative weakness if, for example the large country has already exercised its leverage in negotiating the FTA's original provisions or, later, in an extreme case, threatens to reopen the agreement once it is phased in. In this latter situation, the small country's negotiating position would be weakened because of its vulnerability to the loss of its terms-of-trade and scale benefits from the FTA. Specifically, the small country would face the risk that its newly rationalized industries would lose the export market that they have come to depend on, in particular for economies of scale.

A Partner with a Large Population

Even if such a partner, for example China, is poor, it may offer a large potential future market and a source of inexpensive products.

A Partner with Advanced Technology

This implies a high per capita income in the partner country, and consequently a greater demand for the home country's exports. In addition, the greater the technological excellence of a partner, the more it will challenge the home country's high-tech industries to match this excellence.[18] A partner with advanced technology is also preferred because it will provide knowledge spillovers, as well as high-tech supplies for the home country's consumers and using industries.

Ensure the Partnership Will Create, Rather Than Divert, Trade as Much as Possible

Trade creation should be maximized not because diversion reduces welfare – it has been shown above that it may or may not – but because creation is superior: for example, creation won't leave production in a higher-cost location, but diversion may.

In order to form an FTA that primarily creates – rather than diverts – trade, it is desirable to seek 'natural trading partners', that is, countries that would be the home country's largest trading partners in a world of complete free trade. Because these are the countries that can supply goods at minimum cost, they maximize the opportunities for trade creation, as opposed to diversion. This isn't quite the same as partners with whom the home country has actually been trading most in the past (Wonnacott and Lutz, 1989), but it is close to it. For example, if preferences such as the CBI have increased trade in the past, this increase should ideally be discounted in determining natural trading partners in a free trade world in which such preferences would not exist.

Natural Unions: the Importance of Transport Costs

The countries with trade flows incurring the lowest transport charges – typically the geographically most proximate countries – will be the home country's natural partners, *ceteris paribus* (with this last assumption necessary, of course, because differences in other costs may, in any specific case, overwhelm differences in the one cost – transport – that is being examined).

As a technical aside, the rest of this section illustrates this idea of a natural union. The offer curve example in Figure 10.3 shows the three-country,

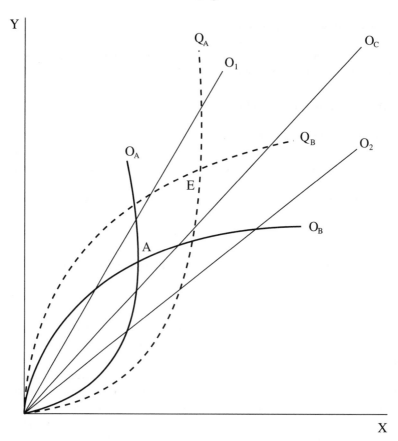

Figure 10.3   An example of a natural union

two-good (X and Y) case, with A and B potential members of a new union. In
the absence of transport or other transactions costs in trading with C,[19] the
offer curve of C – the straight line O_c – determines international prices. The
initial tariff-ridden offer curves of A and B are given by OA and OB (assuming no transactions costs except tariffs in trade between A and B).

Recognition of transport costs in trade with C (and any tariffs imposed by C)
means that C has two offer curves; (C's offer to sell X is O_1, and to buy X is
O_2). Suppose the wedge between the two – defined by the angle between O_1
and O_2 – is wide enough, so that A and B trade within it both before (at A) and
at E after they form a CU (which, in eliminating their tariffs against each other,
shifts their offer curves to Q_A and Q_B). Then it is as though country C did not
exist. With C essentially 'out of the picture', the question of whether countries
A and B should form a union reduces to the standard two-country free-trade

question. In this case a CU can easily be shown to be beneficial under standard assumptions; both countries have a higher welfare at E than at A.

The conclusion is that the higher are transport and other transactions costs with outside countries C, the wider the wedge between O_1 and O_2, and the more likely will be the benefits of an FTA to countries A and B. In this case, transport costs with outside countries C make A and B 'a natural union'.[20] (This and other more complex cases where C trades with the union both before and after it is created have been analysed in Wonnacott (1981).)

Special Issues When an Existing FTA is Expanded

The objective of keeping an FTA open to new members is desirable for three reasons. (1) It is beneficial for new countries to be able to join, since this allows them to escape discrimination in FTA markets (i.e. eliminates members' costly diversion in the past away from these new countries). (2) The wider the domain of free trade, the greater the potential gains from trade for both new and existing members. (3) Expansion of the FTA eliminates the political problems that would arise were an 'economic club' – especially a relatively wealthy one – to exclude new members.

Does this not lead to the paradoxical conclusion that founding countries should be selective in the creation of an FTA; but once the FTA is created they then should become less selective in extending membership to new countries? To some degree the answer may be 'yes'. Even though adding non-optimal partners may not be as beneficial as adding optimal ones (which can't be included for, say, some non-economic reason), the addition of these non-optimal partners may still be beneficial for all members of the expanded FTA, albeit not for those still outside.

The unanimity requirement
In attempting to keep an FTA open to new members, is it appropriate to require, as in NAFTA, that existing partners be unanimous in accepting any new members? While this seems reasonable enough on the face of it, it could raise problems. A protectionist member country may veto new entrants to shield itself from increased competition in its own domestic market or in its export markets within the FTA; that is, the member country may wish to prevent the erosion of its preference in original partners' markets. For example, suppose NAFTA has already expanded to include Central America. Should the unanimity requirement then allow any individual Central American country, in a purely protectionist move, to block the entry of any other new members? True, US pressure would be likely to ensure that such a veto would not be cast. None the less, a useful first step might be made to reform the unanimity requirement by ensuring that any new entrant need not require the

approval of all existing members, but only the approval of each large country, such as the United States, Canada, and Mexico, and each bloc of small countries such as Central America.

To what degree should the provisions of an FTA be renegotiated to accommodate new members?
In the NAFTA negotiations, the energy provisions in the existing 1989 Canada–US FTA were not imposed on Mexico (due to its constitutional constraints) when it joined that earlier Canada–US agreement. How much of this sort of renegotiation should be allowed? A number of reasons suggest that the answer should be 'very little'. Such renegotiation could represent a damaging recontracting of the earlier agreement for some existing members; it could also delay the negotiating process and inflate negotiating costs; or it might even unnecessarily drag trade liberalization back into the political arena of the existing union partners.

None the less, new applicants are likely to request some renegotiation. What should the guidelines be for this – or for any change that existing members may wish to make to the agreement even if new members are not being included? In my view, there are two rules: first, any change should be acceptable to all existing large partners or blocs of small partners. Second, any change should further liberalize trade, rather than protect; this may be a difficult guideline to meet given the desire of special interests to use the renegotiation to make the agreement more protective. In the NAFTA renegotiation of the original Canada–US FTA to include Mexico, this second guideline was sometimes satisfied, sometimes not. For example, it was satisfied in NAFTA's increase in access to bidding on government procurement contracts. On the other hand, it was not in negotiating the increasingly protective rules of origin in motor cars and apparel.

DESIGN GUIDELINES (2): COMBINING THE BEST FEATURES OF A FREE TRADE AREA PROPER (FTA) AND A CUSTOMS UNION (CU)

In the past, there have been two alternative approaches to regional free trade: a customs union (CU) with a CET (common external tariff) imposed by all participants on outside countries; and a free trade agreement proper (FTA) in which each participant is free (subject to GATT bindings) to set its own MFN tariff against outsiders. Each has strong and weak features.

How can one design a new regional agreement – extending the suggestions by the Wonnacotts (1996) – that combines the strong features of a CU and an FTA, while avoiding as much as possible the problems raised by each?

The Problems with a CU

Its relatively sticky and potentially protective common external tariff

The CET which all CU members must impose is often highly protective and difficult to reduce; an example has been agriculture in the EU. Moreover, there is a risk that the requirement to set a CET may provide the negotiating framework for implicit collusion in raising protection substantially above the level possible in an FTA where there is independent tariff setting by each member country.[21] Indeed in an FTA, there is the expectation that such a collusive outcome may be prevented by 'tariff competition' among member countries: e.g. tariff reductions in car parts by an FTA country seeking to attract new foreign transplants and keep its car industry competitive within the FTA and beyond.

The 'captive market' problem

Since a member country can't reduce its external tariff, it is more likely to feel exploited as a captive market for the high-cost protected products made in a partner country. For example, a key question in the Mercosur CU is whether Argentina, Paraguay and Uruguay come to view themselves as a captive market for Brazilian manufactures that are high cost by international standards. When the British joined Europe, they became a captive market in agriculture as they gave up their existing agricultural protection in favour of the far more restrictive protection of the Common Agricultural Policy. Indeed, one important element in the original formation of the European Common Market was the Germans providing the French with a captive market in agriculture in exchange for the French providing the Germans with a captive market in manufactures.

The necessity of joint (perhaps inequitable) decisions

Members' commitment to a CET implies a substantial degree of cooperation and collective decision-making. This closer cooperation may be an advantage: one of the objectives in the establishment of the European Common Market was to promote joint decision-making and reduce destructive nationalism. Or it may be a disadvantage. Joint decision-making in a customs union is precisely why this option was unattractive in North America. For Canada and later Mexico, it would have meant, realistically, that the common external tariff would have been determined in Washington. Moreover, even the USA would have likely rejected a CU if it thereby had to commit itself not to change any of its tariffs unless it first acquired agreement from its partners.

These disadvantages of a CU become advantages of an FTA in which members have a greater degree of political independence and can escape from 'captive market' status by reducing their own external tariffs, thus providing relief to their consumers and their industries using imported inputs.

Consequently, leaving aside some political reason for a CU, an FTA has traditionally been viewed as the preferred form of union. But this was before the increasingly rapid globalization of production.

The Problems with an FTA

Rules of origin (ROOs)

Because each member of an FTA sets its own tariff, there is an incentive for trade deflection, that is, for imports to enter the FTA first through the low-tariff country and thence be trans-shipped duty free into the high-tariff destination country. To prevent this, and in particular avoid its wasteful excess transport and other transactions costs, each FTA has ROOs requiring that shipments across its internal borders contain a certain level of 'domestic' FTA content. However, problems with such ROOs have led some authors to reject FTAs in favour of CUs (Krueger, 1993). One is the compliance cost of bookkeeping[22] – a burdensome cost as production has become more integrated internationally (for example, in the electronics industry). This cost of compliance swallows up some of the gains from liberalized trade between FTA members, and in some cases eliminates these gains altogether – as, for example, in the case of some North American firms that have decided that it is less costly to skip the bookkeeping and instead pay the MFN tariff on their exports to NAFTA partners.

Another difficulty with ROOs is that they may protect an FTA member country in two ways. First, traditionally recognized, highly demanding rules of origin protect FTA member countries from outsiders; e.g., in the NAFTA, Japanese car transplants producing in Canada to export to the United States that have to use more North American content must therefore use less Japanese. Second, demanding ROOs also protect the United States – the large market country – from its NAFTA partners. To illustrate this less obvious effect, note that if a Japanese transplant firm locates in the USA, it has to satisfy any ROO only on its limited sales to Canada or Mexico. But if it locates instead in, say, Canada, it must satisfy a ROO on the bulk of its sales across the border into the United States (and Mexico). The more expensive and demanding the ROO, the greater the incentive of transplants to locate in the United States instead. Thus, more demanding ROOs protect the large market country – the United States – from its 'free trade' partners.

Possible hub-and-spoke complications

One problem unique to an FTA has already been recognized: because each partner country is free to set its own external tariff, it is able to negotiate a tariff-cutting side deal – including the creation of a spoke FTA – with one or more outsiders. Moreover, standard H&S problems can be compounded by

ROOs. To illustrate, suppose some spoke-to-spoke trade is rerouted through the hub because that route alone is duty free. Then the exporting firm has to satisfy two ROOs – the first imposed by the hub, and the second by the destination spoke. Moreover, for each destination spoke, the exporting firm may be facing a different configuration of ROOs. There have even been cases where the exporting firm has consequently had to set up more than one assembly line.

Such problems are far less serious in a CU, since its common external tariff (CET) means that (1) the CU requires no ROOs, and (2) any member is prevented from unilaterally reducing its tariff against any outsider – i.e. from signing a spoke FTA with an outsider or outsiders. However, the *whole CU* can negotiate multiple FTAs, as the EU (a CU plus) has done in creating the H&S in Figure 10.2 made up of its bilaterals with countries in Central and Eastern Europe. Thus a CU eliminates some H&S problems, but not all.

Threats to force acceptance of new members

This problem may arise in the typical case where an FTA requires unanimity among existing members before including new entrants. NAFTA is an example. Even though its accession clause explicitly requires unanimity, this requirement has no teeth: e.g. if Canada and Mexico did not want Brazil in an expanding NAFTA, the USA could initiate a bilateral negotiation with Brazil that Canada and Mexico would have to join, or be left as spokes to the US hub, with the damage to their future trade this implies. Thus despite the unanimity requirement, the USA could – over the objection of its partners – bring Brazil into NAFTA. In contrast, a CU does not allow any member – no matter how powerful – to force its partners into line by threatening to go off on its own and sign a bilateral with an outsider, since this would violate the CET.

Proposal for an Intermediate System that Would Avoid the Problems and Retain the Favourable Features of Both a CU and an FTA

Start with a standard FTA, but then divide all goods into two categories:

1. Products in which all members set their own tariffs, but they must be below some low cutoff rate, for example 2 per cent or 3 per cent – with no rule of origin required. With tariffs so low, there would be little incentive for trade deflection and ROOs would not be missed. Also ensure that ROOs could not be reintroduced; thus there would be little risk that any member would substantially raise its external tariffs, since this would expose it to lost duty revenue from trade deflection.
2. Products in which there is a CET that may be reduced by individual members. This follows the NAFTA precedent in computer products,

where tariffs were set at zero or at a low level that could be reduced without agreement by all parties. When the US and Canada lowered their tariffs in such products in the Uruguay Round, their NAFTA partner Mexico had to follow.

Note how this avoids the 'fortress CU' cost from a high CET that is difficult to reduce, while providing a CU's advantage in eliminating the need for ROOs. At the same time, because some of these CETs would be non-zero, no member could negotiate an independent spoke agreement with outsiders. The idea is to establish the mind-set of a CU in which individual union partners don't even think about signing H&S agreements with outsiders.

Conclusions

Clearly, an 'anything goes' policy toward FTAs is not recommended. While the resulting proliferation of FTAs might eventually be folded into one FTA covering all participants, if this last stage were not to occur the result would be region-wide spaghetti in a hopeless maze of rules of origin.

In the event that the sweeping proposal above is not feasible, less dramatic progress may still be made, for example:

1. Although ROOs cannot be eliminated altogether in an FTA, they can be made less demanding, e.g. by reducing content requirements.
2. To avoid H&S problems, one of the provisions that could be included in any FTA negotiation could be the discipline implicitly and willingly accepted without debate or question by partners in a CU: a provision prohibiting any FTA member from negotiating side deals on its own with outsiders.

DESIGN GUIDELINES (3): REDUCING THE RESISTANCE TO FUTURE MULTILATERAL FREE TRADE

Because of the superiority of MFT over any narrower regional agreement, a high priority in designing any regional FTA[23] is to reduce rather than increase resistance to WTO liberalization. Unfortunately, this is not an easy guideline to follow, since the creation of any FTA, while reducing the resistance to broader free trade in some respects, increases it in others.

How an FTA May Be a Building Block, Speeding Up WTO Liberalization

An FTA may facilitate multilateral WTO bargaining

Because there is a wider set of activities in an FTA than in an individual country, it may be easier in an FTA for protectionist, import-competing interests to be set off against export interests, leaving the FTA in a negotiating position more favourable to WTO liberalization. Moreover, at a very practical level, it may possibly (though not necessarily) be simpler to negotiate multilateral liberalization if the bargaining units are a small number of FTAs rather than a much larger number of individual countries. For example, Lawrence (1991) cites reasons why the US success in negotiating with Europe as a single bargaining unit would almost surely not have been possible on a country-to-country basis. Finally, binational dispute settlement and other provisions negotiated in an FTA may become a useful draft in WTO negotiations.

The creation of an FTA increases the pressure on outsiders to push for multilateral liberalization

This allows them to escape from the discrimination they otherwise would have to face in the new FTA.

Creation of an FTA may in several ways reduce its members' resistance to broader liberalization

Any trade agreement, like the 1965 Canada–US Auto Pact, may demonstrate to the voting public the benefits of trade liberalization. By imposing greater discipline over domestic policies, an FTA may reduce resistance to similar disciplines in the WTO. An FTA, by encouraging foreign direct investment in a member country, may induce its population to be more outward-looking and less resistant to WTO liberalization.[24]

In addition, increased competition between FTA members will reduce protection-based rents and thus the resistance to WTO liberalization that will erode or remove what remains of those rents. This competition – along with cost reductions based, for example, on economies of scale – will move members closer to being competitive on world markets and thus better able to face WTO liberalization. For example, by forcing the United States and Canada to adjust to competition with the low-wage Mexican economy, NAFTA will leave both countries better able to compete with the large number of low-wage countries that will participate in world-wide liberalization. In short, any regional FTA is an opportunity for members to scale up, in a competitive work-up to broader liberalization.

Finally, recall Richardson's argument (1993) that increased competition in an FTA may reduce the size and political power of inefficient industries in a member country and accordingly decrease their ability to retain their protection against outside countries. Any such erosion of protection would not only weaken resistance to multilateral liberalization but also reduce the ability of protectionist firms to finance that resistance.

How an FTA May Be a Stumbling Block to WTO Liberalization

An FTA may, by creating preference-based rents, increase members' resistance to MFT

Such rents are those its exporters earn from trade diversion, based on the preference they acquire over outsiders in partners' markets. If these exporters strongly resist losing this preference in any move to MFT, their natural support for broadening free trade may be tipped to opposition.

An FTA may reduce the benefits available from WTO liberalization

The incentive for FTA members to push hard – often at substantial political cost – for WTO liberalization may be reduced because these countries are already acquiring some of the benefits of MFT from their regional FTA. For example, the improved access to the US market that Canada negotiated in the 1989 Canada–US FTA provided Canada with one of the most important benefits previously available from MFT. With this benefit already cashed, Canada had less incentive to push for MFT. (However, in this case, the FTA has had an offsetting effect in strengthening Canada's support for MFT as a way of restoring more balance in its trade, which the FTA has been shifting more heavily towards the USA).

An FTA may trigger a negative reaction by outsiders

It's true that outsiders may react positively to the FTA by pushing harder for MFT or by seeking to join the FTA. But the problem is that outsiders have a third possible option: create another FTA. While this may encourage broader liberalization (e.g. by facilitating a negotiated entry of its members into the original FTA), it may alternatively discourage it by making trade wars more likely. One reason is that each member country has a larger 'domestic' market within this new FTA and hence some insulation from retaliation. Therefore, there may be less deterrent to members considering policies that risk setting off a trade war. In addition, if the new FTA is in the form of a CU, it may be able to make threats that could not be made by a smaller individual member for fear of the economies-of-scale and terms-of-trade losses it would face in a trade war.

Designing an FTA as a Building Block

The first two guidelines now considered are the same as those required earlier to maximize members' benefits and, in so far as possible, minimize outsiders' costs.

Maximize trade creation by removing internal FTA trade barriers, including easing ROOs

This will reduce members' protection-based rents, thus reducing their political and financial resistance to WTO liberalization.

Minimize trade diversion as much as possible by reducing members' trade barriers against outsiders

Minimizing preference-based rents will not only reduce resistance of member firms to WTO liberalization that will remove these rents, it will also reduce another deterrent to WTO liberalization: the 'double adjustment' cost to firms of first rationalizing to compete in the regional FTA market, followed by a second rationalization necessary to compete under additional WTO liberalization. (There will be this costly second rationalization unless the FTA only creates trade while diverting none.)

Now consider the question: what can be done to increase trade creation, in addition to removing internal FTA tariffs?

Avoid managed trade which typically tends to suppress rather than encourage competition within the FTA

This may not be easy because negotiators who are trying to sell their agreement may want to use market-sharing agreements or other forms of managed trade to enlist the support of protectionists.

Deal with countervailing and antidumping measures

Such trade remedies frequently provide special interests with easy access to the levers of protection. While there is no question that the dispute settlement mechanism in the Canada–US FTA, NAFTA and the Uruguay Round have provided some relief on this score, much remains to be done in negotiating a subsidy code that will make transparent what is, and what is not, beyond the reach of countervailing. Moreover, antidumping laws should be reformed. Specifically, such action should no longer be allowed against imports that are priced below constructed value, an extraordinarily costly provision. Especially in a recession, when damage to domestic firms becomes easier to establish, these firms have a strong incentive to seek protection, and many firms supplying imports operate at a loss and hence, by definition, price below cost and become easy targets. Even in non-recession periods, there are many firms that supply imports priced in the broad range above cost but below constructed value; they also become targets, leaving a relatively small percentage of firms immune from this action. Indeed this constructed value provision would make many US domestic firms a target were they to be located abroad.

More broadly, we should consider moving towards the more drastic reform of antidumping that has been suggested in the US–Canada case: replace these laws with the antitrust (competition) laws of the member countries (Feltham et al., 1991).

THE FTAA AND THE APEC COMPLICATION

Addressing this issue requires drawing together a number of threads from our preceding analysis. If both the vision for the Americas of an FTAA develops as now intended, and the '2020 vision' of APEC as an FTA becomes a reality, a huge hub-and-spoke system would be created. The NAFTA countries plus Chile, as members of both FTAA and APEC, would become the hub, with the rest of FTAA (in particular, most Latin American countries) constituting one giant spoke. The other would be the rest of APEC, i.e. its Asian countries (see Figure 10.4).

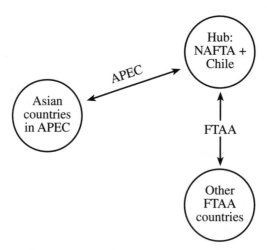

Figure 10.4   The FTAA–APEC challenge

How might the problems involved in creating such a system be resolved in a way that would also ease the transformation of this H&S into a far superior FTA – one that would, in turn, act as a building, rather than stumbling, block towards MFT? Here is a proposal:

1. *Begin by creating FTAA in the hybrid FTA form recommended above.* Thus the FTAA would have the CU characteristics that prevent individual members from negotiating their own special side deals with outsiders.
2. *Create APEC in the same hybrid form.* It is not clear how the political challenges in transforming the present loose APEC into any kind of a concrete FTA could be overcome. For example, how could a US president convince Congress of free trade with China by 2020, let alone the USA granting China unilateral liberalization in the interim period 2010–20? But suppose these difficulties are overcome.
3. *To allow both FTAA and APEC to be thus created, an exception in each would have to be allowed for the hub countries.* Specifically, FTAA would have to include a provision allowing the hub countries to also join APEC; otherwise, these countries would be violating their FTAA commitment to maintain a common external tariff. There would have to be a similar exception in APEC to allow these same hub countries to be in the FTAA. Thus neither APEC nor the FTAA would be able to block the creation of the other.

   So far, all this does is to allow both APEC and FTAA to be created. It would still be in the giant H&S form described above, with one desirable built-in characteristic: individual participating countries would be prevented from concluding any further spoke deals with outsiders.

   How might this then be transformed into an American–Asian FTA covering all of these same countries? One possibility is through a broad FTA negotiation by all participating countries. Indeed this might be included in the negotiation that creates APEC. Failing this, two provisions could provide a strong incentive for individual countries to accomplish this transformation by each acting on its own.
4. *Allow any FTAA spoke country to join APEC, exercising the same exemption already provided to the hub countries.* Any FTAA spoke that did this would become a member of both FTAA and APEC: i.e. it would join North America and Chile in the hub.
5. *Similarly, allow any APEC spoke country to join FTAA, again with the same exemption provided to the hub countries.* Any APEC country doing this would also be joining the hub.

   The more FTAA and APEC spoke countries join the hub, the more pressure would build on the remaining ones to do the same, to avoid the increasing discrimination they would otherwise face in the other union market. If all enter the hub, that hub becomes the giant American–Asian FTA as desired, with CU provisions precluding any individual member from negotiating a spoke deal with any outsider.
6. *Finally, ensure that there are provisions in this giant FTA to facilitate entry of new members.*

Although such a complex sequence of policies would require dealing with a number of detailed problems, this outline sets out the broad framework for a major step in world trade liberalization. In covering over half the world's trade, the resulting huge and expanding FTA could be a key building block in multilateral liberalization, but, it should be re-emphasized, provided its members have low external tariffs and there are generous provisions for the entry of new members.

NOTES

1. I wish to thank, without implicating them in this analysis, Gavin Boyd, Ig Horstmann, Clark Leith, Anne Krueger, Dan Vincent, John Whalley, Paul Wonnacott and members of the Trade Workshop at the University of Western Ontario.
2. The one exception to the US single-track policy prior to the late 1980s was the non-regional FTA with Israel.
3. As an example of how US tariff removal gives Canada a higher price for its exports – and hence a terms-of-trade gain – consider a Canadian firm that exports into the US market, say in Chicago, where price is determined at $100. If the US tariff is 10 per cent, the Canadian firm will receive only $90 from the import purchaser who must pay the $10 tariff. If that US tariff is removed, the price the Canadian exporter gets increases to the full $100, since the good will sell for the same $100 US-determined price regardless. (Note that transport costs, importer's charges and so on are ignored. Once they are recognized they must, like any US tariff, be deducted from the price the Canadian exporter receives. But such costs need not be of concern here because, unlike the tariff, they exist both before and after free trade.)
4. Technically, the simplest illustration of this triangular export gain is in the small-country/large-country case, with the exports of the small country shown in a partial equilibrium diagram similar to the textbook diagram showing its import. When the large country removes its tariff, there is an increase in the price received by exporters in the small country, since they are no longer required, directly or indirectly, to bear the burden of the previous tariff that went to the large country's treasury. (See Box 1, especially the last paragraph.) In response to this higher price, exports in the small country increase, not only because there is an increase in its output for export but also because some of its domestic consumption is switched to higher-valued exports. Each of these creates a triangular efficiency gain for the small country; together they bracket its terms-of-trade gain.
5. In the rest of this section, the special small-country/large-country case is ignored, with any further reference to it deferred to later sections.
6. FTA is used here just as Viner used CU, as a generic term to refer to either a CU (customs union) or FTA proper (which is designated later as FTA).
7. This is not certain because an FTA may offer a member A two possible advantages not available under MFT: (a) members A and B may both get a terms-of-trade benefit in their trade with C (even if their external tariffs against C remain unchanged). The reason is that, with trade diversion, both buy less from outsiders, thus reducing the demand and price of outsiders' goods. (b) The second advantage of an FTA, realized specifically by member A, results from the preference it receives in partner B's market because A gets duty-free access there for its exports while its outside competitor C does not. (Such a benefit for A does not exist under MFT because there are no preferences, i.e. C also gets duty-free access to B.) Finally note that while FTA partner A gets 'preference' in B's market, outsider C views this same thing as the 'discrimination' it faces there.
8. There have been attempts to prove another very different proposition about an FTA – i.e. it is always inferior or no better than unilateral free trade (UFT). However, these proofs have

not succeeded, nor could they, because an FTA provides benefits that UFT does not (from partners' tariff cuts). Nor can an FTA always be proved superior to UFT, because UFT provides benefits (from the liberalization of trade with non-FTA countries) that an FTA does not. Thus it cannot be proved theoretically that either policy is always superior to the other; it depends on the specific case.

9. It has long been recognized that, as A's imports increase with trade diversion, there may be Harberger efficiency gains for A sufficient to more than offset its terms-of-trade loss from importing from a more expensive source. But this is a case in which only A, but not the world as a whole, benefits. Here I concentrate on reasons why both A and the world may benefit.

10. If firms in Canada could have achieved lower attainable costs (from fully scaling up) than firms in, say Europe, why had they not already scaled up to capture US import purchases from European firms even before the Canada–US FTA? One answer was the risks in Canada of the necessary scaling up by perhaps 500 to 1000 per cent to lower costs enough to service a US market which might have then disappeared due to changing US protection – a degree of risk not faced by already large-scale, hence low-cost, European firms.

11. Isn't diversion reversal the same as trade creation between the new member and the original FTA? Much of it may be, but viewing the two terms as synonymous would obscure the way that old diversion is unwound as new diversion is generated in an expanding FTA. (Indeed, as an FTA reaches its limit of multilateral liberalization, all its diversion is unwound.) Moreover, the two terms are not synonymous: e.g. in NAFTA some US trade creation with Mexico is not a reversal of previous US diversion to Canada, but instead is in products like citrus fruits where high-cost Canada never was in the picture.

12. Our example is simplified by the assumption that NAFTA has opened the US market to Mexican goods on terms that are no more favourable than those provided under the CBI. In any cases where Mexico has received more favourable terms, then the result, over this margin, will be standard trade diversion, and the CBI countries have some grounds for complaint.

13. One example arises if outsider C is the least-cost source, while member B is the next-lowest-cost source. Even though partner B gets preferential free access to A's market, A's original imports may continue to be supplied from lowest-cost outsider C – so long as C still retains its original quota rights. (Rents on these will be reduced in so far as B's new free-trade supplies reduce A's domestic price.)

14. While one can't conclude in theory that spoke Q will necessarily be damaged by participating in the creation of an H&S, it will almost certainly be damaged if the hub then adds another spoke. The reason is that, in the creation of the H&S, Q has already achieved the benefits from the only FTA it will be inside (i.e. its bilateral with the hub). When the hub adds another spoke, this creates another FTA that leaves spoke Q outside, with the damage Q can expect as a result.

15. There is also a political and foreign policy reason for the USA to prefer an FTA to being the hub in a continent-wide H&S. As the hub, the USA could be perceived as promoting a system which could justifiably be viewed as not only throwing away some of the potential gains from a continent-wide FTA, but also transferring some of the resulting lower income to the USA from relatively poor spokes.

16. For example, spoke Canada could have faced higher adjustment costs in the US-centred H&S in Figure 10.1 than in NAFTA, the corresponding full FTA – despite less liberalization in the H&S. Canadian firms' lower adjustment costs in the H&S from not having to face duty-free imports from Mexico – a relatively small part of Canadian imports – might have been more than offset by greater adjustment costs for these firms in their much more critical competition with US firms that alone would acquire duty-free inputs from Mexico. For the same reason (i.e. the geographic/income dominance of the USA in Canadian trade), the effects on Canada of its free trade with Mexico in NAFTA are likely to be played out less in Canadian–Mexican trade than in Canadian–US trade.

17. Since this terms-of-trade benefit in an FTA for the small country implies a terms-of-trade loss for the large one, the incentive for a large country, say the USA, to negotiate with

smaller hemispheric partners must be found elsewhere, for example, in (1) economies of scale, (2) spill-over benefit from increased prosperity in its partner countries (a political as well as an economic benefit), and/or (3) benefits to US firms located in smaller partner countries. For example, with their plants in Canada, US car firms – along with Canadian consumers and labour – were beneficiaries of the 1965 Canada–US Auto Pact. Indeed Detroit head offices of these firms provided much of the domestic support in the USA for this agreement.

18. While this, along with economies of scale, are two of the reasons why there may be substantial gains from trade for partners in similar activities, it is important not to forget the traditional comparative-advantage gains from trade for partners in dissimilar activities. The conclusion from an extensive literature on this subject is that there are substantial possible benefits from trade whether or not partners are initially in similar activities.

19. And any tariffs imposed by C.

20. Krugman (1991a) describes the case where transport costs are very low (zero) between members of, say, a continental union, but very high (infinite) with countries outside that continent. This is essentially the same approach as in Figure 10.3, except that assumptions are even more extreme. In this limiting case, all ambiguity is removed: C is now entirely out of the picture, with O_1 and O_2 collapsing on to the Y and X axes. With no trade with the rest of the world, each country operates in its own continental world, with free trade within this world being optimal. Thus, if there are three continents, three blocs are best.

   This result is to be distinguished from Krugman's analysis of trade blocs (1991b) based on different assumptions (e.g. transport costs are the same within and between blocs – or more precisely, the same between any two countries in the world). While this model yields the standard 'one bloc is best' conclusion, i.e. MFT, it also suggests that the creation and development of blocs will reduce welfare until the worst outcome of three blocs is reached. Note the role that different transport cost assumptions plays in reversing the conclusion in this case that '3 blocs are best' to '3 blocs are worst'.

21. Each FTA member is not completely free to change its external tariffs. For example, it typically could scarcely eliminate overnight an external tariff that has provided important preference in its market to its partner, since that could be viewed by the partner as a damaging recontracting of their original FTA agreement. However, such a tariff could be allowed quietly to erode.

22. Herin (1986) estimated that such costs associated with meeting ROOs in the European Free Trade Association were in the range of 3–5 per cent of prices.

23. Note that FTA hereafter – as initially – refers to any preferential regional agreement such as an FTA proper or a CU.

24. This investment effect is far from guaranteed, especially if the FTA is part of an H&S. For example, I understand that some direct foreign investment in the spoke countries to the east of the EU was on the understanding that these countries would not liberalize their trade with each other. Apparently the objective of foreign investors was to ensure against competition from other spokes.

REFERENCES

Baldwin, Richard (1992), 'A Domino Theory of Regionalism', NBER Working Paper No. 4465.

Bhagwati, Jagdish, David Greenaway and Arvind Panagariya (1998), 'Trading preferentially: theory and policy', *Economic Journal*, **108** (449), 1128–48.

Cooper, C.A. and B.F. Massell (1965), 'A new look at customs union theory', *Economic Journal*, **75**, December, 742–7.

Corden, W.M. (1972), 'Economies of Scale and Customs Union Theory', *Journal of Political Economy*, **80** (3), 465–75.

Feltham, Ivan R., Stuart A. Salen, Robert F. Mathieson and Ronald J. Wonnacott

(1991), 'Competition (antitrust) and antidumping laws in the context of the Canada–U.S. Free Trade Agreement', *Canada–United States Law Journal*, **17** (1), 71–166.

Herin, Jan (1986), 'Rules of Origin and Differences Between Tariff Levels in EFTA and in the EC', EFTA Occasional Paper 13, Geneva, February.

Krueger, Anne (1993), 'Free Trade Agreements as Protectionist Devices: Rules of Origin', NBER Working Paper 4352.

Krugman, Paul (1991a), 'The Move Toward Free Trade Zones', Policy Implications of Trade and Currency Zones, a symposium sponsored by the Federal Reserve Bank of Kansas City, Jackson Hole, Wyoming, August, 7–42.

Krugman, Paul (1991b), 'Is Bilateralism Bad?', in E. Helpman and A. Razin (eds), *International Trade and Trade Policy*, Cambridge, MA: Cambridge University Press.

Lawrence, Robert Z. (1991), 'Emerging Regional Arrangements: Building Blocks or Stumbling Blocks', in R. O'Brien (ed.), *Finance and the International Economy, Vol. 5*, London: Oxford University Press.

Richardson, Martin (1993), 'Endogenous protection and trade diversion', *Journal of Internal Economics*, **34** (3/4), May, 309–24.

Viner, Jacob (1950), *The Customs Union Issue*, New York: Carnegie Endowment for International Peace.

Wonnacott, P. and M. Lutz (1989), 'Is There a Case for Free Trade Areas', in J.J. Schott (ed.), *Free Trade Areas and US Trade Policy*, Washington, DC: Institute for International Economics.

Wonnacott, Paul and Ronald J. Wonnacott (1981), 'Is unilateral tariff reduction preferable to a customs union? The curious case of the missing foreign tariffs', *American Economic Review*, **71**, 704–13.

Wonnacott, Ronald J. (1995), 'Regional Trade Agreements: Observations on the How, Where, and Why', North American Forum, Institute for International Studies, Palo Alto, CA: Stanford University.

Wonnacott, Ronald J. (1996a), 'Free Trade Agreements: For Better or Worse?', *American Economic Review (Proceedings)*, May.

Wonnacott, Ronald J. (1996b), 'Trade and investment in a hub-and-spoke system vs a free trade area', *World Economy*, **19** (3).

11. Structural statecraft

Gavin Boyd

Intensifying rivalries between firms striving for larger world market shares have increasing effects on the spread of benefits and costs as globalization continues. The consequences for growth and employment cause governments to adopt measures that are intended to enhance the structural competitiveness of their economies. The structural interdependencies linking their economies can be managed with advantage by administrations whose national firms achieve combinations of efficiencies that result in superior levels of structural competitiveness. The international economic rivalry however also involves uses of leverage over issues of market openness: large states, and groups of states, can discriminate against states with weaker bargaining power, thus in varying degrees limiting any advantages those states may derive from greater structural competitiveness.

Bargaining strength based on the size of its economy enables the USA to exert very powerful leverage against the European Union, Japan and the industrializing countries. How this bargaining strength is used depends primarily on the dynamics of highly pluralistic policy processes which tend to be more understandable in public choice than in public interest perspectives. These processes make the enhancement of structural competitiveness difficult, and limit the scope for measures that might be considered for that purpose.[1] Hence there is an overall tendency to rely on market opening leverage against other states in the international economic rivalry. In policy statements this is justified with reference to the potential benefits of general trade and investment liberalization. It is also justified with complaints that structural policies implemented by European states and Japan distort the operation of market forces.[2]

The structural interdependencies of the USA and other states assume larger dimensions and increasing complexities as US and foreign firms extend their trading and transnational production activities, and as the national identities of many of these enterprises become blurred through mergers, acquisitions and alliances. Competing structural policy endeavours and uses of trade policy leverage influence corporate strategies in the pattern, thus adding to its diversity, and tending to cause adversarial attitudes which limit awareness of potentials for cooperation in the common interest.

The common interest is invoked by US and other trade policy statements advocating general increases in market openness. Advances toward global market integration offer possibilities for higher growth through complementary specializations by firms achieving superior efficiencies while displacing weaker enterprises. Problems of international market governance however have to be envisaged, because of difficulties of competition policy cooperation in the present pattern of unequally negotiated arrangements for trade liberalization under the Uruguay Round agreements, and because of increasing disparities in bargaining strengths.[3] The USA and the European Union are tending to acquire greater leverage against most other states, although lacking capacities for comprehensive management of their rising structural interdependencies with those states.

Forms of international market governance can be imposed by states with superior bargaining strengths. Endeavours of this kind, however, are becoming less and less feasible for the USA because of the vulnerabilities associated with its expanding structural interdependencies: the European Union, in particular, has considerable retaliatory capabilities. Stresses in the USA's structural interdependencies moreover can increase the dysfunctional effects of strong pluralism in American policy-making. Collaborative approaches to issues of international market governance can thus be advocated. Yet these would not deal directly with fundamentals shaping the evolution of what are becoming strained and imbalanced structural interdependencies. For constructive engagement with those fundamentals there must be structural policy endeavours.

Problems of decision-making and implementation caused by strong pluralism do not invalidate the conclusion that structural policy endeavours have become imperative for the USA as a leading industrialized state with responsibilities for promoting order and growth in the world economy. The pluralism clearly necessitates vigorous new efforts to build consensus in the nation's policy communities. The structural policy endeavours, meanwhile, should seek consultative partnering with the major industrialized states, on the basis of full understandings of the interdependencies evolving between firms and governments, and of needs to manage these interdependencies with shared responsiveness for the development of the international political economy as a whole. The purpose would be not to develop collaborative interventionist policies but to facilitate spontaneous entrepreneurial cooperation across borders in line with concepts of partnering in the common interest, identified in consultations with US, European and Japanese technocrats.

The consultative structural partnering would be a shift away from a trade policy orientation targeting structural impediments to complete market openness in Europe and Japan. Interdependent growth would be increased through the concerting of entrepreneurial energies that would be aided by the transnational consultative interactions. Goodwill and trust, if sufficiently encouraged by the partnering, would tend to motivate spontaneous reduction of the structural impediments which limit market access in Europe and Japan for US firms.

STRUCTURAL POLICY

In the pattern of structural interdependencies linking the major industrialized states the USA has a central role, because of its size, the range and technological levels of its external linkages, its bargaining strength and its capacity to relate separately to the European Union and Japan. Macromanagement problems attributable mainly to strong pluralism in a system of divided government hinder the development of a structural policy capability, however, despite challenges to increase structural competitiveness, and the pluralism is a source of pressures to externalize the costs of the macromanagement problems. These pressures, responding especially to balance of payments deficits, are expressed in diplomacy seeking reductions of foreign structural barriers to trade and investment. Associated with these requests are appeals to the major European states and Japan to adopt expansionary policies that will increase internal demand and attract more imports from the USA.

The efforts to reduce foreign structural barriers rely on the importance of the large US market for European and Japanese exporters. Adversarial relationships tend to develop, because of threats that protectionist measures may be adopted. In the Atlantic context, however, leverage has to be restrained because the trade with Europe is roughly balanced and there is a large American corporate presence which serves the European market at volumes much higher than exports from the USA. The interests of US firms in Europe could be adversely affected by unfavourable shifts in the policies of the host countries and of those adopted at the Union level. Against Japan the market-opening pressures are stronger and focus on what are seen to be more substantial structural impediments to trade. The rationale for leverage is felt to have much force because the trade deficits with Japan are large. There is much less basis for concern about the interests of the US corporate presence in Japan, as this is small.[4]

The diplomacy to reduce foreign structural barriers is motivated by very active concerns with export expansion, because of persistently high balance of payments deficits.[5] The foreign structural barriers are expected to be lowered in the interests of fair trade, and are not considered to require US concessions, as the USA's structural impediments are felt to be much less significant restraints on trade. The hopes for export expansion after reductions of the foreign barriers, however, evidently tend to be maintained, at the policy level, without sufficient awareness that the increased foreign economic openness could on balance give more impetus to the expansion of international production by US firms than to their exports from the home economy. American enterprises, it must be stressed, serve external markets through foreign production at volumes much higher than US exports, and those exports include large proportions of intrafirm trade (about 60 per cent). The orientation toward foreign production results from multiple incentives, including the advantages of a manufacturing or service presence in major external markets, and there are compulsions to rationalize international operations as these expand, taking advantage of any reductions in foreign structural impediments.

The emphasis on international production in quests for world market shares has domestic structural significance. Shifts to such production are made with varying reductions of operations in the home economy, and these can affect sectoral and intrasectoral linkages within that economy. There are clear imperatives for coordinated adjustments, but these are generally not met because of considerable fragmentation in the national pattern of business associations and an intense individualism which limits intercorporate cooperation. The need for a structural policy is evident, and although the development of such a policy is made difficult by strong pluralism and by a liberal political tradition, as well as by general corporate distrust of government, the requirement is tending to become more urgent as dispersals of international production processes continue in the global rationalization strategies of American firms.[6]

Structural policy initiatives by US administrations have sponsored cooperation between firms for precompetitive research, in response to perceived needs to enhance the technological capabilities of national enterprises, so as to ensure improved export performance. Investment in new technology by US firms has been below Japanese levels, because of pressures to achieve high short-term profits, and the development and diffusion of innovations has been relatively slow because of inadequate intercorporate cooperation. The sponsorship of technology projects, however, tends to be politicized because of the constituency interests of legislators and rivalries between firms influencing the policy processes. Changes in the bargaining outcomes cause discontinuities in official sponsorship, and can occur before projects have achieved significant results.[7]

Administrative interest in sponsoring technological progress has focused on high-technology sectors because frontier research advances have diffuse effects within those sectors and in medium-technology industries, with potentially very important implications for international competitiveness. The value of intensive information sharing for discoveries in frontier research, and for the exploration of opportunities for commercial application, has been recognized. Comparative studies of technology policies, which have evidently contributed to bureaucratic learning, have in some cases drawn attention to aspects of corporate cultures and structures that can determine innovative capabilities.[8] Intensely competitive intercorporate relations in the US economy, with low levels of trust, have been seen as hindrances to high-technology advances, in effect making these depend very much on the in-house capabilities of major firms with resources that can support wide ranges of potentially interdependent innovative ventures.

The potential utility of intercorporate cooperation increases as advances are made in frontier technology. These advances occur on widening fronts, and while discerning them necessitates collaborative searching, their productive use is difficult to predict. Intercorporate information sharing can thus be seen as a public good that has to be promoted more and more actively by business associations and the US administration.[9] The principal responsibility for the public interest would have to be assumed by that administration, and the nature of the task, it should be clear, would require emphasis on interactive consultative learning between technocrats and corporate representatives. In this process the technocratic involvement could draw in small and medium-sized firms to complement the activities of oligopolistic leaders whose strengths raise issues of market failure.

Technology development and diffusion, as a structural policy task, could be complemented by consultative endeavours to sponsor entrepreneurial cooperation. The encouragement of widely concerted entrepreneurship can be recognized as a vital public good, to be striven for because of the public interest in comprehensive development of the widening range of technological advances and because, in complex industrialized states, potentials for high growth have to be realized through extensive coordination functions.

The encouragement of concerted entrepreneurship, as a structural policy task, has to be considered in the context of market changes affecting high-technology sectors. A concentration trend tends to develop in these sectors as larger and more efficient firms compete as investors in new technology while driving weaker enterprises into declines. Possibilities for entrepreneurial coordination then depend on the information and choices of a shrinking number of decision-makers. They may be linked in alliances, but these are likely to be managed instrumentally, and may become more competitive rather than cooperative, due to the value orientations in the American business culture. Exploration of opportunities for entrepreneurial coordination on a wider scale would be possible in the type of alternative context evident in Japan, where the communitarian business culture causes managements of large firms to respect the independence of small and medium-sized enterprises. In this setting extremely numerous entrepreneurial energies interact, with very intensive communication flows that sustain high levels of trust.[10]

Literature on the Japanese system has stressed its unique culture and the difficulties of introducing it into other societies, but its operational principles clearly accord more with the coordination requirements of a highly industrialized political economy in comparison with the operational principles of intensely individualistic political economies. In those political economies the coordination of economic activities is affirmed to be a 'market' function, but the markets exhibit strong concentration trends in which coordination processes become more oligopolistic.

It can be argued that in highly individualistic political economies the pressures of competition are conducive to radical innovations, and perhaps to higher and more rapid growth, while in communitarian political economies the greater emphasis on cooperation within and between firms is conducive to incremental innovations.[11] The comparison can be suggested because of contrasts between the USA and Germany, but when the differences between the USA and Japan are considered the Japanese system has to be recognized as one with distinctive capabilities for accelerating the pace of incremental innovations and thus opening the way for radical advances. It also has to be recognized that the diffusion of innovations, and, thus, of knowledge relevant for entrepreneurial coordination, is faster and more extensive in Japan.[12]

Structural policy imperatives in the USA that can be derived from closely linked technological and entrepreneurial considerations obligate understanding of requirements for progress in advanced political development. Macromanagement coping with the challenges of globalization has to engage with coordination tasks in the interdependent national economy that tend to become more and more urgent, in the public interest, as independent corporate operations contribute to stresses and imbalances in the home economy and its external linkages, without activating systemic adjustments. Problems of governance, hindering effective responses at the policy level, tend to become more costly for the entire political economy, notably because of accumulations of heavy government debt and failures to control stock market speculation that threatens to become unsustainable. Overcoming these macromanagement deficiencies will be essential for the evolution of a structural policy aligned with the public interest. Initiatives to develop a consultative structural policy, through interactive technocratic–corporate learning, however, could contribute to progress in advanced political development.

CONSULTATIVE PARTNERING

The rationale for developing a consultative structural policy concerns the public good of coordinated entrepreneurship and technocratic facilitating functions that can help to provide that common benefit. The informational complexities and uncertainties about potentials for entrepreneurial cooperation in high-technology sectors, as expected and unanticipated advances are made in frontier research, have to be intensively explored for the development of that cooperation. Market-oriented exchanges of information in the present American business culture tend to be mainly strategic, in terms of individual corporate interests, and are not sufficiently extensive for the development of wide ranging collaboration. Scope for evolving complementary investments and production plans is quite limited, because of problems of informational market failure. The principal government function that can be advocated would be autonomous technocratic analysis of sectoral indicators of potentials for complementarities, viewed in perspectives broader than those of individual corporate managements. Such analysis, presented for discussion at structural forecasting conferences, could be expected to stimulate intercorporate information flows and increase managerial sensitivities to public interest concerns about trends and issues in sectoral interdependencies.[13]

The technocratic involvement could be expected to build on expertise obtained through learning acquired in exchanges with managements. While helping to inspire greater intercorporate trust it could be expected to reduce managerial orientations toward destructive competition, that is through resorts to anticompetitive practices. This would deserve emphasis because of the efficiencies demonstrated by the Japanese blend of competition and cooperation – a blend based on social solidarity which causes cooperation to benefit from rivalries which are intense but restrained by intercorporate goodwill. The constructive technocratic roles that can be envisaged would contribute, through the building of trust, to general reductions of risks in corporate decision-making, and to the generation of synergies in the evolution of intercorporate complementarities.

Pending the development of a community spirit among participating firms, managements, especially those of very large enterprises, could take little interest in the conferencing objectives, and could seek only to identify competitive opportunities, in the context of concentration trends in American industries. Such orientations could be linked with expectations that technocratic roles at the conferences would be influenced by diverse representations of interests and would be negatively affected by conflicts between legislators as well as by shifts in the preferences of the administration.

The encouragement of constructive corporate participation could be assisted by the commissioning of presentations by academics with status as international management experts whose contributions would tend to gain acceptance as impartial assessments and who could be seen to have capacities for informal monitoring of managerial responses to the conferences. The academic involvement would in effect impose informal accountability on the technocratic participation in the conferences, thus limiting dangers that this could become politicized. All this would be helpful for the building of trust and goodwill, but for that purpose the most important role could be that assumed by a structural policy authority, operating as an independent commission with overarching perspectives dedicated to entrepreneurial cooperation.

Political designing for the establishment of such an authority would have to recognize the danger of obstructive and even perverse behaviour by groups in Congress.[14] An educational effort of large proportions by the administration and business groups would clearly be necessary. This, however, could build on the modest rationale for the TransAtlantic Business Dialogue sponsored by the US Department of Commerce and the European Commission in the mid-1990s.[15] It could be explained, moreover, that the conferencing would extend not only the logic of that dialogue but also the logic of enabling policies through which governments provide support for entrepreneurial development through infrastructure projects and the funding of technology ventures.

Linked with the formation of the conference authority there could be an industrial clustering programme, sponsored by the Department of Commerce. This, while risking intensive politicization, would be based on recognition of the advantages of short distances for exchanges that can aid technological and entrepreneurial innovation, and for the development of complementary production processes. Industrial agglomerations, formed mostly through the uncoordinated choices of firms, attract enterprises because of the combined effects of transaction, production and transport cost reductions, opportunities for forward and backward linkages, the scope for economies of scale and opportunities for access to large markets.[16] An indirect effect of the conferencing would be to give more order and stability to industrial clustering in the USA, with prospects of continued administrative support for related infrastructure development.

The entrepreneurial cooperation encouraged by the technocratic–corporate conferences and the industrial clustering programme could enhance location advantages in the USA. Corporate planning could thus give more emphasis to production in the USA for export, and somewhat less to foreign production for external markets. Some reduction of the large balance of payments deficits could be anticipated. Meanwhile the costs of globalization could be reduced, as shifts of production processes to foreign locations could become less active, and industrial adjustments to these could be more orderly, because of intercorporate cooperation.

All this could be assisted by changes in antitrust policy. Antitrust enforcement tends to discourage interfirm cooperation that can be claimed to cause injury to other parties, and accordingly is a factor in the decisions of firms to produce abroad, in environments allowing more scope for productive collaboration. In this respect the balance between external production and export-oriented production in the home economy can be altered in conjunction with other factors motivating foreign operations. Challenges for structural policy thus have to be considered, but the broader problem is simply that the scope for productive – as distinct from collusive – cooperation between US firms is restricted, and that this limits intercorporate communication flows that could be conducive to entrepreneurial coordination.[17]

Legislative action to reform antitrust policy would be difficult, because of the probability of obstructive congressional activity, popular fears of concentrations of economic power and the complexities of accumulated rulings that would have to be considered. The adoption of complementary investment, production and marketing decisions by firms without explicit agreements, on the basis of informal understandings about the benefits of concerting strategic plans, should be possible without vulnerability to antitrust litigation. There would certainly be no risks of such litigation if the concerting of plans were limited to locational cooperation, which could develop through the proposed conferencing, and that locational cooperation could facilitate widening informal collaboration. In the industrial clustering which could be anticipated the natural development of trustful relations could be a restraint on attempts to resort to antitrust litigation.

Entrepreneurial coordination facilitated and encouraged by the technocratic and independent academic contributions to the conferences would extend beyond locational cooperation, multiplying links between industrial clusters within the home economy, and transnationally. In this process the officially sponsored consultative involvement would be all the more important, especially for the benefit of small and medium-sized firms coping with informational uncertainties about opportunities for international operations. Technocratic and academic expertise in structural forecasting, ranging across foreign economies, would be vital for the development of forms of concerted international entrepreneurship by managements lacking comprehensive assessments of trends in the planning of foreign and home country firms.[18]

STRUCTURAL POLICY AND MACROMANAGEMENT

The rationale for a consultative structural policy has to be considered with reference to macromanagement problems and efficiencies in the American political economy, and to the evolution of market forces affecting and affected by those problems and efficiencies. There is a danger that interacting vicious circles of administrative and corporate activity will aggravate macromanagement deficiencies, limiting potentials for progress in advanced political development.

The costs of globalization – the disruptions of growth and employment, and the downward pressure on the wages of less skilled workers – in conjunction with those of a concentration trend strengthening oligopolistic market power – tend to be borne by labour, which is immobile, rather than by capital, while it expands foreign operations.[19] Public support thus tends to shift to groups promising larger allocations for sheltering and redistributive measures, while confidence in the utility of market-opening leverage against trading partners is not encouraged.[20] The rising costs of sheltering and redistributive measures add to corporate incentives to produce abroad, and on balance this contributes to increases in balance of payments deficits that are attributable also to the import drawing effects of the increased sheltering and redistributive allocations. The level of internal demand, accounted for in part by those allocations, motivates increased foreign sourcing by national firms for the home market.

Monetary policy has to cope with the inflationary effects of heavy fiscal allocations and of high-level stock market speculation, which is encouraged in part by the higher returns of US firms expanding their international operations. Threats of and resorts to monetary tightening are intended to dampen the speculation and reduce internal demand. If the currency appreciates, exports weaken and corporate emphasis on foreign production increases; hence the balance of payments deficit rises, thus raising uncertainties about the confidence of foreign investors in conjunction with their concerns about the high level of US government debt.[21]

A consultative structural policy, if implemented with vigour and moral force, could gradually ease the adjustment problems of globalization, moderate the concentration trend in US industries and assist the development of a functional balance between home operations for export and foreign production, thus reducing balance of payments surpluses. A spirit of consensual policy-making could evolve, overcoming class cleavages and introducing greater stability into policy processes and the operations of firms.

The conferencing for high-technology sectors, it must be stressed, would give impetus to intercorporate information flows and cooperation, increasing managerial sensitivities to opportunities for coordinating entrepreneurship and to sectoral and intersectoral interdependencies, as well as to the public interest concerns evident in technocratic contributions to the conferences. Restructuring and relocation decisions would be made with broader informal accountability, and with concerns about the scope for future collaboration, and for the building of trust and goodwill. The burdens of sheltering and compensating groups adversely affected by restructuring and relocation strategies would be moderated while higher domestically based growth would be attainable through the concerting of corporate strategies.

For macromanagement the positive effects would be cumulative. Corporate trust in government would be improved, and constructive corporate–government dialogue would be possible. The development of strong peak economic associations would be aided, with beneficial effects on legislative behaviour because of the breadth of interests that would be aggregated. Increased corporate solidarity and the concerting of entrepreneurship, by contributing to higher growth, would assist reductions of the high level of government debt. Meanwhile the enhancement of domestic location advantages would encourage increased production for export, with somewhat reduced emphasis on the use of foreign production bases.

Greater exchange rate stability would also be in prospect. Higher growth and reductions of the balance of payments deficits and government debt would contribute to this, while assisting management of Atlantic monetary relations. The US dollar's importance for international transactions and as a reserve currency would be maintained. The increased strength of the US economy, moreover, would enable it to cope with financial crises in Third World countries like those which have caused distress in Latin America and East Asia, while providing assistance for resolution of such crises. Meanwhile the enhanced solidarity in the US political economy could generate the political will necessary for resolute engagement with the problems of volatility in world financial markets. Failures to achieve a sufficiently broad and functional aggregation of interests in the financial sector would be overcome, and thus would no longer permit minimal regulation for purposes of competition against foreign financial institutions.[22]

The problem of unsustainable stock market speculation could be gradually reduced to less threatening proportions through the diffuse effects of the consultative structural policy on social capital, the development of consensus on principles of economic management, and institutional progress. A more-community-oriented spirit would tend to develop in the financial sector and in policy communities dealing with regulation of that sector. Corporate identities and performance would be recognized more in term of networks and alliances with pervasive patterns of cooperation. Investors would see reductions of emphasis on short-term profits and the adoption of long-term plans promising stable returns by interdependent groups of enterprises, in which managements would be more dedicated to productive entrepreneurship rather than opportunistic financial management and organizational manipulation.

STRUCTURAL POLICY COOPERATION

A structural policy seeking to promote high-technology entrepreneurial partnering aligned with the public interest, through consultative explorations of innovative structural potentials, could be implemented in collaboration with similar public management ventures in other states. This would promote complementarities and introduce greater stability into the USA's structural interdependencies. The moral basis for the collaboration would be an understanding of shared responsibilities for providing the international common good of collegial globalizing alliance capitalism. As globalization continues economic policies have to be managed with awareness of extended account-abilities for their effects on foreign communities, and this awareness should deepen into consciousness of obligations to work for interdependent welfare as well as shared efficiencies.

Elementary understandings of the obligations of structural interdepend-ence begin with recognition that distinctions between American and foreign firms, and between American and foreign products, become blurred in deep-ening integration. Corporations of mixed composition as well as those that remain distinctly national expand their international operations, and most, especially in higher-technology sectors, join networks and alliances with foreign partners. A consultative American structural policy would have to relate to the widening range of firms operating in the USA, and in linkages with US firms abroad. Cooperation with structural policies in other major states would thus be increasingly necessary in the common interest. To build such an endeavour on a consensual basis moreover it would be desirable to promote very active consultative links between US policy communities and those of the other cooperating states.

American advocacy of structural policy cooperation could emphasize the prospect of increasing strains and disruptions in globalization due to failures of coordination between firms and between governments. The growth of networks and alliances involving mainly US firms tends to be instrumental rather than relational, with minimal regard for interdependent public interests as these are not substantially articulated in the presently distant and distrust-ful relationships between firms and the US administration. Macromanagement deficiencies in the USA and other major industrialized states leave the way open for, and in effect give impetus to, narrowly focused corporate strategies that add to the costs of globalization. Potentials for efficiencies in con-sultative collective management are thus obscured, while problems of internationalized market failure activate only defensive measures. Corpora-tions operating with greater autonomy as their foreign activities expand implement restructuring strategies while becoming more deeply involved in concentration trends, setting up their own interdependencies with disruptive effects on the larger patterns of linkages in the USA's foreign economic relations. As efforts to enhance structural competitiveness and increase the openness of foreign economies, the independent corporate activities have consequences which, in conjunction with those policy endeavours, tend to introduce complex adversarial tensions into relations with the USA's princi-pal trading partners.

The rationale for structural policy cooperation could give prominence to its potential for building international social capital oriented toward widely concerted entrepreneurship, for the development of advanced forms of alliance capitalism. These would promise higher growth and smoother adjustment to changes in corporate structures and activities, blending these into patterns of stable complementary specializations. In the cooperating states, as in the USA, concentration trends could be moderated through respect for the interests of smaller firms, and understanding of the overall efficiencies of dispersed centres of entrepreneurial innovation, exemplified in the Japanese industry groups.[23] A major consequence would be an easing of problem of cooperation in the management of competition policies.

Without substantial structural policy cooperation the problems of harmonizing competition policies are likely to become more difficult in the USA's foreign economic relations. Competition policies are commonly influenced by permissive attitudes to the foreign operations of national firms, and the potential for conflict between governments increases as the international operations of enterprises assume larger dimensions. The constructive effects of the consultative partnering in the USA's structural policy interactions with major industrialized states would focus corporate strategies on collaborative potentials, while subordinating competitive motivations to realization of the larger benefits of overall cooperation. A higher integration logic could thus be given expression in processes of systems transformation: corporate rivalries would become collegial, and destructive competition would be reduced in new coordinated patterns of efficiencies.

STRUCTURAL STATECRAFT AND TRADE POLICY

A trade policy focusing on the reduction of structural barriers to entry in foreign markets, using leverage for this purpose, tends to perpetuate adversarial relationships and, through its negative effects on public attitudes in the target countries, discourages interest in American products. Consultative structural statecraft promoting complementarities through the encouragement of entrepreneurial cooperation would induce spontaneous market openness, and assist the development of a transnational business culture conducive to the resolution of international market failure problems. Representations of interests shaping trade policy would be aggregated transnationally. Meanwhile arm's length and intra-firm trade would assume more balanced and more stable patterns, thus facilitating long-term planning.

Protectionist pressures influencing US trade policy, it must be stressed, tend to be very active because of the persistence of large balance of payments deficits and the openness of the policy process to demands for shelter. The costs of globalization, in popular and elite perspectives, are attributed to the unfair practices of major trading partners, which are seen to justify trade policy activism. Efforts to reduce foreign structural impediments to trade, however, tend to provoke increases in those impediments. These cause US firms to place greater emphasis on supplying the target countries through production within their economies, as the trade frictions are expected to persist due to the hardening of attitudes and failures to deal collectively with the costs of globalization.

The most constructive shift from trade policy activism that can be advocated is diplomacy to promote complementarity in the structural foundations for arm's length and intra-firm commerce as these become more closely related through intra- and inter-alliance trade.[24] Structural conference diplomacy facilitating widely shared explorations of expanding areas of collaborative entrepreneurial opportunities would contribute to the growth of complementarities. This could be expected to happen mainly through corporate responsiveness to structural forecasting in the public interest. That would be provided by the US structural authority and its foreign partners. Extensive corporate adoption of more collaborative and less unilateral strategies, with beneficial structural effects, would meanwhile have favourable effects on interest groups demanding protection and strategic trade policy measures.

There could be foreign suspicions of strategic trade policy intentions in the American promotion of structural conferencing. Direct and indirect subsidies for US firms could encourage such suspicions, and there could be complaints that official infrastructure support at technology-based clusters of industrial activity in the USA was in effect a subsidy programme. Associated with concerns about strategic trade policy intent there could be anxieties about American interest in managed trade, exemplified in the recent history of USA–Japan commerce. With these concerns, moreover, there would no doubt be awareness of the competitive strengths of American enterprises, based on their positions in the home and foreign markets.

Cautious foreign responses to US structural conferencing initiatives would have to be expected. Confidence would have to be encouraged by ensuring very active technocratic and corporate participation in the conferencing by the partnering countries. In Atlantic structural conferences strong roles by the European Commission and the Round Table of European Industrialists would be essential for the building of trust and goodwill.[25] Independent academic participation, moreover, would be an important factor, if this could be seen to be objective and impartial.

To encourage foreign confidence in American goodwill it would be imperative to avoid aggressive unilateralism: market-opening leverage and discriminatory treatment of imports – especially through antidumping measures with overt bias – would have to be greatly reduced. This would require firm high-level leadership and the building of a strong supportive consensus in business associations. Over time the development of the consultative structural policy at home could assist the growth of restraints on aggressive unilateralism. A vigorous and comprehensive educational effort by management institutes could be encouraged by the administration if it were under effective leadership.

STRUCTURAL POLICY AND MACROECONOMIC COOPERATION

Imperatives to reduce trade and balance of payments deficits have been causing US administrations to urge major trading partners, especially Japan and Germany, to adopt expansionary fiscal policies: the anticipated increases in domestic demand have been expected to draw more imports from the USA. The target governments have seen this diplomacy as an endeavour to externalize adjustment costs and as a threat to their own macromanagement performance.[26] With the establishment of the European Monetary Union as a source of pressure for fiscal discipline in Western Europe, the USA now has much less scope for expressing economic advice in Atlantic relations. Japan, however, is exceptionally vulnerable to forceful macroeconomic advice because of its difficulties in adjusting to the financial crises in industrializing East Asia.

Political competition in industrialized states tends to force fiscal expansion, especially to enhance structural competitiveness – through assistance to industries and infrastructure development – and to shelter and compensate sectors and communities adversely affected by import penetration and the restructuring and relocation strategies of firms. In the USA this kind of fiscal expansion has followed a period of drastic spending increases and tax cuts which in combination were intended to shrink the economic role of the state. Strong currency appreciation severely weakened the USA's structural competitiveness before a slow learning process led to an engineered depreciation in the mid-1980s. Large fiscal deficits however continued into the late 1990s and were accompanied by very substantial trade deficits. Heavy debt service was a factor in the fiscal deficits, and associated with this were external vulnerabilities, as foreign holdings of this debt were large, and foreign investor confidence was clearly conditioned on assessments of the sustainability of that debt and of balance of payments deficits attributable primarily to the trade deficits. In this context political competition hindering allocative discipline became a source of pressure to induce the fiscal expansion that has been desired in Japan and Germany.

Since the financial crises in industrializing East Asia there has been strong fiscal expansion in Japan to increase domestically based growth, but as recovery from economic decline has been slow imports have fallen. Meanwhile a loose monetary policy, in conjunction with the fiscal expansion, has caused downward pressure on the yen, resulting in higher exports, especially to the USA. The utility of further pressure on Japan for fiscal expansion has thus seemed doubtful, and US policy has been responsive to proposals for managed trade as well as for increases in restraints on imports from Japan.

Literature on macroeconomic policy interactions between industrialized states has generally focused on their effects, through domestic demand, on external trade, in conditions of shallow integration. Shifts to expansionary policies, increasing domestic demand, have been considered appropriate in states with trade surpluses, while contractionary shifts have been felt necessary in states with trade deficits. As deepening integration continues with increases in transnational production, however, potentials for consultative structural partnering demand attention as well as imperatives for sound collaborative macroeconomic policies.

In the USA's relations with other industrialized states consultative structural partnering, through high-technology planning conferences, could contribute to the evolution of balanced complementarities, with higher interdependent growth. Enterprises based in trade surplus states would increase production in the USA, while American firms would increase production in their home economy and serve foreign markets more through exports. Political competition generating pressures for fiscal expansion in the USA would remain strong, partly because of the continuing costs of globalization. The consultative structural endeavours, however, would gradually orient US macroeconomic policies more toward providing an environment for industrial growth based on concerted entrepreneurship. This could be expected to happen because of the spread of a spirit of cooperation in US policy communities and interest groups. Allocations to subsidize industries in rivalry with such policies in Europe and Japan would be moderated, because of the higher interdependent growth expected from entrepreneurial coordination in the home economy and in the external partnering, especially with Europe.

Monetary policy management would be indirectly eased by the structural effects of the consultative partnering, to the extent that balanced complementarities evolved in the USA's foreign economic relations. Balance of payments problems would gradually assume smaller dimensions, prices in the home and partner economies would tend to become more stable and stock market speculation would recede from levels of doubtful sustainability. The main improvement in the balance of payments would result from increased production in the USA for export, and this improvement would be conducive to increased exchange rate stability. Meanwhile general understanding of the trend in intercorporate cooperation would tend to increase shareholder interests in long-term growth potentials. The cooperative spirit, moreover, could penetrate the operations of financial institutions, reducing their market manipulations and their encouragement of investors' hopes for short-term gains.

Goodwill and trust developing in the consultative structural endeavours with Europe and Japan would assist collaborative engagement with problems of reform in the international financial markets. The lack of progress toward reform has been due to the negative influence of financial groups, especially in the USA, favouring weak regulatory arrangements. Administration of the financial sector in the USA has lacked coherence as well as commitment to stability, and has allowed the nation's financial institutions to be exceptionally active in world financial markets. Opportunities in those markets have been seized mainly by US securities firms which have been gaining strength in the home economy at the expense of banks, taking advantage of regulatory deficiencies.[27]

PARTNERING COMPLEXITIES

A consultative US structural policy operating through conferencing with European and Japanese systems of technocratic–corporate partnering would have to cope with many complexities in collaborative structural forecasting and the exploration of opportunities for entrepreneurial cooperation. These complexities would yield to expectations of coherence for planning only after intensive series of conferences during which technological trajectories and investment paths and options would be recognized. This conferencing would have to proceed with efforts to promote a spirit of integrative cooperation, moderating established orientations that are almost entirely competitive in the policy communities of the participating countries and in their corporate associations.

In the high-technology sectors on which the conferencing would focus, small numbers of mostly large firms are active in international trade and production. These firm operate with multiple interdependencies, extending more and more across borders and innovation frontiers. Entrepreneurial exploration of opportunities and problems in these interdependencies is driven mainly by individual competitive motivations, with varying effects on levels of trust and openness. The breadth and diversity of advances in frontier technology, and the difficulties of predicting these and of discerning their implications for collaborative entrepreneurial planning, necessitate increasingly extensive international networking. Sponsorship of the high-technology conferencing, it must be stressed, would enable the American structural authority to encourage and assist wider information sharing, increasing the efficiencies of the networking and making it more inclusive, in the common interest.

International high-technology networking is part of a larger process in which US firms with varying home country identities, attachments and loyalties relate to European, Japanese and other foreign enterprises as competitors and alliance partners. The densest and most active interactions are with European companies, because of cultural ties, high-volume cross investment, and high-volume intra-industry commerce at medium- and high-technological levels. This Atlantic pattern is exceptionally open to innovative consultative endeavours, and if these are undertaken at high-technology levels, the broader industrial effects, through the diffusion of innovations and general increases in technological capabilities, will be extensive.

For European high-technology firms the Atlantic conferencing, which could be co-sponsored by the European Commission, would provide opportunities for entrepreneurial exploration more extensive than those in the generally specialized information flows within their sectors. These opportunities would provide scope for collaboration that would overcome organizational limitations resulting from the restrictive effects of years of market separation within Europe. Because of those organizational limitations European Union firms have derived only modest advantages from technology enhancement programmes sponsored at the Union level and by their governments. Lagging competitiveness causes many of these firms to seek collaborative ties with US enterprises rather than other European companies. This orientation would remain strong as the proposed conferencing developed, but there would be increased information flows conducive to partnering between Union firms.

The planning of academic contributions to the Atlantic conferencing could draw on the expertise of a very large community of European and American international management scholars, including numerous technology policy specialists. This transnational community could be a very important source of independent analyses that would supplement the roles of US and European technocrats as structural forecasters. The informal mutual responsiveness which would result would be of great value for general confidence building, and for institutional development in the US structural policy authority and in the counterpart organization which could be expected to develop within or under the auspices of the European Commission.

Outside the Atlantic relationship high-technology conferencing endeavours would have to focus on Japan, because of its dynamic role in the USA's structural interdependencies, and the very urgent requirement to build a more harmonious pattern of linkages with the Japanese economy. Crude market-opening leverage has made the policy level interactions rather adversarial, thus tending to increase solidarity in the Japanese political economy and its resistance to disruptive foreign intrusions. The asymmetric interdependence which has evolved, however, clearly demands more collaborative management. Because of unfavourable attitudes on each side, and sharp cultural differences, the scope for productive exchanges at the governmental and corporate levels is quite restricted, compared with that in Atlantic relations, but the prospective entrepreneurial partnering could be extraordinarily dynamic.

The Japanese form of alliance capitalism generates superior capabilities for innovative applied technology and the concerting of entrepreneurship on a wide scale, with technocratic guidance through structural forecasting. These distinctive characteristics invite highly constructive diplomacy to build rapport for entrepreneurial collaboration. Initiatives for this, it is clear, would have to come from the USA, and would have to signal a decisive shift away from aggressive unilateralism, not just as an administrative choice but as a profound change in American policy communities.

Consultative structural partnering in high-technology sectors with the European Union and Japan would greatly extend the efficiencies and system building effects of technocratic–corporate conferencing in the American economy, while assisting the generation of similar dynamism in Europe and Japan. Impetus would be given to high-technology conferencing between Europe and Japan, and, thus, to triangular consultative partnering. The scale of concerted high-technology entrepreneurship could then become very large. Linkages between policy communities and corporate groups in this vast pattern could then provide a structural basis for substantial advances in international collective management.

STRUCTURAL PARTNERING AND MULTINATIONAL INVESTMENT

American structural partnering initiatives demonstrating strong integrative intent, without instrumental political concerns, would encourage greater openness in the world economy, and more positive elite and popular attitudes toward high-technology transnational enterprises. European and Japanese responsiveness would add to the dimensions of these effects. Rivalries to enhance structural competitiveness would become more friendly, and there would be greater understanding of the significance of interdependencies in structural competitiveness.

If integrative intent focused on interdependent growth and welfare were not sufficiently evident, the consultative partnering could be misrepresented by irresponsible media treatment and by social action groups like those which aroused opposition to the negotiation of a multilateral investment agreement during the late 1990s.[28] Apprehensions of increased international high-technology oligopoly power could prevent congressional funding of an independent structural partnering authority. A strongly supportive consensus in business associations and academic management institutes, however, could help to spread rational understanding of the public interest objectives of the consultative partnering.

Formal arrangements concerning rights of establishment and national treatment would be concluded more easily if increased trust and goodwill were developing through the structural partnering between the USA, Europe and Japan, and the settlement of disputes would be more feasible. The USA's status as the main advocate of a multilateral investment agreement would become more favourable, especially because apprehensions about uses of its superior bargaining power would be moderated. The concerns of European and Japanese policy communities with enhancing structural competitiveness and with exploiting opportunities to develop strategic trade policies and strategic direct investment policies would be redirected as the prospective spread of gains from trilateral entrepreneurial collaboration became more significant.

US policy in multilateral investment negotiations has been managed under diverse internal pressures for sectoral exceptions and for wide access to host countries. These pressures have limited interactive flexibility and have affected the credibility of concessions offered regarding transportation, communications and financial services. American administrative interest has given high priority to quests for more liberal European foreign direct investment policies, because of the size of the US corporate presence in the European Union, but the structural policies of several Union governments have tended to become more active because of rivalries to alter the spread of gains in the integrated regional market.[29] Investment bidding competition between these governments is intended to serve rather than weaken their structural policies.

The main policy challenges for the USA identified in literature on proposals for a multilateral investment agreement are that the onset of negotiations would encourage intensified representations by corporate groups and social action organizations, thus complicating administrative efforts to enlist congressional approval, and that problems of competition policy cooperation would demand much attention if the negotiations made progress. These challenges indicate the desirability of taking major structural partnering initiatives and fostering a supportive consensus before entering into negotiations for a multilateral agreement that would increase general openness to foreign direct investment. The political reasons for delay would be valid well beyond the short term, because of the weaknesses of aggregating structures in the American political system that would in effect allow much scope for agitation to disconcert legislators. A further reason for delay would be that the collaborative networking resulting from the structural partnering initiatives would help to form a stable pattern of entrepreneurial coordination which could be expected to remain effective in a new environment of greater capital mobility after conclusion of a multilateral investment agreement.

High levels of capital mobility in Europe, since the formation of the single market, have resulted in complex uncoordinated structural changes, with numerous disruptions, posing many uncertainties for firms and national administrations. Consultative structural endeavours could have provided order and stability for the disjointed systemic evolution resulting from the diverse corporate responses to market integration. Because of the asymmetries in the regional process of deepening integration, and its uncertainties, member governments have been competing against each other to enhance structural competitiveness. The dysfunctional effects of this rivalry would deserve much emphasis in Union level efforts to sponsor consultative partnering, and US initiatives to promote such partnering on an Atlantic basis could identify with the rationale for the Union endeavours.

The functional logic of giving priority to structural partnering in advance of negotiating general increases in openness to foreign direct investment deserves much stress because of the importance of building a foreign direct investment regime within a pattern of supportive and well established policy orientations. Attempting to set up such a regime without a firm basis in international elite rapport, and without activating a system of structural policy cooperation, will risk conflicted observance of the unequally negotiated rules. The increased scope for capital mobility, moreover, with inevitable asymmetries resulting from uses of bargaining leverage, would open the way for increases in the costs of disjointed deepening integration – the effects of accelerated concentration trends, of externalities associated with extensive restructuring and of failures to provide the public good of harmonious growth.

STRUCTURAL POLICY AND FOREIGN POLICY

For the USA deepening integration in the course of globalization has increasingly internationalized the public interest, adding to the dimensions and complexities of policy interdependence and structural interdependence. Moral imperatives and functional logic obligate endeavours to manage the interdependencies cooperatively, to promote synergistic harmony in intercorporate relations at home and externally and similar harmony in interactions with other governments. Liberal and pragmatic elements in the American political culture tend to induce focus on opportunities to assert external interests identified in the nation's competitive policy processes, and to adopt unilateral measures for this purpose, but the continuing expansion of largely independent corporate activities is making the collaboration of other governments and foreign enterprises more and more necessary for orderly growth with equity.

As markets become more closely linked in globalization, it must be stressed, their efficiencies but also their failures assume international dimensions.

Imperatives for collective management thus become evident, to increase and give order to the efficiencies and to overcome the failures – especially the abuses of dominant positions and the externalities associated with restructuring. Unilateralism to extract forms of cooperation from other states is possible for a very powerful nation, but the strains and costs of globalization would remain serious, partly because the domestic sources of unilateralism have destructive internal effects.

Collective management for interdependent growth should not be sought through collective interventionism. Policy cooperation, for efficiency and welfare, has to be guided by the logic of alliance capitalism, and has to extend that logic in consultative structural partnering. Managerial elites drawn into this partnering in high-technology sectors can be expected to become sensitive to international public interest concerns through the informal accountability, the learning experiences and the socialization processes of structural conferences. A pervasive spirit of integrative cooperation spreading from those conferences would help to resolve issues in several areas of foreign economic relations. Transnational knowledge-based policy communities operating in close interaction with managerial elites would contribute to extensive interpenetrations of policy processes in the Atlantic context and in US relations with Japan.

An American structural partnering statecraft, with collaboration from home country corporate leaders and associations, could inspire not only reciprocation but also progress in advanced political development within the European Union. This has become necessary at the Union's present stage of integration, in which regional collective management is hindered by national rivalries. A major negative consequence of these rivalries has been a failure to evolve a common structural policy. Contributing to the evolution of dynamic solidarity-based capitalism in Europe would establish Atlantic relations on sound fundamentals. This, moreover, could provide guidance for reformers in the chaotic Russian transitional political economy, in which there is elite interest in the potential efficiencies of authoritarian capitalism.

For Russians favouring a system of authoritarian capitalism, the Chinese regime has demonstrated how a form of national socialism under hard central control can achieve orderly growth while inducing international firms to contribute to that growth through regulated direct investment. The Chinese have considerable scope to exploit rivalries between foreign governments and firms seeking wider entry to their market. Their regime's growth strategy has dimensions which make it relevant for the security area of US foreign policy. In that area, however, uncertainties about the evolution of Russia have become more ominous problems that demand highly constructive engagement. There is a clear imperative to concentrate on developing a structural partnering statecraft that can inspire Russian consensus for the development of a form of alliance capitalism.

NOTES

1. The basic problems are still those identified in Roger G. Noll 'Structural Policies in the United States', in Samuel Kernell (ed.) (1991), *Parallel Politics: Economic Policymaking in Japan and the United States*, Washington, DC: Brookings Institution, pp. 230–80.
2. See Laura D'Andrea Tyson (1992), *Who's Bashing Whom? Trade Conflict in High Technology Industries*, Washington DC: Institute for International Economics.
3. See Symposium on Competition Policy, *The World Economy*, **21** (8), November 1998.
4. See details of US direct investment position abroad, *Survey of Current Business*, **78** (7), July 1998, 35–58.
5. The 1998 current account deficit approached $225 billion. See *Current Issues in Economics and Finance*, Federal Reserve Bank of New York, **4** (13), December 1998, 1–6.
6. US direct investment abroad at market value rose to $1793.7 billion in 1997 – an increase of $276.6 billion over 1996. See *Survey of Current Business*, July 1998, cited, and general comments on transnational enterprises in Keith Cowling and Roger Sugden, 'Technology Policy: Strategic Failures and the Need for a New Direction', in Jonathan Michie and John Grieve Smith (eds) (1998), *Globalization, Growth, and Governance*, Oxford University Press, pp. 239–62.
7. On US competitiveness in high-technology sectors, see Paolo Guerrieri and Carlo Milana, 'High Technology Industries and International Competition', in Daniele Archibugi and Jonathan Michie (eds) (1997), *Trade, Growth, and Technical Change*, Cambridge University Press, pp. 188–207. See also Rose Marie Ham and David C. Mowery (1995), 'Enduring Dilemmas in US Technology Policy', *California Management Review*, **37** (4), Summer, 89–107.
8. See Parimal Patel and Keith Pavitt, 'Uneven (and Divergent) Technological Accumulation among Advanced Countries: Evidence and a Framework of Explanation' in Giovanni Dosi, David J. Teece and Josef Chytry (eds) (1998), *Technology, Organization and Competitiveness*, Oxford University Press, pp. 289–318.
9. See David J. Teece (1991), 'Technological development and the organization of industry' in *Technology and Productivity*, Paris: OECD, 409–18.
10. See David C. Mowery and David J. Teece, 'Japan's growing capabilities in industrial technology: implications for US managers and policymakers', *California Management Review*, **35** (2), Winter, 9–34. See also Michael L. Gerlach (1992), *Alliance Capitalism: The Social Organization of Japanese Business*, Berkeley: University of California Press.
11. See David Soskice (1998), 'Openness and Diversity in TransAtlantic Economic Relations', in Barry Eichengreen (ed.), *TransAtlantic Economic Relations in the Post-Cold War Era*, New York: Council on Foreign Relations, pp. 8–35.
12. See Guerrieri and Milana, cited, and Patel and Pavitt, cited.
13. Because of the widening range of advances in frontier technology, and the multiplication of industrial specializations, interactive learning between firms has become increasingly necessary for the identification of complementary entrepreneurial opportunities. See Christopher Freeman, 'The Economics of Technical Change', in *Trade, Growth and Technical Change*, cited, pp. 16–54, and John H. Dunning, 'The Advent of Alliance Capitalism' in John H. Dunning and Khalil A. Hamdani (eds) (1997), *The New Globalism and the Developing Countries*, Tokyo: United Nations University Press, pp. 15–20.
14. See Terry M. Moe (1990), 'Political institutions: the neglected side of the story', *Journal of Law, Economics and Organization*, **6**, Special Issue, 213–54.
15. See references to the Dialogue in Brian Hindley (1998), 'New Institutions for TransAtlantic Trade?', *International Affairs*, **75** (1), January, 45–60.
16. See references to agglomeration dynamics in *Oxford Review of Economic Policy*, **14** (2), Summer, 1998.
17. On the restrictive effects of antitrust policy see Lawrence J. White (1993), 'Competition policy in the United States', *Oxford Review of Economic Policy*, **9** (2), Summer, 133–51.
18. On interactive learning in conditions of high informational complexity see Jan Horst Keppler (1998), 'Externalities, fixed costs, and information', *Kyklos*, **51** (4), 547–63 and

Peter Maskell and Anders Malmberg (1999), 'Localised Learning and Industrial Competitiveness', *Cambridge Journal of Economics*, **23** (2), March, 167–85. See also Ikujiro Nonaka and Hirotaka Takeuchi (1998), 'Theory of the Firm's Knowledge-Creation Dynamics', in Alfred D. Chandler, Peter Hagstrom and Orjan Solvell (eds), *The Dynamic Firm*, Oxford University Press, pp. 214–41.

19. See Dani Rodrik (1997), *Has Globalization Gone Too Far?*, Washington, DC: Institute for International Economics.

20. See Geoffrey Garrett (1998), *Partisan Politics in the Global Economy*, Cambridge University Press.

21. On the level of US government debt see Jill Ouseley (1997), 'United States: Primary Market Auctions and Government Debt Management', in V. Sundarajan, Peter Dattels and Hans J. Blommestein (eds), *Coordinating Public Debt and Monetary Management*, Washington, DC: IMF, pp. 341–407.

22. See George M. von Furstenberg (ed.) (1997), *Regulation and Supervision of Financial Institutions in the NAFTA Countries and Beyond*, Norwell: Kluwer, parts II, III, and IV.

23. See Nonaka and Takeuchi, cited.

24. See observations on the structural foundations for trade in Keith Cowling and Roger Sugden (1998), 'Strategic trade policy reconsidered: national rivalry vs free trade vs international cooperation', *Kyklos*, **51** (3), 339–57.

25. On the importance of the Round Table of European Industrialists see Maria Green Cowles, 'Organizing Industrial Coalitions: a Challenge for the Future?', in Helen Wallace and Alasdair R. Young (eds) (1997), *Participation and Policymaking in the European Union*, Oxford University Press, pp. 116–40.

26. See C. Randall Henning (1998), 'Systemic Conflict and Regional Monetary Integration: the Case of Europe', *International Organization*, **52** (3), Summer, pp. 537–74.

27. See von Furstenberg, cited.

28. See Stephen J. Kobrin (1998), 'The MAI and the Clash of Globalizations', *Foreign Policy*, **112**, Fall, 97–109.

29. See Thomas L. Brewer and Stephen Young (1998), *The Multilateral Investment System and Multinational Enterprises*, Oxford University Press.

12. Collective management issues in US foreign economic relations

Gavin Boyd

The management of the USA's foreign economic relations and the international operations of its firms have assumed greater significance for the global political economy since the East Asian financial crises of the late 1990s. Growth in the European Union has remained slow, despite the benefits of internal market integration and monetary union, and slackened commerce with East Asia has increased dependence on economic ties with the USA. The European Union has some potential to develop a leadership role in the global economy, but rivalry and distrust between its member governments prevents the formation of a common political will. The external policy concerns of its governments tend to be confined to their immediate environments. In these the large and highly competitive US corporate presence is a potent challenge, and it has become more important in investment bidding rivalries from which Japanese firms have to some extent withdrawn. These rivalries are factors in a larger context of competing interests which hinder the development of a common structural policy. The structural competitiveness of the USA, and its very substantial bargaining strength, thus sustain a dominant position in the global political economy.

The USA does not have a structural policy, because of a liberal political tradition, and its structural competitiveness is based on the strengths which its firm developed in its large integrated home economy under governments aloof from industry and commerce. Vigorous international expansion by these firms, through arm's length trade but increasingly through transnational production, has activated intensive promotion of openness in the world economy. Japan and European states have been targeted as unfriendly trading partners because of forms of support and protection given to their industries. Shifts by their governments to liberal economic policies have been encouraged, with predictions that the increased commerce would bring large common benefits.

The advocacy of international economic openness derives thrust from concerns about large American trade deficits and balance of payments deficits, and a very high level of government debt, a substantial portion of which is held by foreigners. Trade policy issues are prominent in the US policy process as they directly affect the political interests of the administration and many legislators. Pressures from interest groups obligate continuous efforts to commit major trading partners to market opening measures. Meanwhile these efforts are matched by resorts to protectionist measures in response to demands by sectors adversely affected by competing imports.

The perspectives of policy communities on questions of international economic cooperation tend to be dominated by concerns about unfair trading by other industrialized states, especially Japan. The World Trade Organization is viewed primarily as an institution which should be responsive to these concerns, and its limitations are considered to justify resorts to leverage against the uncooperative trading partners. These limitations are also felt to justify efforts to develop regional arrangements for liberalized commerce in Latin America and the Pacific. Such regional arrangements, it has been argued, could be advances toward global market integration.

Implicit in the treatment of trade policy issues by policy communities, the media, and interest groups, are beliefs that trade should be balanced and that there should be no sectoral disruptions: pressures should thus be exerted against other states to ensure their cooperation. These beliefs, however, are seen to be challenged not only by unfair foreign trading but by larger and more complex phenomena covered by the term 'globalization'. Prominent in this context is an expansion of high-volume foreign production by US firms for the service of the home and external markets. Associated with this is considerable foreign sourcing by American enterprises for the home market.

The complexities of globalization tend to remain peripheral in US policy processes because of the focus on trade – seen mainly as arm's length commerce. Issues of monetary, fiscal and financial policy cooperation draw less attention. The prominence of allocative issues in fiscal policy limits awareness of the extent to which prolonged large-scale budget deficits have contributed to major increases in imports, while indirectly adding to the incentives for US firms to produce abroad. Monetary and financial policy questions, requiring highly specialized treatment of generally little media interest, have much less significance for the political interests of US policymakers. The establishment of monetary union in Europe and the volatility in world financial markets, however, have increased general awareness that levels of interdependence in the USA's foreign economic relations are rising, with consequences that involve vulnerabilities as well as benefits.

CATEGORIES OF OPTIONS

The areas of foreign economic relations given the most extensive consideration in American policy processes concern external trade because the development of this commerce has increasingly significant effects on growth and employment in all sectors of the economy. The average ratio of production for export in the total output of US manufacturing industries in the mid-1990s was 13.4 per cent, having approximately doubled during the previous decade. The ratios were considerably higher for several advanced and mature technology sectors which were making substantial use of imported inputs and which were experiencing large expansions of imports of final products.[1] International trade accounted for 23.9 per cent of GDP in 1996, and, while a modest but increasing proportion of this commerce involved vertical specialization, roughly 60 per cent of it was intra-firm trade related to foreign production by US firms and their affiliates at volumes several times higher than the official figures for US exports.

The overall effects of the deeper US involvement in the world economy are widely recognized to be imbalanced, due to a long succession of large trade deficits and balance of payments deficits, and to disruptions and reductions of industrial output caused by competing imports but also by the movement of US production processes to foreign locations and the sourcing of foreign products by US firms for their home market. The volume of US production abroad and the scale of foreign sourcing by US firms are major factors, but the dynamics of the policy process focus attention on the trade deficits because of representations by interests in the affected sectors. Efforts by the administration to protect and compensate those interests and to open foreign markets for US exports are expected to yield domestic political support. The strategies of US firms moving operations to foreign locations do not evoke public executive or legislative review, in part because of the complexities of assessing the net effects on the trade deficits.

Questions of reciprocity in economic openness thus dominate perspectives in US policy communities dealing with external trade as the politically most visible area of interdependent macromanagement. The principal options recognized are form of trade policy activism, and the utility of these is understood to depend on the responsiveness of trading partners to pressures for reciprocity, Japan being identified as the partner that is most at fault and most vulnerable.

When the policy process is studied closely, however, there are questions about the extent to which it results in rational service of the public interest. To the extent that politicians trade policies with each other and with interest groups in return for favours, validating assessments based on public choice theory, rational choices in the public interest may not be made because of failures in aggregating preferences. There may be pluralistic stagnation, not because of a lack of sentiment in favour of trade policy activism but because of unwillingness to contribute to the likely spread of political benefits, or because of the concerns of some active participants with the interests of US international firms or with the investment bidding hopes of certain states within the USA.

What is in the public interest, moreover, while relativized by complex constituency concerns, may not be clear to politicians functioning under heavy demand overload and information overload, without aggregating guidance from institutionally developed political parties. The organizational weaknesses of the major American political parties hinder the development of aggregations of sectoral and community interests as a basis for policy, and this state of affairs is all the more serious for macromanagement tasks because of a fragmentation of corporate interests. The scope for trading policies in multiple relatively isolated interactions is thus very extensive, and this process can continue in ways that cause administrative initiatives affecting external commerce to depend on numerous side payments to legislators in exchange for their support.

The public interest in areas of foreign economic policy is articulated with considerable objectivity by research institutes offering informed advice to legislators and members of the US administration. This advice urges quests for cooperative solutions to issues in foreign commerce, in recognition of the vulnerabilities of interdependence and the increasing importance of general market openness for the US economy. There are various warnings, however, about the effects of large fiscal deficits on domestic demand, and, thus, on trade balances, and about diversions of investment into the funding of such deficits rather than into productive activity, with negative consequences for structural competitiveness.

How the research intensive articulations of the public interest influence the perspectives of policy-makers is very difficult to assess. Studies of the trade policy process convey impressions that it is heavily dependent on the making of confidential deals in which the overall requirements of macromanagement receive little attention.[2] Conflicts between these deals, it is clear, tend to further obstruct recognition of functional imperatives evident in the research-intensive advice directed at decision-makers. Administrative leadership can contribute to legislative policy learning through persuasive affirmations and explanations of the public interest, but this depends on the status and capabilities of the president and his team.

Within the trade policy area there are bilateral, regional and multilateral choices. The degrees to which these are recognized and assessed appear to vary greatly at the legislative and administrative levels because of the pervasive exchanges of political favours, but it is clear that the main external context seen to be open to effective market-opening engagement is the Atlantic relationship. Interdependencies in this relationship are relatively balanced, and cultural affinities facilitate interaction. Vigorous engagement is seen to be necessary because European governments are believed to be unfairly subsidizing and protecting their industries.

The option of working toward Southern expansion of the North American Free Trade Area is viewed as a choice in which market-opening possibilities are overshadowed by prospects of vigorous opposition from organized labour and low-technology sectors which made ratification of the NAFTA agreement very difficult. The trading of favours by the administration to secure congressional support has profoundly influenced administrative and legislative views on the desirability of striving for an enlargement of NAFTA that could be expected to provoke much more serious domestic opposition.[3]

In the category of regional options market-opening endeavours directed at East Asian states have larger significance, because of the high growth potentials of those states and their greater significance in US foreign commerce. The option of promoting trade liberalization in the Pacific, however, has to be viewed with awareness of the probability of domestic opposition more serious than that discouraging free trade initiatives directed at Latin America. Yet in regional contexts the USA has more scope to press for liberalization, on terms in its favour, than in multilateral negotiations within the World Trade Organization as a forum for exchanges of concessions on barriers to market entry.

Options in the less politicized areas of policy affecting foreign economic relations remain functionally significant while the dynamics of the policy process give prominence to external trade issues. The functional linkages between related policy areas indeed become more important for macro-management in the public interest, especially because of the consequences of large balance of payments deficits for monetary policy and the regulation of financial institutions. Downward pressure on the currency caused by the balance of payments deficits is a problem for monetary policy, which has to combine exchange rate management with the maintenance of price stability at home, together with restraint on potentially destabilizing stock market speculation. The internationalization of financial markets exposes the currency to shifts in investor confidence which can result in volatility that may be all the more serious because of weaknesses in financial regulation in the USA, and inadequate financial policy cooperation between the major industrialized states.

Monetary policy options are difficult choices because of erosions of sovereignty in this area due to the massive growth of largely unregulated international financial markets, but also because of a lack of coherent preferences in the home financial sector to which US monetary policy is informally responsive.[4] The absence of sufficiently substantial cooperation with European and Japanese monetary authorities is a further problem.

The gravity of the closely linked monetary and financial policy problems has to be emphasized because major structural policy options have not been available. The liberal political tradition has allowed wide scope for the market forces of competitive rather than cooperative managerial capitalism. Functional imperatives for the evolution of alliance capitalism in conditions of deepening integration have not been met.

THE CHALLENGES OF GLOBALIZATION

Deepening integration, as it assumes global dimensions for the USA, presents challenges which are commonly identified as its costs. Its opportunities and benefits draw less policy level and media attention, but have great prominence for the managements of American international firms and for research communities studying the world economy. The costs are mainly disruptions of what could be integrated growth processes and can be attributed to coordination failures and destructive competition. The coordination failures are evident in contexts of market failures interacting with government failures. The opportunities and benefits of globalization are increases in interdependent growth with the multiplication of efficiencies in diverse specializations. These, as they become complementary, use wide ranges of innovations at the frontiers of technology.

US policy level perspectives on globalization tend to be dominated by concerns with enhancing structural competitiveness, within the limitations of a liberal economic policy orientation. Recognition of rivalries for higher structural competitiveness has been influenced by concentration on the desirability of maintaining the tradition of limited government, and therefore adopting market friendly approaches, in the interests of efficiency and equity. Other industrialized states have been urged to follow such approaches, instead of subsidizing and protecting their industries. The sizes, resources and generally superior performance of American firms have sustained confidence in the potential benefits of market friendly structural measures, which have resulted mainly in infrastructure development and the sponsorship of precompetitive research and development projects.

The logic of the liberal orientation has been challenged by degrees of deindustrialization resulting from corporate emphasis on building industrial capacity abroad. Issues of structural balance have become evident, and have become more serious because the exploitation of opportunities for foreign production has drawn increasing attention from US firms contending for world market shares. Meanwhile the persistence of large imbalances in the benefits of international commerce for the US economy has been seen, it must be stressed, with a narrow focus on trade policy. Despite increases in American bargaining strength on account of the East Asian economic declines, however, the constraints of rising interdependencies obligate caution in resorts to leverage. In the policy process, moreover, the interests of US international firms in satisfactory working relationships with host governments are further sources of caution, although these firms stand to benefit from increases in the openness of external markets.

While the utility of the liberal policy orientation has been open to question, the policy process itself has been subjected to new pressures because of domestic reactions to the perceived costs of globalization. These have tended to increase popular demands for sheltering and redistributive policies and, thus, for the Democratic Party.[5] The possibility of higher tax burdens, therefore, has made foreign production in lower-cost areas a more significant choice for American international firms. Hence the demands for sheltering and redistributive policies may well become stronger, due to the employment effects of relocation strategies. These employment effects moreover may be all the more important politically because of their association with staff reductions following mergers and acquisitions that increase concentration trends in the US economy.

The prospect of a vicious circle in which policy responses to the costs of globalization lead to structural changes that increase those costs is a complex challenge to the liberal policy orientation. This challenge cannot be met through trade policy activism, because of the strength of the incentives motivating US corporate emphasis on foreign production rather than production at home for export, and because of the restraints that have to be observed in resorts to market-opening leverage. Extensive corporate cooperation in response to administrative and popular concerns about the costs of globalization becomes more desirable, but American international firms relate distantly and distrustfully to their home government, and can bargain more and more effectively with numerous host governments while increasing their foreign operations. Rivalries to acquire and strengthen international oligopoly power tend to become more absorbing for the managements of these firms, although at the same time their interests in alliances also increase.

The challenges of globalization which were first recognized before the East Asian economic crises have become more demanding because of those problems. Competing imports have increased because of the depreciation of East Asian currencies. Opportunities for US firms to expand operations and make acquisitions in East Asia have also increased, while such opportunities have also increased in Europe. Japanese competition in that area has diminished somewhat and European firms, while coping with the policies of left-centre governments, have become more open to alliances and mergers with American enterprises.

TRADE, FOREIGN DIRECT INVESTMENT AND COMPETITION POLICIES

The costs and benefits of globalization are challenges for the USA in several areas of policy between which there are functional linkages that are in varying degrees politicized. Coordinated management of these linkages is necessary in the public interest but difficult because of the strong pluralism which tends to validate public choice perspectives. This pluralism affects the functional significance of decisions within each policy area, and the overall consequences are operative in relations with trading partners.

Trade policy is the most active area in the USA's foreign economic relations, because of the multiplicity of representations from interest groups, demanding protection to reduce competing imports, and also in many cases seeking administrative action to increase the openness of foreign markets. Legislative and executive responsiveness to all the representations has significant effects in all the political competition at state and federal levels. This competition is intense, especially because of the frequency of elections to the House of Representatives and the interests of the executive in gaining political advantages through involvement in trade policy issues. Much of the trading of favours in all the complex bargaining is confidential, and this, together with the relativizing of the public interest in the competition to shape policy, imparts an inward-looking quality to the entire process. Openness to interactions on trade issues with other states is thus limited, and the dynamics of the internal negotiations tend to cause an orientation toward aggressive unilateralism.

The dimensions and complexity of the domestic competition to shape trade policy reflect the aggregating weaknesses of the political institutions, especially the political parties, and the fragmented pattern of corporate associations. The intense individualism of the political culture, which accounts for those problems at the basic levels of the system, tends to prevent the evolution of more cooperative policy processes and the building of stronger institutions. Potentials for policy learning in the public interest are thus kept low in the conflicting trade policy processes. Decisions are outcomes of multiple compromises evolving incrementally and disjointedly.

Protectionist pressures in the policy process maintain a system of administered protection which implements antidumping measures in response to complaints by US firms alleging injury to their domestic market positions by imports claimed to be priced below cost. Procedures in this system indicate tendencies toward bias in favour of the complaining firms, and thus can discourage foreign enterprises seeking market shares in the USA with price competitive products.[6] The risks of triggering antidumping measures are significant for small and medium-sized foreign exporters of low- and mature-technology products, especially those that would be destined for US sectors that already have substantial degrees of import penetration. An indirect effect of the system is that it leaves open opportunities for American firms to source products from foreign manufacturers for the home market. Producers in Third World countries unwilling to face the risks of exporting to the USA at price competitive levels have incentives to deal with US firms sourcing their products for that market. A further indirect effect is that Third World governments seeking to promote export-led growth have incentives to attract US firms into manufacturing ventures directed at the US market and those in other industrialized states. The utility of investment bidding for this purpose can appear to be more significant than the provision of subsidies for home country firms that have uncertain prospects as exporters to the USA.

The trade policy process is not open to consideration of questions of international cooperation in the use of antidumping measures. The established policy orientation, despite all the pluralism, is firmly unilateral, with tacit reliance on the strength of superior bargaining power to secure foreign acceptance of safeguards against unfair exporters. Only the European Union has comparable bargaining strength and it implements antidumping measures with a similar unilateral orientation.

The US system of administered protection is linked politically with unilateral market-opening leverage against foreign governments held to be unfairly restricting US exports. The administration has to comply with legislation mandating retaliatory action against trading partners found to be at fault after investigating procedures under the office of the US Trade Representative. Sentiment behind this congressional requirement does not view the World Trade Organization as an adequate source of remedies against foreign protectionism.

Foreign direct investment policy is a relatively inactive area of the USA's foreign economic relations. Liberal treatment of incoming foreign direct investment is a well-established practice, restricted in principle only with respect to vaguely defined national security issues that are matters for executive discretion. Outward foreign direct investment is influenced by tax policy, but in this respect draws little attention in fiscal policy processes, as congressional interest is absorbed in contests over allocative issues that have more tangible constituency significance than the taxation of American multinational enterprises. Legislators depend very much on corporate contributions to their campaign expenses, in part because of the institutional weaknesses of the political parties. The media, because of dependence on corporate advertising, gives little publicity to problems of deindustrialization that may be associated with outward direct investment. The opposition of social action groups to negotiations for a Multilateral Investment Agreement appears to have caused legislative and administrative opinion to favour careful avoidance of foreign direct investment policy issues which could be taken up by labour unions in ways that would attract media treatment.[7]

Competition policy has become a matter of independent regulatory surveillance and enforcement, while legislative pluralism has prevented change in laws which set somewhat ambiguous requirements for the control of anticompetitive activity. The independent regulatory authorities – the Anti-Trust Division of the US Department of Justice and the Federal Trade Commission – have overlapping and potentially conflicting functions, but the independence of the latter is more significant, as the Department of Justice is part of the administration. The functions of the two authorities in effect encourage the launching of vast numbers of private antitrust lawsuits which contribute to a proliferation of judicial decisions that add complexity to antitrust enforcement. Such enforcement cannot deal with forms of tacit collusion between firms, but by discouraging explicit cooperation that can be alleged to have adverse effects on competitors it indirectly provides incentives for firms to expand through mergers and acquisitions. In recent years guidelines on antitrust enforcement issued by the Department of Justice and the Federal Trade Commission have been influenced by economic theorizing that has identified the possible efficiency and welfare effects of mergers and acquisitions.[8]

The uncertainties and risks of antitrust enforcement tend to make expansion into international operations more advantageous for US firms, as the focus of this enforcement is on the effects of anticompetitive behaviour within the USA on the domestic economy. Competition policy issues however assume increasing significance for governments as deepening integration continues in the global economy, and some cooperation in this area has evolved in US relations with the European Union. This has been considered necessary because of the high volume of cross investment in Atlantic relations, but on each side this has been seen as a process that should remain bilateral, and there has been no interest in cooperating in the establishment of an international competition authority.[9] The collaboration with the European Commission is on a case by case basis, and is not preparing the way for ventures in such collaboration outside the Atlantic context. In the relationship with Japan a standing request is stronger enforcement of competition policy by the Japanese authorities, and their perceived resistance is regarded as a justification for continuing pressure.

The high political prominence of trade policy, attributable mainly to the intractable problems posed by large trade deficits, encourages some executive and legislative interest in forms of managed trade, including managed strategic trade, seen to be feasible through uses of bargaining leverage based on threats of restrictions on imports into the USA. Japan has been the principal target, but an unintended effect has been increased solidarity in the Japanese intercorporate system to limit foreign economic intrusion. Within the US policy process, meanwhile, conflicts of interest have threatened to have disruptive effects. The prospect of coping with corporate rivalries in the planning and administration of managed trade can cause administrative attention to shift to politically more rewarding areas of policy.

MACROECONOMIC POLICIES

The current state of the USA's structural interdependencies, with their imbalances, has been determined mainly by its macroeconomic policies, over the past few decades, through their effects on the trading and location decisions of national and foreign enterprises. Prolonged large-scale fiscal deficits, raising levels of domestic demand and drawing imports while causing diversions of investment into the financing of government debt, have contributed substantially to the profitability of foreign production and foreign sourcing by US firms for the home and external markets, as well as the profitability of exporting to the USA by Japanese and European enterprises. Monetary policy, managed with emphasis on price stability to counter the inflationary effects of fiscal expansion, has in effect been aided by the price competitiveness of imports, especially from East Asia, and by somewhat reduced demand for labour – an unfortunate result of technological advances and of increasing corporate emphasis on foreign production. Monetary tightening, however, it must be stressed, has been seen as a means of dampening potentially unsustainable speculation in US stock markets. This has been avoided because of the adverse effects of the East Asian economic declines, but may well be considered imperative after recoveries in East Asia because of continuing rises in the levels of stock market speculation.

Fiscal policy processes, understandable mainly in public choice perspectives, are not open to considerations of international economic cooperation, but there is a history of administrative efforts to encourage the adoption of expansionary policies by trading partners, especially Japan. These efforts, it must be emphasized, have been clearly recognizable as endeavours to secure foreign cooperation for moderation of the trade effects of US fiscal expansion. The establishment of the European Monetary Union, with its pressure on member governments to maintain fiscal discipline, has reduced the scope for expansionary fiscal diplomacy in Atlantic relations. As directed at Japan, however, that advocacy has seemed appropriate, although in conflict with the IMF's encouragement of fiscal tightening in the distressed East Asian economies.

The strong domestic focus of US fiscal policy tends to increase as the costs of globalization obligate larger allocations for the sheltering and compensation of adversely affected sectors and communities and as subsidies for exporters become important for improvement of the trade balance. If shifts in voter preferences and the demands of interest groups result in pressures for very large outlays to cope with globalization, there could be strong corporate opposition, however, resulting in a polarization which could allow only modest fiscal changes. In such a context a major policy level response could well be increased protectionism and increased trade policy activism.

Monetary policy has to be managed with international cooperation, especially in Atlantic relations, and there are increasing imperatives to extend this cooperation into collaborative control of international financial markets, in which US financial institutions are the most active participants. Domestic price stability is the responsibility of the Federal Reserve System, as a formally independent authority operating with informal accountability to the national financial community, based on professional ties which can become very active if any major institution in that community is destabilized – for example by high-risk speculation. On occasion there is wider informal accountability, as there may be public criticism of the system's interest rate decisions by members of the administration, legislators, interest groups and the media. The Treasury, as a vital part of the administration, is very sensitive to domestic business trends, including especially those affecting the financing of government debt, and those affected by changes in exchange rates.

The implementation of monetary policy through Federal Reserve controls on the banking system tends to weaken because of a decline in traditional banking, as securities firms assume larger financial roles, and as banks move into securities activities that are in effect outside the jurisdiction of the Federal Reserve. The securities industry is under relatively weak regulation, for the reduction of systemic risks, and draws investments promising generally higher returns than those offered on deposits by banks. The Federal Reserve's capacity to lower growth rates and reduce inflation by monetary tightening remains substantial but is limited by the availability of credit through securities firms, which are well placed to use funds from foreign markets with lower interest rates. The US securities industry has exploited the availability of such rates in Europe and Japan.

Monetary policies implemented through the banking system in Europe and Japan are less affected by the growth of securities industries, as these have evolved to a considerable extent as controlled expansions of the banking systems, and those banking system have had very close relations with manufacturing and trading firms. The drift of funds from Europe and Japan into higher yielding investment in the USA weakens the intended growth effects of lower European and Japanese interest rates, and this raises issues in the external dimensions of US monetary and financial policies. The European Central Bank's roles in this context may well become a major challenge for the US administration. Within this context American monetary policy has to adjust to the prominence of the euro in the international monetary system while endeavouring to maintain the confidence of international and home country investors.[10] That confidence, it must be reiterated, is influenced by estimates of the sustainability of upward movements in US stock markets, of large US current account deficits and of high levels of US government debt.

There are strong functional as well as political imperatives for close monetary cooperation with the European Central Bank. These imperatives may well become more evident if the European Union endeavours to strengthen the regulation of its financial markets, for the control of volatility and the channelling of investment into the funding of industry rather than speculation. Political ties are especially important in this relationship because of symmetries in the structural interdependencies and the prospect of considerable expansion in international use of the euro, which will make Atlantic exchange rate management more critical for the US economy. The political ties are also important because planning to cope with possible stresses in the monetary interdependence has been neglected, on each side. Dealing with such stresses is thus likely to require very active spontaneous cooperation, and failure to achieve this, because of inadequate efforts to develop operational rapport, especially for volatility forecasting, could provide occasions for drastically unilateral responses to decisional problems in the European Monetary Union.

Initiatives for effective regulation of international financial markets may well be taken by European authorities, despite decision problems in the European Monetary Union which would hinder crisis management. The USA, as the state that has been mainly responsible for global financial liberalization, has a major responsibility to encourage and cooperate with such initiatives if its own decisional problems prevent leadership for comprehensive regulation in the interests of financial stability and productive use of the investment flows. The US decisional problems are serious, because of conflicting pressures affecting regulation in its financial sector, and they have in effect allowed much scope for speculative manipulation to cause and profit from volatility, while imposing pressures on firms in the real economy to maximize short-term profits.

The future of central banking, in the context of problems of international monetary cooperation, and international financial regulation, demands intensive study by US policy-makers, and has to be decided in conjunction with a solution for the dysfunctional operations of world financial markets. Incremental regulatory endeavours in those markets tend to lag behind the sophistication of products used for profitable risk management by financial institutions.[11] Weak regulation of these markets thus tends to persist, in line with the tacit preferences of the institutions as virtually dominant competitors in those markets. Legislative conflicts, in which those sectoral preferences are important factors, make effective administrative engagement very difficult.

COORDINATING POLICIES

Functional linkages between elements in the US policy mix become stronger with the rises in structural and policy interdependence associated with globalization, and deficiencies in any of the linked policy areas can thus have increasingly serious consequences, with cumulative results. Effective macromanagement however is made difficult by conflicting political linkages, notably those related to the numerous forms of political trading which complicate fiscal policy. An overall knowledge-intensive guidance function might be possible for the Council of Economic Advisors, through contributions to executive leadership, but this group of experts, required to serve short-term administrative needs for practical advice on politically prominent problems, is normally restricted to this kind of activity. Independent advising, focusing on fundamentals, is allowed little scope, and potentials for high-order policy learning thus depend on executive level leadership capabilities. The qualities of these can vary greatly, because of the dynamics of presidential selection in a context of institutional weaknesses.

A well-coordinated mix of rational policies in the public interest is necessary for the collaborative management of interdependencies. The principal requirements set by the recent history of the US policy mix are to achieve allocative discipline sufficient to substantially reduce the heavy accumulation of government debt, and to eliminate major current account deficits. While problems of aggregation and consensus formation remain very difficult, however, because of the system's institutional weaknesses, the dynamics of intense political competition tend to activate attempts at leverage against trading partners. This has to be stressed because those attempts divert the attention of policy communities away from the primary tasks of macromanagement and discourage foreign cooperation for supportive engagement with those tasks.

All the problems of policy coordination reflect the negative consequences of failure to evolve a structural policy to respond to the problems and opportunities of globalization. This failure has been attributable in part to the influence of the liberal political tradition, with its emphasis on individual economic freedom, reinforced by policy-oriented research literature stressing the efficiencies of free market forces. In the USA this literature has had exceptional appeal for corporate managements because of long-standing private sector distrust of government. Studies of the costs of globalization have constituted a separate and smaller stream of literature, and, although recognizing the significance of capital mobility as a source of burden-sharing problems, have suggested only the potential remedies that might be possible through trade restrictions.[12]

The lack of a structural policy can be considered a failure in advanced political development, in conditions in which market deficiencies as well as efficiencies have increasingly assumed cross-border dimensions, and in which the USA's international leadership responsibilities have been increased because of the East Asian economic stresses. The continuing expansion of transnational production which is driving the process of largely ungoverned deepening integration in the world economy is causing governments to seek ways of enhancing structural competitiveness, because of imbalances in the spread of benefits attributable to differences in structural competitiveness, and differences in bargaining strengths that determine degrees of economic openness. US and other transnational enterprises extend their structures and increase their resources in this vast process while the development of linkages between national economic structures involves major costs, due to sectoral dislocations associated with restructuring strategies and concentration trends.

In the rivalries to increase structural competitiveness the USA has the most liberal policy orientation, which is being challenged by the substantial costs of globalization and their effects in the dynamics of popular pressures for sheltering and compensatory measures that can in effect give impetus to further corporate ventures in transnational production. The liberal policy orientation relies on the provision of a market-friendly environment for national firms to encourage location of their operations at home, with apparent hopes that the development of foreign operations by those firms will not lead to any significant deindustrialization. Such expectations are disappointed because of the strength of the incentives motivating expansion of those foreign operations – incentives that become powerful in the rivalries for world market shares.[13]

An interventionist structural policy would not be appropriate in this setting because it would antagonize firms and provoke extensive corporate evasion. Resourceful quests for corporate cooperation in the public interest are clearly required, and can be undertaken through intensive consultations in which firms would benefit from technocratic assistance in the exploration of opportunities for concerted entrepreneurial ventures. As affirmed in Chapter 11, this consultative partnering would have to be sponsored in collaboration with other major industrialized states in which American firms are active.

The rationale for a structural policy shaped and implemented in consultations with US firms would be a key element in the coordination of a national policy mix coping with the issues of globalization. This collaborative structural endeavour would promise improvement in the balance of payments and reduction of the costs of sheltering and compensating endangered sectors and communities. A new spirit of cooperative adjustment and concerted entrepreneurship spreading through the intercorporate system would redirect market forces and increase their overall efficiencies, while providing strong foundations for the development of social capital.

Clear articulation of the structural policy rationale, it should be stressed, would have to emphasize the public interest in dynamic and harmonious entrepreneurship and, therefore, in constructive knowledge-intensive technocratic–corporate consultations in support of collaborative managerial planning. Such consultations would meet the need for flows of tacit knowledge which become increasingly important for entrepreneurial activity in the complexities of deepening integration. This knowledge has to grow with the multiplication of potentials in applied technology as innovation frontiers are extended; and it also has to grow as the scope for complementary entrepreneurial operations becomes evident through collaborative exploration of the opportunities for interdependent planning. Understanding of this functional imperative can bring into prominence the public good of advanced alliance capitalism.

REGIONAL COOPERATION

The most meaningful interactions in the USA's foreign economic relations are with the European Union, on the basis of cultural and political affinities and high levels of structural interdependence, relatively more balanced than those with other areas of the world economy. There is considerable scope for the development of consultative links between American and European policy communities which could lead to interactive policy learning, consensus building and much informal accountability. Outside the Atlantic context the USA's foreign economic relations are managed at arm's length, with much less potential for spontaneous, wide ranging and productive responsiveness, and with more freedom for aggressive unilateralism, across longer social distances.

Potentials for productive management of the Atlantic interdependencies, however, are limited by mutual perceptions of deficiencies in governance, policies, and economic systems. In European perspectives the American political economy functions with dangers of pluralistic stagnation under an overloaded executive chosen through populist contests, with a political psychology more idiosyncratic than those of leaders in parliamentary systems. The USA's external relations are seen to be managed with emphasis on building domestic political support. The strengths of large US firms, evident in the size of the American corporate presence in Europe, are viewed as dangers for the relatively weaker enterprises in the Union, which lack competitiveness in world markets. American elite perceptions, recognizing the differences in corporate capabilities, identify European macromanagement

problems responsible for high unemployment and high welfare costs, reflecting failures to allow sufficient scope for market forces. The Union's system
of collective management is regarded as a cumbersome confederal process
which prevents effective governance of the single market but subjects it to
excessive regulation. As the Union's economic difficulties generate pressures
for protection of its industries, it is felt that the USA must exert pressure for
the adoption of more liberal European economic policies.

The Atlantic relationship has a history of strains but of progression toward
relative bargaining equality as the European Union has absorbed new members, integrated its internal market and established its Monetary Union. The
USA has been the main source of initiatives for cooperation, but European
policy communities have seen US tendencies to impose on the Union adjustment costs for American fiscal and balance of payments deficits. The logic of
monetary integration in Europe has been accepted with the understanding of
its importance for the reduction of vulnerabilities in Atlantic interdependence: intra-Union policy differences were moderated to facilitate monetary
union, on the basis of shared concerns to manage macroeconomic policies in
line with European interests.[14]

For harmonious growth at higher levels in Atlantic relations the USA can
seek to build consensus, through elite networks, on the need for structural
partnering based on the concept of alliance capitalism. Initiatives for the
sponsorship of technocratic–corporate consultations for the exploration of
entrepreneurial complementarities in high-technology sectors at home could
be extended into quests for partnering with similar European forms of collaboration. The rationale for this could emphasize that the consultative
partnering, in the common interest, would help to facilitate more active
communication flows between US and European policy communities, with
an interpenetration of policy processes conducive to integrative cooperation.
The prospect of more comprehensive and more constructive management of
the relationship would help to relieve European anxieties about the concentration on trade liberalization which has been a major feature of US policy
toward the Union. Because of the size of the American corporate presence in
Europe the structural partnering initiatives could evoke cautious Union responses, but this possibility could be prepared for by careful planning to
ensure that the structural diplomacy would be sensitive to European anxieties
and would demonstrate strong commitment to the building of trust and understanding. The credibility of this diplomacy would benefit from inclusion, in
the structural conferencing at home, of European firms operating within the
USA.

Frictions in Atlantic relations may well tend to increase because of intensifying rivalries for world market shares as the East Asian economies recover
and as protectionist pressures increase in the USA on account of employment

losses attributed to globalization, as well as because of a similar trend in the European Union. The rationale for consultative structural partnering may thus become more persuasive, but the necessary sponsorship will probably become very difficult if initiatives are delayed by pragmatic policy debates. Attitudes on each side may harden in disputes over market access, industrial subsidies and preferential trading arrangements with third countries.

Pacific relations are much less open to constructive engagement through conferencing for structural partnering, but demand high priority attention in US policy planning. The Japanese, South Korean and Taiwan economies will probably become more dynamic as they recover from their financial stresses, and will provide very important opportunities for US export expansion, which, with some developments in structural partnering, could lead to more balanced interdependencies. The long records of vigorous growth in these states, before their financial difficulties, had validated the functional logic of their systems of technocratic–corporate cooperation, and the revival of these systems, with more effective financial regulation, will offer possibilities for very productive consultative interaction.

The USA's promotion of regional trade liberalization, in the Asia Pacific Economic Cooperation forum (APEC), has given prominence to concerns to reduce structural impediments to commerce with the dynamic East Asian economies, but the main effect has been to provoke unfavourable reactions. Elites in those countries have seen the US endeavour as an attempt to weaken forms of government–corporate collaboration that have given expression to communitarian values and that have been highly effective. The USA's status in the area, moreover, has been adversely affected by the involvement of its financial institutions in destabilizing movements of funds that caused distress in Thailand, Indonesia, South Korea and Malaysia during 1997/9. Further, unwelcome US influence has been seen in conditions attached to adjustment assistance by the International Monetary Fund which have amounted to forms of market-opening leverage.[15]

American diplomacy to promote structural partnering with Japan would have to seek fundamental rapport with corporate, bureaucratic and political elites in that country's system of alliance capitalism; the efficiencies and equities of that system would have to be recognized and respected, and endeavours to weaken its solidarity would have to be terminated. The necessary reorientation of US thinking about the relationship would have to show understanding that the Japanese system has in effect applied internalization logic *above* the corporate level, notably through the industry groups (keiretsu) as an expression of basic principles in the national culture, and as a means of coping with asymmetries in interdependence with resource-rich industrialized states. It would have to be acknowledged, moreover, that the overt comparisons between the two countries regarding competition policy mask extensive tacit oligopolistic collusion in the USA, outside the range of anti-trust enforcement.

Much effort would have to be devoted to the building of understanding and trust, on the basis of a doctrine of partnership in alliance capitalism which would support intensive conferencing for the concerting of entrepreneurial endeavours in high-technology sectors. The US structural partnering authority would have to seek collaboration with the Japanese Ministry of International Trade and Industry's sectoral forecasting for the development of shared visions of innovative potentials based on technological trajectories. This collaboration would have to be sought with understandings that vigorous efforts would be made to prevent manipulation of the endeavour by US interest groups and legislators. Even more importantly it would have to be well recognized that the consultative partnering would yield beneficial results only after some years of patient endeavours, but that the opening to concerted entrepreneurship on each side would gradually become highly productive. A spontaneous partnering trend would make the Japanese intercorporate system less exclusive, while within the USA there would be increased intercorporate cooperation, with growing receptivity to opportunities for collaboration with Japanese enterprises.

To facilitate the necessary changes in thinking within policy communities and managements on each side much could be done to promote interactions at the middle levels of the policy processes between the USA and Japan, especially through joint meetings of legislative committees. The interpenetration of decision-making systems would result in shared policy learning, the building of trust and acceptance of obligations to show reciprocity. An incidental effect could be a strengthening of aggregating capabilities and an increase in public interest commitments in the American political system.

In the efforts to build mutual understanding the positive US assessment of relational efficiencies in the Japanese intercorporate system and of its potential for spontaneous opening could be linked with understanding of technological complementarities. US scientific institutes have superior capabilities for fundamental research, while Japanese firms have demonstrated superior achievements in applied technology. These achievements have been possible mainly because of the generation of X efficiencies through enlightened management practices in Japanese enterprises and the intensive information sharing within the Japanese intercorporate system. Understanding of the significance of the technology-based complementarities between the USA and Japan would be deepened through the consultative partnering that would bring the entrepreneurial planning of high-technology firms on each side into alignment with each other, in the common interest.

Firms and governments in industrializing East Asian states could become associated with the consultative partnering as it developed between the USA and Japan. In prospect would be the development of structural foundations for more balanced and more dynamic Pacific interdependencies and, thus, for spontaneous reductions of barriers to trade and investment in the region. Harmonious reduction and management of the costs of globalization for the USA, and also for Japan, would then be possible. The increased goodwill and trust in the relationship, moreover, could facilitate collaboration in the transformation of the Asia Pacific Economic Cooperation forum into a system of regional collective management.

Latin American relations, offering potentials for the expansion of the North American Free Trade Area (NAFTA), could be the third major region of structural partnering initiatives. The potential for diplomacy based on the concept of alliance capitalism has great significance because a 'Washington Consensus' that has influenced policy toward Latin America over the past few decades has appeared to be an inadequate guide for constructive involvement. This consensus anticipated that the promotion of economic liberalization in the area would enable freer market forces to increase growth, and that government structures would become more responsive to representations of interests by communities benefiting from enhanced prosperity and educational development.

The expectations of the Washington Consensus have been disappointed because of problems of governance in Latin American states which have prevented the development of market-friendly business environments while diverting managerial energies into clientelist activities and rent seeking.[16] These failings in governance have drawn attention to problems of political development that have not seemed open to resolution through reductions of official involvement in industry and commerce. Such reductions have clearly been necessary, but for enhanced administrative responsiveness to responsible representations of corporate interests there is a manifest requirement for very constructive foreign cooperation with Latin American enterprises to develop hemispheric alliance capitalism.

US endeavours could seek to develop consultative structural partnering through conferencing with Latin American technocrats and corporate elites, focusing on entrepreneurial opportunities identified in collaborative high-technology sectoral forecasting. There would have to be emphasis on the demonstration of goodwill through credible commitments to equality in the development of complementary entrepreneurial planning, so that there would be prospects for secure efficiency gains by the participating Latin American firms. Such prospects would have to be made evident by US corporate restraint on tendencies to acquire Latin American enterprises rather than work with them as partners with agreed specializations and interests in complementary planning.

Social distances in hemispheric relations would present fewer problems than those in the Pacific, because of the influence of affinities related to those in the Atlantic context. These affinities would facilitate initiatives to build rapport with Latin American technocrats and corporate elites, and to develop consultative exchanges between US legislators and their counterparts in major Latin American states. The primary objective of promoting structural conferencing, however, would have to be given great emphasis because of imperatives to overcome difficulties that have caused Latin American development to lag behind that in East Asia. These imperatives will require intensive contributions to Latin American policy learning about the efficiencies of intercorporate cooperation and technocratic–corporate cooperation that have been mainly responsible for high growth in East Asia.

To give full expression to the concept of alliance capitalism the USA's structural engagement in Latin America could invite Japanese cooperation. This can be suggested because the encouragement of Japanese regional involvement would be a dual expression of goodwill and a means of expressing more strongly the functional rationale for alliance capitalism. The positive attitude toward Japanese regional involvement, moreover, would relieve Latin American concerns about possible increases in the inequalities of interdependence with the USA. Japanese contributions to an acceleration of Latin American growth could be highly effective, and could add substantially to the corporate learning and policy level learning that has become necessary throughout the area.

GLOBAL COOPERATION

Much policy literature on regionalism affirms that the formation of free trade areas is against the developmental requirements of the world economy, as all countries would benefit from general trade liberalization. Some of this literature urges the USA to strive for general trade liberalization, rather than work for extensions of NAFTA and for reductions of Pacific barriers to commerce, but it has been argued that through the establishment of regional systems of economic integration the USA can make progress toward global market integration.

The choices open to the USA have great significance for the evolution of the world economy because of its scope to promote international economic cooperation and the incentives for many of its trading partners to seek preferential access to its large market. Such access can be granted, in return for side payments to be expected with bargaining asymmetries. Strong domestic opposition activated by the perceived costs of regionalization and globalization, however, is a powerful constraint, especially on attempts to expand NAFTA. This state of affairs contrasts with that of the European Union, which attracts new members without experiencing significant opposition from within the states dominating its decision processes.

Atlantic cooperation and competition overshadow the global political economy, as attempts at regional integration in the rest of the world have been largely unsuccessful, due mainly to problems of political development. Atlantic collaboration on issues of trade and investment liberalization can confront other states with difficult choices because of the risks of reduced access to the large North American and European markets. Frictions between the USA and the European Union, moreover, can lead to the imposition of costs on other states, especially because the frictions can generate pressures to externalize the burdens of managing those stresses.

For US policy-makers the Atlantic interdependencies absorb much attention, possibly at the expense of tasks obligated by global problems for which the USA has special responsibilities on account of its size and leadership potential. These responsibilities concern order, growth and justice in the globalization process, but efforts devoted to them generally do not bring significant domestic political rewards for the administration. The concerns of interest groups and legislators relate mainly to bilateral and regional issues seen to be of immediate importance and open to resolution through unilateral measures.

Trade policy activism at the global level is not politically rewarding for the US administration, because most of the issues are seen to be remote from domestic concerns and yet susceptible to resolution only through protracted negotiations. There are no significant political incentives for activism to promote reform in the regulation of financial markets or to bring more order into the world monetary system. The policy communities dealing with financial and monetary affairs have scope for autonomous constructive engagement, but, it must be stressed, relate to fragmented patterns of interest representation in which consensus formation is difficult. Highly sophisticated professional interactions in these policy communities often tend to be inconclusive but can be impervious to the concerns of administrative or legislative activists.

Global trade policy is managed, in effect, primarily through retention of scope for initiatives aimed at multilateral liberalization. The European Union does not have comparable scope for initiative, because its involvement in global commerce is smaller and its external network of politically significant ties is thinner. Holding the initiative, with the European Union as virtually a subordinate partner, the USA leaves states outside the Atlantic context with relatively few opportunities for spontaneous involvement in exchanges of trade concessions that could be extended to all members of the World Trade Organization under its formal rules. Regional trade arrangements are concluded by Third World states, mainly in Latin America, but without interest in or capabilities for global extension of the negotiated concessions. The US policy stance expresses no opposition, and does not have to reckon with Third World multilateralizing initiatives because the political bonds that would be necessary for these do not exist.

Use of the USA's scope for global trade policy activism focuses on securing general implementation of the Uruguay Round agreements through active involvement in the World Trade Organization. A leadership role is asserted through attempts at consensus formation which are aided by large inequalities in bargaining strengths and by the virtual inability of most of the member states to press for decision-making through formal voting arrangements. The functions of the WTO Secretariat are in effect restricted by a low level of financing which prevents the development of strong research capabilities that could support an independent advocacy role on behalf of the entire membership.

The USA's status as the principal state working for multilateral trade liberalization is given emphasis by tendencies to adopt aggressively unilateral measures in defence of its commercial interests. These measures add to the significance of bargaining inequalities in the WTO, but also demonstrate that the USA is capable of furthering its trade policy objectives outside that organization. While use of its scope for initiative in the launching of rounds of multilateral trade negotiations depends on the US administration's capacity to enlist congressional support, the international context has become more favourable for US leadership in the promotion of general trade liberalization. Because of the economic difficulties in East Asia and relatively slow growth in Europe, as well as severe problems in Russia, access to the large US market has become much more important for numerous countries outside the Atlantic setting; and the European Union, it must be stressed, has stronger incentives to seek a special trading relationship based on cultural ties and relatively balanced interdependencies.

All this, and the persistence of potentially destabilizing balance of payments deficits, could be seen as a rationale for more aggressive unilateralism. The constructive option, however, is to moderate unilateral tendencies in trade policy and work for more balanced interdependencies through structural partnering, using opportunities in regional contexts. The logic of this choice is tending to become stronger, in terms of the national interest and of the developmental needs of the world economy. The unilateral element in the advocacy of global trade liberalization expresses consciousness of strong bargaining leverage and confidence in the competitiveness of US firms, and can be seen as the basis for a unilateral approach to the structuring of the international economy. A policy reorientation toward structural partnering would invite collaborative responses instead of the defensive reactions normally provoked by aggressive unilateralism. This prospect, it can be reiterated, would help to reduce strains in the world trading system.

International financial markets are evolving with volatility attributable in a large measure to the balance of payments effects of asymmetries in gains from trade and transnational production. The USA is at the centre of this pattern of asymmetries, because of the scale of its balance of payments deficits and the very active involvement of its banks and securities firms in world financial markets. Structural partnering endeavours, contributing to a more even spread of gains from global commerce, could reduce the scope for potentially destabilizing speculation in the financial markets, and could also assist the formation of a sufficiently broad political will to impose effective regulation on those markets. There is a clear developmental requirement to ensure that investment is directed into productive use instead of very high-volume rent seeking; the future of growth in the real economy is at risk.

The rationale for the liberalization of international financial markets has been that savings would move across borders into the most profitable firms, and that these would then be able to make more effective contributions to global growth. A tacit consideration, influential in the preferences of US financial enterprises, has been the possibility of drawing on the high levels of savings in East Asian countries. Instead of the funding of industry on a global basis, however, large-scale high-risk investment strategies by American and other financial enterprises have generated and exploited volatility while increasing pressures on firms to achieve short-term profits and on governments to guard against speculative attacks on their currencies. The exploitation of volatility has involved manipulation of herd mentality among international investors – a major problem of failure in the internationalized financial markets.[17]

In the USA the build up of government debt and the persistence of large current account imbalances, together with levels of stock market speculation that threaten to be unsustainable, entail vulnerabilities to manipulative practices in world financial markets. Engagement with the regulatory problems of those markets is clearly imperative, but there is a requirement to deal with fundamentals, and it must be stressed that these can be changed for the better through structural initiatives. These will not compensate for further macro-management failures, which may have to be expected because of the persistence of problems of governance, but the structural partnering could provide a basis for long-term order in the nation's foreign economic relations.

The consultative structural partnering, opening up opportunities for extensive entrepreneurial collaboration across borders, and, thus, for higher interdependent growth, would tend to induce more stable financing for industry, at rising levels, with beneficial effects on employment that would lower the costs of globalization. A problem to plan against, however, would be the exploitation of industrial interest in collaborative ventures by financial institutions seeking to profit from opportunities opened up by the structural partnering. A partial solution would be the development of cross holdings between firms that begin to coordinate their plans through the interactions sponsored by the structural partnering. A more important solution would be the formation of industry groups, in the USA, Europe and Latin America, in which informal entrepreneurial cooperation would be supported by relational bonds with financial institutions under high principled leadership. The resulting degrees of stability would be especially important for the high-technology sectors that would be intended to be the main beneficiaries of the structural partnering.

The net international investment position of the USA at the end of 1997, it must be stressed, was a negative $1223.6 billion; there had been large increases in foreign purchases of US securities and inflows into the banking system, attributable apparently to the attractions of stock price increases in the USA and to capital flight from East Asia. The net international investment position has indicated serious vulnerability to correction through shifts in foreign investor confidence. This danger demands recognition because available balance of payments data has been becoming increasingly inaccurate, due to the very high volume use of derivatives in capital markets that evade regulatory surveillance and that make assessments of the risks of financial institutions and of the entire financial system very difficult.[18]

The centrality of the USA's difficulties in the surveillance and regulatory problems of international financial markets adds to its responsibilities for promoting order in those markets, and this demands resolute engagement with fundamentals, especially those affected by the manipulative practices of the securities firms. For this purpose increased stability in stock markets has to be sought, in conjunction with large reductions in US balance of payments deficits, and accordingly it can be argued that the logic of structural partnering should receive much attention in the planning of foreign economic policy. While it is clear that the partnering should focus on high-technology sectors, because of the growth potential of concerted entrepreneurship in these sectors and their significance in the diffusion of innovations, the collaborative spirit that would be promoted could be expected to have wider stabilizing effects.

While striving for fundamental change and development through structural statecraft the USA will have to deal more resolutely with the surveillance and regulatory problem in international financial markets. This will require political designing to give the International Monetary Fund and the World Bank more productive roles in the world economy. These two institutions have to reckon with the disruptive effects of high-volume short-term investment flows into and out of Third World countries, and the IMF is being challenged to evolve a supervisory function that would provide advance warnings of threats to stability in world financial markets.

IMF AND WORLD BANK FUNCTIONS

US endeavours to establish more order and more productive functions in world financial markets, with drastic reductions in the scope for high-volume rent seeking, while complemented by structural partnering initiatives, could make the tasks of the International Monetary Fund and the World Bank more manageable. These tasks have become larger because of greatly increased Third World requirements for adjustment and development aid since the East Asian financial crises.

Long-standing criticisms of the IMF have emphasized negative assessments of its balance of payments lending, and more recent evaluations have criticized the conditionality virtually imposed on its clients. The long-standing criticisms are mainly that IMF lending to distressed Third World countries, using resources provided by member states, aids debt repayments to mostly American banks, which have the largest exposures in the client countries, and which have been responsible, it appears, for imprudent lending. The recent assessments of IMF conditionality have questioned its suitability as a pressure for economic reform: market-opening demands as conditions for lending to East Asian states have reflected US trading interests, drawing attention to the major role of the USA in the IMF's system of weighted voting.[19]

External accountability, it must be stressed, is a necessary source of pressure on many Third World governments for more competent and less corrupt economic management. Such pressure can have some effects on the common deficiencies of Third World systems of personal rule which operate with soft but sometimes hard authoritarian methods, imposing clientelism on and exacting resources from subservient business communities. Necessary advances in political development can often be aided by the growth of a strong foreign corporate presence, however, as well as by forms of policy learning induced through dealings with international lending agencies. Large foreign enterprises, with wide ranges of locational choices, can in effect oblige Third World governments to compete against each other in meeting basic developmental requirements. This must be affirmed despite indications that lax labour and environmental standards in Third World countries do attract direct investment into resource-based and manufacturing ventures.

All these considerations can direct attention to potentials for structural partnering through which the USA could became more constructively involved in the harmonization of North–South interdependencies and the promotion of comprehensive development in Third World political economies. What could be expected would be the formation of increasingly extensive, linked forms of social capital, conducive to wider and more active structural collaboration in building systems of advanced alliance capitalism.[20] The structural initiatives that have been suggested for Latin America could become the initial phase of an endeavour which would expand into Africa and other Third World areas. Needs for balance of payments and developmental lending would be reduced in those areas, while vulnerabilities associated with the socially less responsible operations of North American, European and Japanese international firms would be reduced.

Developmental lending by the World Bank to Third World countries would become less necessary yet could be more productive if energetic efforts were made to implement a structural partnering policy. Concerted entrepreneurship in the evolving system of alliance capitalism would make possible greater and more efficient use of domestic savings in the host countries to finance industrial development. This development, moreover, would move into higher technological levels, hopefully with increasing reductions of the discriminatory trade practices through which the USA and other industrialized states hinder outward-oriented Third World growth.[21] World Bank funding could focus more on infrastructure projects linked with the expansion of alliance capitalism.

The World Bank operates with a high degree of centralization, deals directly with governments, but lacks consultative links with corporate groups in recipient countries. There is sensitivity to problems of administrative performance in those countries but little scope to engage with those problems. The organizational interests of the Bank and the career interests of its staff give impetus to its funding operations. These, however, tend to have suboptimal results because of the corruption and incompetence of receiving governments which have cumulative effects that discourage foreign investor confidence in cooperation with local firms.[22]

A firm US orientation toward structural partnering would prepare the way for relational developmental banking: US, host country and other banks could develop long-term advisory as well as financing functions related to the coordination of entrepreneurial activities. The roles of Japanese and German banks in their home economies would thus be replicated in ways that would have very positive growth effects and that would provide better conditions for infrastructure lending by the World Bank. The liberalization of financial markets in Third World countries, although a response to external pressures, is providing opportunities for American and other banks to aid the growth of national firms in those countries through intensive collaboration, in line with the logic of alliance capitalism. It could be suggested that such banks would concentrate on preferential financing for American, European and Japanese corporations active in the structural partnering. Such bias, however, could be guarded against by representatives of the US structural authority involved in conferencing with Third World counterparts on opportunities for aligning innovative strategic plans.

PLANNING FOREIGN ECONOMIC POLICY

Deepening integration internationalizes the public interest while causing the costs of globalization to become more prominent challenges for macromanagement. These challenges have become especially serious for the USA because of its own problems of governance and because its political tradition hinders the development of a structural policy. The management of foreign economic relations relies heavily on trade measures that were effective in contexts of shallow integration, before the contemporary development of large scale transnational production, but that are not adequate in deepening integration. That raises complex asymmetric structural interdependencies to high levels, setting imperatives for collaborative macromanagement that clearly have to be met to a large extent through structural cooperation.

Deepening integration sets imperatives for advanced political development that can cope with tasks of collective management. In shallow integration assertions of demands by interest groups – in the absence of encompassing associations with broad aggregating capabilities – have been the main sources of foreign economic policy measures that have governed the evolution of US interdependencies through controls on arm's length trade. There have been requirements for policy learning, in what could be seen as the public interest, but failures to meet these did not have serious consequences. With the growth of high-volume foreign production by US firms, however, and openness to such production by other enterprises, the deepening integration which has resulted has made intellectual and moral development in policy communities increasingly necessary for the harmonious management of linkages with other national political economies. Decision-making through the trading of political favours has tended to have more serious negative consequences: the narrowly focused concerns that have been decisive have not been sensitive to, or sufficiently knowledgeable about, the functional links between the home economy and foreign industrial sectors. To the extent that the USA functions as an agency-type democracy with a strongly individualistic, pragmatic and instrumental culture, imperatives for responsible management of foreign economic relations are difficult to meet.[23]

Problems in the development of elite political psychology – cognitive and moral – affect the evolution of institutions, especially their potentials for aggregating preferences in line with the common good and for promoting consensus on basic principles of macromanagement. Institutional development, as it becomes more necessary for constructive engagement with issues in deepening integration, can be set back by intensifications of interest group competition and conflicts as a society experiences the strains of generally unguided and ungoverned commercial links with other national political economies.

The greatly increased importance of institutional development, as deepening integration continues, makes it all the more necessary for a nation's institutions of learning and its religious structures to contribute to improvements in the quality of political institutions and the evolution of high-principled political elites. This has to be stressed because of dangerously negative trends in some of the intellectual disciplines which encourage moral relativism, and also because it is necessary for institutions of learning to contribute very actively to the work of policy communities. For this, bias against policy relevant research in the economics profession will have to be overcome.[24] At the same time the flow of economic advice to the administration from public policy research institutes will have to develop a stronger grasp of basic imperatives for a pervasive spirit of integrative cooperation in the social organization of the American intercorporate system. The system of competitive managerial capitalism, operating under strong pressures from investors for short-term profitability, lacks efficiencies because of low levels of intercorporate trust and failures to pursue opportunities for collaboration. Switching investor strategies, maintaining the pressures for short-term profitability, contribute to massive speculation in financial markets, while corporate emphasis on financial management perpetuates myopic rather than dynamic systems of innovation.

Whatever progress can be made in institutional development, in policy learning, the formation of high-principled policy communities, corporate governance reform and improved financial service of the real economy will assist more constructive management of the USA's foreign economic relations. Integrative rather than instrumental approaches to problems of adjustment and development in structural interdependence will be possible because of the new ethos in the political economy. The danger that the independent operations of US and other transnational firms will cause imbalances in the world economy will be recognized, and, with active concerns about the costs of globalization, could make more probable the growth of a consensus for a consultative structural policy.

Comprehensive planning in the area of foreign economic relations is becoming more and more important because of the adverse effects of imbalances in the overall gains and losses from involvement in the world economy and because representations of domestic interests flow mainly into the trade policy process in ways that limit potentials for policy learning. The necessary planning will have to recognize the changing configuration of the international structural basis for commerce, and its significance for the larger context of the global financial system. Linkages, in the entire pattern, are tending to become tighter as market efficiencies and failures become internationalized through the expansion of corporate activities and the interpenetration of national policy environments.

The pragmatism in American political culture is a source of disinclinations to engage in policy planning, but this is becoming imperative because the competing representations of interest groups driving trade policy – the most politicized area of foreign economic relations – allow little scope for policy learning. The limited policy learning that may seem possible can be seen as an opportunity to propose ventures in managed trade which could facilitate improvement in the balance of payments but would make the policy process much more highly politicized and more intensely conflicted. The management of trade would thus tend to become disjointed, while its effects could well be at variance with its objectives because of corporate skills in devising strategies of adjustment and evasion.

Initiatives to introduce a consultative structural policy oriented toward partnering with other industrialized states would help to build consensus for planning in the management of foreign economic relations, with recognition that this would have to be based on structural forecasting and on confidence in the overall effects of the consultative structural endeavours. Advances toward consensus, through policy learning, would be possible because of the prospects for corporate cooperation with the initiatives to facilitate concerted entrepreneurial endeavours, aided by productive technocratic–corporate interactions. Progress along these lines, however, it should be stressed, would have to be aided by intensive educational efforts – especially by management faculties at institutions of learning.

The comprehensive planning necessary in US foreign economic relations, while giving priority to technocratic inputs into a consultative structural policy, will have to set directions for resolute engagement with tasks of regulation and reform in the international financial system. Elementary concepts of the public interest necessitate earnest application to those tasks: the vulnerabilities of the USA are especially serious. What is largely a process of debt-led growth is not likely to be sustainable; high levels of stock market speculation interact dangerously with manipulative practices in world financial markets. These markets have to be brought fully into the service of the real economy, with its international dimensions.

Fundamental orientation for the planning of American foreign economic policy can be derived from principles of integrative alliance capitalism, the basis for consultative structural partnering which can promise harmonious systemic development in the world economy. The logic of alliance capitalism builds on imperatives for cooperation in the development of innovation systems drawing on a widening range of advances in frontier technology; it also builds on imperatives for cooperation in the exploration of opportunities for concerted entrepreneurship. There can be instrumental applications of both imperatives, but there are profound reasons for advocating integrative motivations, in line with moral traditions in the American cultural heritage that have to be made more meaningful in the context of globalization.

Structural partnering inspired by the concept of integrative alliance capitalism can prevent a buildup of pressures for policy-induced demand expansion as a stimulus to an economy under strain in imbalanced and ungoverned globalization. The promotion of structural partnering can give thrust to supply and demand expansion, at home and abroad, through technocratically assisted concerted entrepreneurship; this can promise higher and balanced noninflationary growth. The United States cannot resort to further deficit financing in order to increase growth that has been slackened by diversions of investment into that financing, by tax burdens, by outward movements of industrial capacity and by shifts of competitive advantage to low-cost foreign producers, and that may be endangered by a stock market collapse. The policy learning that has became necessary after an accumulation of macromanagement deficiencies, and of problems in globalization, has to provide orientation for highly constructive engagement with the basic challenge of deepening integration: the development of a macro coordination function to inspire and assist spontaneous ordering of innovative entrepreneurial ventures, serving the public interest as it becomes more internationalized.

NOTES

1. See Jose Campa and Linda S. Goldberg (1997), 'The evolving external orientation of manufacturing: a profile of four countries', *Economic Policy Review*, Federal Reserve Bank of New York, **3** (2), July, 53–82.
2. See Marcus Noland (1997), 'The political economy of the USTR', *International Organization*, **51** (3), Summer, 365–88.
3. See William A. Niskanen (1998), 'A Personal Overview of US Trade Policy', in *Future Visions for US Trade Policy*, New York: Council on Foreign Relations, pp. 38–45.
4. See C. Randall Henning (1994), *Currencies and Politics in the United States, Germany, and, Japan*, Washington, DC: Institute for International Economics, ch. 6.
5. See Geoffrey Garrett (1998), *Partisan Politics in the Global Economy*, Cambridge University Press.
6. See Thomas J. Prusa (1998), 'Cumulation and anti-dumping: a challenge to competition', *The World Economy*, **21** (8), November, 1021–34, and Anne O. Krueger (1996), 'Threats, to 21st Century Growth: the Challenge to the International Trading System', in Ralph Landau, Timothy Taylor and Gavin Wright (eds), *The Mosaic of Economic Growth*, Stanford University Press, pp. 191–214.
7. See Stephen J. Kobrin (1998), 'The MAI and the clash of globalizations', *Foreign Policy*, **112**, Fall, 97–109.
8. See Lawrence J. White (1993), 'Competition policy in the United States: an overview', *Oxford Review of Economic Policy*, **9** (2), Summer, 133–50.
9. See symposium on competition policy, *The World Economy*, **21** (8), November 1998.
10. See C. Randall Henning (1998), 'Systemic conflict and regional monetary integration: the case of Europe', *International Organization*, **52** (3), Summer, 537–74.
11. See Myron S. Scholes (1998), 'Derivatives in a dynamic environment', *The American Economic Review*, **88** (3), June, 350–70.

12. See Laura D'Andrea Tyson (1992), *Who's Bashing Whom? Trade Conflict in High Technology Industries*, Washington, DC: Institute for International Economics, and Dani Rodrik (1997), *Has Globalization Gone Too Far?*, Washington, DC: Institute for International Economics.
13. See Nagesh Kumar (1998), 'Multinational enterprises, regional economic integration and export platform production in host countries: an empirical analysis of US and Japanese Corporations', *Review of World Economics*, **134** (3), 450–83.
14. See Henning, note 10.
15. See Martin Feldstein (1998), 'Refocussing the IMF', *Foreign Affairs*, **77** (2), March–April, 20–33.
16. See Louis Emmerij (ed.) (1997), *Economic and Social Development into the XXI Century*, Washington, DC: Inter-American Development Bank , parts II, III, IV.
17. See Jeffrey Sachs (1998), 'International economics: unlocking the mysteries of globalization', *Foreign Policy*, **110**, Spring, 97–111.
18. See David Folkerts-Landau and Peter M. Garber (1997), 'Derivative Markets and Financial System Soundness' in Charles Enoch and John H. Green (eds), *Banking Soundness and Monetary Policy*, Washington, DC: International Monetary Fund, pp. 290–304.
19. See Feldstein, cited.
20. For general observations on the significance of social capital see Charles Boix and Daniel N. Posner (1998), 'Social capital: explaining its origins and effects on government performance', *British Journal of Political Science*, **28** (4), October, 686–93.
21. See Laura Baughman, Rolf Mirus, Morris E. Morke and Dean Spinanger (1997), 'Of tyre cords, ties and tents: window dressing in the ATC', *The World Economy*, **20** (4), July, 407–34.
22. See symposium, *The World Economy*, **19** (2), March 1996, and Gustav Ranis, 'Successes and Failures in Development Experience since the 1980s', in Emmerij, cited, pp. 81–98.
23. On the dynamics of an agency-type democracy see Anthony King (1997), *Running Scared: Why America's Politicians Campaign Too Much and Govern Too Little*, New York: Free Press.
24. See references to the US profession in symposium issue, *Kyklos*, **48** (2), 1995.

Index